Schoolishness

SCHOOLISHNESS

*Alienated Education and the Quest
for Authentic, Joyful Learning*

SUSAN D. BLUM

CORNELL UNIVERSITY PRESS
ITHACA AND LONDON

First published 2024 by Cornell University Press

Library of Congress Cataloging-in-Publication Data

Names: Blum, Susan Debra, author.
Title: Schoolishness : alienated education and the quest for authentic, joyful learning / Susan D. Blum.
Description: Ithaca [New York] : Cornell University Press, 2024. | Includes bibliographical references and index.
Identifiers: LCCN 2023045877 (print) | LCCN 2023045878 (ebook) | ISBN 9781501774188 (hardcover) | ISBN 9781501774744 (paperback) | ISBN 9781501774195 (pdf) | ISBN 9781501774287 (epub)
Subjects: LCSH: Learning. | Education—Social aspects. | Education—Aims and objectives.
Classification: LCC LB1060 .B585 2024 (print) | LCC LB1060 (ebook) | DDC 370.15/23—dc23/eng/20231027
LC record available at https://lccn.loc.gov/2023045877
LC ebook record available at https://lccn.loc.gov/2023045878

For Estrella

They might make us furious, those teachers incurious,
The ones who are mulish, perhaps even foolish,
Who no matter the reason, the weather, the season,
Still choose to be thoughtlessly schoolish.

KEN SMITH (poem inspired by this book)

When we try to pick out anything by itself, we find it hitched to
everything else in the Universe.

JOHN MUIR, *My First Summer in the Sierra*

CONTENTS

PREFACE

Schoolishness: the characteristic of being made for, by, and about
   school
(1) not real, not from "the real world," but for the self-contained world
   of closed-off institutions, with their own logic, grammar, rules
(2) a form of being that emphasizes packaged "learning," teaching,
   orderly progressions, uniformity, evaluation by others, arbitrary
   forms, predetermined time, artificial boundaries, postponing rewards and use. The reading is finite, the writing has specific rules,
   and the tests have tricks to sort out those who have mastered the
   techniques of figuring them out. There are correct answers, and
   someone knows them. The success is preestablished, the norms are
   bell-curve-like, and the standards are universal.
(3) rhymes with *foolishness*

I thought I had to quit.
   But I'm still here, in the education trenches, digging the holes and filling them in.

I really thought it was over. I had spent fifteen years, at least, learning about everything that is wrong with formal schooling, after spending all the previous decades (maybe four decades, or six, depending on how you count) as a worshipper of formal, abstract, beautiful learning in schools. I had become a typical true believer who had lost her faith, who saw behind the Wizard's curtain at Oz: an atheist, an a-schoolist. I was convinced that homeschooling, unschooling, school without teachers, school without grades, school without requirements and curriculum and stress, school without walls, learning without school, were the only ways to tap into the innate human capacity for deep learning. I recruited all my anthropological training about how humans learn language, walking, kinship roles, social values, learn how to eat and sleep and cook. All these are part of being a person, and all of these vary wildly around the world, yet these things are not truly *taught*. So what is school for?

Not only is school not necessary, went my thinking. It also produces harm. It is the setting for bullying, for stress that leads to anxiety, depression, suicide. It wastes time and money. It entrenches racial and economic inequality. It doesn't usually successfully teach (in the United States) second languages, or science, or civics. Our students may not be very good at writing school essays, and they may not turn into critical thinkers. Some swell with pride at perfect grade-point averages, and grovel at their teachers' feet to earn a tenth of a point. They cheat and lie and plagiarize. Others move directly from schools to prisons.

How could *anyone* defend such an institution?

The Buddha's disciples wrote of the "Eightfold Path," which humans must follow in order to eradicate suffering. Number 5 is *samma ajiva*, "right livelihood." This means avoiding work that causes harm.

My "livelihood"—being a college professor in a system filled with harm—felt wrong.

But I needed my salary. My health insurance. Retirement benefits. (I'm one of the lucky faculty who gets those things.)

I'm too overeducated to get a job at Starbucks—though I did calculate how much I could reduce my expenses, and whether we could live on my spouse's salary alone. (Not easily, at least not without drastic changes.)

I was too young to retire. Too old to begin an entirely new profession. So I'm still here.

But, after undergoing quite a lot of soul searching, experimentation, complaining, talking, and ever-reading, I'm okay with this.

I've learned some things. This book is that story, the story of my progress, as a teacher.

And surprisingly the COVID-19 pandemic helped. It showed how much people, a lot of people, really care about school.

We just have to get it right. And the best way to do that is to get rid of schoolishness.

What's Ailing Our Youth?

People in our world spend up to two decades in schools. This should be understood as a *new and powerful way to shape all people*—to shape them for good or ill. Some people thrive, and many people are destroyed. Some withstand the assaults, and some ride a wave of success. Some love it; many don't. Some argue that students don't learn well. Some argue that schools cost too much, or admit the wrong students. Some argue about what is taught in the schools. Some give insight about how to redesign a syllabus, or how to remove the harms of grading, or how to inculcate more play.

Clive Harber goes further. In *Schooling as Violence: How Schools Harm Pupils and Societies*, he writes that

> formal schooling has often been harmful to children and their wider societies. . . . The irrelevant, alienating and even threatening nature of schooling can play a significant part in low enrolment and school drop out. . . . Most schools are essentially authoritarian institutions, however benevolent or benign that authoritarianism is and whatever beneficial aspects of learning are imparted. . . . Schools, as other forms of modern institution, control through their bureaucratic, routinized authoritarianism—constantly measuring, categorising, ordering and regulating so that control becomes accepted by the majority as normal and natural. The desired result is increased docility and obedience.[1]

For decades after it ends, many people, traumatized, have heart-pounding dreams about negative schooling experiences. In some places, schooling is so terror-laden that students—even high-achieving students, the "good" ones—are driven to the brink, or over the brink, of despair. To medication. To therapy. To costly tutoring. To punishment. To failure. To shame. To suicide.

In March 2017, I got an email out of the blue from a woman whose son had tried two different reputable colleges and was on the brink of leaving school altogether after two students had died by suicide at his second school. He was starting to hate school in general, she told me, after loving learning all his life. He had gotten through high school believing that once he finally got to college, people would appropriately be focused on learning and ideas. No dice. His mother was relieved to have found my book, *"I Love Learning; I Hate School."*[2] This student is far from alone; his experience is shockingly, horrifyingly common.

Students—even or sometimes especially the successful ones—are suffering. All levels of schools, not only universities, are filled with suffering. Individuals experience suffering as part of their daily life—which includes lots and lots of schooling, which exerts power over them. How could it not, given the dominance—in terms of quantity, authority, consequentiality—of schooling?

And the more we push more years of schooling on more people, the more important it is that we get it right.

But I don't think we have.

We have so naturalized our ways of schooling that we scarcely question them. Yet we should. Stronger than *should*: we *must*.

Because surely our goal is not to increase misery. The world has enough for all kinds of reasons and in all kinds of domains. I assume that the grown-ups want our young to be happier, to be more *fulfilled*. And yet, the side effects, the unintended consequences, could not be less happy. They could not be more alarming. If we have students committing suicide because of structures of schooling designed in some way to create the possibility of a better life, then the contradictions must be faced. We cannot ignore the possibility that the structures are not working. And if unhappiness, if misery, if suffering are widespread, then it cannot be that every individual is lazy, coddled, weak, and in need of medication, therapy, self-care, hot baths, aromatherapy, time management, and improvement. If we have created a system that is causing widespread ill-being, or if that system has arisen willy-nilly, however well-intentioned, over many years, then we need to know.

When things are evidently not working, as is the case with regard to so much having to do with schooling—many students don't learn well, and many fail to thrive—then it is necessary to ask: How could it be different? How might the fundamentals change?

What *are* the fundamentals of schoolishness?

This book is manifesto and tirade, pamphlet and prayer, autoethnography and annotated bibliography, lament and dream. I have found this book to be very challenging to write and to finish. In some ways I never stopped writing *"I Love Learning; I Hate School."* I just kept going. Right after that book I submitted a proposal for a project that I called "Well-being, Suffering, Schooling." I got a fellowship to work on that for a semester. What I see now is that I already had the kernel of *this* book. That one was already stuffed, and this one has become overstuffed like a double Oreo. But the kernel—and I say this as someone living in Indiana—the kernel never popped. Though full of starch, it never became white and fluffy. What happened was it took root, and it grew. There are lots of stalks in my cornfield. But just like in Indiana, the cornfield needs to have a path throughout it so that there's a way out. The thread that helps find the way out is understanding, and then challenging, schoolishness in all its intertwined dimensions. It's about education, but it's also about psychology. And it's a moral undertaking too. As an anthropologist, I feel compelled to take them all on—as an observer and participant in this strange human experience.

SCHOOLISHNESS

Part I

TINKERING AROUND THE EDGES DOESN'T CUT IT

INTRODUCTION

The Education Gospel and the Deeply Held Structures of Schoolishness

> To see people properly we need to place them at a reasonable, well-judged distance, like the objects we see before us. Then their many-sided strangeness becomes apparent. . . . In this strangeness lies their truth, the truth of their alienation. It is then that consciousness of alienation—that strange awareness of the strange—liberates us, or begins to liberate us, from alienation. . . . To look at things from an alien standpoint—externally and from a reasonable distance—is to look at things truly.
>
> HENRI LEFEBVRE, *Critique of Everyday Life*

I watched the two-year-old—who happens to be my granddaughter—learn how to work light switches on a panel in my kitchen. She stood on a chair, delighted, as she figured out how the three switches worked: two pushed and one slid. It was complicated: The slider turned on a set of lights overhead; one of the push-switches turned on a different set nearby; and the other controlled outside lights, which she couldn't see. But the switch for the outside lights had a little red light that at least signaled a change as it went on and off. To figure this out took practice, because the push-switches are a little flat, and how to operate them isn't especially obvious. Plus they got out of sync once my husband started goofing around by changing them from another panel across the room that controls the same lights.

Nevertheless, Estrella did it over and over and over until she mastered it.

She taught herself, and she learned. She was intensely focused, and didn't look for any external validation. She was very pleased with herself when she had an effect on the world.

Was this play? Was this work? It was learning—and definitely not schoolish. This was learning via trial and error, with intense focus and satisfactory results. It was purely for herself.

Humans are amazing learners. Learning is our superpower. When we watch children learn to walk, to insert a pen into a cap, or to snowboard, or when we watch adults during a pandemic work to master the art of sourdough bread and post images of their increasing proficiency (that would be me!), or when we hear how thousands of scientists worked together on the CERN Large Hadron Collider to observe evidence of the Higgs boson, or . . . or . . . Once we notice, we see that learning happens everywhere and that we often do it with joy, even when it's hard.

Anthropologists have documented the varied ways people learn. Learning occurs all around the world at all ages and in all domains. It happens without grades or curriculum and often without evaluation. Animals of all sorts must learn too, because our environments have dangers, and the need for survival calls for agency. Unlike most other mammals, human beings are born helpless. We require many years of assistance from many others merely to survive. My biological anthropology colleagues talk about the "fourth trimester" when babies' brains and lungs must continue developing just so they can survive.[1] We have externalized a lot of our knowledge of the world, in the environments we build and the artifacts we create and the texts we treasure and transmit. And we learn it from others; nobody acting alone could possibly invent all the knowledge needed in any human society. We call this "cultural transmission."

This is true for all humans, as far as we know, everywhere, since the first *Homo sapiens sapiens* emerged in Africa perhaps two hundred thousand years ago. Humans have always had sophisticated cultural knowledge, including about the technologies involved in preparing food and creating shelter. And they have learned it, for most of those many thousands of years, without schools, and often without direct instruction.

Our species is indeed characterized by that one supreme superpower: we are excellent at learning.

Building on the work he did in his 2012 book *The Evolved Apprentice: How Evolution Made Humans Unique*, in 2021 in *The Pleistocene*

Social Contract philosopher Kim Sterelny points to the "almost universal consensus . . . that in our lineage, cultural learning has become cumulative, and that is a critical difference between late hominins and almost all the cultural learning of almost all other animals." This is because our knowledge must be socially transmitted. But this makes us dependent on others: "Humans are obligate co-operators": We depend on cooperation and culture, not on specific instincts, because "we have the capacity to acquire new skills for which we do not have specific genetic preparation, and we can re-purpose existing cognitive circuits to new tasks." The only disagreement is about the need for direct instruction and for teaching, as I explore in chapters 3 and 4.[2]

In their first years, young children learn the fundamental aspects of being members of society: how to speak the languages spoken or signed around them, how to walk and jump and run and roll and grasp. They learn how to address elders and which locations are off-limits and how to eat the foods that are considered appropriate.

Adolescents learn to function responsibly in their own communities and how to interact with other communities. They learn about rules for marriage and how to explain the origins of the universe. They learn how to divide labor so that some people become experts in some aspects of their society. They learn about communication and transportation and art. They learn stories, and they learn about modesty. When they encounter new problems and situations, they learn more.

We learn constantly throughout our lifetimes, as we enter new situations and encounter new technologies. We meet new people and learn how to interact with them. We reach new phases of our lives and learn how to act in them. We get new jobs and figure out the local norms and processes. And most of it is without school, without the now-unquestioned schoolish structures.

Questioning Schoolish Structures

I edited the book *Ungrading: Why Rating Students Undermines Learning (and What to Do Instead)*, on challenging conventional grading practices and finding better approaches to giving feedback to help students discover their own motivations.[3] The book was a "bestseller" in the context of academic nonfiction books, selling well over fifteen thousand copies. I was invited to give more than sixty talks, workshops, and podcasts in the two years following the book's publication in 2020. But I was increasingly uncomfortable with these pedagogy workshops.

Often I was invited by centers for teaching and learning. The events varied enormously, from discussions with a dozen people who had spent a year working through the chapters of the book, to online workshops with almost five hundred people who might be skeptical and completely new to the idea. Some of the events were as short as about twenty-five minutes, and some stretched—too long!—to two and a half hours or even three, workshop style. There were podcasts and book talks, webinars and a few in-person events, including two at my university where department chairs invited me. Sometimes they wanted inspiration and food for thought; often individual faculty hoped to get help fixing something for Tuesday. I understood that immediate need but felt I couldn't really meet it. Without changing many things, we can't just remove grades.

It became clear that my discomfort derived from recognizing the limits that any one teacher can challenge. We operate within fairly unchangeable structures that often get in the way of what so many of us would ideally do.

I decided to name this set of structures "schoolishness."[4] We might modify one element at a time, but as long as the rest remain, outcomes will be limited. For instance, we might try to remove grades entirely from all discussion all semester, as I do, focusing instead on students learning, challenging themselves, taking risks, discovering the joy of learning; yet at the end of the semester we have to submit grades. Students are constantly aware of this, and of the consequentiality of the grades, for medical school admissions, for internships. So when faculty are looking for answers, the real answer is that it can never really work well because the structures are problematic. Otherwise we're just tinkering around the edges.

The scholarship of teaching and learning (SoTL), for which I have the utmost respect, occurs within the context of school as it is, the taken-for-granted structures within which we operate. Researchers in SoTL study everything carefully, for instance analyzing test results from two evenly matched cohorts of students who have a single change in the ways they are taught. Such work provides the foundation for the "evidence-based"

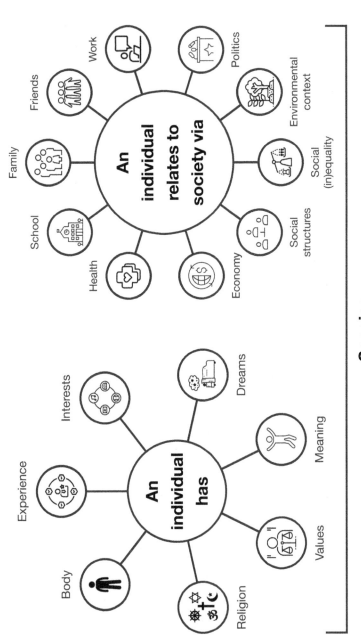

Species

Figure I.1. Units, levels, and dimensions of a learner

practices taught by the growing numbers of centers for teaching and learning and their always-heroic instructional designers and learning specialists, and never more than during the initial months of the pandemic. All of these people have to help their colleagues, right now, tomorrow, improve their classes. They have to figure out how to get more people to pass Chemistry 101 or how to help more students graduate. They have to figure out how to get better critical thinking in First-Year Composition, and how to decide which General Education requirements should be discarded.

I am far less expert than they all are.

But I have my anthropological superpower that I think can also be useful: I can call into question the structures. Taking an *anthropological* perspective, for me, means taking into account all the ways humans are, and have been, and can be, across time and space.

We are individuals—the primary subject of the field of psychology—but also we work as members of groups that have differential power, and specific cultural values, and all this occurs in the context of our own species. All action has simultaneously species-wide, culturally specific, and individual dimensions. And, looking at school, it looks strange.

Anthropology and the Strangeness of Schoolishness

Physics has a "strange" particle. A *stranger* is someone from outside whose practices may be different. *Strange* can also indicate the uncanny, the peculiar, the "off." Anthropology courses often begin by talking about our mandate to "make the strange familiar, and the familiar strange." Making-strange, *Verfremdung*, a focal aspiration of the theater of the absurd, *ostranenie*, defamiliarization—all these allow us to see what we ordinarily take for granted, by causing a sense of wonder. That's one reason anthropologists often begin our training by going to an unfamiliar—a strange—setting, because when things are unfamiliar, we notice much more. The challenge for my readers is to make schoolishness strange, to question the familiar.

The structures of interaction are as significant as, or more significant than, the "content": form often overrides content. But structures are much harder for us to see—they're naturalized—and we have ideological overlays that prevent us from noticing what's happening in front of us. One aim in my classes, no matter what the ostensible topic, is to use anthropological techniques to challenge students' erroneous and disprovable, but widespread, ideas about the way the world is. We use some methods to show what's in front of their very eyes—they record a conversation, grapple with the future-tense-lessness of English, see that fraternity men "gossip," that African American English has "logic," that children in poverty have rich interactions that may differ from those of their rich white counterparts, that snacks and meals have different rules—and that the old myths don't hold water.

The need for, benefits of, and inevitability of schooling as it is, is such a myth.

It's not what you think, even when it's in front of you every day for decades.

So, we'll look at the grammar, the deep structures, of schoolishness, to notice what we usually take for granted. As my friend and colleague Jim McKenna says, once you put on anthropological lenses to see the world, you can never take them off.

You've been warned.

The whole enterprise is strange.

An Institution That Controls Learning

Let's start with the whole idea of *an institution that controls learning*. If, as I said just now, learning is our superpower, how is it that we've come to assume that people need special institutions to help them learn (if learning is even the goal)? Parents who homeschool and unschool their children question this assumption, but largely it's taken for granted.

This book intends to reveal the deep structures, the grammar, of schoolishness, with all its intertwined dimensions. I aim to unsettle our assumptions. I show that what is everyday in one place is not how it is everywhere, and that it could be different—especially if the status quo is harmful.

And *so many* people agree that, at best, much of the status quo is ineffective, and at worst it's harmful. Huge industries have evolved to improve the system: professional development for teachers, centers for teaching,

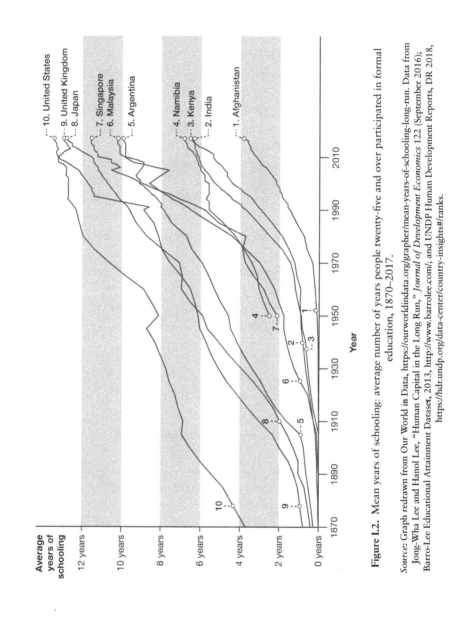

Figure I.2. Mean years of schooling: average number of years people twenty-five and over participated in formal education, 1870–2017.

Source: Graph redrawn from Our World in Data, https://ourworldindata.org/grapher/mean-years-of-schooling-long-run. Data from Jong-Wha Lee and Hanol Lee, "Human Capital in the Long Run," *Journal of Development Economics* 122 (September 2016); Barro-Lee Educational Attainment Dataset, 2013, http://www.barrolee.com/; and UNDP Human Development Reports, DR 2018, https://hdr.undp.org/data-center/country-insights#/ranks.

offices for accessibility and disability, curriculum specialists, testing, advising, amelioration, and coaching through the system.

We know enormous amounts about teaching, learning, and schools—far more than was known at the time of the previous two waves of substantial critique of schooling, during the early twentieth century among people like John Dewey and Maria Montessori, and in the 1960s with progressives like Paulo Freire, A. S. Neill (*Summerhill*), Ivan Illich, John Holt, Paul Goodman, Jules Henry. I have bookshelves full of books about education (and I've borrowed many more), and stacks of printed articles, plus electronic folders full of articles and links and downloaded books. They range in focus from technical dimensions of memory to philosophical views of human agency, from detailed ethnographic accounts of particular classroom interactions to economic histories of schooling. I draw on this, and my three-plus decades as a professor, to make schoolishness strange, so we can challenge it.

And yet—in our era—we have the assumption that most learning has to be accompanied by teaching, and that it should occur in schools. Learning is probably hard, people believe, and maybe distasteful, and has to be regulated and controlled. Not only that: we should extend this learning in schools for over a decade, some compulsory and some voluntary. Though the mean number of years of schooling is still different between high-income and low-income countries, the trend is identical: more, and more, and more.

The Education Gospel

The growth of schooling is connected to the complexity of the contemporary world and is also an outcome of the spread of printing, capitalism, and nationalism. School participation rates are as high as nearly 100 percent in some countries, and this is the aspiration for all, whether we look at the Human Development Index of the United Nations, the Sustainable Development Goals of the United Nations, or the commonsense guidelines for all development work. Why would we *not* want everyone to have as much schooling as possible? One answer is that people often don't like school. There are many other answers. But it's important to note how recent the question itself is in the context of our existence as a species. The dominance of schooling and its foundational structures accreted without a plan. Many of our practices, the most schoolish ones, would not be the ones we would create if we were starting from scratch.

The increase in education—more years of schooling for more people in more places—has been taken as an indisputable good. Grubb and Lazerson termed this "the education gospel," the faith that more and more and more schooling is needed, for individuals and for societies.[5] Others are less sanguine: sociologist Basil Bernstein lamented the pedagogizing of society. Norbert Elias wrote of the "civilizing project." Michel Foucault had his critique of discipline and governmentality.[6] All are connected to the problematic ways that contemporary society controls and shapes all people within it, and forces them to learn, to be certain kinds of people.

Yet people widely believe that remaining in school for years is an unmitigated good and that failure results from individuals' lack of will or fortitude, or lack of grit or character. This assumption may be well-intentioned. It can also be fostered by people standing to benefit materially from belief in the system—college counselors, real estate agents selling houses in "good neighborhoods" (i.e., white) with "good schools," selective colleges wishing to reduce their acceptance rates, test-prep industries. (Race and class are connected through and through.) The assumptions of the education gospel can be the justification for charter, private, and religious schools, or for people selling new professional development packages.

Pedagogical Fever in East Asia: The Education Gospel Worldwide

Because I live and work in higher education in the United States, most of my attention focuses there. However, I also have training in the study of China, and I have read widely about education in East Asia. (I really don't "stay in my lane.") Here I'll just briefly point out some noteworthy dimensions of beliefs about schooling.

In China, education is compulsory until grade nine, with tuition paid by the state. However, fees are paid by parents, resulting in a disproportionately expensive system for the poor. Still, education is cherished. As Andrew Kipnis has shown in *Governing Educational Desire*, parents devote enormous resources to formal education and to higher education, even if the payoff is less than it would be if the children went directly into work.[7] This pattern holds throughout the world, where school's prestige is hegemonic.

In South Korea, something called "education fever" has gripped the country since the end of World War II, especially when it seemed that getting a strong higher education credential was the certain path toward a middle-class life.[8] This was generally true until neoliberal economic policies began to guide the country, making even highly educated people fearful about their prospects.[9] Even college-educated youth without employment prospects tend to believe the myth, though increasing attention is being paid to the costs of this obsession with grades, success, and schooling—when 17 percent of youth (age fifteen to twenty-nine) are unemployed. The popular K-Pop group BTS has created songs explicitly questioning the dominance of schooling.[10]

In Japan, education mamas, *Kyōiku mama*, are blamed for their obsession with their children's educational success, yet they also shoulder the burden of ensuring their children's success in a stratified educational system.[11] Japan has a very egalitarian educational system prior to university. New college graduates had an employment rate over 97 percent even after pandemic hiring fell slightly.[12] And school is dominant worldwide. My colleague Catherine Bolten has shown that in Sierra Leone, despite high costs and lack of payoff for attending school, schooling maintains its prestige over the more-remunerative apprenticeships.[13]

The Elements of Schooling

Many of the features of contemporary schools arose, bit by bit, without a plan. They've nonetheless become part of the enormous institution of schooling. This inheritance is often harmful, because these institutional dimensions don't serve us well anymore, yet they've become part of the intertwined deep grammar of schoolishness. You'll see the dominant, accidental dimensions of schoolishness in the book's central chapters.

Given the enormous variation in schools—from preschool to graduate and professional school, from academic to vocational, from well-resourced schools in high-income countries to low-resourced schools in low-income communities—any generalization is necessarily danger-ous. Not every school and not every classroom has all the elements I analyze. But most do. And prototypical, generic school does. We can speak of prototypes, ideal types, a family resemblance of schoolishness, a broad assortment of similarities, from which we can also discern many deviations.[14]

The Structures

The central chapters of this book present analysis of key elements pres-ent in virtually all schooling. Each element may be harmful and may contribute to a sense of ill-being. Each differs from the ways we observe learning occurring outside school. Each is relatively recent. And they are almost impossibly intertwined, which makes changing any of them diffi-cult unless others are simultaneously changed. An observer—an anthro-pologist from Mars, to use the typical hypothetical outsider—might pop into a setting to determine how schoolish it is, using the handy checklist in the appendix.

We relinquished much of this schoolishness in March, April, and May 2020: attendance was not required; less reading was assigned; fewer writ-ing assignments were required; deadlines became flexible. The academic calendar changed overnight, even though such calendars are usually de-termined a decade in advance. SATs were suddenly nonessential.[15] Classes occurred on rooftops. Debates that had been long-standing got decided in weeks.

We discovered that arbitrary structures could and sometimes should be changed.

This book aims to persuade you that more needs to change.

Axioms, Principles, Values

So much written about higher education seems technocratic. It seems to use "science," "cognitive science," science of learning, learning sciences, neuroscience, "evidence-based practices," as if these were neutral, uni-versal principles.[16] Because I see this whole educational enterprise as simultaneously moral, psychological/experiential, and educational, I've found it helpful to spell out my axioms, principles, and values. People may disagree, but at least we can locate the sources of our disagreement, just as people disagreeing about abortion might at least agree that the fundamental differences lie in ideas of when life begins, of whose life takes precedence, and of who has the right to decide.

These are the axioms, principles, and values, some based on research on learning, that guide my practice, my praxis—a fancy word that reminds us that practices are built on theories, which might be either implicit or explicit.[17] In making them explicit, we can interrogate them.

Here's a preview of my conclusions, both about schoolishness and about humans and the world I hope we create:

Axioms and Observations

- Humans are amazing learners; that's our superpower
- Humans are always learning
- Humans are deeply curious
- People learn for need or interest
- People usually learn by doing (something), not by being talked at or told
- "Banking" information for the future is ineffective
- Threats and fear are not as good motivators as use, confidence, and responsibility
- Giving people responsibility makes them rise to the challenge
- Twenty-year-olds are not usually "children"

Principles

- Multimodality—the use of multiple channels of communication and activity—helps learning
- Internalizing standards takes practice
- Structures communicate more powerfully than explicit "missions"
- Humans are social, emotional, bodily learners in specific contexts
- Democratic *practices* teach democracy better than lectures about democracy
- "The floor" matters in terms of power

Values

- Equality is better than inequality; equity is better than equality
- The principal goal of school should not be mere school success
- Sorting is not my business or calling (vocation)
- Multiple types of variation and diversity are an asset; uniformity of input, process, and outcome is an industrial artifact
- Inauthenticity takes a toll
- Genuine results feed the soul

A Map of the Book

Part I of this book presents a high-level discussion of some of the reasons we need to look critically at schools and then at the complex, sometimes contradictory aims and ends people attribute to schooling. In each of the ten central chapters that follow in part II, I present a familiar but contingent—not necessarily inevitable—aspect of schoolishness, while providing some of the ways I and others could make that dimension less schoolish. In part III, I then present a model of what "authentic learning" might look like, in a far less schoolish form, based on three summers of ethnographic research that I conducted. I conclude with reflections on the nature of change, from small and individual to large and systemic. There's a lot of change, experimentation, and alternatives going on. That should give us hope, but also pause, as wholesale change often occurs slowly—but sometimes, as with an overnight pandemic, shockingly quickly. This book is mostly analytical and diagnostic; it is not prescriptive, though I draw out implications wherever possible. And the question is: can we have school without schoolishness?

Here are some definitions:

- Learning: a relatively permanent change in action or understanding
- Schools: gathering for learning with others
- Education: being guided to learn
- Formal education: education occurring in institutions designed principally for learning

- Informal education: education occurring in institution-adjacent settings, such as museums and athletic organizations
- Nonformal education: learning that occurs without formal instruction
- Schooling: the institution of school
- Student: someone enrolled formally in a school or an institution designed for learning
- Teacher: guide of novices' learning
- Learner: someone engaged in changing their knowledge, behavior, skill, or disposition
- Novice: someone explicitly present to learn something that others know better[18]
- Expert: someone who feels or is recognized as competent in some domain
- Direct instruction: explaining something verbally, and possibly also demonstrating physically

Schools Influence and Are Influenced By . . .

Like any pervasive institution, schools are both influenced by and in turn influence the rest of society. We in schools cannot unilaterally change everything. And fixing schools won't fix everything, either. Schools and schooling exist within multiple contexts, including all the political and economic structures that shape experience; the situation of individual and social health; the social structures; and the environment. Schools are only some domains that affect students. Others include family, friends, and work. There can be others as well.

As school, along with schoolishness, spread across the globe and across childhood and adulthood, it has come to occupy more hours a day and more years for all in all societies. It has more functions, and more consequences. The fact that I engage in critique of schoolishness is not to say that schools alone are responsible for the flaws—but they also cannot themselves fix the social needs that have devolved onto schools. Nor do I deny the consequentiality of schooling in our current context. Like many institutions, schools both shape and are shaped by other social, cultural, political, and economic factors that surround them.

But the negative dimensions of schoolishness now affect nearly all in the contemporary world, to a far greater extent than ever before. People in different societies, and different identities within each society, experience schoolishness differently. But the dimensions tend to be standard, and have come to be nearly universal in their uniformity. Solutions cannot be adequate if carried out one by one. As John Muir said, "When we try to pick out anything by itself, we find it hitched to everything else in the Universe."[19]

Still, it can be useful to analyze the dimensions of a problem. These dimensions are not natural kinds, like those of, say, a strawberry or an armadillo. They are heuristic slices of a desiccated, ravenous sphere.

For short, we could call my approach a PoliticalEconomicPsychoBio-SocioculturalSemiotic approach, or maybe, "It's Complicated."

This book does not prescribe an easy set of techniques that will improve a classroom tomorrow, though in each chapter I present some ways that I and others have tried to improve our own courses or institutions, and some of these might be useful for other teachers. It does not accept the status quo as merely "realistic." In that sense, it's driven by idealism. But surely there's room for that.

I would like to draw an analogy, one that may offend you.

In my earlier academic life as a China scholar, I encountered the strange practices of footbinding—the deliberate effort to shorten women's feet by breaking bones and binding the toes with cloth strips, because small feet were considered beautiful. Much is written about the origins and reasons for footbinding, which I won't go into here.[20] But this practice was dominant for nearly a thousand years (the twelfth through twentieth centuries). It determined marriage, and thus every dimension of life, for aristocratic women. Parents had to do their duty and ensure that their daughters' feet were properly "bound" so they could be regarded as desirable. The shoes were gorgeous—embroidered and fashionable and fetishized. People competed to see whose feet could be smallest. Women too were deeply involved and not mere victims.

There was no opting out, at least for the wealthy. (Women from what are now called "minority nationalities," such as Manchus, did not bind their feet, and poor farmers needed their daughters to be more mobile, and able to work, so their feet tended to be bigger.) It was "just the way it was." If an individual, or a family, decided not to participate in these practices, they would be seen as "unrealistic." Footbinding lasted for many centuries, until it was finally outlawed by the Republican government in 1912, though some families secretly continued to practice it for years afterward. When I did fieldwork in southwest China (Kunming, in Yunnan Province) in the early 1990s, some older women still had feet that had been bound when they were young.

Now, I'm not saying that schoolishness is as harmful as footbinding, or not as evidently harmful. But I'm saying that harmful institutions can endure, and people willingly participate because the stakes are high and real for failing. When people say things like "I know that standardized tests aren't a real measure of ability, but I need to do well," they are acknowledging some of the problems but feel helpless, as individuals, to make any changes. When faculty and students say "I know grading isn't really working, but I have no choice," they are accepting the status quo—even when it makes them miserable, and even when they're aware of the evidence against the practice.

But as I've written in the context of trying to get people to change the dominance of grading: we invented it, and we can uninvent it. And if we don't even try, nothing will ever change.

Scale and Numbers

To give some sense of the scale and scope of schoolishness, I present several numbers here. These won't be my focus; plenty of experts weigh in on them. But without the greater context in the contemporary world, it will be hard to see how challenging it is to challenge schoolishness. The numbers, the scale, involved in schooling worldwide are staggering, whether we look at numbers of institutions, people, years, or funding.

Schools

It's impossible to get a count of schools worldwide. The number of formal educational institutions in the United States is huge, and should give us a sense of the scale.

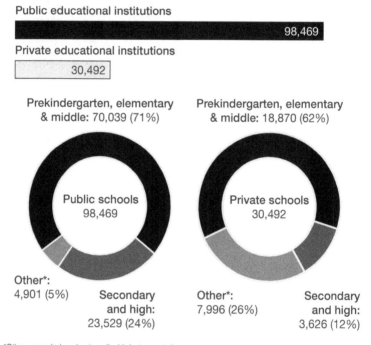

Public educational institutions

98,469

Private educational institutions

30,492

Prekindergarten, elementary
& middle: 70,039 (71%)

Prekindergarten, elementary
& middle: 18,870 (62%)

Public schools
98,469

Private schools
30,492

Other*:
4,901 (5%)

Secondary
and high:
23,529 (24%)

Other*:
7,996 (26%)

Secondary
and high:
3,626 (12%)

*Other, ungraded, and not applicable/not reported

Figure I.3. Number of educational institutions in the US, 2019–2020, by level and
control of institution.

Source: Graph drawn from IES NCES (National Center for Education Statistics) data.

People

The numbers of people involved in schooling are also staggering.

Students

An astonishing 23 percent of the world's population are students. Anything we do or say about schooling affects *nearly one-quarter of the pop-*
ulation of the world. (I know I've just restated the same thing, but as I try
to process this, I have to say it aloud.)

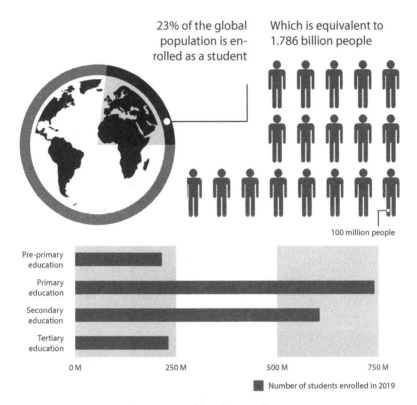

Figure I.4. World student enrollment

Source: PesaCheck, https://pesacheck.org/is-one-fifth-of-the-worlds-population-currently-in-school-cf014d60f59a, http://data.uis.unesco.org/

This has extended so far beyond the teen years that psychologists, especially Jeffrey Jensen Arnett, have coined a new stage of human development, "emerging adulthood," which is completely connected with the extension of schooling.[21]

Teachers

Besides occupying the time of large numbers of students, school occupies the time of large numbers of teachers as well.

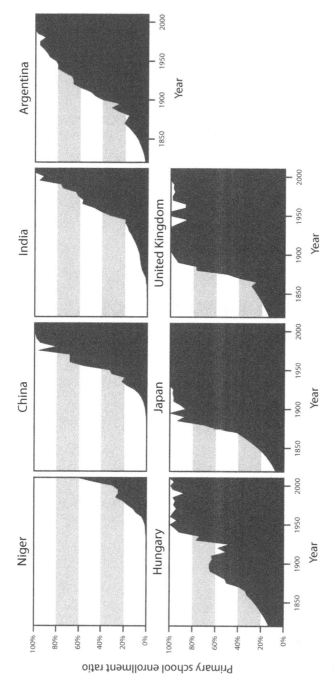

Figure I.5. Primary school enrollment: estimated enrollment ratios of official primary education age. Estimates adjusted with repetition ratios. *Source:* Graphs redrawn from https://ourworldindata.org/primary-and-secondary-education. Data from Jong-Wha Lee and Hanol Lee, "Human Capital in the Long Run," *Journal of Development Economics* 122 (September 2016).

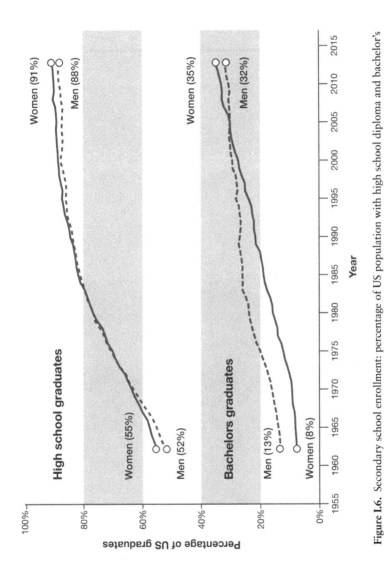

Figure I.6. Secondary school enrollment: percentage of US population with high school diploma and bachelor's degree, 1962–2013; percentage of US population, ages 25–60, with high school diploma and/or bachelor's degree, by survey year and sex.

Source: Graph redrawn from Russell Sage Foundation, from its analyses of IPUMS CPS (Current Population Survey) data.

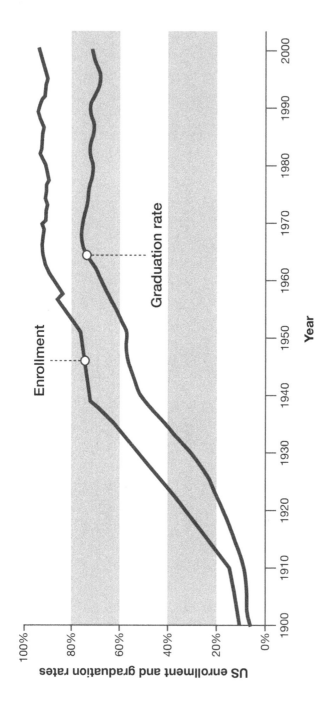

Figure I.7. High school enrollment and graduation: US enrollment and graduation rates, 1900–2000. Enrollment percentage: total enrollment divided by total population ages 14–17. Graduation rate: number of high school graduates divided by total population age 17.

Source: Graph redrawn from Mirel 2006. Data from the National Center for Education Statistics.

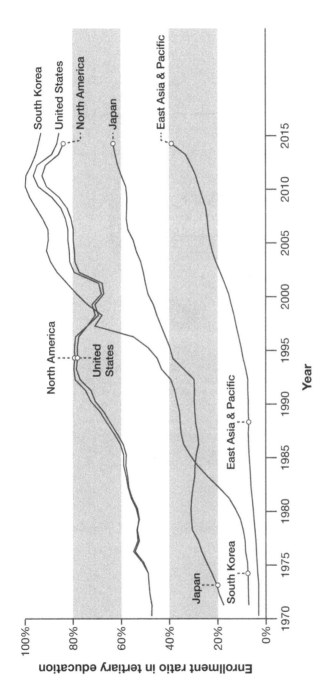

Figure I.8. Gross enrollment ratio in tertiary education: total enrollment in tertiary education, 1970–2015, regardless of age, expressed as a percentage of the total population of the five-year age group following completion of secondary school.

Source: Graph redrawn from https://ourworldindata.org/tertiary-education. Data from UNESCO Institute for Statistics.

Number of teachers worldwide:

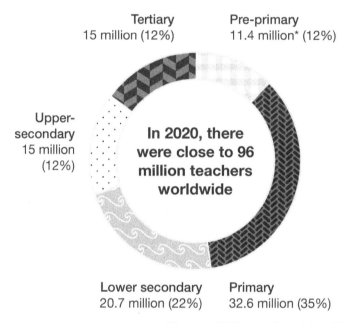

Figure I.9. Number of teachers, worldwide. How many teachers are there?
Source: http://data.uis.unesco.org/.

Time

Individuals spend huge amounts of their lives in school, often legally compelled to do so.

Public: 4.16 M (80%)

Public: 3.176 M (87%)

Public: 984 K (64%)

Teachers of all levels 5.21 M

Primary & secondary teachers 3.661 M

Post-secondary* teachers 1.549 M

Private: 1.05 M (20%)

Private: 485 K (13%)

Private: 565 K (36%)

*Instructional staff in degree-granting postsecondary institutions

Figure I.10. Number of teachers in the United States, 2019, by level and control of institution

Source: Graph drawn from IES NCES (National Center for Education Statistics) data.

Years of Compulsory Schooling

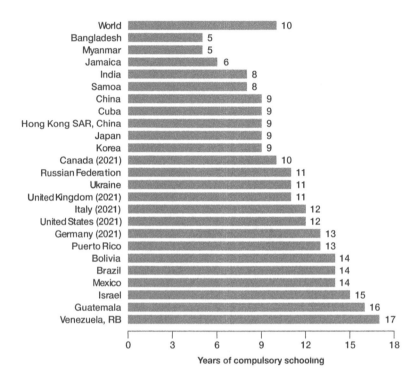

Figure I.11. Years of compulsory schooling, 2020. Sample of select countries.
Source: World Bank IBRD-IDA.

Years of Actual Schooling

Throughout the world, rates of education have increased dramatically during the twentieth century, even if there's still a large gap between wealthy and less-developed countries.

Money and Spending

The amount of money spent on schooling, whether by public or private financing, is huge, but varies considerably worldwide.

Public and private spending do not necessarily predict outcomes; they are often inversely related.

Nuances and Comparisons

In addition to national variations, all these rates and numbers also vary considerably within any nation-state by race, class, gender, ethnicity, religion, migration status, and more. Some figures are easier to attain than others, such as Programme for International Student Assessment (PISA) ratings for Organisation for Economic Co-operation and Development (OECD) countries, comparing fifteen-year-olds' reading, math, and science scores. Gender is always important. In the United States, race and class matter, as does student debt for higher education. To the extent that there is social inequality, schooling will be inequitable, in terms of quantity and quality.

But for the purposes of this book, what matters most is the question of students' experiences with schoolishness. Why is it a problem?

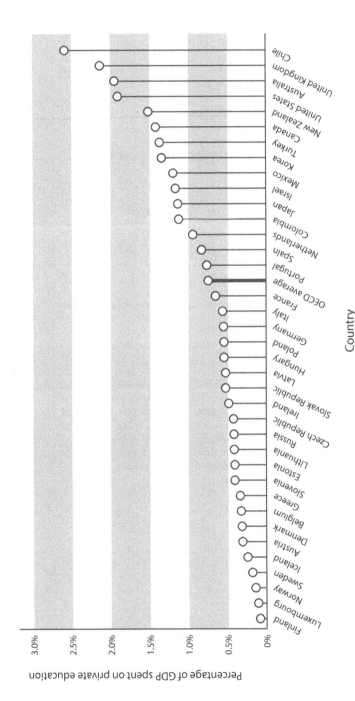

Figure I.12. Public and private spending on education: *top*, public spending on education, primary to tertiary, by percentage of GDP, 2019 or latest available; *bottom*, private spending on education, primary to tertiary, by percentage of GDP, 2018 or latest available

Source: Graphs redrawn from OECD data, from "Education at a Glance," "Educational Finance Indicators," Human Development Insights, https://www.oecd-ili-brary.org/education/data/education-at-a-glance/educational-finance-datasets_c4e1b551-en

1

Experiencing School

What's the Problem?

There are very few children who do not feel, during most of the time they are in school, an amount of fear, anxiety, and tension that most adults would find intolerable. It is no coincidence at all that in many of their worst nightmares adults find themselves back in school.

JOHN HOLT, *How Children Fail*

The statement that man [*sic*] can live under almost any condition is only half true; . . . if he lives under conditions which are contrary to his nature and to the basic requirements for human growth and sanity, he cannot help reacting; he must either deteriorate and perish, or bring about conditions which are more in accordance with his needs. . . . Human nature and society can have conflicting demands, and . . . a whole society can be sick.

ERICH FROMM, *The Sane Society*

Nightmares.
Stomachaches.
Panic attacks.
Medication.
Therapy.
Ice cream rewards.
Payment for success.
Jealousy.
Bullying.

Fear.

Dread.

Debt.

Boredom.

Feelings of inadequacy.

Shame.

Impostor syndrome.

These are all things that students at every level of schooling associate with school. They're not the exception; they're the rule.

Why is it that substantial numbers of people, as adults in their thirties, forties, fifties, still have such strong memories of school that they awaken from nightmares with their hearts pounding, panicked? Even, or maybe especially, successful students experience fear, concern about being knocked down from their perch, dread at the possibility of failure. Those told early in their school lives that they don't measure up, simply give up.

And while not all fear is avoidable or even undesirable—some research shows we learn most indelibly when there is a modest level of anxiety and discomfort ("moderate arousal"),[1] probably because it forces us to pay more attention and provides the adrenaline to fuel it—this amount of constant negative emotion cannot possibly be healthy.

Since every student will eventually have a decade or more of such accumulated experiences, and some will add the negative school emotions to a life already filled with adverse childhood experiences (ACEs) such as domestic violence, homelessness, and family substance abuse, we can't just say that the problem lies in each individual child. Nor does the real solution. Each individual has to figure out a way to *cope*, every day and every year—but that's not a *solution*.

School is all about the experiences and transformations of learners. If so many people's experiences are negative, that is no mere "side effect." As Yong Zhao puts it forcefully in his book *What Works May Hurt: Side Effects in Education*, "Education is universally perceived to be good, so that very few people automatically associate education with any adverse effects. Thus, when people consider educational interventions, they believe they need to know only whether the interventions are effective"— narrowly defined. "The prevalent definition of educational outcomes included in policies, educational studies, and school evaluations today is cognitive abilities in a few subjects, measured by standardized tests."[2]

Zhao uses the example of tension between supporters and detractors of "direct instruction": direct instruction may temporarily and quickly, even efficiently, increase achievement on certain cognitive measures, but it simultaneously inhibits curiosity and creativity.[3] Not good "side effects."

Students may recognize and admit the downsides of schooling, if we ask. Anthropologists worldwide know this. Amy Stambach, for instance, reports on Chagga people near Mount Kilimanjaro who speak constantly of school-related illnesses and are explicit about the cause: "too much studying makes me crazy." David Lancy, in a chapter titled "Taming the Autonomous Learner," catalogs all the ways people around the world lament the introduction of schooling.[4]

When we aim to understand the existential conditions of learners, whether in "ordinary times" or during a global pandemic, we need to understand the fully social, emotional, and embodied nature of learning in each learner. Emotional and personal characteristics are central to educational experiences—even if the ultimate goal is narrowly cognitive.

At the best of times, at all levels of schooling, a lot of the experience is negative. If that's so, we must *examine the structures, not blame individuals*, as so many do, for their frailty, laziness, or worse. Is John Warner right? Is it true that "school is bad for students"?[5]

Experience: The Being of the Learner

Phenomenology, the study of experience, describes how things feel in great detail. It is radically subjective; the *subject* is the one who knows, just as the *subject* is the one who learns. These two things are related.

Experience is shaped by many factors, some individual and some shared. The educational experience is simultaneously cognitive, social, moral, bodily, and affective. It involves every dimension of the learner's being. John Dewey, philosopher of education, wrote about the importance of attending to "the quality of the experience." Most of the focus in education has been on acquisition of knowledge—procedural, theoretical—with other elements seen as contributing to or detracting from that cognitive learning. Yet a quarter-century of research about even cognitive learning shows that *the affective experience is central to the process of education.*

Emotions Rule! Emotion Is the Master over Cognition

Schools are drenched, saturated with emotion and feelings and affect. There are the positive emotions of joy and love, friendship and laughter and excitement, pride and tenacity and hope, wonder and curiosity, attachment and connection—all the stuff promised by colleges like mine, which reopened in person in fall 2020. But simultaneously present are the negative emotions of fear, dread, boredom, isolation, senses of inadequacy, stress, anxiety, depression, worry, and shame that are so familiar in our schools.

Emotions are responses to combinations of external events and internal structures, communications about the nature of what's out there. And they have something to *teach* us; they are evidence, information.

And we ignore them only if we want to avoid reality.

Schoolish Feelings, Affect, Emotion in Schools

I started to learn about the research on emotion in education, expecting a large building filled with rooms. Instead, I opened an ordinary-size door and found that, like a dream sequence in a movie, it opened onto an entire planet, with continents devoted to various topics, all filled with teeming people busily doing their research.

Recent research in cognitive science and the neurobiology of learning has shown that emotion, affect, feelings are central to all experience, including learning information and analyzing complex scenarios.[6] As humans have evolved from our other animal ancestors, as we've added increased cognition afforded by the prefrontal cortex, as we are capable of self-awareness and metacognition and have changed some of the ways brains function at the cellular level,[7] we also *preserve all the other dimensions of our prehuman neuro-architecture*, having to do with sensory input, motor control, and emotion.

In their masterwork, *The Archaeology of Mind*, Jaak Panksepp and Lucy Biven argue that all animals, not only mammals, have seven *emotional systems*: seeking, fear, rage, lust, care, grief, play, self.[8] All are present at all times, even when "higher" cognitive levels are emphasized. These emotional systems help *motivate* (notice this word; we'll return to it) and protect, causing animals to draw near certain things, to avoid certain behaviors, to increase certain activities that produce positive responses, for example to work very long hours to invent a new vaccine for a world-ravaging virus. All these systems contribute to survival, but some are not only about brute survival and reproduction and eating. Many also have to do with security and further with notions of integration, exploration, and connections. Some are responsible for play.

Neuroscience researchers such as Antonio R. Damasio have shown that it's not possible to learn well without some emotional work being managed. We usually think of rational, ethical decision making as something that involves only cognition, but decades of work have demonstrated the essential involvement of emotion: "the reasoning system evolved as an extension of the automatic emotional system, with emotion playing diverse roles in the reasoning process."[9] Sure, emotion can mislead us. But "when emotion is entirely left out of the reasoning picture, as happens in certain neurological conditions, reason turns out to be even more flawed than when emotion plays bad tricks on our decisions."[10] So even if we believe that the goals of schooling are entirely cognitive, we can't neglect emotion; it's not just an added nuisance or necessary adjunct. (Damasio also was interested not only in morality but in aesthetics; the brain is involved in aesthetic experiences as well.) Annie Murphy Paul in *The Extended Mind: The Power of Thinking outside the Brain* shows that bodily knowledge (interoception) can be *more accurate*, for instance in the work of day traders who must juggle huge amounts of information very rapidly, than conscious analysis of explicit data. "The heart, and not the head, leads the way," she concludes.[11] Leslie Shelton puts it bluntly: "Emotion is the master over cognition."[12]

Despite emotion lying at the core of well-being and suffering, despite existentialist philosophers' and existentialist psychologists' interests in human experience, and phenomenologists' focus on what it feels like to be or to do a certain thing, the study of emotion has come relatively late to students of education, especially higher education.[13]

James Zull, a biologist, started learning about how people learn—neurologically. He found, to his surprise, that it was not all cognitive and analytic, though this follows directly from a detailed understanding of how brains are organized and how they learn. His book *The Art of Changing the Brain: Enriching the Practice of Teaching by Exploring the Biology of Learning* includes not just one but two chapters on emotion and feeling: "A Feeling of This Business: In the Business of Reason and Memory, Feelings Count" (chapter 5), and "We Did This Ourselves: Changing the Brain through Effective Use of Emotion" (chapter 12).[14] Based on experiments in his own classes and watching others teach, both well and badly, he learned the importance of getting students' emotions on board. This happens when certain conditions hold: students see the big picture; motivation follows learning; stories help people care; teachers have to be *real*; and students need to feel that the learning is *theirs* and directed by them, not merely by the teacher's orders. He stumbled upon self-evaluation, just as I did.

But in the context of school, being and feeling are often left unexamined. Here's a brief introduction to this broad constellation of negative and positive emotions in school.

Negative Emotions in School

Students regularly experience negative emotions. It's common to read about stress and anxiety in the context of school, but rarely of long-standing, pervasive fear, despite its substantial presence.[15] (Fear tends to have a specific focus; anxiety tends to be more vague and general.) Beyond the exceptionally high incidence of carnage by assault weapons in the United States, students worldwide have experienced fear and trauma in school, terror, shame, boredom, despair, anxiety, stress, depression, and worst of all, suicide.

Fear and Trauma   Flight, fight, freeze. Those are our methods of survival.

Fear has a role to play in protecting us from dangers, by producing negative feelings. Constant fear gives rise to stress hormones, such as cortisol, which bathe the body's cells. Constant fear shortens telomeres, the ends of DNA molecules, and in turn contributes to hastened aging, diseases, and death. Obviously, introducing constant fear into humans' lives, especially the lives of young humans, is undesirable.

Yet students are often fearful in their school life—both academic and social, though this has been little studied, other than test anxiety or exam stress. "The risks of failure are so many and rewards so few," lament John Evans, Emma Rich, and Rachel Holroyd in their study, "Disordered Eating and Disordered Schooling: What Schools Do to Middle Class Girls."[16] Fear of failure is rampant, even built in.[17]

Schoolish Terror   In a novel about a chef (identified as a woman by the use of the new French word *cheffe*), the narrator accepts that she "didn't learn much in school."[18] She experienced bodily terror and panic, which in turn affected her cognitive learning and her ability to demonstrate that learning. This description vividly illustrates the bodily, cognitive, and emotional complexity of schoolish terror. (Fiction is often better at description than social science.)

> As soon as I walked into the classroom I felt a groundless terror contracting my bladder, and also, and worse, draining my memory of everything I'd crammed into it the night before, at home, in many diligent hours of anxiety and desperation to please, to be perfect, and so the precious fruits of my attempts to learn and remember vanished into thin air, the mere smell of the classroom—sweat, leather, dust, chalk—instantly turned my brain into a helium balloon, ready to fly out of my skull if I made just one move, and I knew what that move was, and I struggled in vain not to make it: it was my trembling, breathless little body hunching down as the teacher looked for someone to call on, making me look guilty, like some laggard who didn't even have the nerve to assert his boredom and laziness, when in fact I was yearning to cry out, "I know all this backward and forward, there's not one question I can't answer!," and then the balloon started to rise, drifted out through the open window, climbed into the autumn sky to join all the others that had broken free before it, the balloon of my memory, my work, my intelligence, leaving only the shell of my true being on the chair, tiny, stupid, pathetic.[19]

Here we have everything: fear, shame, anxiety, the need to please another who had power, perfectionism, and the bodily trigger of trauma.

In ordinary times, students experience humiliation, overload, a sense of failure. They experience the schools as punitive, and at many schools worldwide there is still the possibility of corporal punishment.[20] Accounts of indigenous people's boarding school punishment, or the well-documented sexual abuse in some Catholic schools, are reminders of undeniably real sources of fear in schools.[21]

In many schools, especially in higher education, students live with the ever-present fear of sexual abuse and harassment, from fellow students, faculty, staff. The Rape, Abuse & Incest National Network (RAINN) claims that "among undergraduate students, 23.1% of females and 5.4% of males experience rape or sexual assault through physical force, violence, or incapacitation"[22]

In a trauma-filled society—because of abuse, inequality, uncertainty—much of the experience students bring with them to school is traumatic. A trend toward "trauma-informed" or "trauma-aware" pedagogy acknowledges that school isn't *responsible for all of it*, but as an institution with a wide reach, it might be of help, and it certainly should not contribute to increasing suffering and trauma. It's not sufficient—but it is necessary.[23] Understanding that students of all ages and backgrounds may bring truly painful experiences with them—invisible, often—means that teachers should understand that some topics will be especially difficult. Some people nevertheless caricature "trigger alerts" as stemming from "wokeness," the new version of the old "political correctness," and call those who suffer "snowflakes."

And COVID-19? Some of us remain fearful, as of this writing, and traumatized simply from these years' experiences. Fear of being together was added to every classroom for a time, as well as fear of being shut down, the unknown and unknowable adding to everyone's discomfort.

Trauma-informed pedagogy became widely discussed during the COVID summer of 2020, and a crash course in all this distress, including how to teach for inclusion and racial justice during a summer of police brutality directed against Black people, has put a great burden on faculty who themselves, of course, have their own fears.[24]

Even less evident, externally, than trauma, though, is shame.

Shame and Surveillance   Shame is a sense of inferiority or concern about others' negative judgment. It's a powerful means of controlling behavior, and it occurs throughout human societies, often reinforced through gossip. Sometimes compared with guilt, which is more of an internal sensation or a response to a specific misdeed, shame, because of its social nature, saturates schoolishness. Students commanded to perform publicly, in front of others—reading aloud, volunteering insights, being called on—are subject to the evaluations of others, both peers and teachers.

Successful performance leads to a sense of pleasure and pride; unsuccessful performance leads to humiliation and can result in avoidance of the situation that produced it.

Shame stems from caring what other people think, from our human attentiveness to others' mental states and to having a sense of self derived in part through interaction. *Face* refers to the sense of dignity and respect in others' eyes; it's a powerful driver of both our noblest and our most despairing actions. Peter N. Stearns, a historian of emotion, puts shame within a cluster of self-conscious emotions, which require both a sense of self and knowledge of group norms. These emotions develop through interaction with others, unlike, say, fear. (Fear, like all emotions, is also mediated by cognition, which alerts the experiencer to dangers.) Shame provides a "sense of failing or potentially failing to live up to audience expectations," with awareness as to possible "consequences to self and self-image."[25]

School and schoolishness teach us to attend to others' evaluation, which is constant. Schools usually involve surveillance of attendance, of bodily positions, of participation, of interaction and the specifics of language, of comportment. Beyond but including schools, a near-century of humanistic social science, such as Norbert Elias's *The Civilizing Process*, Michel Foucault's *Discipline and Punish* (among other works), and Nikolas Rose's *Governing the Soul: The Shaping of the Private Self*, has shown the ways state and social power and individual consciousness have been intertwined, with harmful consequences.[26] Modernist and modernizing education and the civilizing project and discipline begin early in childhood, with all behavior subject to scrutiny and evaluation, as well as potential punishment.

Shame in schools may arise from making public mistakes, from being bullied, being less highly achieving than someone else, being poorer, heavier, slower, too tall, too short, gender nonconforming, shy, neurodivergent, learning a new language, having parents in jail, immigration status precarious, with disabilities, belonging to a racialized group, being housing insecure, food insecure. . . . The ability to evade shame is rare and precious, and afforded to few people. (Faculty certainly experience shame not only in their own interactions but possibly also in interactions with students. We may all wish to be that "cool" teacher, but few of us are.)

As Shelton writes in a report on the shame felt by students struggling to read and write, "School itself becomes a kind of hell—a virtual prison with no escape (except for running away or dropping out) and the joy of learning descends into a struggle to survive, where the name of the game is damage control—to just lay low until you can get through the ordeal and get on with life after school." She continues, showing that the "seeds of shame [are] sown by the daily experiences of failure and not measuring up in school."[27]

There are also appearance-related dimensions of shame, especially for women, girls, and minoritized students.

> In a modern society in which people lead their lives in close proximity to one another, mechanisms for social control are necessary. Shame . . . may be one of the most powerful of these mechanisms. Unfortunately, our results suggest that these mechanisms may also be activated by cues of physical appearance such as obesity, which may thus become a stigmatizing feature and put adolescents at psychosocial risk. The results also suggest that clinical treatment of obesity should take psychosocial aspects of the condition into account. Treating obesity may not just be a matter of diet and exercise but also of dealing with issues of shame and social isolation.[28]

In an unforgiving system ruled by a single model of the normative, anyone perceived as outside the "normal," such as people characterized as obese, may find themselves shunned or stigmatized—by peers or by the institution itself, including staff such as teachers, counselors, and principals. These experiences of shame and lack of belonging pervade education at all levels.

Schoolish Boredom   Believe it or not, lots of researchers have looked at student boredom. Boredom is deadly to learning. It's also part of alienation and often leads eventually to other troubles such as creating a nuisance, being disciplined, being suspended or expelled, dropping out, flunking. Students are supposed to be engaged, to pay attention, even if it means hours of listening passively every day to someone far away. But most students (about two-thirds) are bored in high school every day, and only 2 percent are never bored.

A teenage poet named Obasi Davis wrote a celebrated poem, "Bored in 1st Period," and of "dreading the upcoming day."[29] WikiHow articles advise how to deal with one's own boredom in class and give parents tips in case their children are occasionally bored in school—as if that were anomalous.[30] A franker treatment, from the Harvard Graduate School of Education, is titled "Bored Out of Their Minds: A Look at Why Students Get Increasingly Bored as They Get Older—and Why It Matters."[31]

Zachary Jason summarizes a Gallup poll from 2013 asking students about their engagement.[32] The younger they are, the more engaged they are. The more years in school, the more bored they are.

A huge, twenty-two-thousand-student survey in 2015 showed eight of ten high school students reporting negative emotions in school; students in large numbers felt "tired" (39 percent), "stressed" (29 percent), and "bored" (26 percent).[33] This is not so different from a 2007 survey of more than eighty-one thousand high school students, two-thirds of whom said they were bored in class *every single day.*[34] They explained it as stemming from lack of interaction with teachers (30 percent) and uninteresting material (75 percent).

When students were asked why they dropped out of school, 47 percent said it was because school was boring.[35]

Some people argue that life is boring, so school shouldn't have to be entertaining. But as Grant Wiggins, a blogger whose piece "Attention, Teachers! Why Students Are Bored" caught my eye,[36] says, "Please don't write me and say that there is always boredom in life; I simply won't post it. We're talking about needlessly boring and improvable teacher practices here." (He says that the top student complaint, in case you're curious, is PowerPoint.)

Perfectionism and Mistakes

One of the messages that schoolishness conveys is that there is an absolute standard of perfection, and somebody is always in a position to assess students' approaches toward perfection and to let them know when they fall short. A score of 100 percent (or more?), an A or A+, means that you've got everything exactly right. (There's no meaningful difference between numbers or letters as evaluation; both are "tiered grading.")[37] Schoolishness teaches inadequacy and perfectionism as it focuses on evaluation and performance.

I'm all for high standards. I have them myself (I call myself a recovered perfectionist and often model imperfection, in both my teaching and in giving talks); I was attentive to my grades and loved getting A-pluses and 100 percent (or higher) scores on assignments and courses. But most students don't get those perfect grades, and the less you get them the more discouraging the entire process is. And the more you get high grades, the less prone you are to risk losing your unblemished record.

But there's something even more pernicious about this idea of perfection. I will use two examples to talk about it, one from writing and one from science and language learning.

Writing courses have many goals in helping students become better writers. In my many decades of teaching I've encountered a handful of students who were extraordinary writers, and anybody reading their work would concur. They almost always came from backgrounds where their families were professionals, and they spoke a variety of English in their households that would be recognized as "standard." They had not only the mechanics down pat, but they were comfortable and even playful with their writing. They might have a poetic opening to something that was then going to be scientific, or they played with the form in a way that was far beyond mechanical and was both responsible and creative. They were confident and sophisticated. They integrated personal positions and theories, quotations, facts, and arguments and evidence in ways that didn't feel painful but nuanced and layered.

But saying that they are perfect writers in their context may sometimes give the impression that they're finished and they don't have to keep working at it. (In fact, many faculty assume that the first-year writing faculty have "taken care" of writing and that students ought to appear in their fourth-year Environmental Studies or third-year Film course with it completely under control.) As a writer myself, one with several books and articles and chapters under my belt, I know that a writer's craft is never complete and never perfect. So evaluating writing on a scale that offers a level of "perfect" or "excellent" gives a false sense of mastery to those who are already good at writing, and this practice discourages those who aren't yet good at it.

In science or language learning it's another matter entirely. Facts—names of elements or chemical reactions, names of geological eras or hominin species, the vectors that govern interplanetary space travel, gender in Romance languages—are necessary foundational dimensions of understanding the world. Someone could get them right or wrong.

But fixation on these sorts of facts often overshadows the much more important question of *what you are doing with all this*, and it conveys the impression that once you get these little things right, that's all you need to do. Further, in the case of second (third, fourth) languages, this fixation on the small and right or wrong often paralyzes novice speakers and prevents them from actually *using* the language while echoes of quizzes reverberate in their heads.

Don't believe me? Believe physics Nobel laureate Carl Wieman. He was so frustrated by the superficial learning of contemporary science students that he's been devoting the second half of his career to science education.[38]

My own students, very successful in their schooling, often bring with them this paralyzing perfectionism—in their schoolwork and in their private lives. And as every therapist and writing coach knows, perfectionism produces procrastination. So my students struggle not only to be excellent at everything but struggle to begin because they're so afraid of judgment. One of my approaches is to model imperfection and error, mistake making, and correction. Because we also know that learning often includes mistakes, but if the mistakes are going to be judged and averaged into a final grade—oh, grades—then making mistakes is not acceptable, and how can one begin to achieve perfection in every facet of every activity? Schoolish selves are perfectionist, and schoolish selves procrastinate.

There's a connection between personal mental health and the emotional dimensions of schoolishness. A study by Evans, Rich, and Holroyd of disordered eating and mental health in a high school demonstrates some of the complex relationships among body images, eating disorders, senses of self, and school. The authors attribute at least some of the disordered body images to schools, quoting one girl who explicitly states that "the depression came from school."[39]

Yet this study has little company. "Research has tended to shy away not only from exploring more negative emotions in schooling, such as alienation and disaffection, but also the potential negative uses of emotion in sustaining social hierarchies and effecting social control."[40] A lot of the work on emotion has rather to do with affective *management*, or control. Such work may argue that students' disordered eating originates from their senses of selfhood shaped by schools.

Yet the schoolish practices themselves, such as the emphasis on "performance and perfection codes" within a more general culture of performativity, including promotion of slenderness and body perfection, not only inside schools but also outside them, make management of emotions impossible.[41]

As students navigate a schoolish world saturated with threats and evaluations, they are only as good as their most recent accomplishments. As students are ranked and sorted in competition with each other, some students surrender and give up. Some struggle to survive.

Evans et al. are told by a student, "Even if you work really hard and get an A, and then someone else gets an A* [equivalent to A+ in the United States], it doesn't matter any more because they have taken [the achievement] away from you."[42] Young people with various kinds of stress manifested in disordered eating become "disembodied": "They feel that they corporeally have less worth, less significance, less substance as they lose their sense of 'authentic' self."[43]

As students are rejected by their teachers if they challenge them, in emotion-laden contexts, they display "dispassion, detachment, distance and aloofness, drivers of the 'empty pragmatic self.'"[44] Competition and achievement are the constant, and sometimes incompatible, imperatives. As students strive to reach high levels of achievement, "the 'perfection' of such performances is ultimately ephemeral, unobtainable and, therefore, deeply alienating and damaging to the persons concerned."[45] Perfectionism combines with desire to please and constant focus on external validation. And those with the greatest "success" often struggle too though, given their outward success, they may not understand this. Lauren Berlant's notion of "cruel optimism," "when something you desire is actually an obstacle to your flourishing," applies perfectly to school.[46] This leads to Bateson's double-bind: you're harmed if you do it (achieve) and also harmed if you don't.[47]

The Risk of High-Achieving Environments: Cruel Optimism   In 2019 the National Academies of Sciences, Engineering, and Medicine declared students at "high-achieving schools" in the United States an at-risk group for poor health and well-being, along with those living in poverty, those under foster care, those recently immigrated, and those whose parents are incarcerated. Students at high-achieving schools exceed national norms in rates of substance misuse, depression, anxiety, and rule-breaking, and sometimes fare worse in these measures than their high-poverty counterparts.[48] (This holds for Germany, too.) In 2018 the Robert Wood Johnson Foundation noted that students subjected to "excessive pressure to excel" similarly suffered. In China, Susanne Bregnbæk has shown the pressures, sometimes leading to suicide, of students at the top schools. In the United States, suicides among students at highly selective elite colleges and universities, as well as high schools, are noteworthy.[49]

Despair   Philosopher Mary Townsend was teaching an Existentialism course at Tulane University when a cluster of suicides occurred. In a surfeit of bad faith, hoping to avoid contagion, the college advised students to have massages and get enough sleep—without explicitly mentioning the suicide. Townsend and her students puzzled over what this meant. They concluded that students had true existential suffering, with no place to "be at home in the world."[50] Middle-class students, for instance, were expected to move from their families for college and later for work. They were supposed to identify with the institution, with its arbitrary branding of college colors and logos. While on campus, the lucky ones created pseudo-families. Those struggling were supposed to go to the gym or take mindfulness class. (Yes, of course they are good things to do.) "Self-care," though, is an individual solution to a systemic problem. Worse—it masks the woes of the system, in what Ronald E. Purser calls "McMindfulness."[51]

Students beyond Tulane and this class, and beyond college, find it challenging to be "at home in the world."

And that's a big problem.

Anxiety, Stress, Depression, and Suicide

Statistics about mental health are bandied about constantly. Mental health of young people is poor in the United States and many other countries, but not all countries. Up to three-quarters of US college students experience psychiatric and mental health disorders.[52] Rates of depression and anxiety have more than doubled between 2013 and 2021.[53] From mood disorders like depression and anxiety to stress and suicidal ideation, children (and adults) experience worrisome mental disorders. The World Health Organization reports that throughout the world, about a quarter of all people, at some point in their lives, will be affected by mental illness. Depression is the illness that causes the greatest number of sick days, worldwide.

(Mental disorders have long been in the top-ten causes of the "Global Burden of Disease.")[54] Most solutions, however, are individual and psychological: better self-care, treatment with therapy and medication, increased numbers of mental health professionals. In the short term, this is necessary and essential. However, we know that cultural and environmental conditions have enormous effects on people's well-being; my contention is that one of these conditions is schoolishness—in the context of other negative social trends.

School Phobia, Refusal, and Resistance

Kindergartners are excited about school. By first grade they dread it.[55] They have stomachaches and visit the nurse (if there is one), or beg to stay home sick. They have nightmares. (School nightmares persist for decades. Ask anyone.) Schools use carrots and sticks to get students to attend: pizza and ribbons for perfect attendance, suspension and expulsion for excessive absences, or even child protective services or jail if the parents aren't doing their part to ensure that children attend.[56] Ever since universal schooling was made compulsory, students, and often their families, resisted.

David Lancy chronicles all the ways students have resisted schooling, going back in the records to Mesopotamia and ancient Rome, medieval Europe and early modern America. Students were beaten; they were shoved into cold rooms where the only chair was for the teacher. Physical punishment was frequent. A truant officer, or "the man nobody liked," enforced undesirable compulsory education laws.[57] Students' distaste of the experience of schooling has a long history—but now more people go to school for ever-longer times daily and in terms of years, as you saw in the previous chapter.

In East Asia, where the consequences of failure may be dire—culturally and economically—student suicide rates are high.[58] "School refusal" is widely known in East Asia, and it occurs in the United States,[59] though it is not technically recognized as a psychiatric disorder and may be considered just resistance. Whether it's a symptom or a syndrome, it's revelatory: Some children have panic attacks, anxiety, depression, phobias; some have been bullied. Some have separation anxiety. Some are dealing with family issues. But it's telling that school seems undesirable to many rather than a safe place to go, in which to cope with problems. School may instead be the setting for increased trauma. Still, for some school *is* a refuge, a sanctuary. During the pandemic lockdown, many students longed for school and were at greater risk without it. Other students' well-being *increased* during the pandemic, as the social misery lessened.[60] But students have varying needs; meeting actual needs is necessary.

Naomi Fisher, the author of a fantastic book called *Changing Our Minds: How Children Can Take Control of Their Own Learning*, posted a long thread on Twitter in August 2022, beginning

> As a clinical psychologist, I'm often asked what to do about school refusal.[61] By which adults usually mean, how can we get the children to go to school and stop protesting? I meet lots of kids who have refused to go to school. When I talk to them and their parents, they always have reasons. Sometimes it's bullying, but not always. Sometimes it is the way they feel at school, or the intensity of the smells and noise. Sometimes it is being prevented from following their interests, or made to do things which they find pointless. Sometimes it's how bored they feel. Sometimes it's how stressful they find the repeated transitions and being with large numbers of other people all day long. One girl told me all about the rules in her school and how arbitrary and outrageous she thought they were. She told me that school felt like a place of unreasonable control to her, and she objected. School trauma is much more complex than school refusal. We need to start asking "What's going wrong here?" rather than "How can we make them go?" We need to see school refusal as feedback, sometimes the only feedback children can give.[62]

We need to take seriously the experiences of schooling.

A psychiatric diagnosis, "oppositional defiant disorder," or not being willing to obey authority, causes problems at home and at school. It develops by age eight and may be lifelong. "The causes are not known."[63]

Could the causes stem from the very oppressive structures within which a self-affirming organism finds itself?

Students who "oppose" and "defy" may end up rejecting school entirely. Some refuse. Some experience "phobia," mostly in primary and secondary schools. The last article I can find about "college phobia" comes from 1965, when college attendance in the United States was about six million (about 51 percent of high school completers), compared to almost twenty million in 2017, about 66 percent of the college-age population.[64] College attendance has been declining since its peak in 2010 but has declined more rapidly since the pandemic; this is regarded as dangerous—to the schools themselves, obviously, but also, given the education gospel, to individuals and society as well.

Even when negative experiences aren't traumatic, students may still experience, for long periods of their lives, lack of meaningful engagement. The trauma carried after schooling is often lifelong.

Well-Being

But it's not inevitable that schoolishness creates misery. Goodness may emerge in schools. At school, children and college students meet lifelong friends, sometimes life partners. They discover passions. They meet requirements for jobs. They laugh and run, especially in other systems such as Finland's, where play and freedom are incorporated into the shorter-than-ours school day, making children's lives less schoolish.

During COVID, almost *everyone* longed for school—but for which *parts* of school? Students missed their friends. Parents needed child care. Politicians, for various reasons, just wanted schools to open.

I see my challenge, as a teacher, as trying to create more of the good stuff. More joy. More well-being. More space. More learning, but also more confidence about learning. More curiosity. More genuine, meaningful, comfortable learning (in the sense of confidence) rather than panicked accomplishment.

Even with the structures of schools, there are opportunities for thriving, which stem from what I see as the most fundamental aspects of schooling—*gathering with others for learning*. Both the "gathering" and the "learning" offer some opportunities, which I elaborate on throughout the book.

So that's why I reject schoolishness but can, gingerly, with the right conditions, consider embracing (in some cases) school. Little tweaks can bring relief and improvement but can't solve the greatest problems. That requires bigger and intertwined changes.

Fundamental Elements and Structures

As Ronald E. Purser puts so forcefully in his critique of the commodification of mindfulness, which he rightly points to as an individual solution to inhumane and brutal conditions, "Anything that offers success in our unjust society without trying to change it is not revolutionary—it just helps people cope. . . . Instead of setting practitioners free, it helps them adjust to the very conditions that caused their problems. A truly revolutionary movement would seek to overturn this dysfunctional system."[65]

It is even starker: "Personal stress . . . has societal causes."[66] Suffering in school has at least some structural causes.

The fundamental elements, the structures and grammar, of schoolishness are the focus of this book's ten central chapters. When all these elements are present, students experience constriction and tedium. When only some of them are present, their experience is more fulfilling and enjoyable. When none are present, then learning can occur in conditions of ease and peace.

We begin with a look at the most basic but very confusing thing: what the whole point is, the big picture—that is, trying to see what this institution of school is for.

2

THE AIMS AND THE ENDS, VALUES AND VALUE

From Games, Sorting, and Exchange Value to Learning, Being, and Use Value

> What counted as education seemed to mainly involve learning to walk in single file and otherwise keep quiet. School meant grown-ups telling you that things had to be done in a certain way, and in no other, that however many obvious and inviting paths might lead from one point to another, only one of them was right. The rest might as well not exist at all. To do well, to earn praise, you had to learn not to see them anymore.
>
> BEN EHRENREICH, *Desert Notebooks: A Road Map for the End of Time*

> There are things that can be measured. There are things that are worth measuring. But what can be measured is not always what is worth measuring; what gets measured may have no relationship to what we really want to know. The costs of measuring may be greater than the benefits. . . . The things that get measured may draw effort away from the things we really care about. And measurement may provide us with distorted knowledge—knowledge that seems solid but is actually deceptive.
>
> JERRY Z. MULLER, *The Tyranny of Metrics*

At great expense, all contemporary societies support schools. The content varies. The forms differ. But the education gospel holds. Societies support schools to prepare citizens, and to promote loyalty to the nation-state. They support worker preparation. Some use schools to promote social integration, perhaps of new arrivals or of minoritized groups. Other goals, perhaps covert, maintain the status quo, even while professing contrary notions of social mobility. Some schooling aims to assist in international competitions: "us" versus the rest of the world, different from the widespread intrasocietal sorting for internal "meritocracy." We must ask deep questions about all dimensions of schooling: Why do we have schools? What do they teach? How do they teach? They're all intertwined.

I'll start with why we have schools. What is school fundamentally for? If schools are part of everyone's childhood, possibly for decades, then we must *begin with the end in mind*, as they say in permaculture and design thinking. The aims for me lie in *fostering confident, independent, joyous, effective learners who can ask questions and do so without harm.* Sometimes school, gathering with others for learning, can help with this.

"The aims of education" is a huge topic. The philosophy of education literature is deep and substantial; social theory often touches on education. The goals differ among different entities, whether society (and taxpayers), institutions, individual students, or teachers. Politicians often weigh in. The goals may be idealistic or pragmatic, explicit and overt, or implicit and covert, core or peripheral. Sometimes the means of accomplishing core goals get confused with the ends. A *New York Times* series in September 2022 about the purpose of school had a dozen responses: school is for everyone; for economic mobility; making citizens; care; wasting time; learning to read; connecting to nature; merit; hope; parent activism; teaching; "us."[1] A 1999 book edited by Roger Marples, *The Aims of Education*, includes as aims liberalism and citizenship, critical thinking, autonomy, national identity, self-determination, well-being, fairness, moral seriousness, and social commitment. One author questions the need for aims.[2] In December 2022 the US secretary of education Miguel Cardona tweeted that "every student should have access to an education that aligns with industry demands and evolves to meet the demands of tomorrow's global workforce."[3] Comments in response were split between outrage and support. Neil Postman, with characteristic sharpness, puns: *The End of Education.*

I've asked many people why they are in school, why they are in college. I've listened to countless discussions to tease out the assumed goals—and they are a mess.

When I ask students why they are in school, their responses include getting good grades, graduating, finding a job, making friends, and having fun. They're also happy to learn, but they rarely volunteer this, and that response has diminished over the thirty-five years of my teaching career so far.[4] That's not what school is about for them. I say that not to criticize or mock the students but to observe that the goals of school have coalesced around pragmatic principles, especially return on investment, for individuals, and sorting for society. Some of my students, in my always ungraded classes, are aware. One said, "I feel that I've lost a lot of my enjoyment for learning. College and academics in general have become so grade focused, end-result focused, distilling four years of studying, learning into a single number as a GPA determinant for employability. This semester I am 'treating myself' to classes that emphasize learning, and focus on interesting material and less about the actual grade. I'm thrilled to be able to take interesting classes, de-emphasize grading and at least for my final semester of college, enjoy actual learning." I found that sad. Only at the end of college, to "enjoy actual learning"?

Some see schooling as the inevitable gauntlet that children must endure. Alternatives would be child labor or idleness (voluntary or involuntary), which, people believe, leads to "delinquency." This was the thinking that brought compulsory high school to the United States in the early twentieth century. "Juvenile delinquency" was one of the first things identified as a "moral panic": All those teenagers—another new category, following "adolescents" in the early twentieth century—hanging around urban streets, consuming the new media of movies and popular music, wearing scandalous clothes. . . . This was not acceptable.[5] Something had to be done about it. So they sent them to school.

As I said—it's a mess. Or, more respectably: the goals are incoherent, contradictory, jumbled, and unclear. We might regard the goals of school as including both the "values" and the "value" driving it.

I'll divide them into two rough halves, inspired by Marxian analysis, in turn inspired by Aristotle—use value and exchange value. *Use value* is connected to the material human needs satisfied by something. In a market, however, *exchange value* is extracted, and connected to the labor value; as labor increases, the exchange value of commodities increases. Then I'll talk about the sorting function and the various accreted functions.

Use Value: Learning (What?)

The concept of *use value* reminds us that schoolish content can be valuable because someone is going to use it, in some way. In this sense, schooling is about *what people actually learn*.

The content of learning-for-use may be a combination of skills, knowledge, and dispositions. And depending on the level, location, time, and participants, all these may differ, and also may be challenged. What is the schools' job? What do schools have to do to prepare citizens to make sense of a complex and infinite world?

Almost all institutions of education have requirements, initially because of use value. Requirements range from learning how to use capital letters in kindergarten, learning to read by first grade, or learning state history in fifth grade in US primary schools, or learning a foreign language for three years to enter highly competitive colleges, or taking psychology if you're going to become a doctor. Here we might see arguments about Great Books, about amassing cultural capital in the service of either social integration or social mobility.

Banking: Content for the Future (Often Fraught and Backward-Looking)

Institutions of education are charged with providing some kind of predetermined curriculum, sometimes with a set of shared "standards" or

Figure 2.1. The banking concept of education

"learning outcomes." Schoolish content is inculcated, "banked" in Paulo Freire's term, against potential use at some future time.[6] It is shoved in, instructed into sometimes incurious minds.

Schools' focus on "content," learning goals, learning outcomes, skills, knowledge, dispositions, standards, presupposes agreement about what must be learned in school at what levels. This content may appear value-neutral as in the allegedly universal math; it may present highly ideological material such as views of the nation-state or religion (or secularism). It may aim to produce individuals with certain traits—docile, obedient, "clean" (as in the immoral Indian boarding schools of the United States and Canada) for indigenous, colonized, racialized, or classed groups. Or it can promote confidence, critical thinking, and creativity for the future ruling class. Students are trained to know their places; in few societies are all groups freely mingled.

Nations Produce Citizens: Citizenship, "Civics"

One reason schooling initially became compulsory was that the community's need for citizens overrode individual parents' preferences, whether to keep their children at home or at work; more recently, parents might wish to keep their children away from required vaccinations.[7] In other words, compulsory education began with citizens' obligations, not individual goals. Benedict Anderson, in *Imagined Communities*, demonstrated how the task of building a modern national polity depends on the shared creation of a story, of literacy, of a history.[8] The most efficient way to inculcate all this is at school.

In the nineteenth century, in the United States and Germany, as well as elsewhere in Europe, nation-building efforts coincided with efforts to create municipality-funded, compulsory primary schools and "common schools" teaching uniform curricula.[9] In the United States, Horace Mann was the architect of this plan, though his ideas built on decades of international attention to the role of education. It's a very complicated story, with issues of religion, scale, funding, content, teacher training, federal or local control, concerns about equality, and continual reforms and reorganization.

Many twenty-first-century disputes in the United States are similar to those a century or more earlier, when many parents had resisted the mandates for schooling. This dispute remains with homeschooling and unschooling. Current US battles occur over control and funding (public, private, religious, charter) and over the curriculum (banned books, critical literacy, social justice, and a right-wing hyped-up campaign against critical race theory, in 2022). In other countries disputes have to do with access and admissions, with costs, quality, inclusion. Given the scale of education and the hopes pinned on it, it's no wonder that it's contentious.

Dispositions: Societies Strive to Inculcate Character, Comportment, Compliance

All young people need to learn their society's norms of behavior and comportment. Humans must have some kind of discipline. Whether this is inculcated simply through incorporation into social groups or through explicit enforcement of discipline, children learn to control their bodies and tongues; people cannot simply do whatever they want to or blurt out every thought whenever they wish. Social and cultural values are always transmitted in schools; these are sometimes explicit ("Respect others") and sometimes implicit (competition and individualism are desirable).[10]

A long line of social critique has shown how pervasive the explicit promotion of discipline is in European societies, with a focus on obedience and punishment for transgressions. Especially for poor children, the goal was to prevent them from sloth, idleness, and dirt. Boarding schools for disadvantaged children—and in North America, for indigenous children—aimed to re-form the poor and culturally other. In younger grades, focus on comportment and discipline are evident: young children learn to line up, wait to speak, raise hands, take turns, or whatever the norms of interaction are. Proper comportment ("soft skills") assures the advantaged of their status. For the disadvantaged, there's a slim chance of mobility.

Whether schools focus on doing good for others or for the self—in other words, on values or value—whether they emphasize diversity or uniformity, docility or freedom, obedience or creativity, social equality or stratification—they both *reflect social values and influence them*. Some schools challenge social values. Some emphasize "critical thinking" or "cultural revolution," while others emphasize conformity.

Schools also promote a "hidden curriculum" of social hierarchy, from language to adornment to aspiration, with more advantaged, majority teachers often unaware of their complicity.

But sometimes the overt goals smuggle in covert goals as well, as with the notion of "cultural capital" and *social mobility for some*, which means *some are not moving*. Some lack this capital. Some noble-sounding goals *assume* ongoing stratification. As David Labaree says, "someone has to fail" in this zero-sum game.[11] And the cliché of obedience training for the working classes and creativity and critical education for the advantaged has a basis in reality.

Pragmatism: Preparing Workers

Businesses need educated and trained workers. The common understanding is that our "industrial" model of schooling was created with the encouragement of factory owners, as Charles Eliot, president of Harvard, conferred with Fordist efficiency experts.[12] Workers in factories had to be docile, obedient. Prior to that, institutions of higher education prepared clergy, but were also a kind of finishing school for the wealthy. Many businesses collaborate with schools at all levels to influence the curriculum. When my children were in elementary school, I was confused about the intertwining and intervention of businesses in public schools, for instance when volunteers came from the Chamber of Commerce to the schools to give presentations; or a teacher-friend was employed by a business-and-education coalition that aimed to influence and provide training at schools; or when corporations (Coke, Disney) sponsored signs, libraries, TVs. They solved the problem of financial shortfalls, as did auctions and candy bar sales, especially in well-to-do neighborhood schools. I should not have been confused. Businesses want workers ready to go.

Acquisition of professional and technical expertise is a necessity when a public depends on experts having certain knowledge. Society depends on students being prepared, which presupposes some expertise: but in what?

This emphasis on worker preparedness sometimes appears "timeless" and at other times responds to events. When Russia launched the Sputnik satellite in 1957, the United States perceived that it had a technological and scientific gap, and this spurred a focus on science education.[13] In the

2020s the COVID-19 pandemic should have prompted investment in public health, virology, and epidemiology.

But disputes are everywhere. In even the most highly regarded profession in the United States, medicine, we can observe detailed disputes over what is necessary to prepare doctors. Organic chemistry? Humanities and communication? Business? In many countries, medicine is a four-year degree; in the United States it's eight—a general degree followed by professional training. It always involves apprenticeship. Assessing the preparation of doctors is an entire industry.

Content, Requirements, Curricula

Schoolish requirements change. We no longer claim that to be educated, people must know ancient Greek or Latin, or elsewhere classical Chinese, but these have been central to creating educated people in some places and times. In Vietnam, Korea, and Japan, for instance, knowledge of classical Chinese was essential, given these countries' roles on the periphery of the Chinese empire. In the 1980s concerns in the United States focused on "cultural literacy," as E. D. Hirsch Jr. noted that few students were familiar any longer with John Milton, or with passages from *Julius Caesar*, or the dates of World War II.[14] He found it especially worrisome that young people couldn't read the work addressed to a "general reader." "Our aim," wrote Hirsch, "should be to attain universal literacy at a very high level, to achieve not only greater economic prosperity but also greater social justice and more effective democracy. We Americans have long accepted literacy as a paramount aim of schooling, but only recently have some of us who have done research in the field begun to realize that literacy is far more than a skill and that it requires large amounts of specific information."[15] Ah. There's the rub. Which specific information?

Content and skills change over time, resulting in tension between groups advocating and groups resisting such changes. How should we teach the theory of biological evolution, astronomical principles, geology and the age of the earth? In many countries, national and international history are contested, such as the Japanese-Chinese realities in the twentieth century, or Japanese and Korean views of the Second World War. In the United States the nature of slavery has been a dominant discourse in the 2020s, with *The 1619 Project* of Nikole Hannah-Jones, critical race theory, and similar touchstones for political fights.

Even for "skills" we have debates both about *what* to teach and about *how* to teach it—including basic literacy ("whole language" versus "phonics," in the US); which linguistic variety should be taught (for example, in Haiti, French or Haitian Creole?); numeracy ("new math"); algebra; use of calculators or computers or phones; cursive.

Values and cultural ideologies are inherent in every decision, whether views of the child, or of human social relations as inherently respectful and cooperative or tense and competitive.[16] Ideas of the place of religion, nationalism, and gender, race, sexuality, are always involved.

Disagreements constantly arise about what knowledge must be included. During the question-and-answer session at a lecture I gave at a regional university, one faculty member expressed her dismay that few students knew how a bill becomes a law. At another talk someone was shocked that a student didn't know who Ruby Bridges was. Granted these are important topics. It's also important to understand how biosequestration works and how much carbon has been released into the atmosphere, and it's important to know what NATO is in the context of Russia's invasion of Ukraine. I think the Chinese revolution is a world-historical event. And it's essential to understand what R-naught is in viral transmission. And for that you really need to understand something about virology, and about evolution. Some advocate real-world budgeting for high-school students. In my day we had shop class and metal workshop for boys and cooking and sewing for girls. (I loved saying "Welsh rarebit.") Some contemporary schools have "life skills." Many privileged college students graduate needing courses in "adulting."

National curriculum organizations and lobbies work hard to get their favorite items included in the requirements, which might be called "standards" or "core" or simply "the curriculum." In the United States, fights about the "common core" in primary and secondary school were an attempt to find common ground among states about what students needed in order to be "career and college ready." As with everything American, tension characterized the struggle between private and public interests. Unlike most countries, the United States doesn't even have consensus about the need for a department of education.

School requirements often backfire. In college these are sometimes called "gen eds," or general education requirements (usually not characteristic of European or Asian higher education). In the United States, with its emphasis on "well-rounded students," we often require every student to take first-year composition and some sort of mathematical thinking, science, and arts or humanities, no matter what individual students' professional goals are. Students often see gen eds as something to get out of the way, obstacles to pursuing their genuine interests. My own institution, a relatively conservative Catholic one, has numerous requirements: philosophy and theology, as well as history, art, math, and science. Students constantly tell me they're eager to get them over with. Some other universities, such as the University of Chicago and Columbia University, still have a core curriculum, where all students have to take a certain sequence of courses. Still other universities are much more flexible, such as Brown, where writing competency is the only specific requirement (beyond the major and a certain number of credits), or Hampshire College, where students have to take something in four out of five distribution areas, plus undertake some kind of "engagement." Graduate education and professional education usually have some sort of balance between electives and requirements.

Students often resist attempts to coerce and compel. Antiracism became a pressing issue at my university in 2020, and colleagues called for the addition of diversity courses as part of the required curriculum, just as several years earlier some people had wanted to include a kind of sustainability requirement. I was dubious.

In the 1990s at the University of Colorado Denver and at the University of Denver I taught required courses in diversity. Like all such courses they were created with idealistic intentions. Given my own background, I taught Cultural Diversity in the Modern World as an anthropology course, with the goal of introducing the idea of relativism and respect for multiple ways of living. It was a very difficult teaching assignment, partly because it was my first time teaching anthropology (I had taught Chinese language, literature, and culture for several years). But it was also difficult because the students had not chosen to be there. Some were quite resistant. I remember one course evaluation where a student wrote "I think Professor Blum hates white people." Now, as a white person, I don't think that's entirely true, unless there's a limited amount of respect available. Students forced to take a sustainability course may already be enthusiastic; they may actually know nothing about it and discover amazing things. Or they may go through the motions because they are opposed to the course but have no choice but to take it. So this kind of requirement can easily backfire. ("Indoctrinating" students is not a simple task!)

Algebra An illuminating case has arisen in the 2020s about the role of algebra, with both use-value and exchange-value dimensions. High schools began to offer algebra after Harvard, in 1820, made it an admission requirement. Fifty years later Harvard added geometry to its requirements—and secondary schools again followed suit.[17]

As high schools have promoted a college-prep curriculum for all students, and as math played a substantial role as a prerequisite for later science and math, in the United States all students were expected to have at least pre-algebra by the end of high school. Math is often seen as extremely difficult. In college, perhaps community college (that globally rare, democratic version of higher education), many students ended up taking what used to be called "remedial" (now called "developmental") courses in algebra. Many students who failed pre-algebra in high school continue to fail the same course in community college, and there are other consequences as well: Students have to pay for these courses, which don't advance them toward their degrees; many drop out. In opposition to the goals, the actual consequences are that students do not complete their associate degree, or they do not transfer into a four-year program. So given the realities of very poor math education throughout the United States, combined with severe inequality, combined with the high cost of increasingly privatized higher education, many jurisdictions, such as the state of California, have begun to question the ongoing requirement for algebra and calculus, and "tracking" students.[18] Further discussion of the merit of this requirement revolves around the actual *use value* of requiring algebra for everyone. Some have suggested replacing algebra with statistics as a universal math requirement.[19] These disagreements have gotten violent; Stanford math educator Jo Boaler received death threats after she challenged the algebra requirement. (Just for the record, Japanese math classes do not have tracking, and Japanese students consistently perform highly in the PISA tests).[20]

I can't come down on one side or another in the algebra requirement wars (I personally love algebra), but this issue illustrates the importance of returning to goals periodically to weigh what is included and what is excluded. Otherwise things just keep accreting. Requirements increase, and then every few decades most institutions revisit the need for them—but by then many other vested interests have become institutionalized; teaching staff has been hired to teach required courses; faculty lobby for their own discipline's importance. Members of the public who took similar courses got attached. But most students take these courses purely for their exchange value: one unit of math fits into the equation that is needed for the credential.

This pragmatic conversation about learning-for-use, *learning as an end*, takes place alongside an entirely different conversation about the goals of school, focused on what schooling can be *exchanged* for, *education as a means*.

Exchange Value: Confusion of Means and Ends

In a stratified, uneven world, maintaining or improving one's social position depends on comparison with others, through competition for limited goods. The *credential*, not the *learning*, becomes a unit of exchange signaling years and prestige of schooling. Students can exchange educational capital and cultural capital, in Bourdieu and Passeron's terms from their 1970 book *Reproduction in Education, Society, and Culture*, for social and economic capital. Dewey called this whole approach that of "social efficiency."[21]

Credentials, Completion, and Signaling

Way back in 1979 sociologist Randall Collins published *The Credential Society: An Historical Sociology of Education*, where he was especially concerned, like Bourdieu and Passeron, with the social reproduction of inequality.[22] He also wrote of the increasing chasing of credentials as leading to "credential inflation": to do the same job workers require ever-higher degrees, not for the knowledge gained but simply through competition for a limited good: decent-paying, stable employment. The credential "signals," represents, knowledge and comportment, to big organizations. Stephen J. McNamee clarifies: "The widespread practice of using educational credentials as proxies for skills needed to do certain jobs is imperfect. Beyond literacy and basic computational skills, most of what people need to know to perform most work tasks is learned on the job, not in the classroom. . . . To the extent that educational signals used as convenient screening devices for job placement are inaccurate, true meritocracy is compromised. . . . The *lack* of particular credentials operates as an artificial barrier to mobility."[23]

In higher education, which is always voluntary, dropping out or failing to complete a degree is considered a major problem no matter how much knowledge gets accrued along the way: the "higher education premium" is attained only when the degree is completed. (In the United States more than 60 percent of high school graduates *begin* higher education, but fewer than 40 percent have even an associate—two-year—degree. The "completion agenda" is an attempt to improve these figures.)[24] Consideration of return on investment is certainly rational when schooling is costly for an individual, and the "return" is calculable in monetary terms. Ron Lieber warns that attending some colleges doesn't result in attendees earning any more than had they merely graduated from high school.[25] Bryan Caplan concluded that the return on investment for higher education is negligible for all but students at the most highly selective, elite institutions, who actually finish their degree.[26] So students who fail to persist or to achieve the degree are likely to have squandered resources without the desired payoff—even if they've learned something.

The Big Sort, Ranking, Gatekeeping

This emphasis on exchange value stems from another function not inherent in learning, but one that has been placed on schools and, in turn, on individual students and teachers: sorting and ranking students.

Gates (Open versus Selective Admission)

Selection, sorting, and ranking lie at the heart of much of contemporary education as a whole. Some families orchestrate their children's entire childhood toward admission to high-status higher education. In the United States, elite colleges and universities have continually reduced the percentage of students they admit, even though the total number of students in higher education has been *declining* since the peak in approximately 2010. As admission to highly selective schools appears increasingly competitive, in a neoliberal context where class anxiety is reasonable, students hedge their bets by applying to more schools, which increases the necessity for each school to reduce the percentage of students admitted. A close friend's child applied to about ten colleges in 2022 and was admitted to only two. The child was on the waiting list for four, and rejected from four. But ten is a relatively low number for ambitious students, when many students having such aspirations applied to twenty or thirty schools. So let's say fifty thousand students each send out multiple applications for fifty thousand positions in the schools, with most of those students capable of succeeding—whatever that means—at any of them. Most will be rejected from any particular school. This high rejection rate, "selectivity," is one of the measures formerly used by *US News & World Report* to rank institutions of higher education, so schools' ranks increase when their admission rates fall.

When admission to college is highly selective—which is the case only for a limited number of institutions, and not in all countries—testing and other high-volume production of metrics may be relevant. During the COVID-19 pandemic, when it was impossible for students to be surveilled safely in standardized admission tests such as the SAT, ACT, or gaokao, there was a lot of concern about what to do about these tests. In the United States several large systems of higher ed such as the University of California began to accelerate their distancing from these exams to the point that by 2022 they were not using them at all.[27]

But when these exams exist, *the exam itself takes on the end of education* rather than being a means to an end. Globally, whether it concerns the college entrance exams that loom so large in East Asia and South Asia or the international baccalaureate or A-level exams in Europe and the Americas, secondary schools devote temporal, financial, and psychological resources to preparing for these tests. Students learn not only subjects but also tricky, schoolish exam formats that incentivize learning a particular way for grounding an answer in evidence, or using certain vocabulary and grammar. Students have to practice working within time limits, just like in sports. In the United States, as well as in East Asia, there are whole industries devoted to preparing for these exams (see chapter 10, "Genres of Production").

Some elite secondary schools also limit entry, especially when there are a limited number of spaces in unevenly resourced (in terms of material and personnel) institutions where attendance may have consequences for life outcomes. Some mechanisms must determine admission: a lottery, home address, ability to pay, connections, or some kind of examination. But that also depends on prior preparation, so the competition begins with preschool.

In higher ed, the sorting is sometimes overt. "Weed-out" courses like organic chemistry for medical school applicants have come under an increased amount of fire in 2022. An NYU professor of "orgo" was let go for—well, different accounts give different reasons, but possibly for making the course too hard to pass for most students. But such controversies have given rise to a central question of what schools are supposed to be doing: are they supposed to be teaching all their students? Sorting the meritorious? And if the latter, what are the useful metrics? John Warner interviewed Dan Singleton from Texas A&M University about this topic. Singleton argued that organic chemistry was one of the first courses that didn't advantage college students from privileged backgrounds, because pretty much everyone begins with the same ignorance, and what helps people learn is perseverance and attention.[28] So if perseverance and attention, as evidenced via outcome of orgo, are useful for medical school, maybe this course, no matter the content, provides useful information to admissions committees. But should that screening happen prior to or within medical school? What do doctors need to know? Who gets to become a doctor? On what basis? Are people born with fixed amounts of "merit"?

"Meritocracy"   The word "meritocracy" was coined as satire by sociologist Michael Young. We observe it in Plato's assertion that "the best" should run things; this reasoning lies behind the old Chinese civil service examination and justifies the contemporary East Asian college entrance examination system.[29] Even where such "meritocratic" sorting is used, people may recognize that it is problematic—but say that it's better than a system of recommendation and connection. In some obvious sense "the best" should oversee the most important and difficult things, in a

stratified society. (Social scientists disagree about whether extreme stratification, accompanied by competition, is inevitable. David Graeber and
David Wengrow, among many other anthropologists, argue that egalitarian notions governed humankind for most of our history.)[30]

In the twentieth century, sorting was tied with "race science," eugenics,
and the notion of "intelligence" as a fixed entity.[31] As Nicolas Lemann
shows so chillingly in his book *The Big Test*, this idea became justification for a continuing aristocracy cloaked with claims of fairness, the assumption being that anyone who can test well can do the job or get into
the school. Yet high scores track almost completely with socioeconomic
status. Advantage leads to more advantage; winners take all.[32]

Critics have focused on the tests' content and structures, showing that
they advantage some groups automatically. Yet context also matters: in
the twentieth century, free or very open colleges, such as City University
of New York, facilitated social mobility, especially of new immigrants.
But as inequality has increased in the United States and worldwide, it's
become ever harder for disadvantaged groups to join the elite—and even
more necessary merely for existential security.

In the 2020s increasingly prominent critics have challenged the idea
of meritocracy, going so far as to term it a myth with racist and classist
origins.[33]

Schoolish Metrics for ALL!

When there's a limit of desired goods, metrics come to be seen as essential. In turn, they govern other practices, in a further confusion of means
and ends.

I like numbers. I took advanced math in college, for fun. My SAT scores
were equal on the math and verbal parts. (The fact that I remember this
nearly half a century after I took this test should astonish us all.) I considered myself "a math person." But some of the ways numbers are involved
in schooling—the schoolish ways—are harmful. Numbers, quantification,
metrics, audits, and accounting play a huge role in policies and claims
about educational success.

"Not everything that can be counted counts and not everything that
counts can be counted," Albert Einstein may have said. So what are we
counting? And what counts?

From global metrics of national school participation to individual grades (cumulative, course, assignment), numbers are collected. As with all metrics, people tend to collect easily collected items: days late on assignments, errors on factual tests. These are often assumed to be correlated with the desired goals—equity, learning—but then often take on a life of their own. And all depend on what someone has decided to count, and what counts as the things in a category. "Every number is born of subjective judgments, points of view, and cultural assumptions. Numbers are filled with bias through and through, because that's what categories do. Categories are ways of seeing and *not* seeing," says Deborah Stone in her fascinating book *Counting: How We Use Numbers to Decide What Matters.*[34] What do we see and what do we fail to see with our schoolish numbers?

Grades for Students: The Quintessence of Extrinsic Motivation   Students talk about grades as one of the *goals*, the *ends*, of their schooling.[35] They aren't entirely wrong. If one of the ends is, for instance, to get a particular job, then one of the means of attaining a job is to be able to demonstrate that a certain degree of learning has occurred in a particular subject area, and one of the methods of demonstrating such learning is through communicating via a credential, built upon a series of particular grades. One applicant's grades are compared to another's. Efficient!

Teachers often think of grades as motivating. "How," we ask, "can I motivate my students?"—that is, manipulate them. "How can I make them do X?" The assumption is that it's the teacher's job to coerce because nothing else will make, or motivate, the students to learn and to do the work that supports learning. Alfie Kohn traces this to 1930s–1960s behaviorist psychology that aimed to control, to motivate; it assumed that punishment and reward were both necessary and sufficient.[36] With or without academic justification, people often believe that children need controlling this way.

The commonsense, widespread belief is that through enough extrinsic motivation, people can be led to develop intrinsic motivation. *Eat your broccoli and then you can have dessert . . .* and eventually you may like the broccoli. *Master the conditional verbs of French, get an A*, and eventually you can discuss your dreams for the future in French. *Get pizza coupons for reading books*, and eventually you'll learn to love reading. *Participate in the online discussion five times*, and you'll come to care about the issues. *Get incentives for quality work* and you'll work harder and better. I used to believe it too: If I could just get my students to write abstracts of complicated anthropological theory, they would learn to love it! But research consistently shows that, contrary to such belief, providing extrinsic rewards does not lead to intrinsic interest. Piling on extrinsic rewards not only fails to increase intrinsic motivation. It's worse: it can destroy or at least *diminish intrinsic motivation.*

Mark Lepper and colleagues sorted children who liked drawing into three groups. One group was allowed to draw as they wished. A second group was shown a certificate that they could win. The third group was not told in advance that they would receive an award, but they did. Weeks later, the group without rewards, as well as the one that received an unexpected reward, had essentially the same distribution of interest in drawing. But—and here is the shocker—the group told to work for the reward saw a dramatic *decline* in interest in drawing.[37]

In another experiment, Edward Deci and colleagues observed college students who wrote newspaper headlines—a real-world activity. Only some were rewarded with monetary payments or praise. Those who were rewarded showed a *decreased interest* in this activity.[38] Since the early 1970s—that's a half century ago!—research both in labs and in "field" studies have consistently shown that students may stop doing activities they formerly enjoyed after an intervention providing extrinsic motivation.[39] In other words, *extrinsic motivation caused decrease in intrinsic motivation.*

Metrics as Goal: Wagging the Dog   As assessments, grades are both "formative," helping people improve, and "summative," or summing up how well they've learned. Because the means of assessing learning looms so large, the means (grades, tests) take on the role of ends; "the tail wags the dog." Schoolish assessment takes on a life of its own.

Another confusion of means and ends is in standardized testing (see chapter 10). If standardized testing has any role to play in formal education, it would be to determine who has actually learned the material. (If the goal is for everyone to learn, this would have different consequences.) Armies of experts try to figure out how to assess learning. Ideally, say assessment experts Kathleen Strickland and James Strickland, "assessment and evaluation [would] no longer [be] the product of teaching, they [would be] the tools that learners and teachers use to support learning."[40] Yet we know that what is tested is what is taught. Standardized, normed tests such as the AP (advanced placement) tests, A-levels, O-levels, the gaokao, the Suneung, or the College Scholastic Ability Test, the Regents Exam in New York, the "Common Core" assessments . . . all these tests drive the secondary-school curriculum.

People who want to change the curriculum often first have to lobby to change the test, like the College Board's SAT and AP exams, which in turn drive curriculum, in a circular round of tests, leading to teaching to the test, leading to test results.

Metrics for Faculty! Productivity and Student Evaluations   Teachers are also evaluated. Teachers submit to the discipline of metrics regarding output, student evaluations, and, in lower grades, PISA and regents' exams and state exams. In higher education, faculty are evaluated by productivity, as in the UK, where the Research Excellence Framework, the REF,[41] aims to ensure that faculty are achieving "excellence" by means of various metrics. Most people believe that because "productivity" is incentivized, others are (1) gaming the system and (2) producing far less "authentic" work.

Faculty are usually evaluated by their students, too, in Student Evaluations of Teachers (SETs), which have been known to be biased for gender and race.[42] Teachers try to improve for the evals.

Metrics for Institutions! Accreditation and Ranking   Educational institutions themselves, like any institution, have goals such as solvency, reputation, and accreditation: outside entities evaluate whether institutions as a whole or programs within them are accomplishing the established benchmarks. Some schools can be "failing." International rankings of high school students occur in the PISA tests, which are international competitions of educational systems, testing some fifteen-year-olds in OECD countries every three years.

Other institutional goals such as rankings contribute to admissions and donations.

Institutions of higher education (and now also high schools and professional schools) are ranked in the United States. One of the prominent sources of such rankings is a formerly second-rate news magazine, *US News & World Report*. In 1983, to set itself apart from competitors *Time* and *Newsweek*, it began to publish rankings of colleges; it added professional schools in 1987. This has become the primary source for such rankings, but deeply contested. Reputation, funding, class sizes, and alumni giving—inputs—are some of the primary criteria in the ranking process. Other ranking systems, such as that proposed in 1900, "Where We Get Our Best Men," consider matters of social mobility and citizenship as desired outcomes.[43] President Obama worked to develop a "College Scorecard" focused more on equitable *results* and costs.[44]

International rankings of institutions of higher education such as the Times Higher Education World University Rankings, the Shanghai Ranking, and the QS World University in turn drive institutional decisions.[45] Following the model of German research universities, at the turn of the twentieth century Charles Eliot remade US higher education to include a focus not only on *reproduction* of known knowledge but also on *production* of knowledge, with the introduction of research agendas and graduate education. Since Johns Hopkins University introduced the first graduate schools, most other universities have followed suit, and international universities as well. The rankings of these institutions are especially about reputation and research fame, usually in the sciences.

The Game and Gaming of School: What Games Make

When metrics drive the system, "gaming the system" becomes fairly simple.[46]

Schoolishness teaches the game of school.[47] Someone made up the rules, which vary all the time. The goal of the game of school, schoolishness, is to accumulate points, ideally more than everyone else. Strategies are the main learning outcome of all those years of schoolishness. Anyone who flunks strategy basically flunks school. In classes the points come from figuring out the specific version of the game that the teacher in that specific class has set up.

Successful students master the arcane rules: penalties for absences (some may sign in for a classmate) or cameras off (they can join the Zoom and do homework for other classes); points for oral or written participation; points off for improper citation (number of sources, format); arbitrary regulations regarding use of notes or "cheat sheets" during exams, collaboration, time and speed on multiple choice, essay, or other elements of tests. In *Wad-ja-get? The Grading Game in American Education*, first published in 1971 and reissued in 2021 in a fiftieth-anniversary edition, students collaborate against the rules to share homework or test and quiz information, trying to regurgitate exactly what the teacher wants.[48]

Schoolishness promotes this "game of school"—not using games to learn, gamification, but "to game the system," to figure out how to get the end result, by any means. The exchange value—points, high grades, credits, credentials—is what matters. What *doesn't* matter in this game is the process, the means, the content, the use value. Some students—sometimes with the complicity of teachers, administrators, parents—excel at gaming the system of schooling. Things like "participation points" and "extra credit" are part of the gaming plan: they may not actually demonstrate learning, and sometimes can be entirely disconnected from the subject itself, like converting unused bathroom passes into extra credit.[49] The "best" are rewarded with a very high grade-point average (GPA) and all that accompanies it.

Students must know all about the schoolish exchange value to master the system of getting points enough to graduate, so they can cash them all in to get the coveted diploma—a credential—just like you trade four houses (plus the cost of a fifth) for a hotel in Monopoly. They need to keep track of the total number of credits, transfer details, distribution and major requirements, possibilities of double counting. They need to have a clear eye on their grades, the worshipped GPA. They have to keep track of how each little chunk of school affects their GPA. This expertise in schoolishness is consequential, to be sure. But is it what we truly want students to master?

Games have certain characteristics. Think of Monopoly, Scrabble, or soccer. They have

- Competition: some will be winners and others losers[50]
- Boundedness and self-containment
- Metrics, points
- Pre-established roles and activities
- Arbitrariness (the values of certain properties, or letters, or goals)
- Pretending, suspension of disbelief

When applied to schools, these gaming characteristics are likely to have some predictable consequences.

Students learn to perform a simulacrum—an appearance, a show of eagerness, a semblance of engagement—to achieve what are often the only topics discussed publicly: points, rewards, approval, praise, high grades, admission to the next level of school.[51]

Successful students show impressive expertise in the game of school. Not everyone is successful, however. This game of sorting begins at birth; those with advantages continue to build on them throughout every level of schooling. In households where formal schooling has been mastered for generations, the knowledge of how to *learn for schooling*, schoolishness, is passed along effortlessly. Others have to pick it up in the course of life, which is one of the challenges for first-generation college students, in addition to the financial and familial obstacles.[52]

Some students miss the socialization into this set of rules, for whatever reason. Some don't get the teacher's jokes. But the system is strong. It maintains its "standards," its "rigor," and no matter what the reason, everyone is subject to the same evaluation. That's "meritocracy." Winners usually take all. Helen Lees, a critic of this type of schoolishness, nevertheless wanted to *reveal* the game to *everyone* but also to promote genuine learning within the system despite the game, so published a book, *Playing the University Game: The Art of University-Based Self-Education*.[53]

Even when students focus on exchange value, they do learn *something*, though, because humans are always learning. They learn, and rehearse,

TABLE 2.1. Characteristics and consequences of games and schoolishness

Characteristics of games (and schoolishness)	Lead to →	Consequences of schoolishness
competition		sabotage
metrics, points		cheating, focus on extrinsic motivation, transactionalism
boundedness, self-contained		nontransfer, nonlearning, nonretention
preestablished activities and roles		uniformity; rejection of diversity
arbitrariness		vigilance
pretending		performance, roles; fakeness, insincerity

being-for-others, appearing one way and actually being another, living with contradictions in their selfhood—beyond just being casual with friends and formal with elders. They learn *sham.*

Sham

Sham has existential, psychological consequences, as we saw in chapter 1, "Experiencing School." But it's also a set of tactics that threatens the integrity of the system. And as Jules Henry told us, schools teach sham. A child's "major introduction to sham, at the institutional level, is school, where he [*sic*] learns to give the teacher what she wants."[54]

Dark, Dark, Light: Faking and Chasing the Fakes

At worst, people in the point-game-credential exchange system resort to dark practices, or are suspected of it.

In contemporary higher education in the United States, alongside earnest, hardworking students genuinely devoted to learning, we see multiple types of fakery: students and faculty writing things that are not theirs at all (fraud, fakery, plagiarism), writing what they think the professor wants to hear, whether they think it or not (bullshit, insincerity), and increasingly "contract cheating," where students hire others to write, take exams, and even attend classes for them.[55] The motivations, or what economists call the incentives, are clearly stacked *toward* corrupt practices; gaming the system is an obvious strategy, for some even a necessary one, just like the incentives and motivations for faculty to publish as much as possible.[56]

When stakes are high, we see the cat-and-mouse game of attempting to get past "invigilators," the monitors of International Baccalaureate examinations, technological identification and surveillance of the SAT, TOEFL, GRE, MCAT, etc. This isn't new. The Chinese civil service examination, which lasted almost fourteen hundred years, was filled with student cheaters writing award-winning essays in the required style, hiring substitute test-takers, or buying forbidden cribs of the responses, while the authorities searched the candidates, and copied the candidates' responses in their own hand so that the evaluators could not be bribed to pass those whose handwriting they recognized.[57] This was fakery all the way down, with fake-detection in hot pursuit.

Given the general environment of suspicion and mistrust, fake detection is a large side enterprise in the schoolish universe, resulting in plagiarism-detection services like Turnitin. During COVID times, online test surveillance ballooned. Artificial intelligence monitored students' eye gaze, fidgeting, bathroom breaks. Test takers were forbidden to look away, to open new windows on their screens, to stand up. For-profit "EdTech" companies like Respondus, ProctorU, Examity, and Proctorio offered to help faculty deal with the anxiety of ensuring that students were not cheating.[58] This isn't going away.

If the goal of college is points, credentials, elements of exchange, then cheating and plagiarism appear logical. If the goal is learning, however, there can be no cheating.

So how *do* we make students learn?

We don't. We create environments and contexts where they want to. Studies of animal behavior and learning theory have consistently demonstrated the unexpected finding that, beyond survival, most animals engage in activities that appear to have no instrumental purpose but are driven by curiosity, playfulness, fun, or challenge—intrinsic motivation.[59]

Less-Schoolish Goals and Rewards: The Idealistic Core

It's clear that, in life, *learning can happen independently*, without schools. So the questions arise: What can be done *only* with schools? What may be done *better* with schools?

For me, the core function of school is *gathering with others for learning*, with the core goal of *helping learners become independent and confident about learning, without damage along the way.* How can we draw closer to this core function and the core goals?

One way to challenge the focus on the game of school, in the context of an individual class, is through the set of practices I call "ungrading."

Ungrading: Switching the Goals

Grades have not always existed and, God willing, will not always exist. Grades are problematic for a number of reasons, including the fact that they are very poor reports of learning. They often *conflate behavioral dimensions with learning dimensions*, averaging together things such as attendance and participation with testable dimensions of particular subjects. They often punish mistakes rather than using them as information. Those who begin with greater advantages nearly always emerge with the highest grades, so grades essentially *perpetuate the inequalities*. Grades often reward social and personal conditions that may correlate with learning but are probably not central: for example, if we know that those who attend courses more regularly tend to learn better, then we may "incentivize" attendance. I used to do this with great precision, but no longer. What are the reasons for students' failure to attend regularly? Is it because they are not engaged in the course? Is it because the course is not structured to afford any meaningful experiences in class that make it inherently rewarding to attend? Is it because they are ill, coping with disabilities, making barriers to attend different for them? Is it because they have responsibilities to care for others, whether children, partners, or other loved ones? Is it because they face economic challenges, and sometimes it's too expensive to attend, or they have competing financial incentives, such as taking on an additional shift for needed additional income? What is the message if students perhaps not only don't learn well, but also haven't learned well because they have so many real-world challenges? And they perhaps scored poorly on so-called objective measures of testing, and are marked down for their poor attendance? Is this double jeopardy?

Along with thousands of other educators, I have taken into my own hands the problem of the dominance of numbers/letters/tiered assessment. I call it "ungrading." For me, ungrading is calling into question conventional practices of focusing on metrics, to focus instead on intrinsic motivation and on learning.

Since 2016 I have given no grades on any assignment, though I'm obligated to submit final grades at the end of the semester. Grades fail to accomplish ostensibly positive benefits (communicating information to students or outsiders, motivating students) and have clear negative effects (enforcing obsession with superficial compliance, leading to an "external locus of control," adding to students' stress, and more). I've been implementing ungrading in various ways ever since I walked into my department chair's office and, with two books on education of my own and Starr Sackstein's and Alfie Kohn's books, and secure in tenure, and my white privilege, etc., I announced that I was ungrading.[60] After that came my "side project" in ungrading, which led to the book I edited, *Ungrading: Why Rating Students Undermines Learning (and What to Do Instead)*. I've tweaked my delivery—now I "show, don't tell," by having students engage first with cool, fun learning, and then pointing out that they did that without any grades. I have midsemester and semester-final conferences, five minutes each, accompanied by students' own reflections on their portfolios (which are just the entire collection of their work, not a fancy tech platform).[61] But other than that, I never mention grades.

My own goal is to make my classes as much like the world I wish to live in as possible: democratic, joyful, calm, cooperative. This is clearly not value-neutral. We can't get this from research, entirely, not from cognitive science or the scholarship of teaching and learning, not from experiments. This can only unfold from ethnographic, phenomenological engagement with the experience of real people learning in complex situations.

In every class I ask students to reflect on and set at least some of their own goals, rather than merely responding passively to me and my judgment. They rise to the opportunity. As one student explained, "[Ungrading] took the pressure off of our classes where you were no longer fixated on getting an A, but on doing good work. This structure allowed me to fixate less on getting a good grade, and more on maximizing my learning. Small elements like leading a class, learning from my classmates leading their class, freely engaging in conversation and doing assignments with no grade attached was very useful!"

If the goal is independent, confident learning, then constantly looking over their shoulders to affirm my approval destroys that possibility. "Democracy" for me includes all members of the community having a voice, being imbued with respect, dignity, and autonomy. The self-determination theory of motivation emphasizes autonomy, competence, and relatedness. We can't start with completely predetermined learning outcomes and pretend students have autonomy.

Most medical schools have gone to pass/no-pass systems for the preclinical portion of their training. In "The Problematic Persistence of Tiered Grading in Medical School," James F. Smith Jr. and Nicole M. Piemonte lament that "grading systems in medical school have been based on tenuous pedagogical precepts" that persist even when some tweaking is attempted. Students are still ranked; the ranking has been moved to clinical internships.[62]

So how *do* I make students learn? I don't. I create conditions and invite them to join a community of learners (more in chapter 4, "Teachers, Students, Classes"). I believe, idealistically, in the true excitement that people can have when they are learning well, in meaningful ways that make sense for their actual lives.

One way is to focus on students' intrinsic motivations. I've seen it work.

Intrinsic Motivation and Incentives

Intrinsic motivation is the impetus to act for its own sake, doing something that a person enjoys or needs. Though there can be many forms of intrinsic motivation, including the desire to please meaningful others, or to live up to a challenge, there are many things that *don't* need extrinsic motivations: unless these are psychology experiments or jobs, people tend to eat ice cream, learn to surf, master the lyrics of their favorite songs, or labor on genealogies because they want to, need to, derive satisfaction from them.[63] We don't pay kids to eat dessert. Parents don't give points to toddlers for picking themselves up when they're learning to walk. We don't test and grade teenagers on knowing all the lyrics of the latest Taylor Swift song, nor sort college students into who knows the most about the Final Four. Intrinsic motivation is easy to recognize through learners' engagement and affect. And the more schoolish the motivations, the more focus on extrinsic rewards, the less intrinsic motivation remains.

Cognitive scientist Daniel Willingham wrote in *Why Don't Students Like School* that when we begin with answers, we shut down curiosity.[64] In fact, the more conventional the schooling, with factual lectures and fact-eliciting tests, the less possibility there is for curiosity.

Schoolishness backfires. It produces exactly the opposite of what it purports to value. The structures of schooling leave no room for the most basic driver of all new knowledge and of all knowledge or understanding that sticks—curiosity.

Curiosity, Wonder, and Genuine Motivation   Curiosity has been treated as an emotion, a drive, a motor, a craving, a stance, an urge. It's a positive feeling that propels people to explore and learn. In their neuro-biology of emotion, Panksepp and Biven call this "SEEKING," an emotional system that drives behavior because attaining it provides its own reward. This is one of the most useful insights for overcoming schoolishness. (I'll go into this more in chapter 5, "Questions.")

"Curiosity killed the cat." Like cats, corvids—crows, jays, ravens, magpies—are curious. They use tools such as straws to prod things they can't reach, and they play. Rats have been understood, since 1925, to forgo food so they can explore.[65] Darwin called this "wonder" and knew that many animals demonstrate "curiosity."[66]

George Loewenstein has been writing about curiosity for decades.[67] An astrophysicist, Mario Livio, wrote of the immense satisfaction driving all humans, not only professional scientists, in his 2017 book *Why? What Makes Us Curious?* He shows how readers are captivated by the mysterious first sentence of a Kate Chopin short story: "Knowing that Mrs. Mallard was afflicted with a heart trouble, great care was taken to break to her as gently as possible the news of her husband's death."[68] *Why?* we want to know. *What? How? Tell me more!*

Anyone who has been around them knows that children have innate curiosity. Yet school dampens it, only to try to reintroduce it artificially—much as industrial agriculture denudes land of nutrients and then tries to spray on minerals. Wouldn't it be better to leave the soil alone and allow its richness to feed the plants? Even if it's harder to standardize and mechanize?

Giving students encouragement to practice their own curiosity is often an afterthought in schools—but it shouldn't be. Building on or creating conditions that permit students to be driven by their own curiosity is one of the best ways to enliven things in school. Students *can* repress curiosity, as they want to be cool, aloof, to show they don't care, to get the job done efficiently, to protect themselves from disappointment. But what if curiosity is cool?

Recent "active learning" experimentation in science classes, big and small, revolves around introducing strange, anomalous, or counterintuitive material and drawing students to attempt to explain it. This can be done with polls—*Do you think the answer is A, B, C, or D?*—or by showing a mysterious video, like a bridge oscillating. Derek Bruff cites the work of Daniel Schwartz and John Branford on "time for telling": don't use the "banking model" of first providing information and later suggesting application. First make it matter. *Then* explain.[69]

Other People and Love: Fostering and Being Motivated by a Community of Learners   Another way to help students be less schoolish is to focus on *being with others*, one of the core functions of school. John Dewey wrote, "The very existence of the social medium in which an individual lives, moves, and has his [*sic*] being is the standing effective agency of directing his activity."[70] In other words, students are motivated by engaging in joint, purposeful activity with meaningful others, communities of practice. When that occurs, it's not necessary for teachers to control the learners.

When we work with others, it may produce strong positive feelings. This should be an aim. Feminist philosopher of education Nel Noddings talks about happiness and love as goals of education, mostly among children, but they constitute another goal that could be considered, especially given the number of years and amount of money that is devoted to schools. *Love* is a term not always used in the context of schools, but perhaps it should be.[71]

Real Use   Another approach is to make the learning *useful* at the moment, to emphasize the *use value*: build something, write something with a genuine audience and purpose, figure out something that matters in the students' lives. Cathy Davidson had her composition students write job applications.[72] In design courses, students enter real contests. Apprentice cooks prepare real dishes.

Less-Metric-Fixated Schools

Challenges to the focus on conventional grading and metrics take many forms, among educators at all levels, from primary and secondary schools through tertiary and professional schools, usually within single courses. Many individual teachers who have some control over the aims and methods of their own courses have introduced contract grading, labor-based grading, specifications grading, standards-based grading, and collaborative grading, whether committed to fully ungrading or to any other form of alternative assessment.[73] Yet some efforts to challenge metrics go beyond individual courses, including larger-scale challenges to schoolish goals, such as reducing fixation on the metrics.

Mastery Transcript   The Mastery Transcript Consortium works within the existing educational system to improve metric fixation on a scale beyond a single course.[74] Beginning in 2017, Scott Looney at the Hawken School in Cleveland created a framework that would present a nuanced snapshot of what students learned and knew, through competencies and a portfolio instead of grades. Like the dozens of colleges and universities that got rid of letter grades in the 1960s, the consortium's four hundred–plus private elite college prep high schools and public schools have a plan to get their students into the next level of education. (In college, one question is always: how do I apply to med school? Colleges like Hampshire have done well with that; they send on the narrative evaluations.) The consortium works with college admissions departments to accept the additional burden of the labor required to read the nuanced transcripts. Their ultimate goal is to reimagine what and how students learn. As always, the challenge is to figure out how to navigate within reality while working toward something closer to ideal.

Saying No to the Tests   During the initial months of the pandemic, it became obvious that supposedly "fair" tests like the SAT were not going to be possible, so many colleges and universities suspended the tests; some have remained test-optional or have no-test admissions. (Even the gaokao was postponed, though it has since resumed.)[75]

Opting Out of Rankings   In the United States, as I mentioned, *US News & World Report* has served as the top source for ranking colleges and universities. It gathers information from those schools, along with publicly available statistics, and determines a ranking. Several colleges, including Reed College, have decided not to play the ranking game. (Reed was given a gift by a wealthy donor in 1995 and stopped cooperating then.) *US News* ranked Reed as number ninety. Students in a statistics class reworked the numbers and alleged that it should be number thirty-six; they also alleged retribution for lack of cooperation, a charge that the magazine disputes.[76] Gaming the system is fairly simple. Opting out has risks.

In 2022 three Chinese universities, Renmin University, Nanjing University, and Lanzhou University, stopped participating in international rankings.[77] In one week in November 2022, six top law schools (Harvard, Yale, Berkeley, Georgetown, Columbia, and Stanford) also opted out of the *US News & World Report* rankings.[78] They still do just fine.

Accretion / Peripheral Goals ("Path Dependence")

Peripheral goals often arise out of necessities that follow from previous decisions, such as a need for fund-raising and development, which clearly does enable some of the other goals to continue. (These consequences are similar to what economists call "path dependence," random decisions that make subsequent alterations more difficult. The key example is the QWERTY keyboard, inefficient but entrenched for a century in typewriters and then computer keyboards.)[79] These choices lead to establishing sports teams and loyalty to institutions, giving preference to offspring of previous alumni (called "legacy" students in admissions to selective schools), to rankings, branding, and other things that support some of the other goals. I acknowledge here that I've been the beneficiary of excellent efforts in these domains in my own professional career, which has taken place at a variety of institutions, most recently at a very well-endowed, highly selective, and generous institution that has made possible my focus on my own research and my teaching in relatively moderate-size classes. It may seem hypocritical for me to criticize this largesse, and I am always a willing self-critic.

Schools Are Charged with All the Leftover Tasks That Society Isn't Taking On

The COVID-19 pandemic revealed how schools are expected to fix virtually every problem: Some schools provide housing; many provide food; colleges have food pantries and career clothing banks. Most provide some referral to mental health counseling. Most provide entertainment, whether arts or sports. We rely on schools to solve inequality and to ensure social mobility. At the same time, they're supposed to teach math, reading, civics, science, literacy, information, critical thinking, open-mindedness, familiarity with the great works of art, music, literature, job preparation, self-discipline, deferral, executive function, teamwork and leadership, perseverance, curiosity, following directions, being creative and innovative, "service" (except for those who receive the service), and to prepare workers for jobs. Is this too much?

Certainly the needs exist; nobody else is meeting them. But is this what schools are supposed to do?

If we keep in mind a core goal, perhaps it can help sort out this and some of the other questions that arise.

Goals keep getting added to the initial ones, whether rightly or wrongly. One of the conundrums for society is the question of how much responsibility schools do and should have for replacing other institutions that might care for children and students. Certainly in an immorally unequal society like my own, that of the twenty-first-century United States, it is necessary to turn to schools as potential safety nets, given the lack of others. But in this book I am addressing not only the current realities, but also the aims to which we might aspire: and that is for a society where the suffering is less great, and where hunger and immoral levels of inequality are not rampant. Yes, I am a dreamer. I confess.

Yet if an image of a just and desirable society is at the core of aspirations for institutional education, we need to clarify which goals are central and which are peripheral.

The COVID pandemic and the role of schools illustrated that our society fails to meet the needs of many. But surely we would not argue that babysitting is a core goal of school, even if we do inadvertently add that to the actual, practical, realistic goals in a society where most adults of childbearing age work in jobs that cannot be done with children around. Clearly the anthropological record is of limited use here, because much of that record has been compiled in societies where adults and children are not separated for most of the daytime hours.

So what are the goals and aims, the ends?

Wendy Fischman and Howard Gardner conducted a ten-year study to figure out what students were actually doing in college, and how students, administrators, alumni, and faculty understood the goals of college. They recommend nontransactional, transformational goals for higher education. A wonderful, idealistic book edited by William Moner, Phillip Motley, and Rebecca Pope-Ruark, *Redesigning Liberal Education: Innovative*

Design for a Twenty-First-Century Undergraduate Education, has twenty different positive examples of what such a design could look like. David Staley has written *Alternative Universities*, dreaming up schemes great and small. My own team of six brainstormed a model of what we called "A Theory of Public Higher Education," as if we were starting from scratch.[80]

Whatever school is to become, it seems to me that we want this institution to foster the desired characteristics in a manner consistent with the aims (that is, we don't want a contradiction between means and ends). And one final aim is more idealistic than all the rest.

Being

Learners are persons, human beings, before they are doers or learners. Robert Bringhurst writes that "the vocation of every human . . . is to be a human being."[81] We can see appeals to authenticity and freedom in the works of Simone de Beauvoir and bell hooks. Where does humanness fit within any educational schema? How can the cognitive and practical goals *also* support the human goals?

Idealism and "Realism"

Institutions, departments, and faculty set apparently noble, if bland, goals. Read mission statements. Some, like Indiana University's CAREER Edge, try to balance ideals and practicality. They aspire to support students as they "explore their values, strengths and interests in relation to degrees and careers; Develop an academic plan that connects with careers that excite them; Graduate with a solid plan for furthering their professional goals, and be employed in a career that they are passionate about!"[82] Not bad goals at all.

But ask students what their experiences are like.

Students Know When They Are Truly Learning: Ask Them

Since I've been ungrading, along with changing nearly every dimension of my pedagogy, students have talked more frankly about my class compared with most of their other classes. Here is what a handful of students have reported about the experience in my ungraded classes during the spring 2022 semester, with written permission to share:

- "I loved this class structure, I have learned in so many different ways in this one course than most of my other ones here. I think this is because of the structure and I was able to learn things through methods that were conducive to holistic learning (rather than regurgitating facts for an exam). The assessments forced me to think about the material in a way that I hadn't tried before."
- "I tend to really rely on grades as a measure of my value as a student and an academic, but this class has helped me unlearn some of that unhealthy thinking, while also encouraging me to still engage with the class content in a genuine and serious way."
- "There is so much value in placing an emphasis on learning rather than a grade."
- "This was never a class that I was anxious to attend and I always felt very safe and comfortable which promoted my learning quite a bit. If this class would have had lots of tests and consisted of mostly lectures, I don't think I would have enjoyed it and I wouldn't have learned very much. Because I had a little bit more control over my education in this class, however, I was able to do the things that worked best for me to facilitate my own learning."

Ordinarily, they know, they "regurgitate facts for an exam," feel anxiety and discomfort, and learn little.

I ask them what they think they'll remember in, say, five years. Two responses stand out:

- "That learning can be fun!"
- "That I had one class where nothing was graded and all I did was learn."

Many Paths to Many Goals

If, as I claim, humans love learning, then it's easy to understand the lament when some are prevented from getting an education. In my own Jewish tradition, we have stories of secret Torah study when it was forbidden to them by the Greeks. Enslaved people in the United States secretly learned to read and write when literacy was literally legally forbidden.[83] In the spring of 2022 I was absolutely awed by demonstrations in Afghanistan against the Taliban for preventing girls from attending high schools or secondary schools. These girls wanted their education. People have been desperate over the years to get an education that was denied to them. People go to great lengths to learn; sometimes, but only sometimes, that learning is schoolish.

The aims and the ends are connected to the means: *why*, *what*, and *how* are intertwined. The central ten chapters of this book focus on the *how*, the structures, in this broader context where the aims are often unstated, and often at odds with the means.

Part II

Key Elements of Schoolishness, with Some Less-Schoolish Variations

3

PEDAGOGY AND PEDAGOGIZING

From Direct Instruction to Independent Learning

> Yanira stood waiting with a small pot and a bundle with two
> dresses and a change of underwear in hand. A member of the
> Matsigenka people of the Peruvian Amazon, she asked to accompany
> anthropologist Carolina Izquierdo and a local family on a fishing
> and leaf gathering expedition down river. Over five days away from
> the village, Yanira was self sufficient and attuned to the needs of
> the group. She helped to stack and carry leaves to bring back to the
> village for roofing. Mornings and late afternoons she swept sand off
> the sleeping mats, fished for slippery black crustaceans, cleaned and
> boiled them in her pot along with manioc then served them to the
> group. At night her cloth bundle served as blanket and her dresses as
> her pillow. Calm and self-possessed, she asked for nothing. Yanira is
> six years old.
>
> ELINOR OCHS AND CAROLINA IZQUIERDO, "Responsibility in
> Childhood"

How did you learn to speak your first language(s)? Did your parents
teach you? How did you learn to walk? Did you have lessons? Did you
get graded? Was there a curriculum? Who taught you the names of your
relatives? How did you learn who the mean kids were and who the nice
kids were? How did you learn to make a sandwich? Did someone teach
you? Why did you learn it? Was it part of the learning outcomes for age
six (or fifteen, if you were especially coddled)? How did you learn to
share? Did you get a theoretical explanation and then unrelated rewards?
You might have.

Most of my students, like most people in North America, believe that their parents, and later their teachers, taught them language, like everything else. But, as N. J. Enfield says, "Our intuitions about language are typically strong, but wrong."[1] So widespread is this misconception that the Linguistic Society of America corrects it in its FAQs: "Children acquire language quickly, easily, and without effort or formal teaching. It happens automatically, whether their parents try to teach them or not."[2] Parents don't even have the technical knowledge to teach the difference between the present simple, present continuous, present perfect, and present perfect continuous tenses/aspects (*I play soccer; I am playing soccer; I have played soccer; I have been playing soccer.*)[3] Usually parents introduce pragmatics ("Say hello to Aunt Felicia" or "What do you say when Gramma gives you something?") or make corrections of especially charged and salient features that may be frequently tested—schoolishly stigmatized items like *ain't*. This is not to disrespect my students' parents, who were valiant champions of their cultivation. My students— high-achieving students in an elite university—almost all had armies of teachers and nurturers and tutors and coaches behind them. They *were* taught. They were *taught a lot*. But they're wrong to think that everything they know was taught.

Language learning is both different from and similar to other sorts of learning: It takes a lot of practice, and once mastered becomes automatic; and there seem to be special abilities for attending to language. (This is actually a big controversy in linguistics: are the capacities for language acquisition built on more general tendencies of sociality and pattern recognition, or are they, as Chomsky says, uniquely focused on language?)[4]

All human beings learn an incredible amount that they use in their lives, some of it technical, some moral, and some practical, without anyone teaching them.

Yet what I call the "instructional fallacy" permeates schoolishness, the assumption that all learning requires discursive, direct instruction, and that the pedagogical relationship is natural, and beneficial.

Public and even *medical* discourse about language learning urges parents to *make the home more like school*, to introduce schoolishness. This means that there should be constant pedagogizing: parental, teacherly, didactic introduction of uninvited, random information, using the banking model, stuffing children's brain with facts, categories, and chatter that isn't authentic. Parents not steeped in these practices can learn to ask schoolish questions, to train their children in schoolishness. This is quite different from the ways questions are often used "in real life" (see chapter 5).

For those who want to help their children "get ready for school," perhaps even in an enjoyable fashion, there is no time to waste. A website (available in both English and Spanish) advises that "Getting Ready for School Begins at Birth."[5] For a child at twelve to twenty-four months, parents are advised, "Talk together. Point out and name the things you see together. Ask what it is, then wait a few seconds until you offer the answer. [Like a good teacher . . . pause.] This gives your child a chance to respond and show you what he [*sic*] knows. Research shows that the more parents talk with their children, the bigger the children's vocabularies." Talking will yield that precious harvest, bigger vocabularies, which will in turn help the child do better in school.

WEIRD People and the "Normal"

In 2010 a paper was published that has challenged the way we think about psychological research and its universalizing conclusions. Most experiments take place in labs with North American, mostly white, undergraduates. The authors cautioned that this population was not only *not* representative, just as no single population could be, but that it was at the very edge of human tendencies—outliers in most of the tests they analyzed. These WEIRD populations—wealthy, educated, industrial, rich, democratic—or at least the subset who tend to be college students, are more individualistic, more likely to focus on abstractions, more likely to need direct instruction. In 2020 the lead author, Steven Henrich, an anthropologist, turned that jolting paper into a 706-page book.[6] And while some of the researchers' conclusions may be challenged on the specifics, the overall point is rock solid: just because something is true of white middle-class North American college students, it doesn't mean that's how it is or should be for all humanity. Just because WEIRD people need direct instruction, that doesn't mean all people do.

The Hegemony of School in the Lives of Children

During the fall of 2020 I taught a class called the Anthropology of Childhood and Education. I had taught it a half-dozen times before, but this time around new realizations regularly struck me. It might have been the pandemic; it might just have been my fixation on schoolishness. One of our biggest discoveries, the shocking one, had to do with the dominance of schools for all of contemporary childhood.

In the early units, those on pregnancy and childbirth, and even on infancy, physical dimensions of family life and health dominated. But as soon as we got to preschool, and especially elementary school ("middle childhood"), school began to dominate. The stages were often *named* in terms of school level (preschool, elementary-age, college-age). In the section on preschool and elementary school, I did a brief slide presentation with a slide filled with the word SCHOOL SCHOOL SCHOOL SCHOOL. The students were shocked, and even a little horrified, at the absolute hegemony of school over childhood. They had never noticed that whenever people talk about childhood, they talk about school. I kept showing slides of the increase in years of schooling over the last hundred years, throughout the world, and I kept being amazed at the naturalization of almost infinite schooling. Psychologist Jeffrey Jensen Arnett has identified a new "stage" of human development called "emerging adulthood," which has everything to do with the extension of schooling well into biological ages of reproduction and productivity. This stage is not biologically universal.[7]

Even though differences remain between high- and low-income countries, all demonstrate the same relentless pursuit of more schooling, especially prominent worldwide during the period since the end of the Second World War, though in some countries especially noticeable since the 1960s.[8] This is connected to the idea I introduced in the introduction, Grubb and Lazerson's "education gospel," the idea that more school is better and that formal education is the best way to aid development, to empower women, and to promote individual and collective prosperity.[9]

Pedagogy permeates life in the United States and in many other countries. So much of childhood is about school, or is schoolish, even at the very earliest ages—at least if you want your children to be successful in the conventional uniform system. The pervasive North American and East Asian parenting advice focuses on how to become your child's teacher, how to make children learn through direct instruction, even when there are so many other ways to learn. Fallacies about the need for teaching have led to some very strange programs that cost a lot of money and occupy many people's labor. Research on the need for teaching in child-hood reflects WEIRD assumptions.

Sociologist Annette Lareau coined the term "concerted cultivation" to describe middle-class US parents' focus—fixation—on their children's activities and achievements, in contrast to other families who aim to give their children conditions for growth ("natural growth").[10] Families prac-ticing "concerted cultivation" work tirelessly, exhausting themselves and their children, to ensure outcomes such as high grades, piling on extracur-ricular activities that will appear impressive on a résumé and college ap-plication. While such cultivation may be required to prepare students for entrance into highly selective colleges and universities, it has significant negative consequences, including stress and mental illness.[11]

Despite Lareau's concerns about concerted cultivation—and it's been shown to increase psychopathology and parent-child conflict—physician-activist Dana Suskind cites it approvingly.[12] Suskind contrasts parents' responses to a child, their praise and directives, with the former vastly preferred to the latter, because it correlates with school success and IQ—and socioeconomic status. Her prestige as a medical doctor helps promote these practices. Yet, worldwide, children are often exposed to much lin-guistic and interactive stimulation beyond the nuclear family; they have many other kinds of interaction beyond a parent instructing them, and they encounter many different forms of literacy beyond reading children's books. They learn to function in environments beyond school and possess values other than individual showing-off.[13]

Yet practices such as praise and direct instruction have been institu-tionalized in our schools and pervade our society, so much so that we take them completely for granted. They've been naturalized.

Pedagogy and Pedagogizing

Pedagogy has been used as a way to speak of teaching in general, or to foreground frameworks for ways of teaching. *Critical pedagogy* reminds readers that pedagogy, ways of teaching, may be coercive or liberatory, discriminating or equalizing.

Pedagogy can mean narrow attention to direct instruction or a broader sense of educational structure; it may have to do with any theory or methods of teaching. By origin—*though origin is not meaning*—it is related to the Greek term *paidos*, meaning "boy, child," combined with *agogos*, "leader," in turn derived from the Greek παιδαγωγία (paidagōgia), from παιδαγωγός (paidagōgos), itself a synthesis of ἄγω (ágō), "I lead," and παῖς (país, genitive παιδός, paidos), "boy, child": hence, "attendance on boys, to lead a child." Turning it into a verb, *pedagogizing* means "making pedagogical."[14] Everything about childhood has become material for pedagogizing—even play. Matthew Kaiser traces this to seventeenth- and eighteenth-century Victorian middle-class campaigns to "pedagogize child play, to transform it into an innately instructional activity."[15] Even play is schoolish. Everything is instruction.

So What's the Problem with Pedagogizing Everywhere?
Control, Coercion, Dependency

Some critical theorists, especially those influenced by Foucault, have linked pedagogy, surveillance, and governmentality. Like anyone under the authority of powerful others—in prisons, cities, medical care, religion—students are subject to external discipline and punishment, and then are socialized to internalize this discipline.[16] Regulation is evident especially in the focus on time (class time, credit hours, semesters, years of school, cost per unit; see chapter 6, "Time") but also the regulation of space and bodies (see chapter 8, "Spaces and Places," and chapter 12, "Attending (to) Bodies").

Basil Bernstein, a sociologist and linguist of education, argues that even so-called progressive and liberatory pedagogy merely masks the *conditions of inequality that inhere in all pedagogy*. Foucault warns against the pervasive judgment using norms, or the normal, in all dimensions of contemporary life, not only school: "The judges of normality are present everywhere. We are in the society of the teacher-judge, the doctor-judge, the educator-judge, the 'social-worker'-judge; it is on them that the universal reign of the normative is based; and each individual, wherever he [*sic*] may find himself, subjects to it his body, his gestures, his behaviour, his aptitudes, his achievements."[17] When we subject our bodies, behavior, and achievements to this constant judgment of conformity with the normative, many and most of us are bound to fall short. Why would anyone *not* find this disheartening?

Nikolas Rose and others have expanded on Foucault's late-career suggestion of the term *governmentality*, internalization of principles of regulation, which include not only metrics and assessment but also *internally incorporated senses of worth and value*. Schools, as institutions to which virtually all young people are subjected, are in the constant process of evaluating students and teaching them to focus on evaluation.

If actions must be initiated by the teacher/parent in pervasive pedagogizing, then in some sense students, novices, don't even exist unless they are being evaluated. The lack of free time and freedom to roam of middle-class North Americans is notorious; all of childhood is supposed to be in the service of schooling or at least competition and cultivation of the brand.[18] "School is your job," don't forget, whether you like it or not.

Schoolish Learning: Childhood Is Schoolish

Middle-class North Americans and East Asians—the societies I'm most familiar with—are taught that the main goal of childhood is school, and only those aspects of life that contribute to school success are really important. For example, in the listomaniacal fever of web enumeration, we find "10 Ways to Help Your Child Succeed in School—the Right Way!" The first way is to "teach them that learning is their 'job'"—*even if they're not interested*, and even if they are miserable: "Parents often ask what they can do to get their child interested in a particular subject or task. Lesson No. 1 is the most important lesson a child can learn about school: No one cares whether or not a child is interested in something. Of course, children learn better when they find the subject matter interesting, but what children really need to learn is that they must also learn things that they don't find particularly interesting. That's the job children have."[19] I concede that school success may lead to economic stability (despite evidence that schools produce failure), given success's hegemonic force in contemporary life and our age of neoliberal tooth-and-claw competition; but such frank, joyless advice to parents is rare.[20] And yes, this is just one website—but others resonate with it.

There are endless sources of advice for parents, often in the form of lists, and once you notice, a good portion of them have to do with school, and schoolishness. "Ten Ways to Raise Your Child," "Talk to Your

Child," "Fifteen Ways to . . ." In case parents find it difficult to figure out what to talk about, such sites also give advice: Talk about things you see when you're out, or just chat and sing while changing diapers. One piece of advice jumped out at me: *"The supermarket is a good place to talk to her and introduce new words, as she is sitting in the trolley facing you.* Gain her attention and then describe some of the items as you put them in the trolley." Still, it should not be an inquisition: "Try not to ask her too many questions. Instead, *tell her about things*, especially the things she shows an interest in, like a favourite toy" (emphases added). A parent can also "talk with her when she is watching TV programmes, about what you see and what's happening." It's a lecture!

Pedagogizing Everywhere and Magic Bullets! Schoolish Parenting and Parenting-for-Schooling

One of these "most important things" is illuminating: even "Eat with Your Child" is schoolish.

Eating together, it turns out, is not just about kinship. It's not just the civilizing process, the commensality that families enjoy. It's not the reinforcement of power dynamics or "the communicative expectations, . . . the symbolic, moral, sentimental meanings of food and eating,"[21] the pleasures of the table, appreciating the Earth's bounty or the work of farmers and field laborers and cooks, the transmission of family lore and social memory, which writers have often described in such loving detail.[22]

No. The true benefit of dinner is vocabulary, high grades, and better health: "For starters, researchers found that for young children, *dinnertime conversation boosts vocabulary even more than being read aloud to.* The researchers counted the number of rare words—those not found on a list of 3,000 most common words—that the families used during dinner conversation. Young kids learned 1,000 rare words at the dinner table, compared to only 143 from parents reading storybooks aloud. Kids who have a large vocabulary read earlier and more easily" (emphasis added).[23] Note the strange competition between reading and eating dinner, at least for that central goal of large vocabulary, preferably "rare words." The Family Dinner Project organization makes this case as well:

> Sharing a family meal is good for the spirit, the brain and the health of all family members. Recent studies link regular family dinners with many

behaviors that parents pray for: lower rates of substance abuse, teen pregnancy and depression, as well as *higher grade-point averages* and self-esteem. Studies also indicate that *dinner conversation is a more potent vocabulary-booster than reading,* and the stories told around the kitchen table help our children build resilience. The icing on the cake is that regular family meals also lower the rates of obesity and eating disorders in children and adolescents. What else can families do that takes only about an hour a day and packs such a punch? (emphases added)[24]

Yes, correlational studies link family dinner to good grades, which in turn may lead to college, and then, arguably, to a happy life. But what does it take to have family dinner? (Correlation is not causation.) Families with predictable schedules, dining rooms, no night shifts *already* have advantages. The main message here is that *every minute from birth on should be about school readiness*, to prepare children for college, just like the KIPP (Knowledge Is Power Program) schools, which emphasize that children's sole goal in school is getting to and completing college. "Essential to creating a great system of schools is having our eyes on the same goal: college graduation."[25] So parents need to prepare their children to encounter schoolish learning, which is the only recognized type.

Only Tested Learning Counts: The Myth of "Learning Loss"

During COVID, when schools shut down or went remote or hybrid, a moral panic about "learning loss" emerged in the public domain. If students didn't go to school, then they couldn't be learning. Right?

Well, it depends what you mean by "learning." This follows if the only thing that counts is direct instruction for assessed outcomes.

Alfie Kohn wrote a scathing refutation of this moral panic. This discourse had predated the pandemic, when many people were worried about children from nonadvantaged backgrounds "losing" their learning during the summer. Granted, they may arrive in August and September unable to do the strange schoolish stuff they were barely pretending to do when they left school in May or June. But (1) it doesn't mean they learned *nothing*, and (2) they probably didn't really learn that stuff in the first place. Kohn writes,

> Warnings about academic loss are not just dubious; they're dangerous. They create pressure on already-stressed-out parents to do *more teaching*

at home—and, worse, to do *more of the most traditional, least meaningful kind of teaching* that's geared toward memorizing facts and practicing lists of skills rather than exploring ideas. Parents may just *assume this is what instruction is supposed to look like*, partly because that's how they were taught (and no one ever invited them to rethink this model). And if standardized tests rather than authentic kinds of assessment will eventually be used to evaluate their children, parents, like teachers, will be inclined to do what is really just test prep. (emphases added)[26]

So if the only thing that counts as "learning" is something that will be tested, because it's easy to test—"What is the formula for the circumference of a circle?" "What year was the Constitution ratified?"—then sure, some students will be lacking. Advantaged students will stay current in schoolish stuff.

In September 2022, results of the National Assessment of Educational Progress, NAEP, showed a decline in test results from the 2020–21 school year. The breathless headlines abounded: "The Pandemic Erased Two Decades of Progress in Math and Reading."[27] Calls for never again shutting down schools, and more, make it seem as if these tests are the measure of worth. Yes, the least advantaged did the worst, which is always the case. Yes, some may flunk out. Yes, everyone will have a harder time catching up with the predetermined curriculum. But the solution is not school-school-school. The solution is greater equality. An ironic tweet from 2022 jokes, "Good test scores are so important we are willing to sacrifice our children's education for them." Are we, indeed?

Schoolishness Is Not the Only Way to Learn

The research on education and childhood in non-WEIRD societies shows an entirely different set of values. Karen Kramer pointed out how little Maya children in the Yucatan Peninsula, among whom she has studied for three decades, are directed by adults.[28] This is a common observation when anthropologists go outside of middle-class North American context: we see people learning without being taught.

David Lancy, an anthropologist of childhood, has been writing for years to challenge the notion of teaching as a universal human practice. His magisterial compendium, *The Anthropology of Childhood*, lists example after example of children learning. Lancy noticed how young children throughout the world were entrusted with difficult and often dangerous tasks, such as using machetes or tending fires, or serving as child nannies. With few exceptions, children learn—how to make tortillas, how to weave, how to collect nonpoisonous plants, how to cook, how to herd animals, how to do almost everything—without teachers. It's voluntary. The children are the agents of their learning. Success is assumed. Occasionally a child will ask for some instruction, but this is rare. Learning could be through trial and error, through what he calls "the chore curriculum," through apprenticeship, with its graduated tasks, through simpler models of tools, through abiding, wide attention, and observation.

This provoked Lancy to ask: is teaching necessary? (He asks if perhaps procedural knowledge, or how to do things, is best learned through activity, and if propositional knowledge, or knowledge about things, is best learned through declamation. A hot topic in archaeology in 2020 is the archaeology of learning.)[29]

In most of human history and in much of the world, and even in much of our day-to-day world, the greatest learning doesn't happen via "direct instruction." And most questions aren't asked to elicit known information.

The ethnographic record shows—a record increasingly precious as schooling comes to dominate everywhere—children learning to be confident, independent learners, or what Lancy calls "autonomous learners" who are everywhere being "tamed" by schoolishness.[30]

A lot of the rest of this book will show how learning can occur in nonpedagogized ways.

For most of human history, there were no schools. Children learned to be members of their families and societies. There may have been some instruction—especially religion and crafts. But most people learned, and in fact continue to learn, most things through observation, trial and error, and more. So it's strange that twenty-first-century human childhood has become one long pedagogical enterprise.

If we observe and catalog all the nonschoolish learning, we find mixes of the following:

Learning by Doing, Trial and Error

As with learning to walk, young children learn by trying things. Scientists often use this method. A documentary about the history of psychedelic drugs, directed by Michael Pollan, shows that many drugs were accidentally produced in labs while someone was trying to do something different, and then the drug was tried.[31] This can, certainly, be dangerous! But much adventurous learning does in fact occur this way. The ancient pharmacopeias were largely derived from trial and error and long and repeated observation.

Observation

Suzanne Gaskins has spent much of her career analyzing the ways Yucatec Mayans learn. She has documented the ways the young watch others with "wide-angle attention" until they have the capability of doing it themselves. This is true for various skills, as Patricia Greenfield has shown for weaving, Jean Lave has demonstrated for everyday math, and countless people have experienced for cooking.[32]

A documentary called *Get Back* shows the Beatles rehearsing and creating in preparation for what turned out to be their last concert.[33] One scene in particular stuck in my mind: John Lennon is trying to play something on the piano. He's not an especially well-trained pianist, but he seems to be game for everything. Paul McCartney, the better pianist, comes over and plays a passage for Lennon. They don't speak. McCartney plays it, Lennon watches, he tries it, and McCartney goes back to doing whatever he was doing. It was all about careful observation of a demonstration—just as needed at the moment. There was no prior instruction, no "banking," no lectures.

Apprenticeship

Human technology has always required learning. In Ireland I visited Dublin's St. Patrick's Cathedral, which had been completed by 1191. Though the spires have blown off and burned, the roof has been replaced, and the interior has been redone many times, the impressive, elaborate stone structure itself remains. Somehow, workers without school or the Internet or calculus designed, coordinated, procured materials, and built this amazing structure.

The Chore Curriculum

Lancy shows that young children worldwide undertake a graduated series of responsibilities as they learn to be members of their societies. They are eager to be useful. At first they do very simple tasks, which increase in difficulty and importance as they master them. The children are expected to take the initiative, often, to jump up and do hard things.

How many middle-class white American children could do any of the tasks performed by the six-year-old Matsigenka girl described by Ochs and Izquierdo in the epigraph of this chapter? Would they even be permitted—by parents, by the law—to work and fish and cook?

Does this seem desirable?

If you have ever watched a young person proudly accomplish something hard, like Estrella did with light switches, you can see that it can be meaningful, authentic, and independent.

And they've often learned it experientially, not schoolishly.

Pedagogizing is assumed as the default condition of learning, at least in WEIRD societies, where schoolishness dominates. We'll see more about the ingredients of pedagogizing in the next chapter.

4

TEACHERS, STUDENTS, CLASSES

From Authorities and Competitors to Communities of Varied Learners

> Perhaps oppression dehumanizes the oppressor as much as, if not
> more than, the oppressed. They need each other to become truly free,
> to become human.
>
> DESMOND TUTU, 1984 Nobel Lecture

If direct instruction lies at the core of schoolishness, as we saw in the
previous chapter, then the agents involved in this process are teachers
and students. Teachers directly instruct students in groups, and then
judge students as individuals. Schoolishness presumes certain roles
and relationships, both between the teachers and students and among
the students.

Schools are interactional settings. Courtney B. Cazden, a linguist
who studied the interaction of language with teaching and learning, put
it beautifully: "Like a group of musicians improvising together, speech
events, including classroom discourse, can only be accomplished by the
collaborative work of two or more persons. In this sense, *school* is always
a performance that must be constituted through the participation of a
group of actors."[1]

The most schoolish interactions are controlled; teachers are always the
gate. They acknowledge speakers, receive responses, and are the beneficiary of all the comments. Students face front. They request permission for

all activities. They do so as individuals. (I recognize that many classrooms operate differently, and to that extent they are less schoolish.)

In this chapter I talk about teacher-student relationships, student-student relationships, and the assumed uniformity of students. As always, I'll introduce the schoolish dimension of each of these three aspects, followed by less-schoolish versions. Classrooms may contain a variety of relationships, including competition and cooperation. If we wish for democratic societies, then we may need to enact the practice of democracy in learning.

Schoolish Interactions: Teacher-Centered Structures

In their roles as centers of authority and control, teachers discipline their students and are the decision makers regarding punishment and reward. They determine the structure, the content, the pacing. At best, they may also serve as kind mentors and guides, either in addition to or instead of as sages, experts, those who know. Depending on the roles played by teachers, students in turn have roles with specific relationships.

Expert–Novice

Schoolish teachers are experts, possessing all the knowledge and skill. Students are "empty," in need of filling up with what the teacher has already determined. Students' lack is constantly reiterated.[2] It makes students *passive recipients* of something *pre-formed*. They develop a false view of mastery, as if they have completely understood something once they pass a test or get a good grade. They are *dependent* and *passive*.

Teachers may not actually feel completely expert, instead feeling like impostors. Or they may know their material so well that they develop an "expert blind spot." When things have become "second nature," implicit, we have a harder time teaching. Some pedagogy experts have urged us to "teach what we don't know," to be learners alongside our students, to model genuine inquiry, not just absorption of completed knowledge.[3]

Judge–Defendant

Along with this role, teachers are usually expected to judge and evaluate—both on behalf of the learner and on behalf of interested parties outside the school. The evaluative gaze of school, as Carol Black puts it, is "profoundly deadening to a curious, engaged child."[4] Whether the evaluation is positive ("Good job!" "A+") or negative ("Wrong." "F"), she continues, "when you watch a child who is focused on learning, and you let them know you're watching, and you let them know your opinion *as though your opinion matters*, you just took that thing away from them." Foucault, Bentham, and many others have written of the panopticon, of judgment, of being surveilled. When this is the principal role of a teacher, students become the objects of surveillance. In my research I've heard a good number of students in secondary and higher education speak of teachers as someone to outsmart, someone to get past, to fool, because they hold the power of the grade. Alfie Kohn reminds us that even rewards can punish.

Parent–Child (Mentor–Mentee)

In lower levels of schooling but sometimes even later, teachers may occupy a parental role, charged with caring for students' multiple needs. Takeo Doi, a Japanese psychiatrist, wrote that this parent-child and teacher-student relationship, *amae*, modeled on the mother-infant relationship, is a universal need of human nature.[5] We wish to be able to depend on reliable, benevolent older others. When seniors accept their responsibility, then the junior in the relationship can be protected, afforded some indulgence, and explore freely. When students indicate their need for help, the teacher is obligated to be responsible, considerate, compassionate. Much of East Asia has holidays celebrating teachers.

Control over Interaction and Attention

Often a good part of teachers' work is managing classroom interactions. In younger grades, teachers are often evaluated on their "classroom management" skills, aiming for quiet, order, decorum, and avoidance of any semblance of chaos. But even in higher education, students constantly seek permission for movement, speech, absence, or deviation from the arbitrary and inconsistent expectations of teachers. Yet schoolish interactions are not universally deemed appropriate.

Linguists and anthropologists have conducted meticulous ethnographic research of classroom interactions, often guided by Erving

Goffman's notion of *participant structures*. Interaction and attention may be conveyed in varied ways. One especially powerful study, by Susan U. Philips, showed that Anglos and Warm Springs Indians in Oregon had different ideas of proprietary and morality.[6] They differed on stillness and movement, eye gaze, expressiveness, speed of speech. For Warm Springs Indians, the Anglo expectations of evidence of attention—head nodding, direct gaze—are not appropriate. The centrality of the teacher, which reinforces hierarchy and control, violates their notions of equality and autonomy.

Analysts of interaction—sociologists, anthropologists, communication specialists, discourse analysts, conversation analysts, or ethnomethodologists (there is a huge amount of research, as you can tell)—generally see the person holding the floor as holding the power. If someone is not only speaking but controlling who speaks, this is a double power. Preventing one from speaking or demanding they speak also requires power. Volunteering to speak is complicated, because, as Senator Elizabeth Warren explained when asked about her commitment to the Socratic method, cold-calling on everyone in her Harvard Law School classes, if "you just rely on voluntary discussion in classrooms, you're only going to hear from the two white guys that love to talk."[7] (Cold-calling, however, keeps the professor at the center, introduces fear and shame as motivation, and involves coercion. It also forces a single type of overt public production of speech in order to foster engagement.)

Hand raising and looking at the teacher as the conductor of verbal traffic might seem simply practical, until you realize how many students address *only* the teacher, as if everything is a test and they want to make sure they get all the points. Participation points. Brownie points.

Hand raising was invented by Pietists, and adopted by Prussians, as a way of enforcing discipline and hierarchy.[8] That is not an endorsement. To promote horizontal, not-teacher-centered interactions, I stopped having students raise their hands to speak—until masks made it harder to jump in or notice who was planning to jump in, perhaps through an inhale. In real-world interactions, we have to figure out who gets the floor. (That's one of our research topics in the linguistic anthropology class every year.) Sometimes two or more will begin together. Technically this is called "trouble," and it is followed by "repair." Only in the most formal of interactions, such as debates (when people follow the rules, not like in presidential debates), is there an absence of overlap.

No Learning without a Teacher?   I met a speaker who had come from another continent to give a public lecture. She was returning home the very next day because "I could cancel class on Tuesday but not also on Thursday. They can't teach themselves!" She said it as if it was the most obvious fact about learning. But I think they can. If I have to cancel my classes, I entrust the students with directing their own activities.

Less-Schoolish Relationships: Learner Centered

Not all relationships in schools are schoolish. When students and teachers are on the same side, not adversaries, even "strict" teachers may provide protection and security.

Most of "progressive" pedagogy aims, one way or another, to, at minimum, *reduce pedagogizing*. Whether it's called "learner centered," "liberatory," or "child centered," the aim is to reduce the absolute power and authority of teachers and to focus on learning and learners. Sometimes the emphasis is liberation, sometimes well-being, sometimes play. Self-directed students in Sudbury schools experience their educations as learner centered, with freedom, equality, and responsibility baked in. Sudbury schools don't even have "teachers." They have adult guides who are voted on by the learners every year.[9] Adult education, both formal and informal, may be self-directed.[10] To be sure, adult learners may also seek coaches or guides.

Coach–Athlete/Performer

Athletes and musicians who care about their work—in other words, people who aren't learning things just because they're forced to in school—want to improve. In order to do this, there's often a coach, someone who shares the learner's aims. This might include sessions where work is reviewed. Skilled coaches know when to sit back and allow the athlete just to work and when to let the musician improvise. Coaches often bring a lot of experience and expertise, just as teachers do, but the desired outcome is always enhanced work. If judgment is involved, it is always formative, even if there will later be some kind of competitive, outside judgment.

Guide–Seeker

In much of the world, people welcome the guidance of gurus and spiritual leaders, appreciating someone who can provide tasks, insight, texts, exercises, and counsel. This is the case for religious traditions and possibly for therapy, though this is a complicated and somewhat nonrelated topic. In Judaism the word *rabbi* means "teacher," with the insight and wisdom that comes from long and serious study.

In yoga, meditation, and many Asian-derived practices, there's a role for a guru or a teacher who has wisdom that the students themselves may not even know to seek. In each case, the curriculum is tailored to the actual needs of the students at that moment. In Chan/Zen Buddhism, originally from India and influenced by Chinese Daoism, Zen masters or teachers give individual students what they need, whether it's the task of cleaning a garden or contemplating a kōan.

Master gardeners help novice gardeners figure out problems in their own garden. Doulas, whether for birth or death, guide a person into a new phase, giving them what they need at the time.

In this sense, it is a great privilege to have a teacher.

Model–Apprentice

In many domains—work, craft, home chores—learners begin simply by modeling themselves on someone who can already do the work, and they serve as apprentices. The work increases gradually in complexity and difficulty.

Partners, Co-learners

Some relationships among learners are simply of partnership. This may be true at work, and in life. In hacker spaces, my colleague Luis Felipe Rosado Murillo tells me, anyone who comes in is expected to participate in the hands-on learning that constitutes the core of the space. Most of the participants, he says, had truly despised conventional schooling, but they love learning new things.

What all these less-schoolish relationships share is that the aims of the teachers and learners converge.

You're the Learner, I'm the Coach: My Teaching Makeover

In my journey from schoolishness to healthy learning, I have often been inspired by the clichés about "sage on the stage" and "guide on the side." I often call myself a "coach." On my syllabi I specify that this course is "Coached by Susan D. Blum." I've come to believe that there is no such thing as teaching; there is only learning. I repeatedly say "I can't make you learn; I can only create conditions in which you want to learn, and then in which it is possible, even relatively easy, to learn." To foster a more egalitarian relationship, for a decade I've urged my students to call me by my first name. But I also recognize that many faculty lack my institutional authority or racial security, or are minoritized and wish to emphasize their earned authority, perhaps to help with representation of underrepresented groups, such as Black women in academia. In those cases, the title "Dr." is extremely important. Similarly, many students have been socialized from birth to address any elder with a title, even if it's an affectionate one: Miss Martha. Auntie. Reverend. Doc. This is true for students from many cultural groups in the US, and for international students as well. I don't *insist* on egalitarian naming, reciprocal naming, but I do *invite* students to call me "Coach Susan" if "Susan" alone is too awkward.

People Interacting Together: Competing and Cooperating

Relationships among students are also a relevant part of schoolishness. If schoolish teacher-student relationships are vertical, student-student relationships are horizontal. As I showed in chapter 2, when sorting and ranking are seen as the primary outcomes of schooling, identifying who attains the limited goods (prizes, admission, jobs), the main relationship among students is competitive, and students are pitted against each other. When there is curved grading—which Melanie Cooper and Mike Klymkowsky in the member journal of the *American Society for Biochemistry and Molecular Biology* have declared "educational malpractice"—the focus is entirely on outdoing others.[11] Ryan Bowen and Cooper followed this with "Grading on a Curve as a Systemic Issue of Equity in Chemistry Education" in the *Journal of Chemistry Education*.[12] These are not fuzzy-headed humanists or anthropologists; these are people who treasure deep and accurate learning. But they argue on many grounds that this "capricious decision to predetermine what percentage of the class must fail" is harmful. Should we not be *pleased* if everyone learns well?

It's far better to have students help one another learn. It's true that as the system is currently structured, many science classes are especially designed as "weed-out" courses, often on behalf of admissions departments of medical schools. A hand-wringing conversation occurred in the fall of 2022 (as I noted in chapter 2) when an NYU adjunct professor of organic chemistry was fired, purportedly for his mockery of some students' poor performance, or because students petitioned that his course was too hard.[13] *New York* magazine had the headline "The Whiny Grade-Grubbing NYU Students Have a Point."[14] But nobody would argue that weeding out students is moral or educational; it's merely a familiar, schoolish convenience.

Students cooperating is, in some sense, the ideal outcome of schools as places where people gather for learning. At best students learn with friends. Some may be uninterested in others, just taking their own individually required classes. But predetermining that only some will succeed begins with threats, antithetical to authentic, joyous learning.

Less-Schoolish Structures and Interactions: Becoming a Community of Learners

Less-schoolish learning involves learners cooperating with one another rather than competing. They may simply enjoy connection and sociality; they may reach moments of friendship and even love, when they have cooperative and supportive relationships. They may learn from one another.

Students Learning Together

Instead of teacher-centered structures, where everything has to be filtered through the all-powerful central authority, I work hard in my classes to create space for students to hear one another's voices and to learn from one another. Why else should we gather, other than for the sake of industrial efficiency, which might be even more efficient if done digitally? What do we gain from being together? And how does this happen?

We have to build a community so students are interested in learning with others, and to choose communicative platforms that enable student-generated questions.

One of the ways I attempt to achieve these goals is to leave lots of time, regularly, for student-generated questions (see chapter 5). This can be done in a variety of ways, through varied, engaging formats, so that students with different tastes and limitations may find ways of learning that are more suitable.

In recounting her own experience of student power, Cathy Davidson writes about what happened after she introduced the idea of "contract grading" to her graduate students. On a day when she had to be absent, she charged them with determining the "standards" for the different grades. When she came back, she found that they had wrenched the task away from what she had assigned and decided instead that everyone (except one) would work for an A, meaning "a perfect, proofread, satisfactory chapter in a book that the students, collectively, would copyedit, design, and publish," and that *they would take responsibility for one another to ensure that everyone did well.*[15]

It is a fact of our nature, our species-being, as Marx termed it, that humans need society, social relations. Humans are by nature acutely attuned to others, and to others' positions. We take our place, or we resist; we bask in others' admiration, or we starve and squirm in mockery. The flip side of caring about other people is that we care when they love us and we care when they mock or disdain or exclude us. (There are different kinds of love, as observers at least since Aristotle have noted: romantic love, friends' love, love of parents, sexual love. . . .) Kathleen Hull writes of *eros* in classrooms, careful to differentiate it from sexual harassment and all that is forbidden. But deep passion and desire must play a role in deep engagement and learning. She warns, "One of the glories of being human is that our thought and imagination create various shades of objects to fulfill our desires. We have forgotten the ancient notion that erotic desire, *eros*, may put one on the road to disruption, change, growth, and according to some, transcendence."[16]

In Japanese schools, without tracking, students are expected to bond with the group. In the project comparing American, Chinese, and Japanese preschools, *Preschool in Three Cultures* recounts a young Japanese child acting improperly and the teacher declining to intervene. American and Chinese teachers disapproved; the Japanese teachers all approved: they believed that students need to learn how to solve problems among themselves. In Japanese math classes, students who learn faster are not praised; they are expected to help their classmates.[17] *The class moves forward as a whole.*[18]

It's no secret that the things students often like best about school are their friends, kind teachers, their cocurricular activities such as sports and arts.[19]

It was clear during the initial COVID year of distancing how much most people missed being around others. Others were relieved. Most schools were able to reconstruct the cognitive part of what they did, but not the emotional part. Humans are actually created to respond to one another, in both positive and negative ways. At best, we like to synchronize our laughter and our bodily movements, as we do with dance, comedy, sport. All societies have dance and music, conversation and humor. We coordinate and share, and at best this brings about what Émile Durkheim called "collective effervescence," that bubbling up of laughter and joy, synchronized.

Anthropologists talk about something called *communities of practice*, groups that interact together with other people for particular ends.[20] But it's more complicated than that in contemporary classrooms, at least the kinds of classrooms that I aspire to shape. In my classroom I attempt to create what I continually refer to as a "community of learners." I try to foster what a lot of the educational folks now call social and emotional learning, and in a frame of mind with Universal Design for Learning, which means that I try to create a place for everyone, knowing that each person will have a slightly different place. I rarely have strict course prerequisites now (other than interest in the topic), to ensure a diversity of backgrounds—mimicking "real life," where we bring different assets to every interaction. I try to make it fun, and safe, and exciting, where collective effervescence can happen at least sometimes. This is physical and involves interaction of bodies in specific spaces. Goals are many, but they include a sense of responsibility to others, so that if people are weighing attending class or not attending class, one of the motivations will be to see people they know. Since I don't grade, and I don't threaten for failure to attend, and yet I want people to attend, it's important to establish from the beginning a sense of community.

We begin every course with social interaction, in which every student speaks, at least to some others, to immediately imprint on their bodies, their memories, their experience, the recollection of having spoken. Quiet passivity is not what they associate with the class. This works, even if later in the semester I give mini-lectures in which students are sitting quietly; but this does not define the experience.

I've developed an array of first-day activities, from tasting weird food together to "speed dating" (see chapter 5) to a human scavenger hunt where students learn of others' varied backgrounds, tastes, and assets (as much as they're willing to disclose).[21] It's always fun, and sometimes loud, and I love it. Students often remarked on how different it is from other courses where they simply go and pick up the syllabus. I don't have "syllabus week"—the first week of class when, apparently, many colleagues simply go over the syllabus, the rules, and the outcomes. Some give "syllabus quizzes," and others annotate the syllabus.

When I taught online during the first COVID year, I modified the human scavenger hunt with breakout rooms, and it went pretty well. I would not categorize it as joyous, but we coped.

Vertical and Horizontal Interactions

I try to encourage students to talk to one another, not only to me, when they speak. They have been trained to think of all of school as doing whatever the teacher/professor asks. But what if they *actually had something they wanted to say to people*, not just to jump because we say *jump*? It is so hard to unlearn the hand raising, and the *speaking-for-participation points*. All semester, I remind them. Sometimes I turn away, cover my face, humorously hide under the desk—anything to get them to stop seeing me as the only audience. After fall and spring break, even the ones who had gotten used to it often revert; it's ingrained in their bodies since their first forays into preschool. The hand raising requires a central traffic director, eye contact, and pausing to get permission. It interrupts any semblance of normal, real conversation or discussion.

In my linguistic anthropology class, I begin every class with one or two students bringing in something they have, independently, discovered "in real life" (we call it "Language IRL") that connects with that day's topics. They become experts. Other students look at them. The day begins with student voices. Students are responsible to their classmates.

Simultaneously, the "Daily Card / Daily N&Q [Notes and Queries] Curation Team" is quickly looking through the questions about the reading, which every student is supposed to write before coming to class. When I switched to teaching remotely, I switched from physical Daily Cards to digital Daily N&Qs. The team selects the questions we'll discuss. Some pick "better"—to me—questions than others. But this makes the students try to write good questions that will be picked, not just anything, to fulfill the assignment. If I'm giving them power, it has to be real.

So as I try to begin class with the students' interests, it's still within a structure I've constructed. I try to ride the discussion, connect it to what we're learning but without controlling it. It's hard, nerve-wracking, like improv. I have to listen, be quick, juggle competing needs (acknowledge someone, make sure we get to "the main point"—unless something else comes up that's really important). And occasionally I correct a factual error, or provide information about research that has already answered the questions students raise. But then there is *a need for the answer*, not just my answer before there is a question. The motivation emerges from the students' interests and experience, not from some predetermined lesson plan.

Some faculty teach their students to cite each other, as they would any academic reference.

Independent Learning in Community

Peter Elbow, among his extraordinarily helpful and powerful books about writing, wrote *Writing without Teachers* to show how a group of writers—what we now call a "writing group"—could give useful feedback about their reactions and in that way help writers clarify what they need.[22] Workshopping drafts is an activity with multiple benefits, including providing an authentic audience and providing practice at being willing to do revision. It also helps foster independence, which is one of my ultimate hopes for my students. I create spaces for my students to do a lot of that. I also have my students meet on their own if I'm away for a conference or a religious holiday. Students *can* teach themselves.

Not Total Autonomy   In the United States, we have ideas of democracy and empowerment, yet the "hidden curriculum" enforces dependence and hierarchy, while we profess independence and equality. We aren't sure, nationally, if we want autonomy or relationship. In the 1980s, in *Habits of the Heart*, Robert Bellah and collaborators wrote about tension in the United States between "individualism and commitment."[23] Maybe we don't want total autonomy, but a sense of efficacy, power, confidence? Whatever the goals, it's clear that we're doomed to fail if we say "be responsible" (like adults) and then take away all autonomy, keeping students dependent on pleasing authority.

Sitting Equally (Yes, with White Tenured Privilege)   The world we wish to create via our education can be professed explicitly (equality, respect) and yet contradicted by the actual structures of interaction. It's true that the world is filled with competition and scarcity; but at least my model ideal society has cooperation and abundance. In order to get students to experience that, it's necessary to develop a structure of safety, where laughter can abound and where a mistake can be shrugged off, rather than leading to shame, humiliation, punishment.

It takes a lot to convince my hierarchy-comfortable students that I really mean democracy, at least as much as possible. I understand that I rely on certain privileges to maintain "authority" in the classroom while simultaneously asking for equality. We sit equally, same height, same importance.

Maha Bali from Cairo curated but also solicited a set of resources about creating community. (I don't have to do this alone. There's a community of educators too!) The science of teaching and learning and research on social and emotional learning remind us that humans are generally embedded in social networks to which they are responsible, which can judge but also assist them.

If we stop *demanding* attendance or participation, the challenge is how to create conditions in which students nonetheless want to attend, feel responsible to their team to attend (as long as they are not ill—a COVID-years concern, but also always important in these compact interactions where people are near each other for long periods). This requires attention, early in the semester, and activities that lead to silliness, purpose, and a range of emotions—not personal confession demanded, but sharing of knowledge and other experiences to help the group succeed in its goals.

When I returned to the physical classroom in August and September 2021, I celebrated our physical copresence, the possibility of "collective effervescence" that synchronized our gazes, our breaths, our gestures, our brain waves, though masks made the rhythms harder to get right. In the fall 2021 midsemester portfolio conferences, many students spontaneously mentioned how much they "loved my team" and that the class was so collaborative, unlike their more typically competitive classes. They had fun and felt safe; I had introduced the concept of collective effervescence, and some applied it to their own lives. Some mentioned how frequently they saw people from our class—at football games, at bars, around campus.

A Note on Introverts: The Hell and Heaven That Are Others, and a Place for Solitude While games, active learning, teams, groups, pairs, and more emphasize social relationships, schoolishness results in a shortage of privacy and solitude. It is impossible to avoid surveillance for most of the time in schools. Many students—and faculty—go to bathrooms for moments away from others' eyes. Any humane education must leave room for a respite for those who want it.[24]

When I taught online, I often gave time (five, ten minutes) for students to turn off their cameras and just write. Many found this a great relief.

Humans need solitude, in varying degrees. Hell is other people—but so is everything, according to Warren von Eschenbach.[25]

We need others but in differing degrees and in different ways, from shy people with severe anxiety who can focus on essential tasks, to life-of-the-party extroverts who flit from enthusiasm to enthusiasm.

> ### When Students Just Want to Get the Task Done
>
> Someone asked me, after a talk I gave about ungrading, about students who
> don't want community or don't want to generate their own questions. They
> want to come in, be told what to do, and then do it. They don't want deep
> and meaningful learning. They don't want a chance to reflect. They want to
> check off this requirement so they can get the credential and then get a raise
> at work. This "transactional" approach is certainly widespread.
>
> In many ways this real and common conundrum is the kind of reason
> for which I wrote this book. A simple trick can't fix what is really a systemic
> problem.

If our classes aim to foster real learning that matters to learners, then
we have to make space, and time, for them. We have to clear away the
unspoken message that our aim is compliance. We have to build a community so students are interested in learning with others, and to choose
communicative platforms that enable student-generated questions. And
we have to think hard about what roles teachers and students are actually playing.

Norms, Normal, Divergent

Communities are not collections of sameness, of mechanical solidarity,
but rather of organic solidarity, where people with different strengths and
weaknesses, different interests and backgrounds, different characteristics,
different roles and functions, can all find welcome, and in fact be needed.
I model an ideal community more on my small, intimate South Bend Sinai
Synagogue, where we have people of different ages and political backgrounds and economic statuses, than on my former synagogue in Denver,
where everyone was young, well-educated, and liberal. I welcome people of multiple political and ideological backgrounds, even when we talk
about political issues. In fact one of my objections to selective college admissions in general has to do with its artificiality. If our education is so
great, why should we confer it only on those already privileged? And if
there aren't enough spots for everyone who wants one, there are three

Figure 4.1. Idealized students and outcome

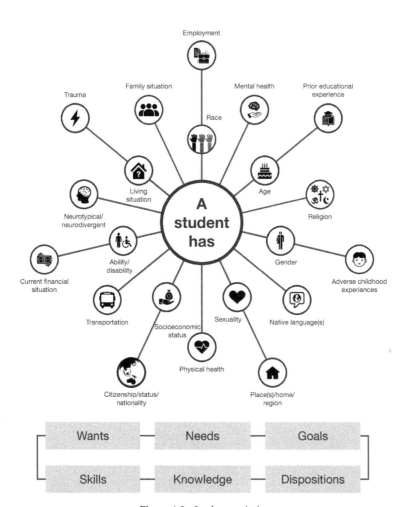

Figure 4.2. Student variation

options: increase the number of spots; have a lottery; or increase the desirability of other options.

The prototypical schoolish experience presumes a generic student moving at a steady pace through a uniform set of educational experiences. At the end, there is a uniform output ("learning outcomes"), and this in turn automatically generates a grade. It is acknowledged that some students are "special," a euphemism for divergent, and need Individualized Educational Plans, accommodations, or some kind of special course.

Accommodation is usually done in response to students' documented intellectual and physical disabilities. But at the same time, diversity, equity, and inclusion efforts have called attention to the other ways students may differ. Usually this includes race, class, gender, and (in higher education), being first-generation.

However, students differ in all ways. Figure 4.2 gives a glimpse of some of the ways. Clearly a uniform class cannot be constructed that addresses every dimension.

So here I would just like to put in a plug for Universal Design for Learning, created along the lines of Universal Design in general. Rather than call attention to the deficits of certain individuals, one must try to design experiences that can accommodate people of all different types.

Is this hard?

Yes. It certainly doesn't fit the students-as-widgets model. But it's what we do in families, in communities, in religious institutions. You'll see this difference-as-asset approach in chapter 14, "'The Trees Need Water.'" First, though, we'll look at a concrete way relationships can be schoolish, or not: through asking questions.

5

QUESTIONS

From Compliance, Control, and Evaluation (Authority) to Curiosity, Power, Wonder, and Effervescence (Democracy)

> The basic purpose of school is achieved through communication.
>
> COURTNEY B. CAZDEN, *Classroom Discourse: The Language of Teaching and Learning*

If schools are built on interaction, human interaction is built on conversation and related *genres* of talk. When we are in a conversation, our brain waves synchronize.[1] We rarely allow much silence between what are called, technically, *turns*. Now, it's true, classroom interactions are not usually conversations. But some of them resemble them. Schools contain multiple genres of interaction: lecture-and-discussion; seminar; question-and-answer; recitation. But conversation is special: it is universal, and part of our social and human nature.

There's a huge field devoted to the nuances of interaction, called conversation analysis, related to something called, not so comfortably, ethnomethodology—EM/CA, for short. I adore this approach because it is so precise and counterintuitive.[2] In linguistic anthropology we speak of *pragmatics*, asking what a given chunk of language *does*, not just what it *means*. The branch of philosophy called speech act theory distinguishes an utterance (the thing that is said, or uttered) from its intended effect and from its actual consequences. (Technically, following J. L. Austin, these are called the *locutionary act*, the *illocutionary act*, and the *perlocutionary effect*.)[3] Language serves social and pragmatic purposes; there's never a mere exchange of information. We can use these insights to examine schoolish interactions and especially that ubiquitous school genre, questions. "Questions are a universal feature of human language," Nick Enfield points out.[4] But in schools, they're strange.

What Are Questions For?

Questions have many forms and many functions. The most prototypical questions solicit new information: *What's your address (so I can find your house)? Why is the road blocked (maybe you know)?* Some questions expect no *actual* information but are conventionalized greetings: *How are you doing?* (United States); *Have you eaten yet?* (China); *Where are you going?* (Sri Lanka).[5] Sometimes questions are essentially accusations: *What time does the concert start, did you say (so why aren't you ready already)?* The functions and effects of particular questions, like all speech, can't be known without knowing their context: *What color is my shirt?* I may ask a friend because I'm color blind, or I may have poor lighting in my bedroom, or because we always joke about our clothes. If I ask a toddler, I'm probably quizzing her.

Why did you do that? This will have a different function if it is from a parent to a child who broke a sibling's art project [= you shouldn't have done that = anger], or from an apprentice learning to bake bread [= seeking explanation], or from a teacher trying to get a student to see that their solution is wrong.

What is that? Such a question could come from curiosity, fear, a need to know, or from the schoolish motive of testing, asked by someone who already knows.

Some questions take the grammatical form of questions—*Has the train left yet?*—and really require answers, depending on the situation. Some questions are grammatically questions—*Didn't I already tell you that five times?*—but don't require answers because they are not, pragmatically, questions but rather accusations. Some utterances function as questions, though they lack the grammatical form of questions—*She was Ukrainian?*—but may have the intonation of questions. Rising intonation at the end of the sentence for yes-no questions seems to be widespread, if not universal, and is acquired very young.[6] (Huddleston distinguishes "interrogatives," which have grammatical form, and "questions," which have to do with meaning.[7] Some languages, like Spanish, don't invert words to form questions; other languages, like Mandarin, Korean, and Japanese, add a "question particle." There are "polar," yes/no questions, wh- questions, and more; it's complicated.)

All human enterprises—especially education—involve interaction. And interaction involves both rights and responsibilities. Questions require responses.

As Nick Enfield points out in his wonderful book *How We Talk*, participants in a conversation have a *moral obligation to respond to questions*. Failure to do so may be seen as incompetence (as for very young people, or people without knowledge), defiance (as in prisoners who refuse to answer questions—or stereotypical US teenagers), or evasion. They are failing to uphold their responsibilities.

The *right* to ask a question, though, is often a matter of power, precisely because it obligates the other to respond.

Schoolish questions are a special category. Teachers ask students these kinds of questions all the time. Some are *didactic questions*, related to the *testing function of schoolishness* (see chapter 10). And they have great bearing on the experiences of schooling.

Who Asks the Questions? What Kinds of Questions?

Asking a question is a power move because it demands an answer and puts obligations onto the conversation partner. In schoolish interactions, teachers have power, and students have obligations—moral and consequential. The moral obligation is the general human one. The consequential one has to do with the power of assessment and its "travel" in the transcript.[8]

Teachers ask a lot of questions. Prototypical schoolish exchanges have questions and answers, already known to the teacher.

What's the Pythagorean theorem?
What is participant observation?
What does a cat say?

When did the first enslaved Africans arrive in the Americas?
How does a bill become a law?
Why does the moon have phases?
What percentage of food is wasted in the US?

These schoolish questions must be answered, because of the power imbalance. (People may believe that only an unprepared, defiant, or otherwise nonnormative student would fail to answer. But can you imagine other reasons? Deafness? Social anxiety? Language learner?) The teacher is not engaging the students to *learn* the answers from the student. The assumption is that the teacher already knows. Schoolish questions have answers. Right answers. Wrong answers. These can be oral, in class, or written, on tests, quizzes, and homework. They can be and often are assessed, counted, marked right or wrong, given partial credit.

Courtney Cazden in 1988 pointed out that the exchanges of schoolish questioning have three parts, sometimes abbreviated IRE (F), for "initiation" (asking the question), "response" (answering the question), and "evaluation" or "feedback" (assessment).[9] These exchanges may be instantaneous and oral, as occur frequently in class, or written and delayed, as occur in tests. The power and authority remain the same.

There is a lot written about the kinds of questions *teachers* should ask, and how long to pause before . . . I guess, reasking, or answering for the student.[10] Pedagogues sometimes distinguish *convergent and divergent questions*: the ones with and the ones without clear answers. These kinds of questions range from the known-answer questions that are prototypical school questions, which exist almost entirely in schools, to more open-ended questions that can be effective or not (*What do you think about Benjamin's argument about mechanical reproduction?* [pretty vague]. *Do you have any questions? I've read discussions about a simple improvement: What questions do you have?*).

Gaps, Deficits, and Testing: The So-Called
Word Gap and Schoolish Parenting

There's a line of thought that tries to put schoolish questions beyond the school walls and into the heart of family life.

The so-called language gap or word gap is the erroneous idea that before kindergarten, children in poverty are exposed to thirty million fewer words, as Hart and Risley claimed in 1995 with terrifying but false precision, than their affluent peers, and that the "quality" of their surrounding language is inferior.[11] In addition to children supposedly lacking thirty million words, their households are said to lack schoolish questions, the kinds that ask for known information and are rewarded with praise, or confirmation of correctness. Well-intentioned "experts," not aware of how language really works, give advice.[12] They teach parents how to ask schoolish questions.

What is this? What does a horse say? The questions are not truly motivated by anything in the environment, or any genuine need to know something, but are simply the parents using their power to initiate a topic and the students, or rather children, having an obligation to respond no matter what else they are doing.

This IRE, or sometimes talk-listen-respond, routine is exactly the kind of schoolish discourse that *puts the teacher at the center of the learning* and *makes the students passive respondents* to *decontextualized and unmotivated material,* to random questions thrown at them in no particular reasonable order, and then teaches the children to *crave this kind of evaluation,* or praise, or reward, or grade, for answering something that is not meaningful.

In real life, vocabulary is usually learned not by drilling, not by testing, not by direct instruction, but by use. Every language learner knows that the lessons that are so difficult in a classroom are made so much easier once the language learner sets foot in a setting where the language is actually used. In that context, the language learning might even be effortless. For most people, young people, it's impossible to *prevent* learning. So despite parents drilling random words with their children, unless the parents are actually using those words, and others around them are actually using those words in meaningful ways in social interaction, they are not likely to stick.

White middle-class US parents ask their children such known-answer questions all the time. Those are *didactic questions* and stem from the *testing function of schooling* that is so familiar to advantaged families that have thrived in their academic lives.

Questions have many effects—as hints getting people to act (*Is it cold in here?*), finding out information (*Where are my keys?*), as encouraging agreement (*Shouldn't we all wish Bruno a happy birthday?*). But asking children to demonstrate their knowledge out of context (*What color is that? What does a dog say?*) is a peculiar speech act that demonstrates performance for a judging audience. This is the principal didactic activity within schools—leading to learning-for-testing, passivity, and many other things that are problematic in the ways children are schooled.[13] So if parents want their children to succeed in school, they have to act just like teachers, from day one: A website, "Talk to Your Child," suggested the use of "name games": "Make it a game: When kids are learning words, play games like 'Where's your tummy?' . . . 'Where's the cat?' . . . 'What's that?'" These are schoolish questions with the appearance of fun and games.

Not only is drilling children in low-income households on colors, shapes, numbers, the alphabet, just as wealthy families do, a strange interaction, but it's also problematic to make the home into a school—not an authentic school but a school with random, meaningless, arbitrary factoids thrown without any order at children. Such attempts to improve children in poverty *makes the children the problem*, rather than a system of education that has only one method of learning, and rather than actually addressing inequality. Far better would be to pay the parents living wages, or to improve public transportation so that low-income parents can get to and from day care and work without having to take multiple buses, as well as to understand the mismatch, as Christopher Emdin explains, between comfortable white teachers and poor students of color.[14]

Schoolish Questions from Teachers to Students and Students to Teachers: Compliance and Comprehension

Some questions that must be answered are initiated by teachers. When permitted, students also ask questions. These often disappoint teachers, who wish for something more interesting.

I hadn't noticed until Michael Wesch pointed it out that so many questions were about students complying with the arbitrary and random requirements each of their many professors imposed:

Is this right?[15] *How many sources do I have to include? Are our annotated bibliographies due on Tuesday? How many comments do I have to make? Is this on the test? What do I have to do to get my grade up from an A-minus?* We could call these "compliance questions."

Students want to be sure they've correctly understood the teacher's arbitrary expectations. This is prudent, of course, given the varying mandates of different courses. But such questions reinforce the role of students not as having to comprehend the reasons for any particular practice but simply as passively responding to authority.

Another kind of question students may pose to the teacher has to do with comprehension or clarification. *I didn't understand how they got this answer on page fifty-eight. What does "heteroglossia" mean?* There's nothing inherently wrong with comprehension questions, but they do tend to emphasize the already known nature of the information, rather than helping students practice finding their own answers, as will be necessary outside school. Outside school we frequently ask questions of others, but we have to figure out, on our own, which particular authority will provide the most trustworthy answer. Practicing this is useful.

In contrast to schoolish questions, there are other types of questions, the ones that drive real learning—even of not-yet-known or not-easily-knowable knowledge. If the key to learning is intrinsic motivation, and one of the keys to intrinsic motivation is space for curiosity, then questions are the embodiment of curiosity.

If our classes aim to foster such questions, then we have to make space, and time, for them. We also have to clear away a lot of the other stuff that communicates the message that what we are after is compliance.

Less-Schoolish Questions from Students to Teachers and Students to Students: Making Space and Time for Questions

"Real questions," or "genuine questions," are those that askers care about and to which they don't know the answer.

How can I get this brochure to be more exciting? How do different marriage patterns across societies affect the well-being of children? How do speakers' brain waves synchronize when they are in a conversation? How do digital platforms add affordances to communication, compared to face-to-face communication?

What's a Real Question?

If students are encouraged to ask questions, and to think about the *types* of questions they're asking (information, clarification, application, explanation), then instead of the model of empty students being filled with information (the "banking" model that Freire named), we can have a model of inquiry.

As a bonus, these questions may be asked of fellow students, not just teachers. They can motivate research and the production of new knowledge. They can motivate the learning of smaller-level items ("facts") and theories, of skills and even difficult material, in the service of some genuine purpose.

To foster an environment that leaves space for questions, we have to grapple with ideas of voice, agency, and the ways educators might design courses, not just to transmit predetermined information to passive recipients but to welcome the active, and possibly messy, generation of new questions.

"Real questions" are interesting, generative, emergent. These are the kinds of questions that could lead scientists to discovery or novelists to speculation, students to absorption:

Are there any societies where young men are the linguistic innovators, instead of young women? Why did anthropologists stop calling their consultants "informants"? Do you think it's more effective to begin with a general abstract statement or a personal experience? How about if I research the background on the Chicago Lab School before we finish the section on John Dewey? How would the world have looked to someone with poor vision before there were glasses?

The Right Question Institute is devoted to questions.[16] Some pedagogy folks emphasize "inquiry."[17] (Their method is a little too controlled for my taste, but I admire them.) I also like to introduce time for students to ask burning questions (*What is the meaning of my life?*) and wicked questions (*How do we solve climate change?*). Burning questions are the ones that matter to a particular person, and wicked questions are so complicated that they can never quite be answered.

Michael Wesch, in his now-dated but still amazing video called *The End of Wonder in the Age of Whatever*, points out that young children ask all kinds of profound questions, like *How high is the sky?* Or *Are you going to die too?* In contrast, his students ask questions like *Will this be on the quiz?* Or *How many sources do I need to use?* Other questions may simply occupy and possibly motivate, drive, the thoughts of the asker. Such *burning questions* may never be answerable. *Why is there evil in the world? If humans do bad things, will they all have guilty consciences?*

I've incorporated Wesch's notion of *burning questions*, the questions that fire us up, into my own classes. In some classes we spend a week just generating burning questions, not necessarily related to the course, to rekindle the sense of wonder that animates all creativity, science, inquiry, and childlike attention. I invite students to let their curiosity go wild! They think it's so weird, at first, and then they catch on to the genuine invitation, and then they realize they can continue to ask real questions—though it may take a lot of reminding, because it's so different from what they are used to. (This is all in the context of an ungraded and thus less-risky class.)

Question Party and "Speed Dating"

Often toward the beginning of the semester I have students generate as many questions as they can or want, on sticky notes that they write at their tables and then post around the room. They can be any kind of question: *Why is the weather in South Bend so bad? What is anthropology? Will I find true love? What happens after we die? Will I get into med school?*

Then I ask them to read and categorize them, often into categories such as "morality and theology," "personal," "technology," "anthropology," or more, depending on the course. This is really fun, and it reminds students that they can be active *askers*, not merely passive re-gurgitators. They find each other's questions surprising and stimulating. They're anonymous, so people aren't usually afraid to reveal too many fears. The questions are about everything, from the class and school to life in general.

I save them. (This can also be done virtually, on Jamboard or any of the many sticky-note platforms and apps.) Sometimes I pass them out again at the end of the semester, just to highlight how far we've come.

Sometimes I pass them out and we do a super-energetic, loud—fun—activity called "speed dating." (One student suggested "speed-friending.")

Sometimes for this activity I have students write questions right then, maybe on index cards, and sometimes I distribute questions that others have written. Like in the romance-seeking version, we put students in random pairs for one or two minutes, and they have to talk about whatever question is on the card. They usually want to keep talking when the time is up. Then they switch—stepping to the left or moving around a circle. We've done it sitting and standing. It sure gets energy flowing in a class! Did I mention that it's noisy? It's often filled with laughter, that cherished "collective effervescence" that arises when people are interacting together in person. (Students with various disabilities can be accommodated with different types of movement or nonmovement.)

Daily Questions, Entrance Tickets, Exit Tickets

As I described in chapter 4, in my most technical, content-filled class, students generate questions nearly every day, and these lead our class discussion. Some choose more engaging questions than others. Sometimes they skip the ones that I would find most important. Sometimes we talk for a long time. Sometimes I give a mini-lecture to clarify or explain something. It's unpredictable, but it gives a sense of what students find interesting in the reading/viewing. I look over all the questions, too, and if there are some that I think are important, I can address them the next day.

This can also work with the more-familiar tactic of having students bring "entrance tickets" or "exit tickets," brief, low-stakes responses to something they've read or learned or need. Students bring the "entrance tickets" to class, often jotting down something that they find interesting or that they would like clarified. "Exit tickets" are often responses to what was learned in class. Both encourage engagement with the material and provide instructors with snapshots of student understanding and interest.

Asking Questions of Classmates' Work

In ungraded classes it's important to have a lot of feedback, but the feedback doesn't all have to come from the instructor. I often have students work with one another's drafts to give helpful feedback. This requires practice and scaffolding, because otherwise students are likely to just give a thumbs-up or thumbs-down response, or to fix superficial elements such as spelling. But two helpful methods to teach people how to respond are TAG (*Tell* me something you really liked; *Ask* a question; *Give* a positive suggestion) and WWW (from Laura Gibbs: *Wow!* I *wonder. . . . What* if . . . ?). Both use questions as the essential element.

Early, Midsemester, and Semester-Final Questions

On the initial "Learning Goals" document that I almost always ask students to complete, there's a spot for their questions: "What questions do you have?" "What do you want to learn?"

Depending on the student and the topic, they may not even know what the class is about at all. Both midsemester and semester-final reflection documents may include the questions "What questions have you answered?"; "What questions haven't you answered?"; "What questions do you still have?"; and "What new questions do you have?"

It's important to know that the world is filled with things to be learned and understood, and that it can't all be completed in one course in one semester.

Unessay Reflections

Very commonly, when students write reflections on their work, which is often but not always an "unessay" (see chapter 10), I include an invitation: "What else do you want to know?" or "What new questions do you have?" I often also say, "You're not committed to doing this, but if you were to pick a final project right now, what would it be?"

Project Jam

In some classes we hold brainstorming sessions when we're figuring out final projects. These can take many forms. One that can be fun is to use sticky notes around the room or a platform like Google Jamboard, which mimics sticky notes. Sometimes students write "topics" and sometimes "questions." Then they categorize them into related groups and meet to talk about their interests. Almost always the questions change once they get to work.

Research Questions, Burning Questions, and Wicked Questions

Still other questions are pressing and urgent, but they are so difficult and multifaceted that they can never be definitely answered. *How do we solve the problem of climate change? How do we balance the need for expertise and the need for openness?*

My class called What Should We Eat? is focused on this single, wicked question. Students enter expecting to be told, for example, whether they should eat a paleo diet or become vegan. They exit with much more complicated ideas of the question. We brainstorm questions throughout, workshop, sort into groups, and create final products.

As Paul Hanstedt states simply in *Creating Wicked Students*, "The end goal here is to develop students who can encounter unscripted or wicked problems, situations that almost by definition they don't see coming."[18] But this requires practice, and a movement away from banking of known information to being able to ask questions of the mysterious world around them. Research questions require time and effort.[19] *How did masking requirements affect COVID transmission in elementary schools?* These questions are conventional questions and have methods of inquiry that may be standard. I've directed maybe fifty or more independent undergraduate research projects at Notre Dame. The hardest part is coming up with the right-size question.

There are many different kinds of generative questions, the ones that lead to deep learning and engagement. But our schools are rarely set up for these. We rarely have time.

6

TIME

From Speed, Uniformity, and Deferral to Need, Variation, and Sufficiency

> Time is a learning trap.
>
> IRA SOCOL, PAM MORAN, AND CHAD RATLIFF, *Timeless Learning: How Imagination, Observation, and Zero-Based Thinking Change Schools*

> The goal [of grit] is to make sure kids will resist temptation, override their unconstructive impulses, put off doing what they enjoy in order to grind through whatever they've been told to do—and keep at it for as long as it takes.
>
> ALFIE KOHN, "Grit: A Skeptical Look at the Latest Educational Fad"

Clocks and calendars govern work, relaxation, and activity for virtually everyone in the contemporary world. Schools especially naturalize industrial time. Schoolish time is fast, long, and uniform. Its payoff is far in the future.

This may not be how people learn "in the wild," but it's how schoolish learning has developed. It has a lot in common with work, of course. E. P. Thompson wrote in his 1967 article, "Time, Work-Discipline, and Industrial Capitalism," about a contrast between "task-orientation" and clock orientation, as timekeeping technologies had become more widely available in industrializing Europe. Task orientation is "is more humanly comprehensible than timed"; disciplined industrial capitalism, in contrast, has "the time-sheet, the time-keeper, the informers and the fines."[1] In the early years of the Industrial Revolution in eighteenth-century England, people deplored idleness and tried to avoid "sloth." Schools were explicitly recruited to teach the "ragged" poor children the virtues of industry, frugality, order, and regularity, whether in their work in the workhouses or the two hours of schooling they were bestowed each day.[2] Children, like factory workers, especially needed to learn the virtue of punctuality. Time, they were reminded, is money. Puritans, Wesleyans (Methodists), and colonialists like Benjamin Franklin stated this explicitly, and the time-and-motion studies of the assembly line of Henry Ford emerged directly from this equivalence, where tasks were broken down into the smallest possible unit so maximal efficiency could be attained.[3] (Piecework can also be inhumane.) As the upper classes aimed to discipline the idle poor, so developed countries imposed discipline on developing countries, because they saw leisure as a problem.[4] Getting people to "be on time" according to timekeeping devices was a profound shift. Our phones ensure that we have access to "the time" at all times, and we no longer need bells, wall clocks, or other shared instruments. Awareness of time and efficiency are everywhere with us. This is true at many levels, in many different senses of time: ages, years, yearly divisions, hours, and futures.

Age Grading and Schools: Age Consciousness and Compulsory Attendance

While all people experience biological and social changes over time, it's only in the past hundred years or so that age has become the dominant mode of reckoning these changes globally. Anthropologists used to report that their subjects didn't know their chronological age, though they knew specific biological markers of change: weaning, deciduous teeth, puberty, childbirth, aging. They recalled seasons and events to track the passage of time.

Schooling did not always require a focus on age. For most of the world until the last century or so, ages were sliced very approximately: childhood, youth, and adulthood. Most people did not go to school, but even in schools, prior to the nineteenth century, learners were grouped together by their level of knowledge and by their need to learn specific skills: literacy, numeracy, languages, manual skills. In, say, Roman or early colonial

US schools, learners' needs dictated their studies; classrooms contained students of varying ages. In China, which had a quasi-system of higher education, those men who hoped to pass the civil service exam studied until they believed they were ready. There are many stories of men who tried repeatedly, well into middle age.

Howard P. Chudacoff, in his book *How Old Are You? Age Consciousness in American Culture*, points out how people learned in the United States in the past:

> Before the inception of age-graded schools in the 1850s and 1860s, the process of educating youths [a vague category that could go from seven to thirty] followed diverse and unsystematic paths. On farms, girls and boys acquired vital knowledge and skills from other family members. Older persons explained, demonstrated, and commanded; younger persons watched, listened, asked, and practiced. Most teaching took place within the context of everyday life, not in classes that grouped together unrelated children and professional instructors. The Puritans, for example, believed every person should be able to read the Bible, but they relied upon parents to teach their children how to read.[5]

But once schooling became universal, then it became desirable to group people together by very precise ages. This coincides with many other changes, including a focus on intelligence, which was measured by dividing the "demonstrated intelligence" by the "average intelligence" for the age, yielding the "intelligence quotient," IQ.[6]

Chudacoff calls this "age consciousness."

Even when "organized schooling" spread, he notes, "there was no uniform age of entry into, or departure from, these schools, and it was not uncommon to see very young children in the same classroom with teenagers."[7] From 1790 to 1850, even in colleges, age was not all-powerful. Harvard and Yale might have students from age fourteen to their mid-twenties. In the 1820s a coordinator of seventy "young men's Christian societies" in the United Kingdom, France, and the United States had members from age fourteen to thirty-five.[8] Nor did age determine consumption of alcohol, industrial labor, farmwork, artisanal crafts, marriage, dress, or comportment. Precise age was scarcely mentioned.

In the United States, especially since about 1850, education has made age, and increasingly narrow age strata, important.[9]

Age restrictions vary worldwide for "adult" responsibilities, rights, and consumption: voting, driving, serving in government or the military, marrying, consuming alcohol or tobacco. Precise reckoning of age, age consciousness, comes from the increasing importance of bureaucratic practices and especially schooling.

Students are expected to attend and progress at specified ages, with stigma attached to exceptions, such as failure to be promoted with others of their age cohort ("held back"), or delaying entry in order to give them advantages as they may then be more mature than others in their same educational cohort ("redshirting").

I sometimes ask my students how many friends they had who were more than a year older or younger than themselves. Depending on the sizes of schools they attended before college, it might be as few as zero. With the spread of these new gradings via then-new media like movies and radio, connected with consumption and bureaucratization, age as a category took hold as a dominant dimension of life. People of each age came to have appropriate clothing, foods, activities, knowledge, music, and other activities.

Globally, compulsory education begins between five and eight years of age and extends until somewhere between thirteen and eighteen. Secondary education is compulsory in some societies but optional in others (see introduction, figure I.11.) Goal 4 of the United Nations' Sustainable Development Goals is "Quality Education," which means ensuring "inclusive and equitable quality education and [promoting] lifelong learning opportunities for all." Target 4.1, "Free Primary and Secondary Education," specifies that "by 2030, ensure that all girls and boys complete free, equitable and quality primary and secondary education leading to relevant and effective learning outcomes." The guidelines state explicitly that twelve years of publicly funded education should be provided to all, "of which at least nine years are compulsory, leading to relevant learning outcomes."[10]

Tertiary education, higher education, is voluntary virtually everywhere, with varying sources of funding; in the United States the sources are a mix of direct public support (both national and state), indirect public support through loans, private funding in the form of tuition and fees, and funding by corporations and not-for-profit organizations. Some advocate making at least the first two years of tertiary education if not legally compulsory then socially obligatory for any sort of decent employment. This is currently contested in the United States, with increased discussion of technical training as an alternative. (Class considerations are relevant here: those who opt for the greater immediate payoff of vocational training are more likely to be in less-advantaged groups. The US "democratic" possibility of everyone potentially being able to prepare for college is idealistic, if unrealistic.)

Not all students, or learners, are children—especially at community colleges and regional universities. An entire field of study is devoted to adult learners, and *andragogy*, the teaching of adults, is sometimes contrasted with *pedagogy*, the teaching of children. But the fact that "adult learners" is a marked category reminds us that they are the anomaly.[11]

Years, Terms, Rhythms

Schoolish time is divided into years, with varying naming and numbering schemes: Year 1, Grade 1, first grade, first form, sophomore, second-year, and so on, and organized into two, three, or four sets, possibly primary school, grade school, grammar school, or small school, followed by secondary school, which is sometimes divided into middle school or junior high school or lower secondary and a higher secondary school, followed by high school or A-levels, or gymnasium. These divisions are unstable, because they're artificial. If there were an obvious way to divide up the years, then surely by now someone would have found it. Alternative schemes include Montessori schools, which group together multiple age cohorts. Some high school students may also take classes for college credit at the same time ("dual enrollment").

In higher education there are different degree schemas, with two-, three-, four-, and five-year first degrees (associate, bachelor's), and one-, two-, three-, and four-year next degrees (master's). Doctoral and professional degrees may take between three and many more years, possibly up to twelve or even more, though this is increasingly prohibited. Each year has a beginning and an end, and possibly distinctive fees that must be paid each time. The school calendar originated during a time when most people were agrarian, but countries' start- and end-dates and lengths and timing of breaks vary considerably.

There are often gates between levels, even at young ages. Schoolish sorting occurs, for example, in Germany where students take examinations at the end of fourth grade to determine which sort of upper elementary school (Hauptschule, Realschule, Gesamtschule, Gymnasium) they will attend, which also largely determines whether they will aim toward vocational or academic schooling.[12] In many countries, school uniforms, privileges, ceremonies and rituals, degree conferral, buildings, daily schedules, and subjects mark changes in year.

School years are usually further subdivided into segments that may be called terms, semesters, trimesters, quarters. Sometimes at lower levels of education these do not include much substantive change, though they may be marked by report cards, marking periods, or a change of subject. If students proceed in their schooling, the terms might also include a complete change of schedule, focus, or courses.

Each semester or quarter in higher education usually begins with introductory activities and familiarization with each new course and each new set of teachers, classmates, and rules, and usually culminates in some sort of end-of-term activity, whether a research paper, an analytic paper, an examination, a project, or a performance. As Brandon Moskun has shown, schoolish terms have rhythms, with beginnings, middles, sometimes with scheduled breaks, then a climax of examinations and the end, followed by a break and then another beginning.[13] The COVID-19 pandemic disrupted many of these familiar rhythms, as many universities eliminated breaks to discourage student travel and thus inhibit the spread of COVID from outside back to campuses.

I have lived with schoolish time almost my entire life, and I experience a kind of bodily knowledge about seasonal change. The stimuli and my responses involve things like temperature and food and clothing, and also where in the semester I am and what kind of work I will be doing. For example, at the end of the summer, as it's hot and the cicadas begin to buzz before the asters bloom and the grasses develop plumes, I'm busy planning my fall semester courses. Despite casual attention to my upcoming courses all summer while I focus on writing, family, and house repairs, by the end of the summer, as the term nears, I'm usually anxiously trying to firm up the daily schedule. Then, at the height of August, when it's still hot and the air conditioning is still functioning and the garden is still quite lush, and tomatoes are still delicious, I go inside with sweaters, to overchilled spaces, to meet my new students, who are tan and fit and excited about the coming term. It used to be the case that there was a new batch of notebooks, pens, and school supplies that accompanied each batch of new courses, but even I have switched to mostly digital materials. At the end of the term, we're all stressed (I do anonymous surveys!) and eager for breaks.

Time in Seat, Credit Hours, Carnegie Units

The current system of education is governed by "time in seat," or "Carnegie units" and "credit hours." Learning is parceled out in predictable temporal packages. The history of this metric is shallow and a little odd.

In 1906, Andrew Carnegie, then the richest man in the world, gave a ten-million-dollar check to the president of Harvard, one of the Carnegie Foundation's trustees, for a pension system for college professors, then very poorly paid. There was enough money to support only postsecondary faculty. At the time, high schools had uneven curricula, and colleges had loose admission requirements. Carnegie decided it would be necessary to differentiate secondary and tertiary education, with clear definitions of precollege preparation. The committee, inspired by the "scientific management" craze that was sweeping the United States, with its minimal units, uniformity, and quest for efficiency, defined what specific high school preparation would be acceptable for colleges and what amount of learning would be expected from colleges: there would be fourteen "units" required for admission: four of English, three of history, etc., each taught five days a week. If students met daily for forty to sixty minutes, for thirty-six to forty weeks a year, they would have had a total of 120 hours per subject.[14] Thus the pension of the Carnegie Foundation for the Advancement of Teaching was created; many contemporary teachers' pensions, if they have them, are still run through the descendant institution, TIAA-CREF.

Universities too were made uniform and efficient, based on these industrial models. Industrial engineer Morris Cooke posited that each unit required three contact hours a week, for three and a half months of a semester, to maximize building use and to standardize workloads. This unit is familiar to all in US higher education (with some exceptions, as you'll see at the end of this chapter).

The usefulness of this unit as a measure of learning has been repeatedly challenged, even by the Carnegie Foundation itself. "Time in seat" might loosely correlate with learning but neither guarantees nor necessitates it.

In 2015 the Carnegie Foundation commissioned a study called *The Carnegie Unit: A Century-Old Standard in a Changing Education Landscape*. The questions guiding their inquiry were: How much of an obstacle is the Carnegie unit to educational change based on new understanding of how people learn? Are old practices intertwined so thoroughly that the unit can be eliminated only with wholesale transformation? Authors Silva, White, and Toch state one aspect of the problem: "By stressing the amount of time students spend in the classroom rather than their mastery of subjects, the Carnegie Unit discourages educators from examining more closely students' strengths and weaknesses. It masks the quality of student learning. And by promoting standardized instructional systems based on consistent amounts of student-teacher contact, it discourages more flexible educational designs."[15]

The Carnegie unit and the credit hour are necessarily intertwined with the various metrics that are central to institutional education in the current moment. Carnegie units measure how much "instructional time"—schoolish time—a student has experienced. This is known to be faulty, since learners learn at different rates. But it's baked into the institutional structures. We could regard this as "path dependence"—a random decision was made and continues to have consequences, the way the QWERTY keyboard has persisted.[16] Such decisions include what constitutes a "full-time" student eligible for financial aid, aimed at ensuring progress toward degree completion—a metric with implications for equity, debt, funding, and return on investment. In the United States, four-year institutions average only a 60.4 percent graduation rate; the number may be higher among students who take longer than six years to graduate. Two-year institutions average a 31.6 percent graduation rate. (Some students transfer; some get jobs; some never intended to complete a degree.) Overall, at two-year and four-year institutions, the graduation rate is 46.2 percent—not an impressive figure, especially if the economic premium for college derives from the credential rather than from the learning.[17]

Time governs most public school structures. "Most [public schools] require . . . a minimum of 900 instructional hours over a period of at least 180 days, and some set standards by minutes-per-day or even per-class-period."[18] The need for extra days added at the end of the school year for "snow days" stems from these requirements. Whether anyone is learning or not, the hours must be accumulated and documented.

But is it a measure of learning?

The Carnegie Foundation established the Carnegie Unit over a century ago as a rough gauge of student readiness for college-level academics. It sought to standardize students' exposure to subject material by ensuring they received consistent amounts of instructional time. *It was never intended to function as a measure of what students learned.* Teachers and professors were left to gauge students' actual learning through grades and tests, papers, and other performance measures. Many current indictments of the Carnegie Unit as a poor proxy for the quality of student learning ignore this important distinction." (emphasis added)[19]

Transcripts and grades, along with credit hours, are supposed to provide evidence of learning.

It used to be the case that schoolish time especially characterized institutions of higher education in the United States, but European countries have been changing their systems to align with that of the US and with one another. A different system to track students' movement through higher education began in Europe but has essentially converged with the Carnegie unit system. The European Credit Transfer System began in the late 1980s as a combination of grades, learning outcomes, and workload, but because grades are not standard, and outcomes are hard to measure, it has largely defaulted to a time-based measure just like the credit hour. In 1999 an agreement called the Bologna Declaration, resulting in the Bologna Process, aimed to "ensure more comparable, compatible and coherent systems of higher education in Europe." As a consequence, time has become one of the key dimensions of recognition for learning, facilitating mobility across countries and institutions. The credit transfer system is spreading, through Latin America, West Africa, and Southeast Asia.[20]

Such a unit is portable and easily measured. It may be a *proxy* for learning, but it is not learning.

The Carnegie Foundation report acknowledges that "students learn in different ways and at different paces"; some of the "competency" approaches to learning have directly challenged the Carnegie unit's dominance.[21]

Despite the good intentions that underlie these indicators, they can be obstacles as well. Students working full-time but required to take full loads are exhausted and stressed, and sometimes able only to skim the surface of their work. Humane "progress toward degree"—less than a "full load"—would likely result in more completion. But the "completion agenda" is all about making progress toward the degree based on normative assumptions of how much time a "regular" student should take.[22]

Hours

Do students spend enough time in school? Too much? Not enough?

In the United States, something called the National Center on Time and Learning is arguing for expansion of the school day.[23] David A. Farbman has written an article, "The Case for Improving and Expanding Time in School: A Review of Key Research and Practice."[24]

Schoolish time, globally, is—as it were—all over the map, with inconsistent outcomes not correlating with amount of time spent. While some in the United States advocate longer hours, later start times, or shorter hours, in East Asia the problem for high-aspiring students is overlong hours. (In poorer and rural areas, they may have shorter hours.) In South Korea, children spend virtually every waking minute in school, mostly on academic work, going from school to after-school classes, called *hagwon*; it's common for students to stay until midnight, or later.[25] This had become such a problem that the government passed a law forbidding school to go past 10 p.m.—but people often break this law, with children getting home at midnight or 1 a.m. Education is highly valued in South Korea, with noble ideals: "The well-educated person—according to the curriculum and perhaps shedding further light on what is valued in Korean society—is healthy, independent, creative, and moral."[26]

In China too the government has cracked down on online tutoring and private schools, with something called "dual alleviation": reduced homework and reduced after-school training.[27]

Yet there is no consistent correlation between school hours and performance, at least according to conventional testing measures such as the PISA (Programme for International Student Assessment) test, administered in OECD (Organisation for Economic Co-operation and Development) member states, mostly high- and middle-income countries. Fifteen-year-old students take the exam in reading, math, and science every three years. Estonia and Finland tend to be very highly ranked, yet Estonia has an estimated 175 school days a year, and Finland a *maximum* of 190 days, in contrast to South Korea's 220 days. In the United States, most states require an annual average of 180 days. In Finland students are in school about five hours a day, and in Taiwan about 8.5 hours a day. Yet students in both systems do very well in the 2018 PISA exams.[28] In reading, Estonia and Finland ranked higher than South Korea. In math, Taipei and South Korea out-tested Estonia (US was thirty-seventh). In science, of these countries, the order was South Korea, Estonia, Finland, Taipei, and the United States (at eighteenth).[29]

A Downside to Too Much Schooling: Myopia

The idea that students should spend *more* time in school has an unmentioned downside: the increase in myopia that accompanies being indoors. A 2017 metastudy of myopia has shown that a decrease in time spent outside accounts for the onset and severity of myopia (though adding time outside later cannot halt the progression).[30] This is one of many "side effects" that Yong Zhao urges we attend to.[31] China's myopia rate has been seen as a national crisis.[32]

Schoolish time is not just uniform and measured. It also has other characteristics: it is fast and full.

Speed and Busy-ness: Too Much of Everything but Time

Schoolish time places a premium on speed, efficiency, and productivity. Students who complete things fast are seen as "quicker" intellectually, and others are "slow." "Efficiency" is a measure of productivity per unit of time.

In schoolish time, "students are expected to arrive on time, absorb information at a particular speed, and perform spontaneously in restricted time frames."[33] In contrast, disability studies scholar Margaret Price talks of "crip time," the amount of time something actually takes given the realities of each person's abilities and disabilities.

Timed tests reward speed; even the "accommodations" given to students are connected to time. And lest someone says, "Everything in life has time limits," I would like to note that at work and in life in general, people take variable amounts of time to accomplish things, whether writing an email, editing photos, learning to bake, or writing a novel.

Students' lives (teachers', too) are often packed with activities, homework, other obligations, plus all the living challenges that have made things harder in the twenty-first century: work, housing instability, general increased inequality. This leads to stress and the need for "management." When my daughter was looking at middle schools, one of the teachers at the Montessori junior high boasted that they emphasized "time management." Many courses designed to introduce students to college emphasize exactly this. Yes, given the realities of having too much to do and feeling great stress about it, it's important to manage the activities. (And yes, some students "waste time.") But the idea of packing activities into pure wasteless efficiency is not necessarily designed to promote learning and well-being.

Deferral and Waiting: Noseless Grinds and Rotten Cake

In 1984 when I was in Taiwan, studying Chinese for the year, a little homesick despite my late-twenties' independent-mindedness, my mother sent me one of her special baked masterpieces: chocolate-chip banana cake. Not only did she send it; she spent a then-unthinkable $37—worth about $109 in 2023—to ship it to me, fast. I was so excited to have it that I savored it. I ate a quarter piece every few days, to stretch it out, to make it last.

You know how this ends: the last pieces were rotten. Sorry, Mom.

So good am I at delaying gratification that a piece of my mother's being, her love embodied, went to waste.

In this sense (not every sense!) I'm the ideal successful person, filled with self-control. I would have passed the marshmallow test at any moment in my life. The marshmallow test presents a very young child, three or four years old, with a treat such as a marshmallow and asks the child to wait, maybe as long as twenty minutes, to eat it, with the promise of a second one if the child manages to wait. It measures trust, but mostly it measures the ability to delay gratification.[34]

According to US educators and educational psychologists, one thing children must learn, and young adults continually practice, is to defer.[35]

To delay gratification. To exercise self-control, executive function. To manage time and keep their eyes on the eventual prize, whether it's a second marshmallow, going to the bathroom, uttering a comment, taking turns feeding fish, getting a high score or grade, entering an excellent school, going to medical school, getting a good job. Or eating treasured chocolate-chip banana cake from home.

In discussions about the purpose of schooling, the length of school years, and the purpose of particular elements of a curriculum or even of a particular activity, the emphasis is usually on the future. And as with many things, taking it too far can be harmful.

Clearly all humans practice the discipline of curbing our impulses. Every society teaches waiting to eat until the proper moment, or avoiding sex with certain prohibited partners.[36] Living with others, the sine qua non of the human condition, requires—as Freud lamented, given its inevitable contribution to our unhappiness—subduing or denying our most basic urges, our id.[37] We—in the contemporary US, or at least a large segment of white middle-class folks—celebrate people who can discipline themselves and climb the Himalayas, or run fast marathons, or write two books a year, or code software in garages. (Some people are beginning to question the whole addiction to stories of individuals overcoming insane odds—walking twenty miles to work, working with disabilities and illness—and ask not so much how these few individuals managed to overcome adversity, but rather how to prevent such adversity from occurring in the first place.)[38]

Certainly one dimension of living a worthwhile life is some degree of self-control, and that requires, sometimes, waiting. But student experience suggests that this discipline, this denial, this delay, this deferral, has frequent, perhaps unavoidable, negative effects, and that these may be central, not peripheral, to the project of increasing schooling—a feature, not a bug.[39] Rather than brushing these consequences aside as imperfections to be sorted, or implementation to be improved, or as inconveniences to be outweighed by benefits, we should look at the ubiquitous downsides of this ever-more universal mandate for increasingly distant-future orientation, the infinite deferral that characterizes schoolishness.

The schoolish emphasis on future payoff should be familiar:

> *You need fractions now, in third grade, so you can take geometry and algebra, so you can take four years of high school math and get into a good*

college. This will grant you entry into or security in living in the middle class, with a decent job and reasonable income, which will allow you, finally, or still, to live a decent life.

Or this:

Give a talk in your anthropology class, and in ten years when your child is in school you'll have experience with public presentation and can talk to the school board. (I've said this myself.)

Or

Learning "soft skills" like getting along on a group project will make you attractive to employers.

All over the world, equity-committed people advocate increased years of schooling.

Graduate from a good high school, take your entrance examinations, go to college, accumulate debt or deplete the family savings because it will be worth it; probably attend graduate school as well, as you pile up credentials.[40]

Those who trust, who have the emotional fortitude to do something that is presently not compelling, keep their noses to the grindstone.

But what if we end up with noseless grinds, twenty years later? Is that a good, worthy, desirable outcome? And what is harmed in the process?

We must ask: If much of schoolishness is premised on a future orientation, a promise, a hope, aspiration, optimism, waiting for later, deferring, how long must this deferral last?[41]

Students show that this deferral is too long, through their evident uneasiness.

Marshmallow Test

Walter Mischel can't resist temptation. He used to be a heavy smoker—three packs a day. He studied children's self-control as a way of understanding his own failures, in part (he may exaggerate slightly), and to understand the variations among his own daughters. What explains divergence in self-control, ability to delay gratification? Why did my banana bread rot, while other people devour a tub of ice cream in one setting? In my house, the half-empty cartons of ice cream usually sit untouched for months and sometimes years, until our daughters come home and wrinkle their noses and shriek *eww!* and tell us to throw them out.

But "self-control," while a trope of Judeo-Christian thought, as Mischel states—don't forget Eve's inability to resist temptation—also raises questions: How much control? For how long? And for whose benefit?[42]

Sure, it is necessary, sometimes, to hold off on impulses. But if the delay is decades? Surely that's far too long. Psychologically this is not at all simple, even if the lab experiments are elegant.

Mischel's book *The Marshmallow Test* recounts his decades of research on small-reward-now, bigger-reward-later.[43] He and others researched self-control and executive function—"the cognitive skills that let us exert deliberate, conscious control of thoughts, impulses, actions, and emotions"[44]—trying to figure out which children were able to distract themselves, and how. They learned that some children visualized the eventual reward; others engaged in reminders about the eventual reward. Some reveled in their pride at being able to hold off, and then getting rewarded. These studies have shown substantial correlations between ability to wait and later success, even happiness and health. This study, and others like it, have served as the basis of much practical intervention in schools.[45]

Entire schools are built on the basis of teaching delay and discipline, especially to students from "chaotic" family backgrounds. "No-Excuses" charter schools, KIPP academies, are established almost always in low-income populations. (I have a wise and humane friend whose son goes to one and is apparently thriving. A former student taught at one, and though he had reservations, he believed in the benefits of the discipline and consistency his son was learning.) As the educational narrative of "grit" develops, it tries to inculcate what we might even call "discipline for discipline's sake."[46]

Mischel tells the story of George Ramirez, who was "saved" by KIPP academies, with their repeated goal, "Everyone is going to college."[47] They have long hours, lots of discipline. It is all about the future.[48] To emphasize this future orientation, some charter schools in Los Angeles have names like "Aspire" public schools; Chicago and Minneapolis have

Christian schools named Hope Academy. My university has a program called the Alliance for Catholic Education, which helps underresourced Catholic schools prepare students for "college and heaven."[49] Talk about the long view!

Critiques abound, especially from people disillusioned with the fixation on individual "grit" and "character" and denial, with the authoritarianism, discipline, and focus on college and tests.[50] While I am sympathetic to the important contrast between *fixed mind-set*, which views "intelligence" as an inborn and unchangeable endowment, and *growth mind-set*, which regards hard work, rather than something inborn, as the key to success, there are downsides. It may feel good to *believe* in the nearly superhuman powers of a few individuals to overcome everything that is keeping them in their places, but are the long odds really just a false narrative? Are they bad faith? Alfie Kohn points this out in his article "Grit: A Skeptical Look at the Latest Educational Fad":

> Because we can't always be there to hand out rewards or punishments as their behavior merits, some dream of figuring out a way to equip each child with a "built-in supervisor" (as two social scientists once put it) so he or she will follow the rules and keep working even when we're not around. The most expedient arrangement for us, the people with the power, is to get children to discipline themselves—in other words, to be *self-disciplined*.[51]

And while nobody doubts the intentions of those who encourage the "rigorous, supportive learning environment" that "characterizes schools that promote student tenacity" and which may include a cooperative and caring atmosphere, the "rigor" dimension and focus on the future, requiring "60 percent more time in the classroom" than neighborhood peers, classes on Saturday, during the summer—this is a lot of investment.[52] It may in fact pay off. But at what cost?

This whole discourse emphasizes individual discipline, rather than structural changes, what Kohn reminds us is called by social psychologists "fundamental attribution error": the "tendency to pay so much attention to character, personality, and individual responsibility that we overlook how profoundly the social environment affects what we do and who we are."

The "grit" discourse tends to emphasize that kids with self-discipline will endure the unengaging dimensions of education, the schoolishness, for the promise these things hold, eventually. What if instead we first fill the kids up with food and joy, and then have them wait for some things, or figure out how to have them work on problems so interesting that they persist, "the kind of purpose and meaning that will sustain students' commitment when the going gets tough"?[53]

The Happiness Deferral Chain: Music versus Test Prep

Over one Thanksgiving weekend long ago, my then-college-student daughter started singing. She knew, and claimed that her friends knew, hundreds of songs. My father, a pediatrician, asked what he thought was a rhetorical question. "Why do kids know the words to every song, but they can't memorize something for a test that will get them a higher grade?"

This is, actually, a real question.

Alfie Kohn and the folks who ruminate on the differences between intrinsic and extrinsic motivation would easily explain that kids love music and derive genuine pleasure—happiness, flow—from being able to sing it.[54] Nobody has to force children to learn songs. They willingly repeat them, to the point of adult annoyance or even hysteria.

What my dad wanted to point out was how lazy, foolish, and short-sighted children were. They could surely use their abilities to do something more useful than simply to sing popular songs for fun. They could study. They could make flash cards, they could settle down and focus on what their teachers wanted them to learn, and get good grades.

But the reason this is a real question is not only that the test preparation is, sometimes, boring. It is that the gains are so remote, via such an extremely long chain of causality, that any ordinary person would refuse to endure such an exchange. We are not talking about waiting to eat the brownies until the broccoli is finished, or even about drinking milk as a teenager to avoid osteoporosis as a postmenopausal woman. (Wait! How long a deferred benefit is this? Maybe it *is* similar.) Psychologically, existentially, this is harmful.

We are talking about a chain of causality that goes like this:

I will stay in one place even though I'm fidgety so I can sit and learn the order of the elements / which Greek philosopher was associated with which school / the founders of the state of Indiana / the Krebs cycle. If I do well on this test, I will get a good grade. If I get a good grade, my parents will be happy and my teacher will like me. I will get into the next level of courses. I will graduate from high school, and with more good grades and with more days spent like this, I will get into a good college. In college I get to do the same thing all over again—though with parties on the weekends. Once I graduate from college, I will find a good job. This job will get me money, and if I'm lucky it will not be as boring as most jobs. All this will make me happy.

What should amaze us is that huge numbers of children *do* actually engage in this process. They do study, for the purpose of getting those sacred grades. Some learn to enjoy the process of learning. Yet there are others who engage in this long process in less-than-ideal ways. Some cheat. Some live in despair, medicated, in therapy, suicidal. Chinese students preparing material for the all-powerful gaokao neglect sleep, even food. One student, Shan, told Xin Xiang, a researcher on rural education in China, that he studied in a cold room to stay awake. "Sometimes I also get sleepy in the classroom. I need to stand, squat, or kneel on my chair to get my muscles tensed up and keep myself awake."[55] His younger brother, at an urban boarding school, was even better at such grueling self-discipline than Shan himself.[56] Strange, no?

I agree in principle that "deferring gratification" and using "executive function" are worth learning and practicing. But to be surprised that children have trouble seeing rewards decades out, in comparison with the meaningful satisfaction derived from freely chosen activities, is to ignore the nature of humans.

And often our schooling does just that.

Hope and Delaying Gratification: What If Tomorrow Never Comes?

Paulo Freire says that hope is a human ontological need. It's what brought us Barack Obama.

Hope leads people to spend their rare dollars on lottery tickets. To play slot machines that are programmed so the house always wins. To click on a Tinder profile or to apply for a job as an assistant professor.

It's what drives us to do things that are difficult. Or foolish. Or magnificent. It's easy to exploit.

Hope is what provokes people to leave their homes in times of dire strife and walk or take a raft or trust in a *coyote* and approach a new place that may thrust them out or despise them. My recent ancestors (three of my four grandparents) did that, on boats from Europe.[57]

It's what parents feel when they have children, ideally, and it's what has families invest their life savings in schooling for their children, doing without pleasures or luxuries, working multiple jobs, trusting their children to the guidance of strangers, perhaps seeing their children only for short periods each summer. It's what allows parents to prod their children to grow away from them. Hope leads a young Haitian who can't read to believe she can become a doctor, a student at a school with twenty-two thousand students to believe she can be a change agent, a Latin American youth to send remittances to her family from a country that is working as hard as it can to spit her out.[58] Hope is also what's lacking when a generation believes it will be worse off than its parents, economically, and that the environmental situation will be dire. Hope may entice, may mislead, may motivate, may appear deceptive.[59]

Hope may be a pipe dream, or a mirage. It may be a solid projection from all the signs, or a carefully nurtured image. Paradise? Rags to riches? A necessary fiction? An advertising gimmick? A huckster's product? A therapist's goal?

Hope is a dream, possibly deferred, and it is always forward looking, always a search for a better or at least a positive outcome. Is the past a guide, a promise? What is the evidence for the hope? Is the dream manipulated by someone who profits from it?

When does it explode?

How much suffering is adequate evidence?

Infinite Deferral: Everyone in the Academy Is Waiting

Sue Clegg, a prominent writer about the shortcomings of British higher education, writes movingly about the "present future." She describes the future as open and empty, arguing that "dominant discourse" in British higher education entirely "discounts the [realities of the] future for present gain."[60] Clegg invokes feminist ideas of "real embodied persons" and urges readers to recognize that one reason for the general anxiety is that what was once focused either on learning or research has now become "the enterprise university," where benefits are phrased "entirely in terms of private benefit" and "in which future rewards are discounted against the present investment that students are required to make."[61]

False Promises

If the effort needed by individuals is, essentially, superhuman, then the future-orientation discourses are at best a distraction from the need for systemwide transformation ("fundamental attribution error") and at worst a cynical lie. Structural factors intertwine with affective and psychological factors, as well. Nabil Khattab writes, "Policymakers and educational authorities will not be able to improve educational attainment of students from certain backgrounds (working class and minorities) by simply raising their aspirations and/or expectations." Indeed, raising expectations and aspirations—to attend higher education—"has to be accompanied by other activities at the community level, such as enhancing community bridging and bonding social capitals, enriching community 'ethnic capital' and providing greater resources to meet the basic educational needs of families so that they are able to uphold high expectations for their children, and most importantly to help fulfil these aspirations."[62] In other words, don't lie, and provide needed support.

This is a tall order, and it might be true only if jobs are abundant and pay more. Cathy Davidson, in her magnificent book *The New Education*, writes of John Mogulescu, the dean of the School of Professional Studies at the City University of New York (CUNY). Mogulescu works extremely hard to prepare his students, doing his part, but he points out that "society has to do its part and make sure those jobs are worth having, that the people who do vital, important work in our society are compensated for that work."[63] "Education pays" can only be true if jobs pay.

Always a Day Away

> Once I . . . get 100 percent on the test / get into the IB program /
> get accepted to the "reach" college / get the residency / get into a
> good firm / get into graduate school / pass my comps / finish my
> dissertation / find a job / get a real job / get tenure / get promoted /
> get the article and grant and book and invitation and endowed chair.
> . . . then I'll finally be happy.

The benefits of endless delays are not limitless, as even Walter Mischel acknowledges: "I can't end this discussion without reiterating: a life lived with too much delay of gratification can be as sad as one without enough of it. The biggest challenge for all of us—not just for the child—may be to figure out when to wait for more marshmallows and when to ring the bell and enjoy them."[64]

Yet he can't quite let it go without insisting: "But unless we learn to develop the ability to wait, we don't have that choice."[65] Beckoning just around the corner is the payoff, the thing that will validate all the work that has preceded it, and which will finally allow the striver to calm down, accept life, take stock, rest.

It's always a day away.

But there is always something near at hand, something that can nurture, feed, fuel. It could even be a treat. Like the waiting marshmallow, there within reach.

Most important here is the question: Does focus on the future prevent well-being in the present? If mindfulness involves focus on *now*, and aspiration on *later*, what tradeoffs are acceptable, and for how long?[66] It's not all hopeless. Though our current overall approaches are harmful, insights from positive psychology, Buddhism, and permaculture might alter the conversation.

Less-Schoolish Time: Problem-Driven and Goal-Driven Time

In my actual teaching, what I have the least control over are time and space. These apparent unchangeable structures provide the very framework for everything we can do.

Yet we can also dream.

In contrast to the "time in seat" mandate of Carnegie units, less-schoolish time would focus on what needs to be accomplished. Yes, it would be far less uniform—just as children learn to walk, worldwide, between about eight and twenty-four months, depending on their conditions, bodies, contexts, and more. Novelists spend six weeks or three decades finishing their books.

Instead of prescribing the number of hours for a credential, learning could be done in units. Once proficiency or mastery or adequate interest is demonstrated—depending on the goals, as always—then this particular structured experience could be completed. The online Western Governors University (established in 1997) with its focus on competencies, not time, has challenged the conventional time-bound model.[67]

Colorado College organizes its courses in three-and-a-half-week blocks, with classes meeting all morning, four days a week. Because they take only one course at a time, students don't need to constantly switch attention and juggle priorities.[68]

There are many other ways to challenge the conventional focus on time, all to help provide the "luxury of time."

Luxury of Time

Theses, some internships, yearlong projects, are all ways to enjoy something like "the luxury of time," where things are activity driven, task driven, or question driven, not time driven, at least moment to moment. It's often hard for students to learn how to deal with such amplitude. My own students often do a senior thesis or an honors thesis—replacing only *one other course*. At Hampshire College, students' entire final year is devoted to something they call Division III, where they focus entirely on a single project, problem, question, performance, research, or exhibit of their own. Dissertations are luxurious in the sense that writers can ask big questions and focus on them, without the distraction of other obligations, ideally. In practice, though, given the realities of funding and personal life, many students feel that their time for completing their dissertations is inadequate. (I took many years to finish my dissertation, but I had no funding from my doctoral institution for writing and lived halfway across the country, working as an adjunct and teaching full-time at a variety of institutions, and also having both my children before I defended my dissertation.)

Audacity and Dreaming

My university had a provost in place for a brief eighteen-month period, during which time she called for audacity in faculty ideas for change. With colleagues Hugh Page, Laura Carlson, and Maria McKenna, I proposed the following, in which an alternative conception of time was central:

A New Educational Model beyond the Course at Notre Dame   The structures of higher education are centuries old—a lecturer, dispensing wisdom from a single discipline, students passively absorbing it, tested, rewarded or punished with a definitive simple grade at the end, all measured by time-in-seat over the course of semesters, with preestablished curricular paths, requirements, and juggling of multiple obligations. Some Notre Dame courses use problem- and project-based approaches, or community-based projects, but this proposal aims to go far beyond such course-constrained approaches by creating a school-within-a-school built on principles of progressive, student-directed education. Students would apply to this school-within-a-school with a proposed problem, perhaps a wicked problem, and would be guided to amass the skills necessary to address this problem. Students would form two-year cohorts of fellows (students) and a faculty guide, grouped on similar interests. The students enroll in the equivalent of seven courses—one the first semester and two each in the subsequent three semesters. The faculty guide assists students in locating relevant consultants, including other

TABLE 6.1. A new educational model beyond the course

Semester	Main focus	Deliverable	Assessment	Number of credits
1	Developing a research question, a bibliography, and a list of potential consultants Learn about design thinking	A research question A tentative plan for the next 2 semesters	Successful completion of tasks Student self-assessment Written narrative assessment by faculty guide	3
2	Deepening expertise on research question Amassing necessary skills and knowledge	Preliminary findings, proposal Revision of plan	Student self-assessment Written narrative assessment by faculty guide	6
3	Consultation with relevant experts and constituencies	Draft and preliminary research findings Revision of plan	Student self-assessment Written narrative assessment by faculty guide	6
4	Creating the final product	Public presentation of research findings	By outside experts	6

faculty, community members, and alumni. Students have funds that they can use to pay consultants, travel, purchase materials, or whatever they deem necessary, with faculty guide approval. There are frequent opportunities for feedback, reflection, and revision. There are no letter grades, but simply robust feedback, along the lines of the practices of the New College of Florida [until 2023], Hampshire College, and Brown University. They emerge with portfolios and projects demonstrating the robustness of their learning, and with confidence in themselves as learners and collaborators in the creation of new knowledge.

This was an attempt to be audacious within the structures of units. As of this writing, following that provost's resignation, nothing has happened with this proposal.

Here, Now, This

Permaculture is agricultural practices that do not destroy the planet and do not require ever-increasing inputs but instead are endlessly, permanently, sustainable because they work with nature, not against it. In *I Love Learning* I wrote of a comparison between industrial agriculture and industrial education, on the one hand, and permaculture and what I've taken to calling "permeducation," on the other. One of the twelve principles of permaculture is "obtain a yield." This is to say, there must be both planning for the future and something to nourish now. Similarly the more years of schooling, the more essential it must be to gain a harvest now.

Humans can experience not only dread, fear, hope, aspiration, expectation. We also have curiosity, enjoyment, pleasure, pride.[69] This happens *now*, not later.

While planning for the future is inescapable, so is a touch of *now*, a focus on *this*, on being *here*. With *these people*. Doing *this thing*. Getting *this reward*. Feeling *this sense of accomplishment*, satisfaction. Eating *this marshmallow*. Savoring the banana bread.

In her wonderful book *Happiness and Education*—a title that only cynics, or perhaps realists, would find contradictory—Nel Noddings writes of the need for teachers to offer an abundance of "free gifts."[70] Using a feminist perspective, from which she considers the relations of "care," she argues that, as with permaculture, we have to obtain regular, current yields. The payoff cannot only lie in the future.

Buddhism, while simultaneously urging relinquishing attachment, teaches focus on the present through the practice of mindfulness. Even those who have now divorced these teachings from their spiritual ground, like Jon Kabat-Zinn, argue for the psychological benefits of learning to focus on the present.[71]

Educational systems that are principally future oriented—with high schoolishness indicators and lots of grinding—thus are missing one of the long-standing insights into human needs—the need for attention to the present moment.

Slow

The food system provides additional inspiration, in the context of the "slow food" movement, in contrast with fast food. Slow learning would involve learning that functions at its own speed. It would make the efficiencies and uniformities of the current large-scale educational sector much harder to manage.[72] But it fits much more appropriately, equitably, and morally with what we know about all the circumstances and variations among learners.

As a participant, a teacher, in this system, as well as an analyst, I have a tiny bit of power, agency, control. I can't single-handedly change the ways people push the narrative of "more school is always better." I can't change the "you need this required class" structure. But I have some control over my own classes. I try to make them enjoyable in the present, with some nourishment for the soul, mind, spirit, as well as fulfilling whatever other aims I may have. This is my small contribution to the revolution, to make the work meaningful.

7

WORK, LABOR, PLAY

From Toil and Exchange to Worth, Meaning, and Use

A vocation is a call, but the call is not a command; it is a question.
. . . Vocation is fascination, not ambition; it is work emancipated
from time: a dialogue with being, not a program of predation and
control.

ROBERT BRINGHURST, *The Tree of Meaning: Language,
Mind and Ecology*

Analysts sometimes, but not consistently, distinguish *work* and *labor*.
Work might be its own reward, or may be compensated, or both. Labor
is usually effort expended for a return in wages, and is sometimes connected to capitalism (Marxist social theorist Raymond Williams, in his
Keywords in 1976, includes entries for both *work* and *labour*). Work may
be effortful but not necessarily. Labor emphasizes effort. Jobs are regular
relationships between employers and employees, ongoing and relatively
permanent, or one-off temporary gigs. Even the "self-employed" are paid
by someone for their work, whether calculated by the job/task/product or
by time expended.

Farmwork in the past often had both *use value* and *exchange value*:
farmers produced food for themselves and sold a surplus, if any, to others. Much of contemporary farmwork is pure labor, with *exchange value*:

workers produce commodities that owners will sell to others for profit, while farmworkers themselves exchange their wages for food, which may never have anything to do with what they themselves produce.

Work can be a moral and psychological undertaking: in social justice circles, it's common to hear people talk about "doing the work." I've found articles and websites with these titles: "Doing the Work Externally and Internally: Race, Equity, Diversity and Inclusion"; "Doing the Work of the Social Justice Movement through Storytelling"; "A Calling to Do the Work of Social Justice in New York."[1] In therapy, it's also called "doing the work": "What 'Doing the Work' In Therapy Looks Like"; "What Does 'the Work' Mean in Therapy." One person titled her whole project, positively, "The Work."[2] Writers and artists have "work." Musicians have an *opus*, plural *opera* (these also just mean "work"). When things go well, actors "are working." Work is connected to vocation, to calling, to meaningful engagement in the world. It is also something that requires off-setting with "life" ("work-life balance"). Work is something people go to ("going to work"), and people have "work wives" and "work romances." They also have work hells and work illnesses.

The English word *work* has Germanic and ultimately Greek origins; *labor* has French and Roman origins. The resonances in different languages, the semantic webs, are both positive and negative. For example, in Hebrew, *avoda/avodah* (עֲבוֹדָה) means "work, worship, and service." In Chinese, the word usually translated as work is *gongzuo*, but also *laodong*, "physical labor." The Greek term, *ergon*, had affinity with the ideas of punishment. Labor camps still exist, for example in Xinjiang. *Travailler* in French and *trabajar* in Spanish share roots with "suffer" and "torture" (*Guardian* journalist Jeremy Seabrook reminds readers that "labor/labour" have "tortured" roots.)[3] *Arbeit*, "work," in German, is forever associated for me with the saying inscribed in iron above the entrance to Auschwitz, *Arbeit macht frei*, "Work sets one free." Except of course it didn't. And while "freedom" is constantly touted in US circles, right and left (from bell hooks to Rand Paul), schools rarely look like places of freedom. One of the aims of the "free schools" of the 1960s and 1970s, such as Summerhill, was freedom from coercion. Summerhill's website in 2022 specifies "freedom not licence" and "freedom with responsibility."[4]

Etymology is not meaning, for sure. But often these affinities, indexicalities, indicate something about the affective dimensions of terms, especially key terms like these.

Child Labor and Child Work

The UN Convention on the Rights of the Child permits child work but forbids hazardous child labor and child labor that interferes with proper development. Some "light work" is acceptable for teenagers.[5] Increased years of schooling in the contemporary world comes from deliberate reduction in child labor as well as avoidance of child "idleness," as we saw in the "Time" chapter. In the United States, the return home of military personnel in World War II was followed immediately by the Servicemen's Readjustment Act of 1944, also known as the GI Bill of Rights, or simply the GI bill, an enormous increase in higher education funding and participation. It was an attempt in part to cope with the disgruntled population that might have resulted from widespread unemployment, as had occurred after World War I.[6] In the United States, enrollment in higher education tends to trend opposite employment trends.[7]

But is schooling itself a form of labor? Of work? Should it be?

School-for-Work, School-as-Work

The cliché has it that schoolish work is modeled on factory work. Students are often said to be engaged in preparation for future work, and anything that contributes to future work, jobs, is justified. (More "radical" educators challenge this assumption and say things about play and citizenship.) Schoolish work is drudgery and must be rewarded by extrinsic motivation—usually grades—just as factory work is repaid by wages. (This is the *alienation of labor*.) Journalist Jay Caspian Kang, a former teacher, writes to defend homework and says that he thinks "there's a lot of value in saying, 'Hey, a lot of work you're going to end up doing in your life is pointless, so why not just get used to it?'"[8]

Schoolish work is boring, and hard, people know. It is—and should be—difficult, challenging, rigorous. It requires surveillance.

Work and labor have peculiar relationships with school. *Schoolwork* is a common term, as is *homework*. In Montessori schools, which I generally admire, children have their "work," which they engage with happily.

Yet schoolish labor is often seen as alienated, done purely for the exchange, and it is often tabulated in terms of time. Students do it *for the teacher* or *for the grade*.

Profession, Calling, Job, Employment

Though I'm not mostly talking about faculty, I just want to note that when people regard work as a "calling" they may work long hours without extra pay, provide additional emotional labor, and endure harsh conditions because their focus is on the meaningfulness of their work. The tension between teaching as a job and teaching as a vocation is evident in the existence of teachers' unions in the United States and resistance to calls for improved teacher pay. In many countries teachers are paid well. In Australia, college faculty are limited in terms of work hours and committee involvement. Each activity is assigned a typical number of hours, and the annual total is limited.[9] My former Notre Dame colleague Greg Downey, now at Macquarie University in Australia, says that key to this system is that it prevents rewarding work with more work. This has all been made possible by a robust union. In the United States, K–12 teachers often belong to unions. In higher education, most faculty are not tenured or tenure-track, and the number of conventionally secure jobs is falling. Unionization has increased with the pandemic but is still not the norm.[10] Most faculty feel that their labor is inadequately uncompensated. We teach, do research, write and administer grants, advise undergraduate and graduate students, serve on committees both at our own institutions and in the discipline. We give conference papers and edit journals. We engage in usually uncompensated peer review. Those with a great sense of responsibility and who are competent tend to be "rewarded" with more work.

Less-Schoolish Work

If one of our aims is to improve the educational conditions to permit focus, engagement, and well-being, then having less work pressure can be useful. If we permit *questions* to motivate the work, and the work needs to guide time, then pressure derives only from authentic conditions within which learners operate, rather than arbitrary external metrics.

Labor-Based Grading

Progressive educator Asao Inoue, a professor of English whom I hold in great regard, has tried to focus on equity by using something called "labor-based grading." This is a form of "contract grading," where grades are determined not by assessment of "quality" along some single scale but by students' labor, to rectify the overall observation that "since grades do not equate neatly to learning or even to quality of writing, there is no sense in trying to make them equate." He argues that "standards are reifications" and that "the idea of maintaining standards . . . in a classroom is an illusion." Labor, he argues, is much fairer. Labor is *measured in units of time* and avoids some of the racism embedded, for instance, in conventional writing classes where students from minoritized backgrounds often speak different home languages from the dominant class. Writing classes usually use a "standard" measure reliant on an often-implicit notion of "standardized" language, or what he calls "white supremacist language." Also, we know that *labor is associated with learning*, especially in endeavors like writing, where it is essential to "put in the time." Labor is also simple to calculate: "the more labor you do, the better your grade in the course will be." The aim is to encourage students to undertake revisions and produce high quantities of writing, which indeed tends to correlate with improved quality, especially in introductory courses. Quality is addressed through detailed feedback, discussions, and activities, not through a simplified metric, a grade.[11]

Ellen Carillo's short—sixty-page—book challenges Inoue's approach from the perspective of disability studies and intersectionality: people with economic and social advantages are likelier to be free to invest more hours, while those who are working more hours, or have care responsibilities, or have disabilities, may be unable to do so. Or they may need to spend more time than an "ordinary" student would to do the work. As Carillo points out, the labor-based approach assumes that "labor is neutral."[12] It substitutes one standard for another: "quantifiable information . . . gives the appearance of objectivity. Numbers carry with them a certain air of objectivity, yet we know that numbers are not inherently objective and don't tell any kind of story on their own."[13] She points out that Inoue's preference for labor as "a reference to doing things, to acting, to performing, to working in honorable, embodied ways" assumes a kind of "normative" body, which this whole approach to equity has been designed to avoid.[14] "The students whose bodies are most like the normative body [and mind] at the center of the labor-based contracts are most likely to be rewarded through this approach to assessment."[15] In 2015–16, almost 20 percent of US undergraduates had a recognized disability. Many students of color and those from minoritized and disadvantaged backgrounds are *less* likely to be diagnosed with a disability, which is usually needed for "accommodation"—the most common of which is extended time on exams in a testing center.

Then it becomes a numbers game again, with transactions concerned with quantity.

Determining the "effectiveness" of labor-based or contract grading depends on how "success" is measured: does it result in a more equitable grade distribution? In student satisfaction? Engagement? Self-efficacy? Achievement on standardized instruments? Some people may also find a focus on labor instead of quality to be problematic, especially readers concerned with "rigor."

Despite overall sympathy with the approaches that aim to challenge the problems of conventional grading systems, in what I call the "ungrading umbrella," I have some reservations about labor-based grading on metaphoric grounds.[16] For me, the associations of various terms, the metaphors, the indexicality, are powerful. I can't stop thinking about childbirth, and forced labor. Is all academic activity work? Can one learn without feeling that it is labor? Can one learn effortlessly? What is "the task" to which labor must be directed? Who determines it?

I love Carillo's discussion of multiple forms of engagement, including a variety of formats (what you'll see in chapter 10). "Focusing on engagement rather than labor also addresses my contention that labor-based grading contracts perpetuate a normative conception of time, as well as the unnecessary and unfounded connection between time and willingness."[17] Carillo cites the work of Jerry Won Lee, which resonates with Malcolm Knowles's idea of "self-directed learning." Lee has students generate their own goals, and students choose how they would like their writing to be assessed: according to conventionalized notions of "standard English," or to creativity? In that sense, students may *work* on things that are meaningful to them.

Play

One contrast with the worst, most coercive sense of work-as-drudgery and work-for-other-ends is play. The literature on schooling is filled with advocates of play. (I would distinguish between "games" and "play." Sometimes there's overlap, but not necessarily.)

Psychologist Peter Gray has written extensively about play and childhood. His 2013 book, *Free to Learn: Why Unleashing the Instinct to Play Will Make Our Children Happier, More Self-Reliant, and Better Students for Life*, spells out his argument, much like mine, about human beings being born with "extraordinary capacities for learning," which emerge naturally through play.[18] Anthropologist David Lancy has been examining play in the context of work, learning, and growing up in most of his writings. The Association for the Study of Play (TASP), established in 1973 and renamed in 1987, convenes annual meetings and publishes a journal called *Play and Culture Studies*.

Defining "play" is difficult, but fundamentally the spirit of play involves *enjoyment in the process*. The activity is in some sense its own reward, even if other benefits also accrue. Noncompetitive games, role-playing games, gamification all contribute to the absorption that erases time consciousness, known as flow. (In chapter 10 I give an example of the gamification of higher education in the set of techniques known as Reacting to the Past.)

A research project called "Pedagogy of Play" at Aarhus University in Denmark (with the collaboration of the LEGO Foundation and Project Zero, from Harvard) is focused on researching and promoting "playful learning" even in school settings. The Pedagogy of Play posts on its website dozens of projects that include playfulness, and conducts its own research, contending that "play is central to how children learn."[19] Because they believe this is so central, they want to foster putting play "at the center of formal schooling" so "teachers and learners can experience joy and agency." (I'm generally sympathetic, but I'm forced to ask: are the goals still schoolish, merely achieved in a more palatable way?)

It's clear that outside school, when given the opportunity, many children play. But can school be play? Can learning be play? *Should* it be play? Nonschoolish learning may be playful; schoolish learning certainly isn't.

Still, it's important to note that while play is wonderful, many people learn well without what we could call play. Lancy summarizes a lot of this research, which includes learning through observation, trial and error, the "chore curriculum," and more methods.[20]

Even in settings where children learn early to contribute to their community's and their family's needed work, there's often time for free play. Rarely are adults involved; usually the children play among groups of near-peers, sometimes on what Lancy calls "the motherground," a cleared space around which adults may be engaging in productive work but the children can be safe.

In higher education, play is less evident. Higher education is so *serious*. We have assessment and learning outcomes and rubrics and all kinds of high stakes. Futures are determined by school success, everyone believes, and students are pitted against one another in a kind of Hunger Games zero-sum game. It *is* possible, though, to introduce elements of play—meaning both the space for movement and the enjoyment of the unexpected—into classrooms, but it requires a rethinking about structures that appear timeless and unyielding.

But if one of the goals of nonschoolish education is to promote learners' engagement with their own learning, in community with others, then play, not merely work, has a role to play.

In my fall 2022 Anthropology of Childhood and Education class, we were talking about play. I set up the room with two sets of chairs with their backs together. The students entered the room and immediately remarked on the setup, suggesting that it looked like musical chairs. That was indeed my intention. I told them a story: at my older daughter's fourth birthday party, we planned to play musical chairs. We explained that we would put chairs for every person and then would remove one chair each time, so each time another child would be out. A one-year-younger friend said, "Why?" We realized we had internalized the competitive core of musical chairs, and decided to replace it with cooperation. We played the music; the children ran around; they sat down. When I told this story to my college students, they nodded. I said we'd play. I found a song for "musical chairs." And the students, despite the story, removed a chair each time, until there was a single winner. I hadn't wanted them to be competitive. We talked about it, and whether they felt bad at losing. I had watched them carefully. Several had looked deflated at discovering that they were the one without a chair in that round. It was a great conversation. They learned about competitive play through enacting it with their bodies. Several mentioned it in their midsemester conferences: it was fun, and they learned. And almost all of them mentioned it again at the end of the semester. They remembered.

But just as schoolish *time* and schoolish *work* define the prototypical schoolish experience, so do schoolish *spaces and places*, which we can challenge only with great determination.

8

SPACES AND PLACES

From Separation to Connection

Attachment is . . . a word of ambiguous meaning, whether it is
applied to people or place. On the dark side, it is bondage and we are
glad to be freed of bondage. On the bright side, it is a mutuality such
that people pour affection into a place and that place in turn imparts
its qualities to people, making them into the sort of human beings
they are.

YI-FU TUAN, "Letters to Colleagues"

It's a truism that our activities are influenced by the spaces and places in
which they occur. Sitting in a quiet park near a redwood forest is not the
same as sitting in a rattling subway in a cold city. Running in a gym is not
the same as running along a beach. Learning in an operating room is not
the same as learning in a classroom.

Social scientists have written enormous amounts about space and
place.[1] The shorthand is that places are spaces imbued with meaning and
experience. Space is "objective," while place is "subjective"—or experienced by subjects. All humans create places through our experiences and
our intentional crafting of "built environments," where we engage in activities in them, remember them, chafe against them, and change them.
Academic spaces are made by architects and planners, sometimes aware of
the ways spaces may ideally become significant and positive places.

The Particularity and Materiality of Learning in Places

We learn in and through our particular bodies with particular other bodies, and we do this in particular spaces and places, in what architects call the built environment: buildings and chairs and rows and tables and sounds, with or without screens or windows or microscopes, and in the physical environment, which includes the smells and sounds and the temperature and the humidity and the threat of flooding and the imminence of destruction.

Everything matters: the time of day and the materiality of the desk, the ergonomics of the chair, the number of seats you can hear people speaking from, the fixed or free nature of the furniture, the walls, the windows or lack of windows, the windows' ability to open or not, the airflow, the sound of the HVAC system, a shadow cast by a tree swaying in the welcome breeze, or the sleet banging against the window unexpectedly, when no one has a winter coat, or a bird flying past on its way south, or a truck beeping as it backs up, ready to imbibe the trash of a compost-generating campus. It matters if the video screen is in the front or the back or both, and it matters if there's one tiny whiteboard, or a room filled with old-fashioned chalkboards that you can lift and write on until your heart is satisfied. It matters if the screen is small or big, and if everyone has to strain to read the text on the PowerPoint, and it matters if the acoustics are terrible or marvelous.

The beauty or squalor of the room matters. It matters if there's stained glass or if there are cinder blocks. It matters if there are narrow tables bolted to concrete floors, or if there are modular up-to-date tables that can be configured to foster optimal small group or team projects. It matters if there are cracks in the window, or if the ceiling is low in the basement room, which is too hot. It matters if there are six of you, or if there are four hundred.

The time of day matters. Is it eight in the morning, and most people, but not the larks, are barely awake; or is it one in the afternoon and everyone is sleepy from lunch? Or is it five in the afternoon and everyone is distracted by where they have to go next, or is it seven in the evening and most people have already worked a full day, and now they are squeezing in their precious education, which will get them to a better job or to a more meaningful life?

I've taught at all these times, and in all these conditions, though I've only ever taught in my own body. True, my body has changed over time. I've aged. I've been pregnant twice. Once I had a young male student comment that he had noticed that my usually flat stomach had been protruding, so when I confessed that I was pregnant he was not surprised. I was surprised that he was paying attention to my stomach.

The room bakes in, commands, controls interactions. I've learned to request certain rooms on my campus, having had experiences with particular walls, particular windows, particular tables and chairs, particular configurations. Sometimes my request is granted, and sometimes it isn't. When you're in a fixed-seat auditorium-style room, trying to facilitate small group discussions, you have to work very hard to fight the room. Ask students to help figure out how to cope with the room when it's not flexible.

You can sit on the floor, but that brings up all kinds of issues for people with disabilities, visible or invisible, or different bodies than an agile young one. You can go into the hallway, maybe. You can have people stand up and cluster in the corners of the room, again with caveats. You can, ironically, have people interacting online while they're also physically co-present.

Most college campuses have poor learning spaces. Most assume the default as lecture, and many campuses lack the resources for anything but the most utilitarian forms of walls and lighting. Most seats are uncomfortable, most tables are not big enough, most walls are boring, and there is little beauty.

Beauty, when available, can transform everything.[2]

I dream of learning with students outdoors in mosquito-free green spaces with everyone soothed by gentle breezes. Not too hot, not too cold, and filled with natural inspiration. I have never done that. The closest I've come, other than occasional classes outdoors where there are often bees or mud and we can't actually hear very well but it's fun because we've escaped, is the room with two walls made mostly of windows and with movable furniture, where a few of my most positive teaching experiences have taken place. There are screens front and back, and there are ample whiteboards.

During the height of the pandemic, during 2020–21, I heard that the tables became immovable and the chairs restricted in this and all classrooms. (I taught remotely.) All the nourishing close interactions fostered by movable tables, all my own wandering up and down the room, in and out of chairs, getting close to the students, all active learning was suspended so that everyone could keep their distance.

Well, distance is the enemy of co-learning.

So I opted to try to create closeness digitally instead.

We had no visible bodies. We had no texture, we had no breath sound that we could share, unless I introduced it in some form, or unless students introduced it themselves.

And then there's Zoom. Even when we're using devices, we're *somewhere*.

Brandon Moskun's dissertation examined the ways academic spaces on one college campus were transformed during the first year of the COVID-19 pandemic.[3] He connects this with the ways institutions attempted to navigate the contradictions between gathering people and keeping them apart, using an image from the philosopher Peter Sloterdijk of "foam"—the idea of our interiority being completely connected to others, proximate but also separated. Institutions—prisons, hospitals, commerce, industry—always control space, sometimes with benevolence and sometimes with antagonism.

Social theorists such as Foucault have written about the control of space as the control of bodies and in turn of human subjectivity. The most vivid image came from the then-hypothetical panopticon of Jeremy Bentham, in which a guard had the potential to observe any of the prisoners in all the cells facing a central observation point, but the prisoners never knew which cells would be observed at any time. This fear and uncertainty of the possibility of surveillance, control, and punishment controlled their actions.

Here I'll just show some of the ways schoolish spaces and places function to create separation and alienation. Schools share many dimensions with other institutions, but some aspects are theirs alone.

Schoolish Spaces and Places: Separation

There may be "schools of thought" and "schools of fish," but most of us envision *schools as buildings set apart from the rest of life.*

A dedicated space for learning is often considered the first, basic dimension of schools. Walls may be absent in warm climates, but it's likely that at least something, possibly a roof, will delineate, demarcate, inside and outside.

Sometimes schools are in single buildings, or even single rooms.[4] I've been in a community college located in a single building. Sometimes a school is composed of multiple buildings, in which case we may speak of a "campus." Sometimes schools are scattered in buildings throughout cities, as in many European universities. Sometimes radical, progressive schools are deliberately "without walls." Sometimes developing countries wish they could have something that looks like a "real school."[5] One line of research inquires about the potential contribution of built infrastructure to learning.[6] Radically, people suggest that pedagogical and students' needs should lead the design, from the inside out.

Yet the familiar dimensions of schoolish schools persist.

Walls, Gates, Doors

College campuses and larger schools usually have some sort of signage, sometimes with the year of the institution's founding, and often have gates—literal walls and gates with guards, or such separation as the walls imply. Most college campuses in the United States are open to the public, and some become tourist destinations. In other countries they may be closed to outsiders. I once tried to enter Peking University with a driver and a guide, but because Chinese universities are not generally open to the public, we had to invent a reason for entering. There were several gates; our lies became more convincing with each one.[7]

The best-resourced schools may have attractive brick walls or wrought-iron fences (in the United States), with inviting, though possibly secure, gates. In China, where virtually every "work unit" (*danwei*) has walls and gates, schools share the same fortification. Some campuses in China and the United States and elsewhere are wooded, parklike environments. Some are concrete-lined yards. Urban US high schools have metal detectors. Inside and outside are clearly differentiated. Sometimes visitors sign in, or wear identification, or are escorted.

Whether there is a single building or several, most of the buildings that are for "school" (in contrast, say, to faculty offices or research labs) share many features.

Rooms

Prototypical schoolish rooms are lecture halls, conventional classrooms, or seminar rooms, and in some fields, labs. Each type assumes particular structures of interactions, based on particular models of pedagogy. (Rooms in other buildings are much less schoolish: those for alumni associations and admissions might look like hotel spaces, while those for accounting could serve any bureaucracy.) Schoolish rooms assume a teacher, and a front. They have doors, to close them off from the outside world. And they tend to immobilize the students.

Depending on the school's level and geographic location, teachers (US) or classes of students (East Asia) may have responsibility for maintaining and decorating a room. At some levels, students rotate through the rooms. At others, teachers rotate. At universities, generally, both converge temporarily for a session, so no one has control. These rooms tend to be bland and institutional. (Labs are different.)

Lecture Halls   Lecture halls are unchanged, really, since medieval times, other than the sound and sight tech. They stem from a period when printed material was scarce and expensive. (See chapter 9, "Genres of Consumption.") Those who had access to these materials—books—literally "lectured": read or summarized from the reading material. Students took notes on the content of these presentations.

Lecture halls' seats are in fixed rows, holding as many as hundreds of students, so those students can observe the performing and declaiming teacher. Such rooms are "efficient" at processing the large numbers of students who are encouraged to partake of higher education.[8]

Conventional Classrooms   Conventional classrooms "look like school." They have a front, for the teacher, a central area, for the students, and a back. There may be a board for the teacher to write on, or a dais on which the teacher stands. There may be technological items for the teacher to control.

Usually students face forward, looking at the teacher. Sometimes the furniture is movable and flexible, and sometimes it isn't. The furniture tends to be movable, by default, in classrooms for younger ages, but varied for older students.

I ask to teach in rooms with flexible desks and chairs. We often set up the room so all of us can face one another, but sometimes we change it to be in small groups. There can be small groups that go off into corners. When others teach in the room, they often rearrange it to be more like a conventional classroom, with rows facing a single direction.

During the 2020–21 pandemic school year, at my university, which was determined to hold classes in person, with seats arranged schoolishly and all chairs ideally six feet apart, students were assigned seat numbers, and nobody was allowed to move.[9] That reason alone was enough for me to request an "accommodation" so I could teach remotely. (That wasn't why it was granted; it was granted, in accord with various policies, because of my spouse's health risks.)

Seminar Rooms The assumption in a seminar room is that there will be "discussions," with participants seated at equal distances—though in many classes I've found the students try to avoid the seat next to the professor. (Proxemics, the study of distance, would explain that students are at "personal distance" from one another but at "social distance" from the professor).[10] This then presumes that whole-class discussion will be the dominant mode of interaction, usually with the professor directing traffic, for the entire class period.

Laboratories and "Active Teaching" Rooms There are many types of laboratories, and some teaching occurs in them. Depending on the discipline, labs may be "wet" or "dry," but there will be many types of materials stored around the room, with lab stations spaced throughout the room and the day's materials already set up. (This presumes a known inquiry method within a given predetermined discipline.) In recently designed classrooms, sometimes designated as "active teaching" rooms, there may be computer terminals, or accessible outlets, or larger monitors that can be attached to students' laptops.

"Active learning" classrooms are a very hot topic among architects who work in education. A colleague of mine, Alex Ambrose, has been involved in creating something called the "Learning Space Rating System" to provide "a set of measurable criteria to assess how well the design of classrooms supports and enables multiple modalities of learning and teaching, especially that of active learning" within conventional classrooms, "spaces centrally scheduled and designed for face-to-face meetings of all course participants."[11] Clearly this is not the familiar default.

Furnishings

Whole industries are devoted to producing schoolish desks and chairs, bolted to the floor or movable. For younger students, they may be colorful and smaller-proportioned, but they're always durable and uniform, and rarely comfortable. Some tablet-style desks have a small surface attached to what is mostly a chair. Some tables, especially for seminar rooms, provide larger surfaces for materials to be spread out. Sometimes there are benches, in many places shared.

In younger grades where bodily comportment is being taught, students are often required to be still. This is extremely difficult for some. "Classroom management" is considered a teacherly skill; it works in tandem with the furnishings.

Schoolish Places

Some schools become "places" in the sense that they become meaningful locations in the lives of their participants, as do many workplaces. Some elementary schools serve to anchor neighborhoods or contain sports and arts activities (and when they close, possibly in the name of economic efficiency, this may devastate a neighborhood); some are meaningful places in poor neighborhoods, with "wraparound services" such as providing food, health care, and parental training (Harlem Children's Zone)—often supplying needed societal services that are lacking.[12] This was especially evident early in the COVID-19 pandemic, when students attending remotely lacked the meals provided at schools. In the United States, high-resourced schools offer PTA friendships and a place for eager parents to devote their energies and donations.

At the secondary level schools may simply contain academic learning (as in France), or they can be the site of activity during virtually all daylight hours and then some, with two-a-day sports practices, including early morning swim practice, weekend theatrical performances, evening sports meets, social events such as dances and clubs, and virtually all other social activities. In South Korea students arrive early in the morning and leave late in the evening, though the government has tried to force reduction in hours students spend in school.

At the level of higher education, community colleges may be located in standalone buildings or occupying old repurposed urban spaces. They can be in malls or hospitals. They can have their own beautiful campuses, like Bakersfield College in California.

And the prototypical residential campus becomes what Erving Goffman called a "total institution" (in China a *danwei*), an entity that provides much more than the single central function and meets virtually all its inhabitants' needs—not unlike prisons, mental hospitals, the military, and boarding schools.[13] Such campuses provide food, health services, and entertainment, along with housing and sports facilities. Some universities are like cities, with their own security forces and their own zip codes, and populations as large as forty thousand or more for the very largest, though some people may come and go for particular activities rather than living there. When universities provide everything students need, they may struggle to integrate into their neighboring communities. Other universities, meanwhile, might be places where just some classes occur—much more like the online learning that is constantly promised as a coming replacement for on-the-ground education.

Athletic, Arts, Libraries, and Other Facilities

Athletics is not necessarily required for learning school subjects, but in the United States, athletics has been integrated into schools at all levels for about a century and a half.[14]

Some universities and colleges—and even well-resourced secondary schools—have athletic facilities with areas devoted to single sports: a football field and stadium and a baseball field, a soccer field, and a basketball arena, often a hockey rink and a swimming pool. These can be sources of school pride, student solidarity, and public support for otherwise not-open institutions; that's why some of these programs started in the first place. Most schools have school colors and teams, often with names. These can serve as impetus for profitable paraphernalia. Cheers, music, pride days, and more may attract enthusiastic support—especially from students otherwise alienated from the educational missions of the schools. While "mind" may be seen as the more worthy goal, "sound mind in a sound body" may justify the commitment to athletic places and funds.

Additional facilities may include museums, theaters, concert halls, hotels, restaurants, cafés, botanic gardens, and arboretums. Virtually all schools have some sort of library, from a rudimentary repository of reference materials to breathtakingly beautiful archives.

I'm a passionate adorer of libraries (public and academic). During the worst of the pandemic, when libraries closed, I was bereft. Libraries have become information hubs, locations for gathering in groups of various sizes, for studying and retrieving resources, for consulting with information experts, and much else. Some have their own cafés, with varying rules about consumption. A school without a library might not seem complete.

Online "Spaces"

The metaphor of "cyberspace," "sites," and "online spaces" which we "visit" and to which we "go" shows that virtual interactions have in part been understood as a kind of "space" and "place." (The internet has also been called "a superhighway" and "the cloud" and more.) Users have their favorite "places" on the internet. We have "site maps" and "corners" and centrality.[15]

As "places" to gather and interact, even as "virtual town squares" with "netizens," online or virtual spaces share some schoolish dimensions but are also in some ways distinct. All spaces and places have locations in both "objective" and "subjective" dimensions. Embodied spaces and places have histories, temperatures, costs. Smells. They facilitate certain kinds of experiences and interactions. Cyberspaces lack the embodied dimensions, clearly, but have associations, histories, affective experiences. In both embodied and virtual places, some things are far easier to accomplish than others. (See chapter 11, "Tech and Media.")

School Safety and Danger

As places that contain gathered people, schools have responsibility for their occupants' safety. Besides being a place for learning, schools have been settings for shootings, fires, hysteria outbreaks, bullying, suicide clusters, vaccination campaigns, feeding, and joy. They have served as polling places in the decentralized US election system, and have been community gathering places. A survey in 2018 showed that in K–12 schools in the United States, just over half the students *felt* safe at school.[16] On college campuses, the US Department of Education, mandated by the Clery Act, tracks crimes—violence against women, hate crimes, property crimes—and posts these statistics.[17]

As Audrey Watters points out in a detailed post about school bells, a popular belief is that school bells were initiated as a way to prepare students to become factory workers; but though plausible, this account is not accurate. Bells have been used in schools for a long time—prior to industrialization, it turns out. "Bells, primarily handbells, have been a technology of school since their outset, well before 'the factory' they were purportedly modeled on. They were used, as were the bells in churches, to summon students to ye old one room schoolhouse for the beginning of the day." When the Common School movement of the nineteenth century, founded by Horace Mann, aimed to construct school buildings, every school was urged to invest in a bell. And this had effects, as Watters reminds us: *"The architecture of the school building informs the pedagogy that takes place therein—the same goes for the technologies that are implemented inside them.* And that includes the school bell" (emphasis in original).[18]

But really one of the primary functions of bells in school was to warn about fire, which was a common occurrence. Watters cites a report that there were as many as ten school fires a week in the US in 1911.

Policing and the nature of surveillance and control in schools are fraught topics in the United States. From a tiny 1 percent of US schools having on-site police officers in 1975, by 2018 that proportion had increased to about 58 percent.[19] These officers are often called euphemistically "school resource officers." (Urban schools tend to have metal detectors; virtually all have cameras and gates.) During the height of the pandemic, many people were calling for the immediate reopening of schools. "Children belong in school," they said. Is this because schools serve as day care? Because parents are not at home or otherwise busy? Because kids need social life and our isolated nuclear families of the middle class don't provide it? Because schools provide social services? Are schools "the safest place for children"?

"School shootings" is a category of news in the United States. Students practice "active shooter drills." When I was a child we practiced tornado drills, fire drills, and air-raid drills in case of attacks from the Soviet Union. Students in California practice "drop, cover, and hold on" in their earthquake drills. Some of my students have revealed how traumatized they are by a decade of active-shooter drills and school shootings.

Diseases and pests spread when people are concentrated together for long periods. The COVID-19 pandemic made this impossible to ignore. For all the benefits of gathering to learn, schools also can transmit not only the usual "plagues" of transmissible illnesses, like flus, RSV, and hand-foot-mouth disease, plus other transmissible afflictions like lice and hysteria. Epidemiologists study "epidemic hysteria" and "mass psychogenic illness" in schools. The more current term is "social contagion."[20] Social contagion can induce bullying, self-harm, suicidality, as well as sociolinguistic change, fashion, secret languages, and gossip.

Less-Schoolish Spaces and Places

Learning doesn't require schoolish spaces and places and in fact is often artificially limited by the expectation that it occurs primarily within schools. Environments constrain, control, lead to tendencies.

Bountiful examples of learning outside schools can inspire even those teaching within schools to add dimensions of spaces and places beyond the fixed classroom. Susan Hrach's book *Minding Bodies* has several chapters focused on the environment and ways to evade the room's and the building's constraints: even on campus, students can move within a room, or everyone can go outside the building; faculty can, with difficulty, arrange for everyone to go off campus, in what used to be called field trips.[21]

Schoolish places and spaces are frequently addressed in ways both modest and grand. Hrach lists a few of these ways, and I have also found others.

Modest Improvements

In both lower levels of education and in higher education, individual teachers or departments can aim to improve the rooms and spaces. Teachers of children can decorate the rooms with inspirational or comforting posters. My "Theory of Public Higher Education" colleague, Mays Imad, in her efforts to make her own community college classrooms into "sanctuaries" for her multiply-traumatized students, brings cloths and beautiful items and sets up her classes each time.

Other modest improvements might include temporarily leaving the classroom for a session, or essentially fighting the structure by rearranging the furniture, standing up and disregarding it, walking around.

Intermediate Improvements

Efforts in the twenty-first century have focused on improving rooms and creating "active learning" classrooms, which in the earliest years of the century were essentially computer labs and in the third decade are becoming more like Google campuses, with flexible spaces for brainstorming and groups of varying sizes, with huge whiteboards and screens that can project everyone's ubiquitous laptops.

Moving beyond classroom learning, community-based learning and community-based projects are ways that students, usually in a class but sometimes outside the curriculum, can work *with* or *for* some segment of the local community on a project. Several of my colleagues partner with local organizations. Their students provide some academic expertise and labor while also learning from local people in their communities.

Grander Change

The most radical of all nonschoolish learning spaces are outside, with no dedicated building or place. This could involve something like the peripatetic Greek teaching of Aristotle, who taught informal, voluntary groups of learners as they walked around the Lyceum. This method of reflecting on experience and making sense of it, with an informal collection of learners, is only loosely considered a "school." Martin Bloomer's work on Roman schools notes that the first Roman schools had no dedicated spaces.[22] David Lancy shows how in at least one "traditional" society, the Kpelle in West Africa, children of multiple ages are loosely supervised on the "motherground," a cleared, relatively safe central plaza around which parents can engage in their work. This is set-aside space, but it is not schoolish.

Classrooms have changed over time, certainly. Some, such as Reggio Emilia schools, as detailed by Caroline Edwards, are aesthetically beautiful, with natural light and materials.[23] Some current examples of nonschoolish spaces include "forest kindergartens," usually for preschool and kindergarten, in which students spend the entire day outside, even in cold weather. Denmark and Scandinavia have pioneered this, but forest kindergartens exist throughout the world. Children climb trees, slide in the mud, and *learn from the environment*; they are not just contained within it. Students in my Anthropology of Childhood and Education class, 2022, became obsessed with this after we watched a video of such a Danish "school."

People who unschool their children, in contrast to some who engage in homeschooling, often use "the world as their classroom," rather than mimicking a classroom in their home, or in a consortium of like-minded people's homes.

Richard Louv, author of *Last Child in the Woods: Saving Our Children from Nature-Deficit Disorder*, encourages families and schools to increase children's time outside, as they do in Sudbury schools in the United States and elsewhere. Merging interests in science and sustainability education with student well-being and active learning, some schools integrate on-site agricultural or farm programs into the curriculum, as in the Good Shepherd Montessori School in South Bend, Indiana, and the Edible Schoolyard Project established by Bay Area chef and educator Alice Waters to "transform . . . public education by using organic school gardens, kitchens, and cafeterias to teach both academic subjects and the values of nourishment, stewardship, and community." Such programs take students out of schoolish places so they can enjoy learning in less-controlled, more bodily, and more multifaceted ways.[24]

Outward Bound programs of outdoor experiences, often in rugged settings, are used for students who have struggled in their schoolish experiences. Expeditionary Learning—which I had thought was a philosophy but turns out to be a brand of a nonprofit, a partnership with the Harvard Graduate School of Education and Outward Bound—is an approach that uses progressive principles of partnership and discovery, with a priority on experiences outdoors. "Whenever possible and appropriate, students are encouraged to be active and outdoors during the school day."[25] Prescott College in Arizona often has students engaged in off-campus activities, taking as one of its core values that "classrooms extend beyond four walls," as it encourages experiential and field-based learning. The college emphasizes its "breathtaking natural setting" and aims to help create "a beautiful future for all."[26]

Many students in K–12 schools who find their schoolish experience alienating, harmful, or unsuccessful may complete some or all of their required schooling online. Nearly everything can be transferred online, as we saw during the first months of the COVID-19 pandemic, including kindergarten and physical education.

Prototypical schools and colleges, even when located in urban settings, often attempt to re-create the isolation of the rural campuses that constituted the elite ideal of protection and isolation from the evils of urban life, as Steven J. Diner explains in his fascinating *Universities and Their Cities: Urban Higher Education in America*.[27] Reintegration with the surrounding community is often professed, but as with so many other goals, the literal architecture structures experience in direct contradiction to other professed goals.[28]

Schoolish time, work, space, and place shape expectations for schoolish learning, which is carried out in a variety of schoolish genres, both those consumed and those produced.

9

GENRES OF CONSUMPTION

From Scarcity, Artificiality, Constraint to Abundance and Variety

> We have always needed to be able to curate and discern content
> across media. The need to do so just grows more immediately
> centered in our consciousness when the various options for reading,
> writing, and communicating with each other are easily accessible
> to us.
>
> JENAE COHN, *Skim, Dive, Surface: Teaching Digital Reading*

I like the term *genre*, usually applied to things like fiction and nonfiction, mystery and fantasy, because it basically means "kind." Each genre, form, platform, has its expected formal dimensions. Fiction has dialogue, set off in quotation marks (except when modernist writers challenge the conventions). Mysteries and rom-coms have formulas. Greek tragedies, sonnets, haiku, Instagram posts, texts about getting home late . . . all these have expectations and formal constraints, *conventions*, agreed-upon stylistic and rhetorical features, that govern how any item is conceived, received, and evaluated. Genres exist in ordinary life, for instance with folk labels such as *yelling*, *promising*, *telling*, *secrets*, *lies*. Conversations are different from interrogations, interviews, or lectures.[1]

In both ordinary life and work people are concerned to master particular genres. Teenage friends gather around their phones to craft the best snap or TikTok. Employees are trained in genres when they enter new workplaces: Do they file reports? Create proposals? Send spreadsheets via encryption? Each has subtleties of tone, amount and format of citation or linking, use of images and text, fonts and sounds. If someone wants to attract followers on Instagram or TikTok, they play with their approach until they get things right, the difference between having four or four hundred or four hundred thousand followers. Genres are constantly evolving. If you look at books written two hundred years ago, or even fifty years ago, you'll see that they vary in terms of sentence length, vocabulary, and syntax. The best way to give technical presentations in 1998 was different from controlling the social media branding of a particular company in 2022. All this is related to how writers write and readers read.[2] By the time you're reading this, no doubt new platforms, genres, and conventions will have arisen; the speed of change has increased. Schools can never keep up; most don't try.

Of course, there's always more than just *written* texts, and there always has been. I took my Zoom Text Talk Insta Sing Chat: Modalities and Media of Interaction class to our library's rare books room, and we looked at the illuminated manuscripts and other treasured artifacts prepared enthusiastically by our expert subject librarians. We admired the intersection of image and text, and the materiality of each of these works: on parchment (= skin), leaves, boxes, made beautiful with gold and ink and paint. *Images* have powerful influence over the *affective* and *aesthetic* dimensions of the experiences and make them appealing. The relationship between formal and informal genres, speech and writing, and digital formats is in constant flux. Yet you would scarcely hear a whisper of this in schools.

Schoolish genres, like everything else schoolish, are sets of rhetorical and interactional practices and materials that essentially exist only in schools. They don't really have a place outside school except for the spilling over of schoolishness into all of life. And they are unloved, for good reason, so the only way to ensure students' engagement with them is through threat or rewards (grades). They are not their own reward. I'll talk about consumption ("the lecture" and "the reading") in this chapter and production (tests, writing, and games) of schoolish genres in the next.

"The Lecture"

As we saw, schoolish places presume the centrality of lectures, especially in higher education. Students sit, facing forward; the teacher stands. In large classes there may be a literal platform for the performance. The speaker, the one who commands the floor, is elevated as "expert" about to "fill the minds" of the listeners. Paulo Freire's image of the "banking model," where information is stuffed into empty heads, theoretically for later withdrawal, is built into the very architecture of prototypical classrooms. Increasingly speakers employ multimedia aids, with slides projected onto screens. Classrooms without such technology are increasingly rare, even in rooms designed for seminar or lecture-with-discussion classes, at least in high-income countries. I've been involved in observing colleagues for tenure and promotion; the general focus is on what the *teacher* is doing and how good "the lecture" is. (More recent guidelines in higher education point out that it's also important to note what the *students* are doing.)

The lecture has medieval origins. Prior to the European development of the printing press, lectures were literal *reading* from texts, for the purpose of textual preservation, since only the speaker possessed the text. The speaker was merely the "animator," in Erving Goffman's helpful distinction among speakers' roles in his essay "The Lecture."[3] What was transmitted was not only the *information* in the text but the literal verbatim text itself. The lector literally read aloud.

After the printing press made books more affordable and available, lectures played different roles. Media and education scholar Norm Friesen points to the Romantic notion of hermeneutics in which what was important was not the text itself but *the spirit behind the text*. The text was merely the vehicle for transmitting the thoughts of the speaker into the mind of the hearer.[4] The authority of the text had been transformed into the authority of the lecturer, and the more "authentic" the lecturer appeared, the more of an "event" occurred.

This charisma remains as an ideal in the twenty-first century—both in education and in the edutainment world of TED talks and spinoffs—whereby listeners treasure the appearance of spontaneity and a lecture delivered as what Goffman terms "fresh talk," rather than something memorized or read aloud. Experienced lecturers know that some balance between memorization and consultation of notes *written to be spoken* will provide this "fresh talk illusion," or the *"illusion* of pure orality."[5] The embodied self of the speaker/performer provides charisma and inspiration, as well as personal interpretation, not identical with what can be derived from other sources. Friesen writes that "the lecture . . . transforms the artifact of the text into an *event*" with multimedia capabilities and a combination of textual and visual materials, along with the embodied presence of the authority.[6]

Some of these events are more compelling than others. As Goffman wryly observes, the speaker has the authority to hold the floor; the attention of the audience is another matter.[7]

In many college classrooms, especially when there are large numbers of students, as soon as PowerPoint begins, students settle back, take out their laptops and phones, or zone out, and wait for the lesson. Slides (Power-Point, Google Slides, Prezi) present material in fixed order; a question may send the lecturer scrambling to find a later or earlier slide that addresses it, but it must be prepared in advance, without any possibility of responsiveness. "Information Delivery Mode" assumes that classes are all about "content." (I sometimes get drowsy in presentations, especially when the room is dimmed. I don't know how students do it, actually, sitting and being talked at all day.) Many students welcome the option to access "the PowerPoints" so they can skip the lecture entirely. Now many lectures are recorded, in the "flipped classroom" model; students watch "the lectures" on their own time (or they don't), and in class they do more "active learning" activities. Barbi Honeycutt has left her own academic career to host a podcast series downloaded 125,000 times by October 2022, called *Lecture Breakers*; the publications associated with it are called Flip It.

One of many critiques about "the lecture" is that it occurs at the wrong time. It begins by stuffing incurious minds. Instead, what should happen is to really figure out the right "time for telling"—once learners *want* to know.[8]

In Goffman's, and my, view, the action is really in the *interactions* among speakers, hearers, and setting, which includes all the media and technology involved. A performer's "success" often depends on "backchannel feedback" from the audience: laughs at jokes, gasps at shocking revelations, eyes facing the speaker, nods, frowns, comments, questions. Recorded lectures may get comments in the affordances of web 2.0, with a temporal delay.

Virtual lectures, of which I've given countless, for instance on the Zoom platform, may have cameras on and the chat enabled, which permits feedback in the form of facial expressions, nods, "reactions," or comments and questions in the chat. They mimic the actual copresence at singular events that constitutes the importance of a live lecture, or a class. The webinar version allows only the speaker and perhaps a few panelists to be visible; sometimes the chat is enabled, but often it is not. This is surely an efficient management strategy for controlling hundreds of potential audience members, but that audience has thereby changed from active participants jointly constructing the event to passive recipients.

In the twenty-first century in the United States, heated arguments have revolved around the benefits and detriments of lecturing, and whether lectures should be retained, improved, or scrapped entirely. Many pit lecturing against something loosely termed "active learning." Examples include the use of polls to gauge initial student beliefs about topics, think-pair-share exercises, exit tickets, small-group discussions, problem solving, project- and problem-based learning, or more.[9] It's challenging to determine which methods have "the best" outcomes, because the easiest way to assess learning, or some component of it, is simply to test recalled information, and classes may differ about what they emphasize. But a meta-analysis, studying hundreds of studies, has shown that *lecturing is consistently less effective than active learning*. In fact, so strong was the evidence that the authors said the following, much quoted: "If the experiments analyzed here had been conducted as randomized controlled trials of medical interventions, they may have been stopped for benefit— meaning that enrolling patients in the control condition [lecture] might be discontinued because the treatment being tested [active learning] was clearly more beneficial."[10] What that means is that lecturing is like a less-effective medicine, and students should only get the better one.

That doesn't mean that students uniformly *embrace* active learning; in fact the prototypical schoolish version of teaching is so central and familiar that students often *believe* they're taught better via lecturing even when results, on similar tests, show the opposite. Deslauriers et al. showed that "comparing passive lectures with active learning using a randomized experimental approach and identical course materials, we find that *students in the active classroom learn more, but they feel like they learn less*" (emphasis added).[11]

Faculty are often reluctant to try something unfamiliar, fearing students will receive it poorly and that their course evaluations will suffer. Some mimic active learning without understanding what lies beneath it. For that reason, Gary A. Smith suggests that college faculty learn at least something about how students actually learn—something that is not taught in most graduate programs.[12]

Note Taking

The click-bait controversy about whether handwriting or using a device is optimal for note taking presumes passive reception and information retrieval—the schoolish goal of stuffing, banking, information into empty brains in "the lecture."[13] Are students merely "transcribing" the lecture, or are they actively processing it? (There's a side controversy about equity and accessibility and all the people who can't write by hand and need laptops.)

I'm all for hands-on everything. Amy Weldon's *The Hands-On Life: How to Wake Yourself Up and Save the World* is marvelous (see chapter 12, "Attending (to) Bodies").[14] Handwriting, as Tim Ingold notes, produces a different kind of thinking.[15] Lots of writers suggest mind-mapping by hand, journaling, sketching, all kinds of things.

But the question of "which is better for note taking in lectures" presumes schoolishness all the way down (and uniform, generic students), testing information retrieval as delivered in classrooms.

Mini-lectures on Demand

Some people engage with less-schoolish genres of the lecture.

I often now provide mini-lectures to "deliver" quick, easy-to-use bits of information *when it is desired*, attentive to "time for telling." Having taught for so long, I have a lot of these ready-to-hand. (When I first taught, I remember spending twenty or thirty hours preparing to deliver a one-hour lecture on kinship. I've come across those notes, cleaning up my piles, er, files. And wow, they were so detailed and so irrelevant!) It's easy enough for me, given my decades of experience, but still I have to be attentive to what I can observe about student interests.

But students are not only supposed to absorb information from "the lecture"; there's another principal schoolish genre: "the reading."

"The Reading": Distraction, Scarcity, Limits, Control

A lot of what students have to read in school is created for students. Primers have long existed, simple works that young readers can make sense of. The most famous English-language primer in the United States was McGuffey's Reader, technically McGuffey's *Eclectic First Reader*, *Eclectic Second Reader*, and so on, a series of graduated, easy-to-read texts for children learning to read, especially in the "West" of the US (Ohio, and further). Estimates are that 122 million of these readers were distributed between 1836 and 1920.[16] I was raised on "Dick and Jane" books. (Only with my discovery of the Beverly Cleary *Ramona* books in third grade did I become the voracious reader I've been my whole life since. This is relevant in the vicious "whole language versus phonics" fights.)[17]

The most schoolish of all are textbooks, written purely for students; for many students they are the primary genre they encounter. Textbooks are a big, though declining, business. They're lucrative for publishers and sometimes for the writers themselves, especially in STEM fields where textbooks can cost hundreds of dollars and where revisions are undertaken frequently. Textbook revenue in the United States has fallen from a high of $11.97 billion in 2015 to $7.85 billion in 2020, because of the growing secondhand and rental markets.[18] Most are available online. But, as Barrett points out, to make up for the loss in revenue, each textbook has to become, initially, more expensive.[19] In higher education, specific classes vary enormously: some assign a single big textbook, others a textbook plus supplementary material, others just articles, and increasingly some use only open educational resources.

Textbooks are political. In some countries (France, China) textbooks and curricula are uniform nationwide; the primary reading material is also common throughout the nation. Australia, Bangladesh, India, and the UK have uniform national curricula.[20] Papua New Guinea developed national math textbooks with the help of Japanese consultants. In the United States, Congress has inquired into the costs of textbooks; and textbook content and perspective are the focus of the "culture wars." Some of the battles have been in K–12 school districts, especially in Texas, which has for years prohibited the robust teaching of evolution or at least insisted that textbooks challenge it.[21] Currently (2022) "critical race theory," "complete sex education," and LGBTQ discussion are driving elections, legislation, and the creation of new textbooks. Whose history gets told? Who gets to write the story?

And why should students read it? Is it inviting? Fascinating? Fun? Useful? Necessary? Textbooks are often dull, even spruced up with boxes and images. And other schoolish reading, academic stuff that's always on the list, isn't always a pleasure to read. That's become true for me too. Some items I used to assign to my students now feel boring, tedious, or difficult to get through. Is it because I have world-events distraction? Is it because I'm waiting to check the Twitter-Facebook-Instagram-email round again? Is it because of my to-do list sitting there beside me on a table? Is it because the textual rhythms have become out of sync with the ways we talk now? Is it because, like my students, focus is challenging? The reasons are not all clear, but the effect is undeniable: I don't like reading boring things. I don't like reading things that take forever to get to the point. I don't like convoluted syntax, or something with a lot of dependent clauses. I don't like sentences that occupy eight or ten lines of text on a printed page. (On a phone—the way many students read—it would go on seemingly forever.)

And I grew up in a completely different era. So, if I don't like this, surely my students like it even less. One thing that many faculty have noted is that over the years students have been calling books that are not textbooks "novels." Novels, to us old folks, are fictional genres. But for young people in school, a novel is a less-schoolish genre that may even be enjoyable to read. A real book.

What to Read: Artificial Impression of Completeness and Containment

Schoolish reading is controlled, as if it were scarce, or complete. This comes from the medieval experience of limits, when print was precious and rare, and when all that was known about a particular topic could be contained. As Carl Wieman wrote in a piece called "Stop Lecturing Me," most of college, with lectures and textbooks, appears not yet to have come to terms with the invention of the printing press.[22]

Many students do all the reading; some do none. Some see it as optional, accustomed as they are to "the lecture" that summarizes or replaces "the reading." Schoolish reading is often a chore.

My diligent students often come with their physical or digital highlighters and look for the kind of information that will be tested: facts, figures, statements. They haven't been permitted to engage in different kinds of reading, from skimming for interest to seeking an argument. Sometimes

I tell my students to skim a certain item—just get the gist of the argument, or the style—and they say they feel guilty. Schoolish reading is dutiful and thorough, time-consuming and hard.

Honesty about the overwhelming abundance of information and material—far beyond the printed word—should force us to address the opportunities but also the challenges of less-schoolish reading and gleaning.

How to Read

We read differently depending on the purpose: for information, for facts, for arguments, for style, for voice. A student once asked me, "What are we reading for?" I think she meant: "Which facts do we have to know?" Given that I had *assigned* the reading with something in mind, it made sense that she wanted to know what I had in mind. In many ways, that's only fair. So I went back to the syllabus—always a liquid syllabus, a living document—and inserted some questions. This was my What Should We Eat? class, which had the triple goal of introducing a discipline (anthropology) in the context of interdisciplinarity, addressing a topic (food and culture and sustainability), and focusing on speaking. So here are the entries early on:

Reading comprehension questions on syllabus

- *The Omnivore's Dilemma* Introduction (pp. 1–11)

  —What IS this dilemma?

- Michael Pollan Explains Caffeine (27 min)

  —Why is coffee a drug food?
  —How are coffee and tea tied up with slavery and imperialism?
  —Is Michael Pollan a good speaker? Why? Is Terry Gross a good
    interviewer? Why?

But these are not good questions; they're basically comprehension, what-questions. I would prefer that students ask their own questions. But for students used to mining material for facts, this was a reminder that I was hoping for more general understandings, especially at the beginning of the semester, as we were warming up. In her practical book *Skim, Dive, Surface: Teaching Digital Reading*, Jenae Cohn writes that different kinds of reading are *all legitimate* but that instructors need to make explicit the different purposes of different types of reading.[23]

Annotation   A fun new trend in higher education is "social annotation"—kind of like sharing marginal notes or comments on social media posts. Some of the entities helping to facilitate this are Hypothes.is and Perusal. I'm a fan of Hypothes.is because it's not-for-profit and because its aim is beyond a single course. If students choose, they can interact with anyone, anywhere, who has commented on particular items. It could be like sharing notes across the whole internet—something that can help people cheat or can help people learn.

Remi Kalir, author of *Annotation*, has done a Twitter project showing 231 examples of annotation and its widespread existence in the forms of graffiti, marginal notes in old manuscripts, pasting on lampposts, doodling on a paper, glosses of sacred texts, and more.[24] It's a reminder of the *social* nature of learning, in which reading plays a role. Some instructors may encourage their students to engage beyond their own classes. Others may limit it artificially, counting the beans—comments—in the Learning Management System, for points or grades.

Less-Schoolish "Reading": Abundance and Attention

Schoolish genres are familiar. But people learn from all kinds of materials: texts and TikToks, ads, TV, YouTube videos, podcasts, diagrams and text, friends' explanations, Wikipedia, and TED talks. We switch effortlessly among them (though apparently "multitasking" is really just super-rapid and frequent switching).[25] We skim and we learn, we misread and we believe falsely. We go down "rabbit holes" in vortexes of fascination. I sure do.

And while it can be efficient to have a teacher or a committee vet the material to ensure some version of quality, if the goal is preparation for a lifetime of learning, then we should provide opportunities for students to determine *what* and *how* to read, other than following instructors' instructions.

What to Read? Abundance: Navigating and Curating, Media Literacy, Information Literacy

I used to start my syllabi with lists of books. Old classes are especially hard to redo because they require relinquishing my favorites. But when I'm on top of things, I remember to start with: "What is the goal? How do we get there? What are students supposed to be able to do? What *doing* (reading, writing, testing) will help them get there?"

If the goal is learning, then the choices are clearer, if not easier. And one goal is independence.

When my students lead class, they have to *find material* that they think will be relevant, of high quality, and compelling to their classmates. They sometimes reflect in amazement that they'd had to spend three to six hours trying to decide what to assign. As do I. This *information curation* is a necessary skill in our life of abundance. I often list a large number of items and ask students to choose one or several, giving the length in time or pages. Isn't that how all of us make decisions about what to read?

"Novels," great writing, high production values are abundant. Why force students to suffer through dull material?

If we aim to help students develop skills to navigate a world of overwhelming abundance and uneven quality, throwing them into it blindly is not helpful. Nor is doing it *for* them. It is responsible to provide some tools. Many such tools have been developed under the heading of "information literacy," or "a set of abilities requiring individuals to 'recognize when information is needed and have the ability to locate, evaluate, and use effectively the needed information,'" and many are from experts in information, librarians.[26] Most college libraries provide lists of resources. There are tool kits, frameworks, guides, and other ways to discern the truthfulness, quality, and relevance of sources.

Some critical literacy approaches have clever mnemonics and acronyms: SIFT (Stop, Investigate the Source, Find better coverage, Trace claims, quotes, and media to original context); CARS (Credibility, Accuracy, Reasonableness, Support); REAL (Read the URL, Examine the site's content and history, Ask about the author/publisher, Look at the links); TRAAP (Timeliness, Relevance, Authority, Accuracy, Purpose). They aim to sort "fake news" and facts, and can also be useful for determining the respectability of a source.

In theses and projects, students are sometimes asked to create annotated bibliographies, and in some projects a "literature review" is expected. These are essentially *curating* relevant and high-quality sources, with summaries and annotations to facilitate returning-without-entirely-rereading.

Given that relevant and high-quality sources might exist in multiple platforms, modes, and formats, if we truly believe that one of our tasks is helping students *foster independence* for their own *lifelong, authentic learning*, then incorporating these activities into classes seems necessary.

Closed or Open? Open Everything: OER   The cost of educational materials, added to other high costs, including tuition and housing and forgone wages, is high. Some educational resources, including textbooks and academic journals, are so expensive that it's hard to fathom. Some are produced by for-profit entities like Elsevier, Springer, and Wiley-Blackwell, which publish journals and books. Both enjoy enormous revenues and profit margins (Elsevier's and Springer's profit margins are 36.8 percent and 22.8 percent, respectively). Three companies control half the scientific journal market (24 percent Elsevier, 12 percent Springer, and 12 percent Wiley-Blackwell).[27]

The Open Educational Resources (OER) movement exists to help. Advocates of OER address the costs of educational experiences and in the name of equity try to curate or create educational resources that are "open" or free. This includes both locating materials that others have freely posted, and facilitating the creation of always-open new resources. One source is a nonprofit called OpenStax. In 2019–20 alone, 2.7 million students, at 6,600 different colleges and universities, used OpenStax.[28] A new model of bundling, like Netflix, has arisen; for example, Cengage Unlimited sells subscriptions that provide access to everything that Cengage publishes.

However, I have a concern, and even an objection: all these materials are produced by the labor of many people.

Materials have costs, mostly in terms of labor (creating, editing, hosting, marketing, maintaining websites, but also paying for servers, electricity, water, software). The costs are borne by or shared among these four entities: (1) the consumer/reader, (2) the producer or publisher, (3) the author, or (4) a subsidy. If the materials are produced by volunteer labor, then it is unpaid, part of an unspoken "gift economy" on the part of writers, reviewers, and editors, few of whom are paid. This is often added to the already large burden of unpaid academic labor. Currently academics provide reviews of manuscripts with no compensation.

Some academic authors or their institutions pay to have their work published, in what is called pay-to-publish, or subvention.

Fees charged to authors may be as high as 9,500 euros for the journal *Nature*—costs included in some large scientific research grants. Some journals, not all technically "predatory," may charge either manuscript-submission fees or article-processing charges, or both.

It's worth it if this is then compensated by higher wages or increased employment possibilities—both of which are decreasingly true. When we call something "free" it masks the actual labor. And while I'm not such a capitalist that I think all work should be paid, the production of scholarly materials seems different from baking a cake for a neighbor. "Gifts" of one's time doing one's job are a confusing mix. The scholarly publishing industry relies on a kind of gift economy combined with the deferred benefit of prestige. I've learned that some faculty are given grants, often by foundations or their own institutions (which are funded by whatever specific mix of state, federal, and private funding they receive) to produce and develop such materials. Many are true believers in open education resources for their promise of greater equitable access.

Since 2018 in Europe, there has been something called "Plan S," mandating open access for publicly funded research. It's fascinating and also quite a substantive change from previous ways of funding student reading materials.[29]

My more general message is this: We have to try to understand the short-term and long-term changes in the context within which learners live. The more we cling to assumed "eternal" practices, the less effective our work will be. Unless it's a literature or deep-reading text class, there are multiple forms of reading, and each type requires analysis, just like film and TV.

I have a colleague, Jim Collins, in our Film, Television, and Theater Department. Jim is a film and television theorist, and generously for about twenty years each May has been offering, free, a one-week full-time course in how to "read" and use film and television in teaching. He does a crash course in visual semiotics, and each afternoon the learners watch a film or TV show. He constantly changes the course, adding new materials and approaches, because the ways we watch, consume, "read" visual media depend on all the other experiences we are also having. We consume within specific, ever-changing contexts. And also produce within them.

10

GENRES OF PRODUCTION

From Artificiality and Control to Authenticity and Freedom

> Increasingly, writing is a public and even collaborative act, but
> school often keeps ideas walled off from the world, shared only
> between student and teacher, and sometimes only shared between
> student and an anonymous grader. It's almost worse than having
> students practicing the training wheels version of writing. It's more
> like we haven't even let them on a bike.
>
> JOHN WARNER, *Why They Can't Write: Killing the Five-Paragraph
> Essay and Other Necessities*

Once students "consume" schoolish knowledge, they usually do something schoolish with it, often for the schoolish purpose of assessing or demonstrating their learning. Critiques are multifaceted: students "can't write" (itself a multifaceted complaint that goes from sentence-level grammar and spelling to analytic thinking and creativity); they do poorly on tests; they cheat and plagiarize.[1] They forget. They can't "transfer" what they learned in one context to another.[2] When we look more deeply at the schoolish nature of these learning activities, at their artificiality, at the control exercised by teachers, it is not surprising that students often find school learning alienating, not engaging or even useful. Sometimes—not often enough—they contribute to the learning. But many of the schoolish genres students are expected to produce simply exist within the schoolish universe.

Tests: Learning for Sorting and Assessment

There's nothing more schoolish than tests. It's not accurate to say that tests (and mini-tests, or quizzes) exist *only* in schools. Lots of places in life have tests; we find tests in self-directed language-learning apps such as Duolingo, or the qualifying boards for accountants, nurses, lawyers, engineers.

Tests are not new. Their purposes vary. Some are "formative," in the sense that they help students learn by assessing what they need. Others are "summative," issuing a final judgment. Some are "norm referenced," and others are "criterion referenced" (explained below). Some are primarily for gatekeeping, to determine access to a limited good. Some determine qualification for credit, to assess what people have learned as determined by a specific format. Some compare test takers with other test takers. Our grading system arose in part through an at-first minor addition to examinations. But grades via tests have come to function as one of the *aims* of schooling.

Tests are the quintessential schoolish genre, despite widespread acknowledgment that they tend to be imperfect measures of professional expertise and practice. According to assessment experts, ideally tests are (1) reliable (consistent across assessors and times taken), (2) valid (they measure what they want to know), (3) precise, and (4) fair. But few tests succeed at all four dimensions simultaneously.

The more "reliable" they are, with consistent results from subsequent iterations by the same or different teachers or evaluators, the less "valid" they tend to be in terms of actually measuring what people should have learned. It's easy to test for facts and information, and appeals to the need for "rigor" and "objectivity" lead to testing manageable chunks of information. It's harder to test for application of principles, generation of new knowledge, or asking new questions.

The use of *tests for learning* ("formative") may not be consistent with their use for final judgment of individual students ("summative"), nor may they be useful methods for evaluation of programs, teachers, or entire institutions—though they are used this way.

High-stakes tests frequently result in teaching to the test, in that confusion of means and ends I mentioned in the introduction. "What is tested will be taught" applies to all levels of schooling, however much experts deplore it.

Entrance/Access, Progress, and Exit

Examinations and tests—the terms are sometimes used synonymously and sometimes differentiated—are forms of *assessment in its most general sense*: to take stock, to learn where students stand, either before, during, or at completion of a course of study. Tests may be a subset of examinations, which can include written and oral forms, though it's also possible to have an "oral test." Oral examinations have long existed and remain, for instance, in doctoral examinations and dissertation defenses (a defense is called *viva voce*, or just *viva*, in the UK).

Examinations can serve multiple purposes: to determine which students are worthy of entering an institution or of earning credentials; to ascertain students' successful mastery of a body of material; to determine placement or next steps for learning, or gaps.

Thomas Kellaghan and Vincent Greaney state in their useful *Public Examinations Examined*, "All education systems are faced with two major tasks. The first is to certify the achievements of students, both to maintain standards and to provide evidence that individual students may need to pursue further education or use to seek employment. The second is the selection of students for further education in a situation that prevails everywhere: the number of applicants . . . exceeds the number of available places."[3] So: for entrance, exit, and sorting.

I've learned that it's not true that Europeans first learned of examinations when the Jesuit missionaries Matteo Ricci and others brought back news of the Chinese examination system in the sixteenth century; but this provided inspiration for amplification of a system that already existed. Demonstration of qualifications following or during education already existed in Bologna, Paris, Cambridge, and Oxford, via examinations modeled on debates, using the Greek and Roman model. At the University of Bologna, oral exams were introduced in 1219; theses and other written elements were presented at some medieval universities, including Padua and Cambridge. Examinations existed at the University of Paris in the late fifteenth century and in the Collegium Romanum, founded in 1551 by

Ignatius of Loyola in Italy, as well as in Latin schools, grammar schools for boys age six to eighteen, usually at the completion of a course of study, to ensure that students were qualified.

Universities too created entrance exams, because universities were the path toward the civil service. The first was the German Abitur (still given at the completion of secondary education), in 1788. Napoleon introduced the baccalauréat in France in 1808; it switched from oral to written in 1830. Exams to determine knowledge continually changed in universities. The Cambridge Mathematical Tripos, oldest of a series of written undergraduate examinations, began in the late eighteenth century. It was developed from oral exams, which became the Senate House Examination, and lasted at various points for four or five days.[4] The General Certificate of Education (GCE) exams in the UK are given at the completion of secondary education, in year 13, though Scotland has its own system.

Civil service selection through examination began in Prussia in 1748 and in France in 1793.

Though it was not the basis of all further tests, the best-known systematic and enduring examination system was the Chinese civil service examination, *keju*, which lasted at least fourteen hundred years. For the last several hundred years of its existence, the primary form was the "eight-legged essay," *baguwen*, a little like our "five-paragraph essay," with precise formal requirements—think *rubric*—which required compositional skill. Those who passed the *baguwen* were assigned to administrative posts in the civil service. The *keju* reflected applicants' training and commitment. But it did not directly apply to the applicant's later occupation, which consisted of dispute adjudication, tax collection, law enforcement, record keeping. Its task was sorting—like the test to win the princess in a fairy tale. It was ended in 1906, and a more modern version, the gaokao, was established in 1952, suspended from 1966 to 1976 during the Cultural Revolution, and reinstated in 1977. The gaokao was significantly reformed several times, most recently in 2015.[5]

College entrance exams worldwide are often single high-stakes tests, such as the Chinese gaokao, the Korean *suneung*, the Japanese *center*,[6] the French baccalaureate, the British A-Levels. Some countries have secondary-school leaving exams, and some even have exams upon completion of primary school.[7] Standardized tests such as, in the United States, the SAT, with their vocabulary, testable knowledge of formal grammar rules of a version of standardized English (or whatever language), and school math may correlate with other school success because they are schoolish through and through.[8]

Examinations and tests may determine entrance to higher education, with two different functions: the notion of discovering "aptitude" and ensuring adequate prior preparation. The notion of "meritocracy" is often involved.

Some note that high school grades are the best predictors of college grades. This should be no surprise: master schoolishness early to keep succeeding schoolishly.

Ranking test-takers against others is used especially when there are limited numbers of positions, such as slots for students in particular programs. US college admission is a fraught, contentious topic that includes tests, grades, "character," and identity, and people disagree about whether admissions should be selective or open. "Recruiting" universities have lower requirements than "selective" universities.

Norm-Referenced Tests   Norm-referenced tests compare individual test takers against a hypothetical "norm" or average. By fiat, 50 percent of test takers must lie below the 50th percentile, and 50 percent above. If many students perform poorly, the bar for proficiency can be lowered, even if students aren't learning more. For instance, in 1994, by fiat, a 430 on the verbal section of the SAT became a 510, and a 730 became an 800.[9]

Norm-referenced tests include the SAT, ACT, GRE, MCAT, LSAT, GMAT, gaokao (in China), the California Achievement Test, the Iowa Test of Basic Skills, the Stanford Achievement Test, the Terra Nova—anything designed to rank, including intelligence tests. Some tests administered in primary and secondary schools are norm referenced, with some nations having periodic national exams, and in the United States various state or district exams. Secondary-school-leaving qualifications in India, South Africa, the UK, and Italy are norm referenced. (A confusing article argues that A-Level examinations in the UK are not norm referenced or criterion referenced, but "attainment referenced.")[10]

Exit: Criterion-Referenced Tests   Tests that measure students against a body of predetermined knowledge, such as licensure tests, are called criterion-referenced tests. In such tests, it's possible for all students to do well. In schools, tests usually are in reference to a certain grade level or age, not an abstract generic person.

Examples of criterion-referenced tests are the Advanced Placement tests, the Regents exams, the National Assessment of Educational Progress (NAEP), bar exams, ABET (engineering) tests, language proficiency tests, or medical boards. Anyone qualified can pass. In many graduate programs there are exit exams, or comprehensive exams. The most important thing to know is that *criterion-referenced tests' results are not affected by other students' results.*

Formative Tests: In-Class Tests

In individual courses many classes have exams and quizzes, usually but not always criterion referenced. (Grading on a curve is always norm referenced.) Quizzes are smaller, less consequential versions of tests. (One faculty member reported on Twitter that students' anxiety diminished when the professor relabeled *tests* as *quizzes*.) Tests and quizzes have arbitrary rules associated with them, from the right to consult outside materials ("open book") to the sequestration of each individual in a testing center with "invigilators" (or an electronic counterpart) surveilling them.

Formats

Tests have varied formats: true/false; multiple choice; fill-in-the-blank; short answer; essay. There may be math, science, logic, or engineering problems. In graduate medical education symptoms may be presented. College entrance tests tend to be essays in Europe and multiple-choice questions in the United States and Latin America.

It's difficult to learn how to construct quizzes, tests, and exams. There are many helpful guides, such as in Barbara Gross Davis's *Tools for Teaching*.[11] Multiple-choice tests are time-consuming to create but a snap to grade. The hard part is crafting plausible-sounding options that are nonetheless wrong, or to be sneaky and write confusing multiple-negation questions. But I stopped giving tests, as I wondered what real-world skill they were assessing. The ability to outsmart the writers of bookcase-building instructions?

Most tests have time limits and reward speed. In the United States some students get "accommodations" to allow them extra time—usually 50 percent more—on tests, proctored by a testing center. In the reformatted SAT (since 2021), both essays and subject tests have been eliminated, and the length of the test has been shortened, recognizing that rewarding endurance may disproportionately reward neurotypical people. (The SAT is increasingly under assault and has become optional or no longer preferred at more and more universities.)

Some critiques revolve around the culturally specific nature of standardized tests. Even if such tests are visual, interpretation of visual material is a culturally influenced ability. Cultural references might include the built environment, foods, animals, plants, relationships.

Given the ubiquity of tests, how can schools eliminate the schoolish properties of such measures?

Less-Schoolish Tests: Assessment for Learning

One of the responses I constantly get from my talks about progressive pedagogy, and especially about ungrading, comes from faculty in STEM. "How can we be sure our engineers/doctors/chemists are really competent? Unlike you fuzzy humanists, there are real consequences for our students' knowledge." The assumption is that "objective" tests are the only source of evidence of learning. But those who create "objective" tests have made arbitrary selections, because one can never test everything.

Alternative or additional ways of assessing student learning include portfolios and observation (think of the road test in driving), and other schemas such as specifications grading or mastery-based grading, which tend to be improvements on conventional tests but still assume (1) there is an "it" that students need to know and (2) we know how to measure "it." It's easy to measure whether students know the strength of a metal, but it's harder to measure how they decide which metal to use, given that one may be strong and another expensive, and another may have environmental costs while a different one is unattractive. What's the right answer? Untimed tests may reveal much more about what students know and can do, and this mimics a lot of real-world experience. Some things take some people longer. The prototypical test is closed-book, meaning students can't consult any materials. Yet open-book tests are much more like real projects in the actual world.

The thing is, the tests that students tend to take in STEM fields rarely reflect the kinds of activities undertaken by actual professionals in these fields. Carl Wieman, the Nobel laureate in physics that I mentioned, has spent the second half of his career focused on pedagogy and created something called the Science Education Initiative. He was dismayed by the evidence he had seen for so long that students who performed well on the tests given even at the best universities had no idea at all how to think or act like scientists. They knew how to take tests, having mastered a set of skills often hidden from less-advantaged students. Wealthy students can avail themselves of costly test-prep services, which involve strategies: *how many multiple-choice questions have been "C" lately? Cross off the double negatives.* These are useful for these actual tests, true, and the tests have schoolish consequences, and ultimately real-life consequences. But they're not in the service of learning the material.

Wieman worked with the University of British Columbia, the University of Colorado Boulder, Stanford, and other institutions to create schoolwide initiatives, with pedagogy consultants who also had disciplinary expertise (Discipline-Based Educational Research, DBER), to revamp the curriculum and pedagogical models and to ensure the buy-in of administrators. It's not that there were no tests. But *the tests were in the service of learning*.

Testing Effect

The developers at the language-learning app Duolingo have evidence from millions of learners. They analyze the effects of their tests, the types and frequency and length of tests, the responses to tests, and the persistence of learners, given certain feedback. I open Duolingo every morning, while the water for my tea boils and then while the tea steeps—and do lessons for maybe fifteen or twenty minutes. I'm working on Spanish right now.

Sometimes I do a review lesson with three questions, and I may get one wrong—a score of 67 percent. But Duolingo keeps telling me I'm great! So I persist. If this were a language class in school, that would be a D, and I would surely be discouraged by now. Anyway, I can always go back and fix my mistakes—which also reinforces the information. And I get points for that too!

The "testing effect" and "retrieval practice" with "spaced repetition" have been studied and demonstrated as especially effective for *remembering information*, especially discrete, disconnected, nonauthentic, simple information. Psychologist Michelle D. Miller has a fabulous book, *Remembering and Forgetting in the Age of Technology*, in which she challenges the alarms about "kids these days," talks about the realities of using technology, the types of attention and distraction that are currently relevant, and how memory actually works.[12] She discusses the effects of testing-for-learning.

In my classes I sometimes do "check-ins," no-stakes surveys to figure out (assess) what my students know. We see the anonymous results together. If many people do poorly, I need to address it for the class. If a few do, then they learn on the spot.

So testing can be done, especially for the kinds of right-or-wrong information that is the conventional province of schoolishness: students can master definitions and terms, dates and authors, outcomes of known processes. But this can hardly be the ultimate goal of learning, even if it is a sometimes necessary step.

As Tamara van Gog and John Sweller note, the testing effect diminishes—or even disappears—as the material gets more complicated. They provide science and language learning examples:

> When learning about the mechanics of a hydraulic car brake system in engineering, it is not only necessary to learn the individual components in the system (e.g., pistons, cylinders), but also how these components interact with each other (e.g., principles of hydraulic multiplication and friction). Moreover, the aim is usually not just to learn how the system works, but also to be able to apply that knowledge to real-world tasks (e.g., being able to diagnose and repair faults in a system).[13]

Such assessment may require more qualitative measures.

Portfolios

Tests may be a dominant schoolish genre, but increasing attention has been paid to another way of assessing learning: portfolios. Assembling a portfolio for each student not only provides evidence of learning but is itself part of the process, not simply the product. This is especially useful for classes that include creation such as writing, on the model of an artist's portfolio, but could also be evidence of engineering projects or science experiments.

Schoolish Writing and Doing

The story goes like this: Student writing is often considered terrible. Students often hate writing. Teachers lament its quality, and the kind of writing done in school doesn't seem to really improve learning; yet schoolishness demands some kind of proof of learning either in tests or writing, and teachers usually feel an obligation to correct it in depth. Students feel anxious; one told me she felt "suffocated" by the requirement to write a schoolish essay, but delved in when she had the freedom to choose a genre for herself—an "unessay." Complaints abound that students cut corners, and they plagiarize. The product is formulaic. It's "bad." It's uninspired. It's fake. It's deadly. It's schoolish. No wonder students hate it. And no wonder teachers hate reading it.

This is a sad story.

Panic: What's Wrong with Kids These Days, Version 257

Despite the public alarm about texting and electronic communication, the moral panic, terror of technology, the eternal question about whether students "nowadays" can read or write, it's important to note that whenever experts actually investigate, they find both a lot of reading and a lot of writing, of a variety of types, even if it isn't identical with the forms of their parents or grandparents.[14]

Laments about student writing are not at all new. We could call them "evergreen": they are always relevant. As one example, Harvard instituted mandatory first-year composition courses in 1885; eleven years earlier, sophomores had to take them because their writing was considered poor. The story of attempts to remediate student writing is long, fascinating, and also dispiriting, where the focus was often on mechanics, and the courses were often taught by poorly compensated employees with little job security or prestige. Little has changed in that regard; the strong field of rhetoric and composition is central to undergraduate education but still underfunded and underrespected while expected to perform miracles.[15]

Current research on writing, rhetoric, and composition is plentiful, productive, and persuasive. I've been influenced by much of it, but also by my own trial and error and by student responses and reflections. Some of the key authors in the field who have helped my thinking are Andrea Lunsford, Peter Elbow, John Warner, Michele Eodice, Anne Ellen Geller, Neal Lerner, Kate Pantelides, and Cathy Davidson. All of them enthusiastically embrace students, rather than echo the common lament, "Why can't they write?" Warner even titles his brilliant book *Why They Can't Write* and proceeds to show that the conventional wisdom about writing is the *source* of the trouble. In fact, he lays the blame precisely on the *teaching* of writing. Yet without acknowledging the expert (yes, I'm appealing to authority) understanding of what writing really is, the laments keep coming. In 2019, literary biographer and historian Robert Zaretsky, in the *Chronicle of Higher Education*, mocked a student's "word salad," as if the core dimension of writing is the sentence.[16] Common sense tells us it is. Research tells us it isn't. Like so much else, our automatic understanding is often flawed. Studies have shown for a century that studying grammar, however venerable the practice, has almost no effect on writing—except to make students dislike it.[17]

Not only don't they write well, the story goes; people worry that "nobody writes" at all anymore. They don't write cursive—don't get me started on the silliness of this moral panic—and they don't write thank-you notes, and they don't write term papers. And they use *abbreves* in schoolwork! For shame! What is the world coming to lol? (Read the brilliant and funny Gretchen McCulloch's *Because Internet: Understanding the New Rules of Language*, for an enjoyable and linguistically *informed* discussion of contemporary writing.)[18]

Well, if you look at "writing" the way experts in writing do—which is to say, taking *ideas* and conveying them in a medium divorced from the moment of speech—then everyone now writes a lot. Students/teens actually do a lot of writing, and have done so since the advent of the digital era, as, despite the panic, respected researchers have shown. The Pew Research Center reports that "most teenagers spend a considerable amount of their life composing texts, but they do not think that a lot of the material they create electronically is *real* writing."[19] You know why they don't see it as real writing? Because of school.

English, writing, and rhetoric professor Andrea Lunsford conducted a study at Stanford from 2001 to 2006.[20] She and her team followed several cohorts of students for several years to track their writing. They identified eighteen different kinds of writing that students engaged in, in a single semester. When outside judges evaluated the writing in different genres, using writing standards such as fresh vocabulary, structure, and clarity, they found that when students felt freer to write, as in a blog, they made *fewer* grammatical mistakes and wrote in *greater quantity*. That's partly because they've been paralyzed by schoolish writing rules.

Students are largely terrified of school writing. They know they'll get things wrong because that's what their teachers have always focused on. They believe that if they are given the formula, the recipe, the rubric, the standards, the rules, they'll be saved from mistakes. These rules are often doctrinaire, apparently arbitrary, and irrelevant to good writing: they provoke questions like *How many sources do I need?* and *Can I use the first-person pronoun?* or *What font?* or *How long?* or *Is this OK?* or *Do I have to cite classroom texts?* This fear stems, understandably, from years of trying to satisfy the arbitrary demands of dozens of teachers. So, of course, students don't like writing.

A host of arbitrary rules paralyzes confidenceless writers who would do anything to avoid the task—procrastinate, cheat, do it as fast as possible by following any convenient rubric like a paint-by-numbers template. Like drowning people clutching at a life raft, students are desperate for a rubric, a recipe for writing, something to guide them through schoolish dangers, from genre to number of sources to rules for font, use of *I*, and countless other minutiae. They see their singular task as assembling enough pages to satisfy the requirement and all the various rules. If it results in "BS-ing" their teachers or in writing something they don't believe in, it doesn't matter. Students equate dull, repetitive, zestless formulaic writing, schoolish writing, with writing in general.[21] When first-year writing teachers ask how their students feel about writing, all too often the reply is they largely dislike it.

Another methodical study of student writing in college by Michele Eodice, Anne Ellen Geller, and Neal Lerner, titled *The Meaningful Writing Project: Learning, Teaching, and Writing in Higher Education*, admonishes faculty to look beyond the limited "goals" we often have for students' writing and think instead about how writing connects with students' own actual goals—"where students might choose to take their writing and why they might make those choices." That requires "allowing them the agency to make those choices and encouraging them to take hold of who they have been, who they are, and who they want to be in their futures."[22] You'll see soon, in a few pages, that this can be done very effectively.

Fake Writing

Academic writing. Writing for school. Schoolish writing. Schoolish learning. When high-achieving students aim to stuff impressive vocabulary and convoluted syntax into their writing, John Warner calls it "Pseudo-Academic B.S.," or PABS,[23] the kind of writing that is rewarded on standardized tests because of its ten-dollar vocabulary words (*plethora*) and complex grammar. It may have nothing to say, but it says it in twisted, fancy, schoolish ways. Contrasting the writing students do for teachers with writing they do (if asked) for a hypothetical reader who needs to have something explained, David Bartholomae observed that "when students are writing for a teacher, writing becomes more problematic than it is for the students who are describing baseball to a Martian."[24] It's completely fake. (But work like this is highly rated by the increasingly popular computer-graded algorithms, or Automated Writing Evaluation, AWE.)[25]

In 2022 a new version of AI, ChatGTP, is able to generate text and also to detect copying. This will continue. It's fascinating, complicated, and connected to the goals of schooling.

Students recognize the differences between schoolish and other writing. The Pew study of teenage writing showed its sophistication: "Yet despite the nearly ubiquitous use of these [digital] tools by teens, they see an important distinction between the 'writing' they do for school and outside of school for personal reasons, and the 'communication' they enjoy via instant messaging, phone text messaging, email and social networking sites."

We tend to discount the skill required to construct all the types of writing students do—skills they could build on in more formal settings. Pew reports that "fully 93% of those ages 12–17 say they have done some writing outside of school in the past year and more than a third of them write consistently and regularly. Half (49%) of all teens say they enjoy the writing they do outside of school 'a great deal,' compared with just 17% who enjoy the writing they do for school with a similar intensity." So, if teens write so much, and even happily, why is it that teachers at all levels conclude they write poorly? What is schoolish writing, and how do students think about it?

Pew, like Lunsford, noted the many functions and domains of writing: "Teens write for a variety of reasons—as part of a school assignment, to get a good grade, to stay in touch with friends, to share their artistic creations with others or simply to put their thoughts to paper (whether virtual or otherwise)." These are all *writing*, though only some "count" in school.

This research also highlighted students' conscious understanding of both their motivation and their enjoyment: "Teens said they are motivated to write when they can select topics that are relevant to their lives and interests, and report greater enjoyment of school writing when they have the opportunity to write creatively. Having teachers or other adults who challenge them, present them with interesting curricula and give them detailed feedback also serves as a motivator for teens. Teens also report [that] writing for an audience motivates them to write and write well." Having an *audience*—a real audience, not merely the teacher—is especially powerful. But in most schoolish writing, the sole audience is the teacher-judge.

Less-Schoolish Writing

In contrast to schoolish writing is another kind of writing, and learning, that we might see as authentic, with different goals and different audiences: writing to woo, writing to entertain, writing to persuade, writing with consequences. Learning to fix something, learning to build something, learning to understand something pressing. But the kind of writing, and learning, we force on students, generally, is not their preferred writing and learning, and professors are not generally their preferred audience.

So we create a relationship of insincerity and bullshit. Of schoolishness. But only the students know that.

It turns out there are many blog posts and articles with titles something like "School Writing vs. Authentic Writing." One especially wonderful one is by Ken Lindblom, who writes of "The Authentic Writing Effect": "It's pretty easy to tell whether students are engaged in schoolish or authentic writing," he writes.[26] He identifies questions that emerge only from schoolish writing, just as Michael Wesch does when he asks students, "What do you want to know?"

- "Does spelling count?"
- "How many sources do I need in my works cited?"
- "How long does this have to be?"
- "Can I use the word *I*?"
- "Do I have to write in complete sentences?"

Lindblom emphasizes the *central role of the teacher* in schoolish writing: questions directed to the teacher, who has authoritative answers and adjudicates right and wrong. This already known quality of "school writing" makes it especially uninspiring. He compares the questions asked of teachers about school writing with those asked about "authentic writing":

- "Can you help me make sure I get the spelling right?"
- "Will my audience think this evidence is convincing?"
- "Will my audience be willing to read this much, or should I make it shorter?"
- "Would using the word *I* be too informal for my audience?"
- "Would this sentence fragment be effective for this audience, or should I write only in complete sentences?"

I witnessed this difference firsthand, at the Bowman Creek Educational Ecosystem, where students cared a lot about their writing—because it was not for school. It was real, for real people.

Authentic Writing outside School: Revision! Feedback

In the Bowman Creek Educational Ecosystem (BCe2) project I will present in more detail in chapter 14, writing played a surprisingly central part. At least four of the eight community projects undertaken by the thirty interns, students ranging from age fifteen to fifty, in 2017 were essentially writing projects or incorporated writing as essential.

One group was interested in the problem of lead in the water and soil in the high-poverty neighborhood. They had learned about lead abatement and wanted to create a project for the city, only to discover that others—a long-established neighborhood association, in partnership with researchers at Notre Dame (many of whom lived in that same neighborhood)—had beaten them to it. This is a typical hazard for student projects: when students with no background discover something and want to plunge into the work, they're often disappointed to find that someone has already done it, or that they can't complete something in the course of a semester or summer, or that the local residents aren't grateful for the students' sincere, if amateur, help.

But after initial despair that their summer would be wasted, this group figured out a way to be useful. Having learned how other cities produced user-friendly documents, they rewrote the 151-page EPA technical document about lead, to make it more useful for the residents who might actually consult it. They learned to assess and reduce the reading level dramatically.

During their week 9 update, they reported that they were "going through the document with a fine-tooth comb." They wanted to get it right at every level: proofreading; making sure they used updated data and information; links. Nobody was grading them on it, but they felt a weighty responsibility to the neighborhood where they had spent the whole summer. And then they revised again, got feedback, and revised again. They felt urgency, and care, and responsibility because somebody real was going to use it. They also prepared a press release.

Another group had created a website to consolidate all the city data about the four hundred vacant lots in the neighborhood. One of the team members was learning HTML, and someone else was learning another software program ("That's been a lot of fun; it's really cool"). They were pretty happy with their work, but after they showed their story map to an outside consultant, they had another four-hour meeting to make revisions based on her feedback. They were going to be featured in a company's presentation, so they wanted to get it right.

A group writing a "white paper" about the pros and cons and considerations of "daylighting" the covered, polluted Bowman Creek and restoring it to healthier visible conditions used a "decision matrix" template but were incorporating feedback and waiting for more information. They had to pause the work.

The team working on an interactive map with information about affordable housing was trying to get synergy among several neighborhood organizations; they had to rename and redo the domain, which took five hours. They also prepared a one-page document to present to the city council.

In contrast to how they would deal with schoolish writing, the students welcomed feedback and revised several times. The formats were quite varied, and some—like the press release—popped up as events unfolded. The only due date was the real one of the end of the internship and the interns' return home and then back to school. They did have an obligation to complete something.

This demonstrates *the power of authentic work for specific purposes and audiences*: the motivation was to help, and the methods—writing, learning, revising, getting feedback—were subservient to the goal.

When students aren't paralyzed by the lists of rules they had been given in high school and earlier, when they are invited to *say something* and maybe even to have choices about what to say, when they *care* about their topic, then the actual writing, even as measured by conventional criteria such as grammar, improves. The key insight is that "the sentence is not the basic skill or fundamental unit of writing. The idea is."[27] You don't start with grammar. You start with ideas. In much student writing, the order is backward. We shouldn't, then, be surprised by poor quality.

The main point is to *use the writing* for some purpose other than simply to get a grade. When students care, they can find help in improving their writing. In the actual work world, we are scarcely ever prevented from getting assistance; I have people read my drafts (grant applications, articles, books, sometimes even assignments for my students) to make sure I haven't overlooked important aspects. Students should learn to seek feedback too, not merely judgment.

Yes, many students need to improve their "skills," but if this is seen as the principal focus, accompanied by a litany of assumptions that everything they do is wrong—or, heaven help us, by *grammar worksheets*—they aren't likely to actually learn what they need to, and they aren't likely to be more inspired. If we set aside the assumption that we need boxes to check, then students can start to care about material once they are given a chance to bring up something about which they are curious, or have views about or experience with. *Then* they can incorporate feedback, which should be both *useful* and *usable*.

"Unessays," or Format Freedom

If our goal is to prepare students for life, which might include various kinds of work and various kinds of school, we might incorporate all these insights about learning. We can't begin by berating our learners.

In contrast to their experience with the limited number of genres of school writing, students, like professors, teachers, and just about everyone else, spend their lives immersed in a dazzling variety of genres. It's helpful, in my experience, to explicitly work with students about what we call *genres*, and to teach several. Despite assumptions about how adept "born digital" students are in every form of technology and media, research shows that students are less proficient at digital writing or digital literacy than we often assume.[28]

Digital platforms are here to stay. If we can help students learn to write blog posts, op-eds, infographics, we are helping them in ways that they will use in the future—in work or personally. I encourage my students to try new things: movies, scripts, podcasts, documentaries. The first time isn't usually perfect or may not even be very good. But I want them to try. And if it takes ten times to make it better, well, there has to be that first time, right? Sometimes I try to learn something new, along with the students, to challenge myself and restore a sense of what it's like to be clueless. The first time I created an infographic, one of those visual representations, with fonts and colors and icons and arrangements to convey my understanding of students' diversity of preparation, of experience, and of goals, the not-very-good image took me about two hours. Unlike more familiar schoolish production in which students stick with the recipe, the formula, the rubric, making work predictable, deadly dull, it can be an absorbing adventure. But it may be risky. Schoolish genres are safer.

Yet, given the centrality of the digital and various forms of writing in the world—as employees, as citizens, as humans living in the world—it is only responsible for us to help them understand the conventions, constraints, uses, and styles of a variety of forms of writing, of *genres*. Few of them come easily, whether we create space for students to choose freely or to choose within a limited range of options, or whether we assign specific forms. Some of my graduate students, socialized into schoolish writing, have a hard time with things like blogging (short paragraphs, simple sentences), even when they try. Some of them have recognized that in their future work—say, as an archaeologist attempting to garner public support for a project—they may very well have to write something like a popular blog, *in addition to* their more formal scholarly writing. It's now called, sometimes, *science communication* or *public-facing scholarship*. Some flourish and see a future for themselves in this domain.

If we can show students how to think *consciously* about the options for writing, something they often do unconsciously as they alter their speech and texting for different audiences, we will have provided a lifelong set of skills.

There's no shortage of inspired assignments out in the world of academia. Especially but not only in the humanities and social sciences, some go under the umbrella "unessay."[29] (In K–12 this is sometimes similar to "voice and choice.") My former colleague Marc Kissel has taken inspiration from the unessay idea and created a range of options for his students in his large (one hundred–student) introductory courses on biological anthropology. He writes that his students have created a cross-stitch of a human skull; Buzzfeed-style lists about evolution, gender, feminist movies; a Dungeons-and-Dragons-style role-playing game about evolution; a magazine-style story about *Homo floresiensis*; YouTube videos; and many more creative *and educational* projects.[30]

In my own classes, students have done interviews, podcasts, videos, poems, letters to birth mothers, infographics, shopping-and-cooking videos, games, songs, short stories, surveys, observations, paintings, photo montages, cartoons, storyboards, Kahoot! quizzes, *Jeopardy* games, and more. That's in addition to the variety of assignments—conversation analyses, ethnographies of speaking, landscape mapping, interviews, observations—that I have also dreamed up. (A student in my introductory linguistic anthropology class wrote on his self-assessment for one project that he had so much fun doing an investigation in linguistic anthropology with a friend that *he forgot it was for school*. Oh teacher joy! Oh rapture! It can happen!)

My biological anthropology colleague Cara Ocobock assigns her students "hominin dating profiles," modeled on the Tinder dating app. Students have to get right the nuances of the different hominin species but also have to get the nuances of the genre right. It looks great; it's fun for the students; they learn a lot; and it's fun for classmates and the professor who evaluates it. She also uses unessays, and she generously posts examples of her students' work, with their permission, of course.[31]

Almost always, unessays are accompanied by reflection (sometimes called "self-assessment"), a kind of "artist statement" explaining what the creator had aimed for—and as with all the ungraded work, this contributes to the practice of metacognition (thinking about thinking) that all independent learners must ultimately develop. I also ask my students to workshop drafts, and then to create "Appreciation" for one another's finished work. The teacher is not the sole audience nor the sole provider of feedback.

My Students Worked Hard and Wrote a Book, and Were Excited about It

In fall 2021, fresh back into the classroom after eighteen months away, immersed in talking about ungrading, authentic learning, and more, I taught a new class (a completely new invention of a class I had last taught in 2010 on New Media) that I titled Zoom Text Talk Insta Sing Chat: Modalities and Media of Interaction. I conceived of it as media studies meets linguistic anthropology, in which we would learn, academically, about all the ways humans have found to interact with each other—first speech itself, then writing, followed millennia later by printing; then a host of new forms (telegraphy, photography, radio, TV, movies) and then newer forms that built on the previous ones (internet, mobile phones, social media, video sharing). I knew students would come with a lot of familiarity with the newest forms, and a lot of taken-for-granted assumptions about all media, new and old. In typical anthropological fashion, one goal was to defamiliarize them. Others were to introduce methods of actual observation and to question the provocative headlines blaming media for all social ills.

Students sat at tables and created "teams" that led the class twice, once on "old" media and once on "new" media. We frequently generated questions, asking "If you were to conduct research into a topic right now, what would it be?" and "If you were going to convey information about something you learned, how would you like to convey it?" I suggested things like infographics, podcasts, games, videos. They were interested, but nervous.

I had been trying to figure out some kind of authentic project with an authentic audience, and I had scheduled the last day of class for that—maybe a kind of poster session or presentation of our products, or something. And then I was reading various things on Twitter from my active educators' networks, and somehow, at some point, I proposed the idea that we could create a book. They were enthusiastic.

A book made sense. The Pressbooks platform (sadly changed in 2022) made self-publishing easy and attractive. David Buck, who runs the Ungrading book club, and Laura Gibbs, who has been writing "tiny stories" for years, had both written about it. It supports a lot of Open Educational Resources (as you saw in chapter 9), and each chapter could have multiple types of media.

I told the students, "We'll write a book, in whatever format you want. You have *format freedom*. You have to figure out a topic, a question, and then a genre that suits your topic and audience. This will give you a searchable item in your online profile, which everyone should have. It will be public. What do you think you have learned that the world would benefit from knowing?"

Starting right after fall break, we spent time generating topics, combining obvious ones. We spent one class period early in the second half forming groups that seemed to have related topics, and worked, bit by bit. The group sizes varied from two to five, depending on how many wanted to work on each topic.

I scaffolded the project, in part because if students learned how to do long projects in small units, this would be an antiprocrastination and antianxiety set of skills they could take with them. We worked for short, fifteen-minute bursts, on titles, opening sentences, epigraphs, outlines, answers to "what?" "how?" and "so what?," consideration of genre, and criteria for that genre.

Once they were on their way, I put the six groups into pairs and had them answer questions about evidence, topic, etc.

We kept working, with the end-of-class work time stretching to twenty and then twenty-five minutes. Students switched seamlessly every day from whatever activities the team leading the class had us engaged in, to forming their groups and getting to work.

Working back from the authentic end-of-semester date, we had deadlines for "predrafts" and for drafts. Each draft, on Google Docs, got read by two students and me, with varying kinds of feedback. Students had to write biographies that were appropriate for the public and for future employers.

We brainstormed titles; a student happened upon the final one: *Communication Complications: Constraints and Affordances of Media*.

Then on a Sunday, six students and I worked for three hours on Zoom, trying to figure out the Pressbooks template—essentially the WordPress platform—and get the chapters uploaded. Some groups still were working on their drafts. When their classmates asked them, via Slack, to finish them so they could upload them, they responded.

There were some technical complications, but on the last day of classes—scheduled as Book Launch—students and I figured it out. When I hit "make public" and "update," students filmed the moment (and posted it to our class Instagram).

They were so excited!

They had told their parents, friends, about it. "Why don't more teachers do this?" one student asked me. They are published authors. You can read it here: https://communicationcomplications.pressbooks.com/front-matter/title-page/.

It was imperfect. We had trouble figuring out how to get graphics imported (they have to be high-enough resolution; but also our account had to be upgraded to allow enough storage). At first we couldn't figure out how to get all the authors' names imported, along with their bios (pro tip: there are two places—under "Profile" and also "Contributor"—where people can post bios). It turned out our account didn't allow us to track views or downloads. I knew no more and no less than the students; we learned this new platform together.

And many of the students didn't incorporate all the feedback, especially substantive feedback (sources, supporting material), but they did revise as much as they could.

And overall, this was a truly wonderful experience.

We all became, horizontally, contributors, learning together how to do something that felt worthwhile; and even though it ended up taking a lot of time, it was absorbing, and nobody seemed to complain. The elements that seemed to work are as follows:

- Cooperative learning atmosphere
- Lots of brainstorming about topics and genres
- Format freedom
- Ability to form their own groups, with size determined by interest
- Twice-weekly mini writing sessions (not even pomodoros, at first!)
- Scaffolding of the elements of any writing (fundamental questions of audience, question, method, etc.)
- Accountability to others
- Workshopping in class
- Authentic audience
  Authentic deadline
- Safety/ungrading

As Patricia Slagle states, "Authentic writing implies that the student is writing in his or her voice to a real living person or group about a matter of concern."[32]

One of the key dimensions that enabled this happy convergence is that the class was ungraded.

The students' work went into their portfolios—simply collections of their products throughout the semester, evidence of their learning. (I don't use any commercial educational technology products to assemble the material.) It's just on Google Drive (granted, a commercial platform), and they refer to it in their portfolio conferences (midsemester and semester-final) with me, upon which they reflect.

My Students Created a Public-Facing Website

I loved that experience and tried to repeat it the next semester but didn't want to dictate it. I asked the students in my spring 2022 wicked-problem class, What Should We Eat?, what kind of platform they wanted. I had hoped for an open science-fair-type event. The year before, which was entirely remote, the class invited our two guest speakers to attend the final presentation. (Both did.) In 2022 they decided upon a website. I asked my Twitter crowd for the best platforms, and we ended up using Google Sites. Some tabs were stronger than others. But it was a very positive experience.

Some students worked for many, many hours, planning, conducting research, meeting, compiling. You can see that too: https://sites.google.com/nd.edu/what-should-we-eat-spring-22/home. It's public too.

When we acknowledge the true abundance of possibilities, of formats, of "ways in" to the material, of important things to convey, of people who would benefit from the learning, then we are honest. We're preparing students for their actual lives. It's far messier and far more complicated than most schoolish writing. And far more effective.

Entirely different but equally engaging and absorbing approaches to learning, which some of the unessay creators also did, involve games. Not the game of school. Not gaming the system. But good games, the kinds that draw you in and make you want to keep learning, and playing.

Good Games and All the Good Stuff

"Reacting to the Past" or "Reacting," as it's often called, is a role-playing immersive "game" designed by Mark Carnes at Barnard College to teach history. It's been used since 1995 by professors in at least four hundred colleges and universities. It explains itself as "active learning pedagogy of role-playing games designed for higher education." It can be the entire course, or a supplement to more conventional materials.

Students are given premises, roles, problems, limits, and primary materials, but they're in charge, with the instructor merely watching, serving as "gamemaster." Based on the given premises and their different roles, students learn and make decisions; they become actively involved in historical inflection points, such as the immediate aftermath of the French Revolution; the class becomes the National Assembly with conservatives, moderates (Feuillants), radicals (Jacobins), indeterminates, and a loud crowd of Parisian revolutionaries.[33] They're embodied in their roles with costumes, sets, other rooms. It's social and absorbing. They conduct research—but in order to be convincing, not for a test. They perform at the end in front of a genuine audience. It includes both cooperation and competition; some students "win."

Reacting's design is based on deep understanding of how students learn: actively, and when they care deeply, and often socially, about something. There are now dozens of research studies, showing positive results in terms of self-efficacy, content, skills, confidence, persistence. The only thing that seems not to be correlated are student grades (and I take that as an indictment of grades, not the use of Reacting).[34]

From everything I've heard, students overall "really get into it." The reviews are fantastic; faculty claim it revives their teaching; that it motivates students to do far more than they are required to do; that it's fun. Students lead the class. There are celebrations. This is "flow," that absorption into an activity in which people lose track of time. It is one of the best kinds of well-being.

Students are learning with others—in ways that would not be possible alone, or from reading or hearing about it.

This contrasts sharply with conventional "banking" education. It's not very schoolish. In fact it's more like Renaissance fairs, Civil War reenactments, and complex video games like Minecraft or Fortnite. It's Dungeons and Dragons meets Mock Trial or Model UN. Not like a history lecture.

These kinds of games—and all that individual teachers also invent—lead to all the good stuff: collective effervescence, ritual, laughter, joint attention, love, exuberance, purpose, safety, movement, rhythm, eros, intrinsic motivation, desire, relationships, connection, and that central part of well-being, flow. These lead to deep learning but in ways that cannot be controlled by the teacher.

In this discussion of genres—both consumed and produced—the key questions are: What are learners *doing* in order to learn—both about a subject and about how to communicate about their knowledge of the subject? How does the *doing* contribute to the learning, not just demonstrate it? Learning usually requires some kind of action. This might mean conducting an experiment, making observations, baking a cake, solving a problem. In turn learning and its goals might require conveying some information to someone.

In contrast, *schoolish doing* is for evaluation and compliance and is often entirely predetermined, with rubrics, recipes, formulas. In science, problems or labs often are already constrained and teach particular algorithms within a topic. If these are known, there's little excitement.

Schoolish genres have expectations and constraints. Students worry about getting them right within the schoolish universe, where consequences spill out beyond its boundaries. Particular professors' genres and rules differ and thus may feel arbitrary to students, but nevertheless powerful because consequential. Schoolish genres include rules such as page lengths, fonts, prohibition of using the word *I*. (Every year I get several students asking if it is acceptable to use *I*.) Students typically have no idea, absolutely no idea, why in one class *I* might be prohibited and in another it would be welcomed. For students, this is simply another of the alien set of rules that they must constantly attend to—like whether you get double points for starting in Scrabble—in the game of school.

Each of these rules can be justified as the "training wheels" for real kinds of writing and learning: If students can learn to produce a paper with evidence and argumentation and structure, or can answer a set of questions very fast on a test, the argument goes, then they will be able to think clearly and be persuasive in their lives beyond school. Yet the evidence doesn't support these claims of "transfer."[35]

With its focus on what we might call schoolish genres, schoolishness prepares students poorly for life beyond schools.

In contrast, in the less-schoolish genres, we help make explicit, available to awareness, the conventions of an ever-expanding universe of genres. If the best use of precious gathering-for-learning time is helping students to expand awareness and helping them to add tools to use beyond this period of schoolishness, then helping learners decide on the effectiveness of and rules for specific *authentic* genres seems central, not an afterthought.

Besides, I want *everything* my students do to be valuable for learning in as many ways as possible: in content, skills, experience, connections, enjoyment, and confidence.

So then, we have to consider, which technologies help with that? How do we decide?

11

Tech and Media

From Clunky to Vibrant

> Technology embraces all aspects of the process of action upon
> matter, whether it is scratching one's nose, planting sweet potatoes,
> or making jumbo jets.
>
> Pierre Lemonnier, *Elements for an Anthropology of Technology*

"Tools" are a fundamental part of our species. We are tool-using and tool-creating hominids. Our lineage has been using tools from the very beginning, afforded by our opposable thumbs. (Some species of corvids and other animals also use tools, though in a far more restrictive sense.)[1] Tools are everything from clothing (allowing us to inhabit harsh environments) to buildings to knives, from stairs to pencils to airplanes. Every human interaction is facilitated and mediated by tools, to varying extents, and anyone setting up an environment in order to facilitate learning must include tools, though they're often presented by default. The built environment, which for most educational activities includes buildings, classrooms, and labs, dominates (see chapter 8, "Spaces and Places"), but it also exists within a natural environment. Walls are powerful in keeping out the rest of the world, but they have doors and windows. (Forest kindergartens reject even this basic assumption about the desirability of being separated from outside.)

Archaeologists and geologists use *technology* to include everything we make that intervenes between our minds and the world, from writing and speech to pencils and smartphones and projectors. Our world is permeated by technologies of all sorts. It's essential for all members of society to have facility with using as many types of technology as they need, and awareness of the affordances and limits, the possibilities and the dangers of each. At the same time, we know that new forms will be created in coming years, so we certainly can't give students every possible tool that they'll use in their lifetime. But we can prepare them by giving them a mix of already-familiar and not-yet-familiar technologies. Some technologies may require some learning, demonstrating that students are capable of using these various technologies.

A "medium" is how we communicate. It's something that is between two entities—in this case humans, but also the world. There is no mind-meld for us mortals, only various types of mediums, or media. Spoken language, writing, and images are all media, though popular usage often focuses on so-called new media.[2] Communications and media studies investigate various media, including radio, TV, phone, and more, but the principles are identical: something between entities, conveying a message, has properties that affect, constrain, enable, limit, facilitate (maybe not quite *determine*) the interaction. Marshall McLuhan said "the medium is the message," but that's too simple. That's *technological determinism*, often connected to *technological dystopianism*, in turn connected to moral panics about the destruction of civilization, or at least individuals, because of technology, often communicative technologies (in contrast to *technological utopianism*, or the view that all will be solved via technology).[3] Face-to-face communication is not the only kind of genuine or important communication. All communication is mediated—whether through speech or writing or devices. We never have direct access to people's intentions. People longing for the good old telephone forget the vitriol and panic surrounding that particular device.[4]

Similarly, "modalities" is a fancy way of talking about the various types of interaction and the ways these occur. Some modalities are speech, writing, images, or bodily movement, and these can be channeled via face-to-face interaction, via a tangible physical object like a codex (a book with pages bound together) or a scroll, or an electronic interface such as a computer, tablet, or phone. In the stream of nonschoolish life, these are often combined unconsciously. Someone telling a story may punctuate spoken sentences with gestures and nonlexical sounds, with physical objects or via images, possibly on electronic devices. We point out objects and directions without explicit exposition, especially among familiars. Basil Bernstein talked of "restricted code"—pointing and relying on shared knowledge to convey a message, without a need for explicit explanation (elaboration).[5] Schoolish telling, though, usually must be explicit. This is taught beginning in the ritual of show and tell, as Courtney Cazden demonstrated so brilliantly in her book *Classroom Discourse: The Language of Teaching and Learning*: communication is at the center of schools.[6]

Affordances and Constraints

Every bit of technology and every medium has what analysts call "affordances," behaviors facilitated without too much friction by the technology.[7] A chair affords a person to sit. A pencil affords writing. But they can also be repurposed. A chair can block a doorway. A pencil can retrieve a bead in a straw.

These concepts can be helpful as we analyze each technology: what does it permit? What is made easy? Difficult? What is it preventing?

Schoolish Tech

Some technologies used in schools are just the same as those outside schools: texts, computers, writing, numbers, books, and so forth. Some tech is unique to schools, including so-called Learning Management Systems (LMSs) and attendance software, proctoring software. Blackboards. Gradebooks that parents can check daily. Primers. Google Classroom. Computer labs. Or not so unique: lined paper, typewriters, Chromebooks, calculators.

Schoolish tech may include slates, pencils, pens. We recognize novices in the archaeological record through clumsy flintknapping, through tablets, rudimentary copying, slow script. When I was a child, we weren't allowed to use pens until perhaps fourth or fifth grade; pencils marked us as very young—as did the pre-cursive printing that we had until we were introduced to the mysteries of cursive in third grade. (The cursive moral panic . . . don't get me started again.)

Default assumptions about schooling begin from a position of control and limitation. What's permitted? What's prohibited? Familiar school-ish exclusions include prohibition of laptops in classrooms, calculators in examinations, consultation with others on exams, outsiders in rooms, prohibition of or use of food as reward, and at lower levels no free ingress and egress—including limitation of bathroom breaks.

Teachers are often overworked. A profitable industry sometimes called "ed tech" (educational technology) has arisen, offering to provide tools that help ease the lives of teachers by removing the necessity to choose among available options. These tools are usually expensive, profit-motivated, standardized, and designed with schoolish practices at their core. Some have come under intense scrutiny because of their surveillance practices (e.g., for remote "proctoring" to ensure no cheating—which presumes that no tools can or should be consulted—developed by companies with names such as Proctorio and ProctorU), even worse than the "plagiarism detection services" such as Turnitin, which at least assess only the texts produced by students, not their bodies and faces.[8] These companies often sell students' data, rely on racist algorithms to monitor students, and build in the worst of schoolishness.[9] A critic, Ian Linkletter, was sued in Canada by Proctorio for his tweets.[10]

The critics are brilliant and terrifying. Audrey Watters, historian of educational technology, talks about *The Monsters of Education Technology*, showing how ed techs do things *to* students, and treat them as objects. Shoshana Zuboff, sociologist, writes in *The Age of Surveillance Capitalism* about the general principles that surround our technology, which makes money by selling our private information. Ben Williamson has taken the very profitable educational technology company Pearson as a paradigmatic case of market devices that "can affect how universities, staff and students are translated into calculable objects, evaluated and ascribed value, with significant implications and effects on how they operate and function."[11] All these people point out that we need systemic legal protection, not simply the consent of individuals.

There is a lot of control. It's unequal, and it's dangerous.[12]

All these technological tools bake in assumptions about teacher-centered structures. Those who wish to teach in more student-centered ways can create workarounds, just as we can find ways to overcome the limitations of schoolish spaces. But the easy direction is in following where the tools lead. When everything is programmed, it's like a board game with its internal rules. Everything you need is included, including batteries. Schoolishness is built in.

Less-Schoolish Tech

In my quest to make my classes as "real" as possible, I've eschewed the school-only tools as much as possible. I reject the schoolish Learning Management System (LMS), whether Sakai or Canvas or Blackboard or Moodle. (Yes, yes, I know. Many faculty are obligated to use it. Laura Gibbs has a solution: she posts completion points for assignments.)[13] There is the LMS with its dreadful, revealing "Management" smack dab in the middle. I don't want to "manage" the learning. I want to *free* my students: from the tyranny of domination by systems, from pleasing the rubric, from placing emphasis on the game of school, the grading game. From schoolishness. If, as bell hooks said, the classroom is a site for liberation, then we have to work hard at that, right?

Students often go looking for the LMS in my classes. Why shouldn't they expect to use it in my class, given that they use it in all other classes? I continue to tweak my approach to facilitate the finding of class materials. (The latest iteration, 2022, has everything linked on the syllabus, a Google Doc that is constantly updated, as a "liquid syllabus.")

It's not only the name of the product that makes me shudder, and it's not only that students have no access to it, or to the work and discussions posted there, once they graduate.[14] It's also that these systems are created with a top-down default model of learning—the schoolish model. Teacher disseminates, students receive, unless the teacher bestows the obligation to discuss. Grade books, point distribution, quizzes . . . all is built in, baked into their fabric, as are conversational structures.

I tried to use Google Classroom, but there's a tab at the top of the website for "Grades," and I couldn't figure out how to remove it, even after consulting forums to inquire about using it.[15]

I don't need this system.

Instead I use "real" tools—things that were not developed for schools, but for life. I'm never completely satisfied, but here's what I've made work (in 2022; surely newer things will also turn up), and why.

Communication

Email is the bane of faculty members' existence. Students scarcely use it at all. It's hard to keep track of everything that I get on email, and I don't want students' fates connected to something that risky. The formality required of email is off-putting. It's not an enjoyable medium; students can't initiate conversations with one another.

Instead, we communicate with a tool called Slack. You've probably heard of it by now. Yes, it's a Silicon Valley tool for business, but it's a real-world tool, something outside the school-iverse. It looks pretty good, works great on phones, has a playfulness about it.[16] And once students get used to it, it *fosters student-to-student communication* about the urgent but not burning questions: "Where is the reading?" and "When is that interview due?" Sometimes it leads in unexpected directions. In fall 2021, two students from my class happened to see each other at an out-of-town football game and posted a photo on Slack. Students have used it to create places for their project teams, and some classes have suggested channels on their own. When I get the same questions from several students, I direct them to the "logistics channel," where I may have already answered it for everyone. Eventually, some individuals acknowledge their power to answer classmates' questions, and maybe, just maybe, I get some other questions. Maybe burning questions about the nature of life, or the ways our actions make us who we are.

After I returned from pandemic remote teaching in 2021–22, students were absent in large numbers. I created a channel called "Summarizing for Absent but Not Forgotten Classmates." When I remembered to do it, the students and I might spend one or two minutes at the end of class jotting down a few notes about what we had done. Reviewing is good pedagogical practice, anyway. The fact that students would get multiple perspectives on what we had done is valuable; they appreciated the chance to find out what they had missed.

Sharing Work

Because it's important for me that my students learn from one another and have an audience beyond me, I've tried to figure out how to get students' work available to others. In pre-COVID days I still sometimes circulated physical copies of papers, though increasingly students shared electronic versions. In recent years I've been using a Google Drive system, in which projects are posted within a folder to which others have access. (There's also a "Private with Susan" folder for reflections on work, and also for any work that they may be reluctant to have other students see.)

If students make movies or podcasts, they can post the link. (Google as a corporation is not blameless; it certainly has search algorithms that have been critiqued, and it sells our information, besides running ads.)

When I used to ask students to do blogs, I used Blogger; Weebly; Word-Press; Google Sites. I'm constantly seeking beautiful, intuitive tools that facilitate student ownership of their own learning, individually and collectively. Intuition and facility change over time. After assigning blogs, I suddenly noticed that blogging was over. In fall 2020, online completely, I used Google Sites for my syllabus. I toyed with the idea of having the students create individual websites too, a skill useful beyond the class. But in the pandemic context, one more thing was just too much.

Starting in 2021 I've been trying to get students to create some public-facing work, at least at the end of the semester. As you saw in "Genres of Production," students have posted on Pressbooks and Google Sites. Other faculty use many other platforms.

But the principle is simple: Anything that's just learning-for-school is rejected.

Remember the Goals!

If one of the goals of schooling is to create conditions for independent, confident learning together, then the best tools, tech, media will contribute to that goal.

We find excellent discussions of *principles* for making decisions about which particular tech should be used—what Derek Bruff calls "intentional tech"—in the works of Bruff, Jenae Cohn, and Michelle D. Miller, among many others.[17] Bruff ties technology to pedagogical goals and likes to shake things up by saying, for instance, that wheels on chairs are a kind of tech that makes a big difference. Cohn is interested especially in reading, but some of the questions she asks of reading tools are relevant to any tool: What does this tool do? What are its core functions? Where does the tool work? Who is using it? How is privacy protected? What kinds of bodies can use it? She asks how users can keep their own intellectual property after the course ends.[18] Miller is interested in remembering and forgetting in the context of contemporary technology. In her chapter called "The Devices We Can't Put Down," she explains how memory and distraction work; she admits that the handwriting-versus-laptop debate has often overstated the results. But still she warns us to reduce reliance on always searching for information on smartphones, which she says are "uniquely distracting." She's enthusiastic about tools such as Kahoot! and Quizlet, for retrieval practice, or polling applications (Poll Everywhere). She suggests that faculty really learn how different technologies support or reduce deep learning, which depends on memory—but goes beyond merely remembering.[19]

Miscellaneous

Here's a list of some of the tech and some of the media I've been playing with in the classroom:

- Sticky notes on walls and whiteboards
- Colored markers on whiteboards
- Furniture movement
- Zoom
- Chat on Zoom
- Polls
- Surveys
- Face-to-face interactions
- Small groups
- Pairs
- "Speed dating"
- Index cards
- Notebooks

- Pens
- Books
- Printouts
- Laptops
- iPads
- Phones
- Handwriting
- Slack
- Instagram
- Google Drive
- Google Forms
- Google Sites
- Google Jamboard
- Poll Everywhere
- Canva
- WordCloud
- Flip
- Hypothes.is

Many of these items, these tools, modalities, technologies, have been much discussed, whether by enthusiasts and entrepreneurs or by detractors alarmed to the point of moral panic. Each new technology, especially communicative technologies, has given rise to a period of dissent, from the very first technology of writing (we have no records about the tension over spoken language), to printing, telegraph, radio, telephone, movies, and more. The list I've put here will be outdated by the time this book is published.

Yet many of the issues are the same, even while the details change: How expensive? How is it paid for? Who pays? Who profits? Who controls it? What are its psychological and social effects? What about surveillance and privacy? What about persistence? What are the aesthetics?

In Wendell Berry's piece "Why I Am NOT Going to Buy a Computer," he argues from first principles that any tool replacing an old one should have the following characteristics:

1. The new tool should be cheaper than the one it replaces.
2. It should be at least as small in scale as the one it replaces.

3. It should do work that is clearly and demonstrably better than the one it replaces.
4. It should use less energy than the one it replaces.
5. If possible, it should use some form of solar energy, such as that of the body.
6. It should be repairable by a person of ordinary intelligence, provided that he or she has the necessary tools.
7. It should be purchasable and repairable as near to home as possible.
8. It should come from a small, privately owned shop or store that will take it back for maintenance and repair.
9. It should not replace or disrupt anything good that already exists, and this includes family and community relationships.[20]

My major principles are that any tech should contribute to and not impede my largest goal of helping students foster independent, confident, engaged, enjoyable, and cooperative learning.

Zoom Exhaustion (from 2020)

Twitter, Facebook and the news media are filled with people lamenting their weariness after Zoom class sessions. I feel that, too.[21]

The first day I had two Zoom classes in a row, I ended up bleary-eyed and exhausted. I just sat and watched something silly on Netflix, drank a glass of wine, and did nothing productive until I could finally go to sleep. I'd had countless Zoom meetings previously, many of which I had hosted. Some were almost joy filled. So what was different?

I have spent a lot of time thinking, posting, talking about this. And it is clear: the essential difference is that videoconferencing is *nearly* a replication of face-to-face interaction but not quite, and for that reason it depletes our energy. And anthropology can help explain what's different. (I'm using Zoom to represent videoconferencing platforms in general. And I treasure and appreciate their benefits for connecting distant loved ones, despite the critique that follows.)

In a Zoom classroom with thirty students, we see faces—just like in a classroom. We see eye movement. We can hear voices. It can even be enhanced by chat—almost like hearing people thinking out loud. It is multimodal, to some extent. We see gestures, at least some big ones. All this is information used by our human capacity for understanding interaction. So far, so good.

Zoom works well for faculty members who lecture, or for groups that have formal meetings, with rules for who speaks and how to signal an interest in speaking. As long as the symphony is directed by an authority figure, order can be kept. The trumpets come in on cue. It is calm. Information and views can be exchanged. It beats a long email exchange any day!

But in the more interactive, active classrooms that I aim to create, this is terrible. When a classroom aims for (doesn't always achieve) democratic, nonauthoritarian conversation, rather than orchestrated teacher-centered pedagogy, all the tools of human interaction are recruited.

Over my decades of teaching, I've learned to read a room pretty well: the harmonized posture, the breaths, the laughter, the eye gaze. My classes are successful when students are so excited that they want to speak over each other out of sheer exuberance. When people sit up straight and say, "Wait! Do you mean . . . ?" because they have a brand-new way to understand the world—that's the superpower of anthropology. When students huddling around a text point to it, their gazes converging, and create a document they're proud of. When people laugh simultaneously. When the affect and the cognition and the interaction work together.

I have also analyzed conversation quite a bit. In "ordinary" conversation there is often brief overlap, as one speaker ends an utterance and another begins. And when it works well—when the hearer is successful at matching the prosodic contours, the rhythms and speeds of the speaker, and anticipating the ending of the utterance—it's like a symphony. And even when we need to repair the interaction, it's incorporated into the conversation, sometimes with humor. Conversation has rhythm. Even our brain waves synchronize in a conversation.[22] "The emotional/aesthetic experience of a perfectly tuned conversation is as ecstatic as an artistic experience," Deborah Tannen writes. "It is a ratification of one's place in the world and one's way of being human . . . 'a vision of sanity'" (quoting A. L. Becker at the end).[23]

Anthropologists, linguists, and sociologists who analyze conversation, which varies around the world, have shown some common traits. N. J. Enfield's recent book *How We Talk* and the work of conversation analysts such as the late Charles Goodwin point to multimodality, rules about eye gaze, patterns for rapid turn taking, and near-universal reliance on microsecond timing.[24] Goodwin reminds us that "co-operative action sits at the center of human language, and symbols are essentially co-operative structures in which one party is operating on another."

This is not what my Zoom classrooms are like.

There is constant need to repair, to apologize. People are constantly talking at the same time and interrupting someone else's signal. I am constantly switching views from one screen to another, to scan the faces (at least of those who haven't chosen to post a blank screen, permitting rest, multitasking, or even absence). I am watching the eyes, listening for completion, listening for that intake of breath that indicates readiness to talk. I am continually repressing my lifelong, trained habit of uttering simultaneous encouragement through "continuers," those back-channel cues that encourage the speaker to go on. *Mmm-hmm, yeah, I know*. None of that works; the platform is made for a single speaker at a time. It's the folk model of how conversation works, but not what we actually find in practice.

In regular classrooms, we notice heads nodding, distracted, gazing in one direction or another.[25]

Humans use eye gaze as communicative information; that's why we have the whites of our eyes, the sclera.[26] (It's not only to look *at* someone; sometimes looking away is proper. Many primates, including many humans, see direct gaze as threat.) On Zoom, people may generally nod, but eye gaze can't be tracked. We seek "joint attention"—that confirmation that everyone is sharing the focus. We get stares, or looking down or away, or watching the image on a screen. *What does it mean?* We always want to know. *Why did they do that?*

That's because, when we interact, the meaning is not just about the content, the semantics. Meaning is always also pragmatic: it does things. Did she say *I'm confused about the assignment* as an accusation or as an inside joke or because she needed clarification or to show leadership or simply to invite clarification? Was the laughter *with* me or *at* me?

In the prototypical usage of these platforms, everyone is looking forward. A camera is broadcasting (unless people turn off their video), but we're not really looking at each other.

So all the communicative signs that embodied humans rely on are thinned, flattened, made more effortful or entirely impossible. Yet we interpret them anyway.

Technology does not completely determine our interactions. The medium is not always the message. Writing, *pace* Socrates, has brought some good to the world.[27] We can write hymns of praise or also calls to hate. A hammer can build a sanctuary—or can murder an innocent person. These technologies, though, have *affordances*, as Gibson pointed out.[28] It is easier to sit facing forward on a chair, though you can also sit backward. It is possible to use

Facebook for lyric poetry. Users can contravene the designers' intentions.[29] I'm sure there's a way to *hack* Zoom—and I don't mean Zoombomb; I mean to roll up our sleeves and find a way to improve from within.

Pedagogy and interaction are quite nearly baked in, though, to our platforms. Banked classrooms with lecterns assume a single central speaker and multiple listeners—though a determined teacher can have students turn around even in stadium-type seating. Learning management systems usually presume that the instructor controls all the communication, unless a discussion board is enabled.

The "pivot to online learning" or "online teaching" affords a number of different opportunities: for asynchronous interaction in discussions, for posting of brief video messages. Many brilliant pedagogues are using these options well. I embrace this, and surely we all need to learn about more affordances of more platforms.

I have used Zoom's small-group breakout room for some tasks to some effect, though it is cumbersome. In one class, where they are in project teams, I have to manually put the students into groups, and it takes measurable minutes, and then joining groups takes a little while, and then exiting each group takes time. . . . I haven't counted, but it definitely takes time, and students are frustrated with all their teachers having to learn the intricacies of Zoom. The dead time is, well, deadly to the rhythms.

When I use technological platforms like Zoom that provide some imitations of face-to-face interaction, what I miss most is the three-dimensional faces and the bodies and the eyes and the breaths.

Humans are delicately attuned to each other's complete presence.[30] If a perfectly tuned conversation provides a "vision of sanity," then it is no wonder that an awkward, clunky, interrupted conversation provides the opposite. We are constantly interpreting others' movements, timing, breaths, gazes, encouragement. It is our beautiful endowment. So we're interpreting the misaligned gazes, the interrupted conversation, as stemming from the technology, not from the interlocutor. And that, my human friends, is a tale of human-technology-semiotic mismatch.

When I returned to the classroom after teaching remotely for a year, I found myself struggling to juggle all the tech. I had grown very fond of the "chat" feature in Zoom—something that permitted even socially anxious students to volunteer to talk. I liked the ready access to interactive documents (such as Google Docs), whereas if we were together in a room, I had to have students pull out their computers.

The tech is a set of possibilities, temptations, limitations, and guidance. The more we can understand intentionally about it, the more humane and effective it can be.

Attending (to) Bodies

From Stillness, Isolation, Normativity, and Control to Action, Connection, Variation, and Agency

> Even as scientific evidence of the link between social interaction and intelligent thought accumulates, our society remains mired in a brainbound approach to cognition; our activities at school and at work still treat thinking as the manipulation of abstract symbols inside individual heads.
>
> ANNIE MURPHY PAUL, *The Extended Mind*

> Being-for-itself must be wholly bodily and it must be wholly consciousness; it cannot be *united* with a body.
>
> JEAN-PAUL SARTRE, *Being and Nothingness*

D. W. Winnicott writes that "the True Self comes from the aliveness of the body tissues and the working of body-functions, including the heart's action and breathing."[1]

In contrast, schoolish bodies are still. They serve the brain. They're separate from each other, not touching. They're confined and have no needs except on schedule. They're healthy and present and visible. They're predictable, and they are never disruptive. They don't need to leave the room, and they are not distracting. They're dressed "appropriately," and they are able to do whatever is anticipated by the teacher. They're of a certain standard size, and often of a particular racial, ethnic, and national origin. They're not too attractive nor too unattractive. They fit in the furniture. They obey on command.

In the early years of school, activities such as clapping and running around and dancing draw on the body. But most of the exuberant bodily actions occur only in officially sanctioned time slots, such as the dwindling recess or gym class. Later on, schoolish bodies also function effectively in athletic competitions in order to bring honor and glory to the institution itself. But this athletic prowess must be channeled. Until university, all bodies at school are regulated. Eating, drinking, and attending to needs such as going to the bathroom or needing a break from the visibility of others require permission. Permission requested may be denied.

Schoolish bodies are still, isolated, uniform, and controlled.

Bodily Beings

"Embodied" sounds like there's something (a mind? a brain? a self?) placed within a body. But our minds are bodily. Three books published in 2021 emphasized this point, two of them directly concerned with education and one with implications for it: *Minding Bodies* by Susan Hrach, *The Extended Mind* by Annie Murphy Paul, and *Foundations of Embodied Learning: A Paradigm for Education* by Mitchell J. Nathan. Hrach (pronounced "rock") summarizes what we need to know about the body and learning in six principles:

1. Like clouds or waves, our bodies are in a state of constant motion.
2. Our ever-moving bodies prize efficiency.
3. Our efficient bodies engage tools, technologies, and other people to extend our capacities.
4. Each of us affects the embodied ecosystem of others.
5. Knowledge is constructed through embodied experience.
6. Our bodies reward learning.[2]

Her book is filled with support for these claims, with examples and suggestions for how to take advantage of these principles in conventional schools, such as by taking field trips at least around campus, if not off

campus, incorporating movement in the classroom, incorporating mul-
tisensory dimensions, and more. The book is superb. I build on it, and
many others, as I continue here.

Hunger for the Body: Alienation from Physical Experience, and
Restoration for Well-Being

Human beings are not "souls in the machine." Our bodies reflect and
cause our well-being. Even calling them "our bodies" makes a distinction between the "we" who have them and the "bodies" that we possess. We are bodily beings. And as bodily beings we have certain basic,
fundamental needs in order to function well. When these are missing, we
are alienated. Certainly the stereotypical Cartesian dualism—mind versus body—contributes to a sense that the body is not the person. A Christian asceticism argues that the body is to be overcome with discipline,[3]
through biopower.[4] And a modernist fable of postbody, postmaterial essence, like food that could be consumed in a pill, or a magic, minimalist
potion, while we don't ever have to touch the ground or work, feeds into
the sense that the body is troublesome and has to be shed so that we can
become just a brain, maybe watching video games.

I'm not a physiologist, not a doctor. But when the body is neglected—
I don't mean by eating fried food and not exercising, but by doing
nothing—the automatic inputs of experience are lacking. And hence something else needs to replace it.

I'm not quite persuaded by Robin Dunbar's grooming hypothesis
that language evolved to replace physical grooming, but it's significant
that primates, and most animals, use their bodies in contact with the
environment and other beings.[5] My colleagues Jim McKenna and Lee
Gettler studied the brain waves of mothers sleeping with their babies.
We change with physical contact. We relax. We exhale when we are
touched.[6] Humans live for the satisfaction and pleasure from endor-
phins, oxytocin, serotonin, dopamine.[7] The pop culture boiled-down
message that "oxytocin is the happy drug" or "love hormone" is
oversimple.[8] But it is certainly the case that many of our most profound,
and intense, experiences are physical, mediated through our semiotic
and cultural interpretations.

"Physical activity" doesn't have to be gym class. In the recent past
it included walking (culturally variable though it is), walking up stairs,

opening car windows, chewing, carrying. . . . All our "labor-saving devices" (we don't call them that anymore, of course) have also been body-deprivation devices.[9] If you don't have to get up to change the TV channel, and now you can command Alexa to turn on the water . . . what is the use of the body? Since teachers, as early as kindergarten, are forbidden to touch students, and students can't touch each other during the day, and colleagues are afraid that hugs will be taken as assault, and we don't use our bodies to walk and convey information across town, and we don't have to scrub clothes against rocks or carry water miles across town or whittle tools or butcher animals or chew tough plants to extract some nutrients, our poor bodies are useless, appendages, alien.

Authentic *use* of the body for work is part of our nature. But in the contemporary world we are largely alienated from our bodies. They are being-for-others, where appearances, not efficacy, are the measure. "The gaze alienates subjects from themselves by causing the subject to identify with itself as the *objet-a*, the object of the drives," writes Phil Lee in an annotation of Jacques Lacan's psychoanalytic analysis of the difference between the "eye" and "the gaze."[10] We look into mirrors to anticipate how we will appear to others' gazes, of which we (especially women) are constantly aware.[11] Our bodies are not for ourselves, but for others. We engage in activities so we can post images of them on social media.

Beyond that, we scarcely need bodies. Our lives lack texture. Even our food is so smooth we scarcely need to chew it. Our jaws have literally shrunk; our teeth don't fit in our mouths.[12] We have no processing to do. Our food arrives premade, in smooth plastic packages. And we scarcely have appetites—unless we're among the billion food-insecure people on a planet of food waste, human-made political famines, and diseases of overconsumption. We are manipulated by advertising, marketing, so our appetites are alienated.

Our lives lack sensation—the texture of fabrics, the roughness of furniture. We shun smells. Our feet, with all their sensory receptors, become carriers of branded status, never feeling the ground. We don't jump, reach, roll, carry. All is done by devices. (Some people still do physical labor, of course.)

And our screens smooth out communication. During COVID times, even things that were previously unremarkably physical and social—funerals, weddings, communion, naturalization ceremonies, dinner parties, bat mitzvahs, saying a last goodbye to a loved one—migrated onto screens. Yay because connection became possible; boo because it felt the same as everything else. No wonder so many people disregarded the public health mandates and plunged too quickly into gathering.

Our senses deprived, they nevertheless crave something, so people resort to cutting, adventure, eating in quantity.

We need to use our feet; bipedality (walking on two legs) is one of the key features of our species. We need to chew our food. We need human interaction: physical, visual, verbal. We can have some of it on screens, in the smooth world of new media; dana boyd writes of the importance for LGBTQ youth outside big cities of the communities they have found online.[13] People fall in love online; they maintain relationships; they learn. But there must still be something for the body to do. There is a body even in online learning—possibly stiff, possibly invisible, possibly miserable, possibly anxious.[14] We develop "tech neck," dry eyes, frozen shoulder.

I reject the technological determinism that fetishizes face-to-face communication and lambastes digital communication.[15] This line of thought, technophobia, is the same kind of thinking that emphasizes the importance of taking notes by hand and of learning cursive rather than keyboarding.[16] I love new media, and technology. But as they smooth our world, we crave using our bodies and brains, which evolved for movement, for touch, for eye gaze, for breathing, for a lot of actual use.[17]

During the COVID-19 interlude, when all over the world students shifted, "pivoted," online, we had a chance to experience the positive and negative dimensions of living entirely virtually.

There were benefits.

In my own family, we began to have Friday night Shabbat Zoom celebrations, twenty-eight of us connected and checking in regularly. (We've continued for three years, and counting.) Other friends had extended-family Passover seders, with participants from three or four continents. I've mourned with people half a continent away, and watched a cousin's wedding, recorded on Facebook live.

And while there were terrific moments, weddings, proposals, checking in with grandparents, there was also something profoundly missing.

Living on screens is hard on the eyes, and starves, while immobilizing, the body.

The "digital divide" also became a thing. So many students had no up-to-date equipment, or couldn't afford broadband. They lived in crowded conditions, or didn't have access to reliable private spaces. School buses provided internet hot spots. People did homework outside public libraries, or at McDonalds. Many just disappeared.

And—as one student was reported on Twitter to have said, though I've been unable to track it down—"It's like someone took a sieve and ran school through it, straining it of all the parts I like."

I bet eleventh-grade English grammar tests are not the parts they like best.

Humans need to engage their bodies.

Without claiming expertise or simple solutions, I mention here merely that abundant research shows that exercise and movement are helpful, and possibly necessary, for treating many challenges: depression, anxiety, attention deficit hyperactivity disorder. When the mind is returned to its role as serving the body and making connections with the environment, benefits of all sorts accrue.[18]

Schoolish Bodies: All Body, All the Time

Some subset of a group of marine invertebrates (animals without backbones), closely related to vertebrates, called tunicates have a rudimentary, flexible backbone-like structure (notochord) when young. Once one of these tunicates finds a place to plant itself for the rest of its life, it doesn't need the structure anymore. It finds a location in the sea, sets down a root within its "tunic," and loses its pseudo–spinal cord. Then it reproduces. Movement is no longer needed. If we didn't have to move, we would not need brains, which are largely in service to motion. Our brains exist to serve our actions.[19]

And this is true, whether we are acting or not.

So if we aren't acting, part of our brain and part of our body are, as it were, revving the motor without going into gear (to use an old automotive image; I grew up outside Detroit, which used to be known for cars). What happens to all that torque?

We use it somehow. If we aren't moving from office to classroom to restaurant to gym, or goofing around with friends in the cafeteria, or running up and down stairs, or even just walking to the parking lot, what is that hungry body doing?

Standardization and Uniformity: The Pathologizing
and Stigmatizing of Difference

Factories require uniform inputs. The "inputs" of schools are the learners and the teaching, and it's quite convenient to assume singular, generic
learners. "The learner," "the student." The problem is that this isn't how
learners, students, or humans actually are.

We learn with our bodies, in our bodies, through our bodies in particular contexts and in particular places. This has relevance for things
like race and ability and age and size; a shorthand is "positionality," with
reminders that they all intersect. All human learners bring their full bodies
to all their experiences—even when bodies are treated as impediments, or
nonexistent, or must be controlled and stilled.

It matters if the teacher is a five-foot-tall, sixty-seven-year-old Chinese
woman with glasses in a wheelchair, or if the teacher is a six-foot-seven,
forty-year-old Black man in a leather jacket. It matters if she's a twenty-
five-year-old TA or if he's an endowed professor in a corduroy jacket with
leather patches on the elbows. It matters if the professor is a knockdown
beauty in a pencil skirt, or an athlete in sweats. It matters if the professor
speaks with an accent, or looks like someone who speaks with an accent.
There's research that even looking at a face that appears to be from another race impedes comprehension from a largely white audience.[20]

Race. Ability. Age. Size. Gender. Sexuality. Nationality. Beauty.

The teachers' characteristics matter.

The co-learners' characteristics matter.

Multiplicity and Universal Design   You know that idea of "learning
styles"? Auditory, visual, kinesthetic learner? Maybe you took a workshop on it, or did a quiz. Well, cognitive scientists have shown it's not real.
People may have preferences, but they don't necessarily actually learn best
in the ways they are comfortable with.[21]

But what *is* real is that people learn best when many modalities are
simultaneously recruited. Because it helps everyone.

Universal Design for Learning, UDL, reminds educators to employ
multiple—readable, audible, academic, popular—ways to get the material and the experience. The more ways students have to enter into the
material, for a wide range of bodies, abilities, interests, tastes, and prior

experiences, the better. This is not to stigmatize those who specifically are granted "accommodation" by the office of disabilities, but rather to acknowledge that there's always bound to be a range. We only need Universal Design for Learning because our structures are so clearly designed for a single type of person.

Abilities, Disabilities, and Other Considerations   The largest "minority" group in the world is people with disabilities.[22] Estimates are that about one billion people—15 percent of the world's population—have some sort of disability: visible or invisible, physical, mental, intellectual, sensory, or other. If we include myopia, the number rises quickly.

Yet schoolishness presupposes all no-disability students. As an afterthought, some accommodations may be made. In the past, some students were often excluded from schooling entirely; but with the notion of schooling as a human right, schools—public, not private—are obligated to find ways to meet the needs of all students.

Students with learning differences often are permitted, with proof, to develop an Individualized Education Plan (lower levels), or accommodations. Those with physical disabilities might be permitted an assistant, or different accommodations.

Uniforms, Dress Codes, and School Gear   In many settings, from primary through secondary school, students are often required to wear uniforms. The name gives it away: students are to be "uniform," the same, in clothing that identifies them as members of particular classes of person: age, gender, institution. Students sometimes love their uniforms because they evoke feelings of belonging. Some deplore them. Some resist actively, by defying the rules. Some fight over them.

Control of clothing, like bodies, has many elements, including regulating gender and sexuality through dress codes. Until I was in junior high, girls at my public schools had to wear skirts. I remember being cold, in southeast Michigan, standing and playing on playgrounds. But when I try to dredge up memories of protest, I come up short. In 2022 in the United States a charter school—publicly funded but under local control—lost a lawsuit challenging the requirement that girls wear skirts.[23] Infringements of clothing codes are often punished. And someone is always watching.

Of course there can also be voluntary identifications through athletic wear and logos, which bond students through the "brand." (My father wears his UM gear whenever he travels, to attract like-minded University of Michigan fans.)

Surveillance Another aspect of pedagogy is surveillance, to ensure (1) compliance and (2) lack of deviance. This deviance can be simply eating or drinking something not permitted at a certain time or place, or playing the game of school and possibly cheating.

During COVID, this all reached levels predictable but not quite envisioned by most faculty.

A clearly pressing issue arose in spring 2020, when courses that had been planned to be in-person had to "pivot" to online. Exams that would have had physical proctoring had to be conducted online. This was complicated; few faculty could possibly redo their assessment instruments (= tests) overnight; sometimes the tests were uniform for many sections of the same course.

Here's where a number of "ed tech" companies were standing ready. They had digital proctoring apps and algorithms, with names like Proctorio and ProctorU, and materials all prepared. The only hurdle was to get universities to sign up. These proctoring applications work in different ways, from tracking eye movement (to ensure that students look only at the single screen) to having human proctors pop into the Zoom exam at unpredictable times. It was uncannily like the panopticon that Jeremy Bentham hypothesized would keep prisoners from misbehaving and that Foucault extended to all modern life, where we are not only surveilled by governments, doctors, teachers, and priests, but by our own internalized judges, in a kind of self-government that destroys our more humane freedoms to act without second-guessing ourselves.

This pedagogical and panoptic eye extended deeper into the pandemic semester of fall 2020, as faculty continued to test students and try to figure out ways to ensure "academic integrity."[24] Critiques of monitoring of bodily functions cite ethical principles of trust versus suspicion. They also highlight technical problems such as the failure of artificial intelligence and facial recognition software to differentiate Black faces.[25] A further critique involves the ownership of personal information, which could be monetized in the context of what Shoshana Zuboff calls "surveillance capitalism."[26] A Canadian librarian, Ian Linkletter, was sued by Proctorio for publicly sharing training material from the company, as a warning to others (though the suit alleges only unauthorized sharing, in violation of rules of service). He has had to raise enormous amounts of money for his legal fees, including through organizing a teach-in, Against Surveillance, on December 1, 2020, which I attended.[27] As of the time of publication, the suit is ongoing.[28]

Schoolish Attention and Distraction

When I ask in talks "What would you like to improve in your classes?" a common response is "engagement and participation." Consternation about students' attention and focus abounds, for example in books about the distractedness of life in general, and of life in college, or about ADHD and the temptations that pull us from what we're trying to focus on.[29] Headlines blame smartphones and technology, with their quick, addictive rewards and "likes" and other attention from others, but also poor food, lack of exercise, lack of free play.

Attention is a physical matter. Michelle Miller points out that attention is required for learning, observed through bodily comportment. But we should admit that paying constant attention is exhausting.

Entrepreneur self-help guru Tim Ferris advocates a four-hour work-week. June Huh, the 2022 winner of the Fields Medal mathematics prize and a MacArthur "genius" grant, does three hours of focused work a day.[30] Yet we expect our students to be attentive for many hours every weekday, and even after school.

Time for daydreaming, for resting, is known to support learning—and well-being—but it's stigmatized in schoolish settings. (The default mode network, operating in doodling and wandering, is known to support creativity and integration of new knowledge.)[31] Yet schoolish attention is supposed to be constant, and visible to those surveilling it.

Anthropologists have shown alternative forms of attention. Suzanne Gaskins, with Ruth Paradise, has been showing that "open attention," which is both "wide-angled," such as scanning the environment, and "abiding," or sustained over time, is common in the Mayan communities where Gaskins has conducted fieldwork for four decades.[32]

Lack of attention has been medicalized as "attention deficit (hyperactivity) disorder." It's a serious problem affecting millions of children and adults, and sometimes treated and treatable by medication. But it's also a consequence of the need for stillness. As Johann Hari writes in his thoughtful investigation into attention problems, *Stolen Focus*, comparing children in schools with polar bears in zoos, and quoting a reluctant zookeeper,

> The problem is you've taken a polar bear out of the polar environment, and you've stuck it in a zoo. . . . Polar bears in nature will walk for miles across the Arctic tundra. They look for seal places, and they swim, and they eat seals. The exhibit . . . is nothing like real life. . . . [In zoos] they pace to appease the inner pain of being denied a real life. . . . They've got all these instincts that are all intact, that they're unable to utilize. The long-term solution is to shut down zoos . . . and to let all animals live in an environment that is compatible with their natures.[33]

So while medication can help polar bears, and children, cope with being stuck in zoo-ish, schoolish settings, it's not a solution. The solution is to change the settings to fit better with the residents' nature. Some propose movement as best medicine for depression; it also helps learning. Jessica Zeller studies dance education and embodiment.[34] Judith Lynne Hanna argues in *Dancing to Learn* that "dance in itself is more than just valuable. Learning to dance contributes to brain development, knowledge, mental and physical health, and fun."[35] Anything engaging bodily beings is an improvement.

Gaze and Faces   Schoolish bodies house brains, and the action of those brains is assumed to be readable via the faces, and especially the eyes, of the dutiful, attentive student.

Masks, veils, and cameras-off are evidence that revealing faces is uncomfortable, especially with individuals with any form of anxiety. In East Asia a focus on *face* is a reminder that facing others, having one's face viewed, is powerful and meaningful and fraught with peril.[36]

Much effort in socializing students from diverse backgrounds—Indigenous, urban, East Asian—into white middle-class US norms forces them to "look people in the eye." In so many other societies, this is impolite or downright dangerous, yet it's so normalized that students can be punished for failing to fulfill this mandate. Susan Philips showed in her beautiful ethnographic account of the Warm Springs Indians, *The*

Invisible Culture, how Anglo and Indian norms of interaction conflicted, in part on this point.[37]

A sixteen-year-old girl who had moved from Nigeria to Tasmania, Australia, reported, "Teachers here expected me to look them in the eye when talking to them but coming from Nigeria, that was a sign of disrespect. I have learned to look teachers in the eye because they think it is rude not to."[38] Neurodivergent students, such as the ten-year-old autistic boy Brandon Strong, may be punished for failing to "look teachers in the eye."[39]

Cultural expectations about bodily interaction vary considerably, and when students from one setting move to another, they may find themselves at a disadvantage. Lee Arbouin in *The Nottingham Connection* noticed teachers' lack of understanding of cultural differences, such as Jamaican-heritage children being unwilling to wear other kids' swimsuits or children from Southeast Asia not looking teachers in the eye because they *were demonstrating respect to elders.*[40]

Severe Anxiety Many students report severe anxiety, and not only about the ability to get their work done. Many are anxious about social performance, about speaking in public. So when "discussion" and "participation" are required—even in the name of democracy and "active learning"—some people are uncomfortable, sometimes to the point of acute panic. Sarah Rose Cavanagh, a psychologist who researches affect in the context of education, wrote a stunningly honest piece in the *Chronicle of Higher Education* about her own struggles with anxiety, her inability to counter them through willpower, or in the face of threats.

Cavanagh's social anxiety in high school transformed into full-blown panic attacks in college, when she started working as a volunteer on a hotline for parents experiencing stress, and heard horrific accounts.

> A true panic attack is all-encompassing and utterly incapacitating. When one strikes, every single biological system in my body rebels—the respiratory, the digestive, the neurological. Most times, I have to confine myself to a bathroom, laying on the floor shaking and gasping for air and repeatedly sick to my stomach, the cool tile against my forehead the only balm. The physical symptoms would be more bearable if they didn't also come with an unnerving sense of being separate from my typical waking

self (depersonalization) and unmoored from ordinary reality (derealization), my swirling thoughts a deep, dizzy tangle from which there is no respite.[41]

This is the kind of thing that a threat of a bad grade can't combat. Requiring someone with this kind of response to public presentation to give a presentation is not going to help.

Cavanagh is now a college professor and a public speaker. She attributes her own transformation to her women's studies classes, where discussion and participation were required but the conditions were not threatening. She says this is the ideal way out for severe anxiety: "controlled exposure in a safe setting. The safety of the setting is key."[42] Safety doesn't mean isolation from challenge; it has to do with an ineffable sense of being welcome—whoever you are. This can be especially hard for people from underrepresented groups.

Cavanagh quotes Sean Michael Morris, who writes of "an orientation toward nurturing not just the intellect of your students but also their emotional lives." Morris speaks of *love*: "Love in pedagogical work is an orientation. . . . It is a decision to commit first to the community of learners and second to the material we've come to teach."

There are so many ways that schoolish practices are harmful. Cameras-on mandates—while understandable if the goal is to ensure student attention—stigmatize students with social anxiety, or unstable internet connections, or physical settings that they feel ashamed of. Such mandates may be especially difficult for international students, first-generation students, or others without advantages.

With a UDL (Universal Design for Learning) approach, by creating caring situations, the hope is not that some students will outtalk others, that some will be cowed into silence, but that all students will have opportunities, which will give them courage. That requires taking care, early on—I start from the first day—to ensure that people feel that they are members, valuable members, in a community of diverse learners.

Food and Feeding   In the earliest years, bodily needs are cared for as a matter of course. In France, for instance, children are served four-course lunches at school. In Italy children are prohibited from bringing their own lunches and are provided with regional specialties cooked on the spot.

In Japan children are taught to eat every morsel of the *obentos* that their mothers prepare for them. In South Korea, students are fed sometimes up to two or even three meals a day, with the cost included in tuition and fees, without their needing to pay additional money.[43] Students who will be present for six, eight, ten hours must be fed, so every institution has to sort this out. (As an aside, when I was a child in the 1960s, I actually went home for lunch, often walking alone.) During the pandemic shutdown of schools, the lack of food provided by the school was an enormous problem for many students, because families were unable to feed their children adequately. This of course is not an intrinsic function of schools but is one of many societal functions not being fulfilled by society, so it falls to the only institution universally charged with caring for children. In the United States we have many college students—like so many other residents of this country—who are food insecure and housing insecure, so caring for their bodily needs is pressing; but again these responsibilities are not inherent to schooling itself, just a consequence of the broader context that includes high fees, enormous inequality, and an inconsistent social network. Food pantries, clothing closets, housing assistance, can all help with the basic needs of food, shelter, and safety, but ideally these would be provided by entities other than schools. Schools take up the responsibility only because someone has to do it.

Attendance, Health, and Care   Many schools require attendance, ideally in person, although during the pandemic and even subsequently much conversation revolved around the possibility of virtual attendance. Failure to attend is usually penalized, though absence because of illness may be excused if properly documented. (At many community colleges, I have learned, faculty are not allowed to include attendance in the grade.) Students are sometimes rewarded for good attendance, which clearly disadvantages anyone with a chronic condition or other health challenges.

Sometimes bodies get sick during the day, and in lower years of school those bodies must be cared for; but this depends on the resources of the particular school, and many schools in the United States lack nurses and social workers. In many other countries schools may have full-on clinics; the benefits of school-based health clinics are multiple.[44] In higher education there are usually clinics and sometimes even hospitals, depending on the size and type of institution. Universities with medical schools often have hospitals on campus to which students and staff and faculty may have rights. Small or underresourced colleges may have clinics with limited hours, in which case students may need to turn to outside emergency care or other community resources. In the United States, with our model of a total institution, and given the number of hours typically spent on campus, the ideal is that health needs are cared for on campus; but in its lack of public health care, the US is an outlier among the leading industrialized nations. A study by the *Washington Post* documented "scores of problems . . . at college health centers nationwide."[45] Student health is essential, but caring for it is a challenge.

Less-Schoolish Bodies

Bodies in schools may be a challenge to care for, but they may also be a resource for learning. My classes have increasingly incorporated bodily movement. Whenever possible I have students move their seats, rearrange the furniture, stand up and talk to someone else, put sticky notes on the wall, circulate around the room. I try very hard to get the students, on the first day of class, to speak, to move, to avail themselves of many modalities: writing, speaking, reading, moving, drawing. The more modalities, the more likely it is that experiences, and learning, will stick, and that they will reach everyone, one way or another.

In most classes before COVID we had occasional snacks; in my Food and Culture class eating is a part of the curriculum, though we analyze as well as eat. (Sometimes I ask students to taste something to which they initially have an aversion, as long as they have no medical or religious reason to avoid it. So it can be educational "work" and thus virtuous.)

As I faced the fall 2020 remote-only classes, I saw none of the effervescence that arises from lively movement and interaction. I hoped to get students moving around on their own. When I returned to in-person classes in fall 2021 I was delighted to have all these resources again. We did on-campus field trips to the library and to our media center, had scavenger hunts in our hallway, went out to do ethnographic observation, rearranged everything in the room. In 2022 we went outside on the first and last days of class to do a "barometer" of student attitudes toward class-relevant topics. They moved to the left for "yes" and to the right for "no."

On the last day of the spring 2019 Person Self Body Mind class, we were doing a kind of "speed dating" in which students generated questions about the whole semester, either on one of the main topics we covered or on their connection to other topics. I brought in index cards—five by seven inches—which were bigger than we needed. I asked them to fold them and tear them in half and write their questions. Then we put some chairs in the center of the always existing circle, and people moved to their left to meet another conversation partner. Afterward, I explained that it was not that I was lazy, but that I wanted them to have the tactile memory of tearing the cards. One student was amazed; she hadn't even noticed how much a part that played in the whole exercise.

I also cherish the multiple voices and the loud excitement of intense, engaged interaction.

Individual Conferences and Meetings   I have many conferences with my students. They are short (often five minutes), preceded by preparatory reflection, and comfortable. I am shy. Speaking openly in front of big groups of people is something I've cultivated over my decades of teaching, but I'm not a natural at it. (I do enjoy it, once it's happening). And many students are shy. So for those students, meeting one-on-one with a professor eases the strain somewhat. It's not that we necessarily become best friends; but we get nearer, physically (there's what Edward Hall called "personal" vs. "social" distance in his study of *proxemics*, and "public" distance is what often happens in classrooms. We can't see each other's pores). At the beginning of the semester, nobody wants to sit in the seats right next to me; they're always the last filled, until at the end of the semester, we're okay with the nearer proximity.

Collective Effervescence

Anthropologist-sociologist Émile Durkheim explained religion as, at base, social. One of the effects of ritual is what he called "collective effervescence," which I've mentioned earlier, where the coming together in rhythmic and multisensorial experience leads to a kind of alignment, at-one-ment, a synchronization of body-minds. Examples are religious ritual, dances, sporting events, and musical performances. In my experience, it can also happen in class, when everyone simultaneously bursts out laughing at something. This shared experience has neurocognitive dimensions. Brain waves, breathing, eye gaze, and bodily posture often align. This can be the best moment of a class—when a joke occurs, when people are collectively satisfied with an experience, and when attention is aligned. It's not individual. There are ways to make it happen virtually as well, but it's far more difficult than in person.

Anything that draws on the genuine bodily involvement of learners, not through coercion or threat but through complexity and design and purpose, giving options and variations, can improve the engagement, enjoyment, and overall experience of fully bodily learners, moving from alienation to authenticity.

Part III

FROM ALIENATION TO AUTHENTICITY

From Is *to* Ought

13

SELVES

From Alienation to Authenticity, Wholeness, and Meaning

> *Random*: The most annoying word ever. You'll say something that
> relates to your previous topic, yet they say it's random because they
> can't comprehend it.
>
> Urban Dictionary

> There are those with great gifts, often precisely the most gifted, who
> suffer from severe depression. One is free from depression when self-
> esteem is based on the authenticity of one's own feelings and not on
> the possession of certain qualities.
>
> ALICE MILLER, *The Drama of the Gifted Child: The Search for the
> True Self*

Schoolishness does more than convey knowledge. It also shapes experience, and that experience shapes the very selves of those in the schoolish system. Schools are not perfect factories; few students emerge exactly
stamped with the intended measures. Yet even those who do may suffer.
Lauren Berlant's cruel optimism, Yong Zhao's side effects—there's a lot
that the structures of schoolishness shape no matter what the professed
aim. In part II of this book we've seen ten dimensions of the ideal type
of a school. To the extent that formal education has these dimensions of
schoolishness, to that extent it creates alienation; as we improve each dimension, we make more authentic learning, being, and living possible.

Alienation

Alienation is a sense of estrangement, of separation, of being different from, outside, disconnected, other than . . . as in a worker alienated from the fruits of her work, or a student alienated from schoolish goals. Alienation is a feeling of not belonging, and of not connecting. It is profoundly painful. People can be alienated from their families, or from friends, from communities or countries. It's psychologically harmful and can lead to ill effects, including self-removal such as skipping or dropping out of school, crime, despair, helplessness, anomie. Philosophers, psychologists, anthropologists, sociologists have different versions of it, but the shared message is the same: alienation is undesirable.

Alienation because of schoolishness can arise from having to do meaningless tasks but perform them in apparently enthusiastic ways. Alienation is connected with extrinsic motivation and can stem from arbitrariness. It can be related to artificiality and the kinds of schoolish games that have unpredictable and randomly decided rules. When events occur at random, it's difficult to feel connected or safe.

Schoolish learning is alienated from the setting within which it will be used, as learning is set aside from its moment of need to an institution devoted to learning. People are divided artificially into those who know and those who do not know, into roles of teacher and student, or expert and novice. In other domains we may be simultaneously both. Schoolishness produces reams of data that are separated from the context in which they are used, and then they have consequential effects. This is true for individuals learning in particular courses, where the product of their learning is often a simple, uninformative boiled-down number or letter, and it's true for the entire set of learning experiences in a degree, where a grade-point average is the summation of all that is learned. It's true for entire schools, entire districts, and entire countries, where findable data is produced in order to do things with it.

We find alienation in the spaces within which schools are created: utilitarian buildings and rooms set aside from everything else, where the assumption is that nothing will happen there except some kind of purified learning separate from the world. We find alienation in the time structures, where the amount of time to learn is determined in advance, and it's uniform, as opposed to motivated by the task itself and the ways particular learners learn, or the speed at which different learners learn. It's alienating because the ages for the learning are also predetermined no matter what individuals need, and the payoff is far in the future, so that waiting is the nature of schoolish time.

We find alienation in schoolish relationships and interactions. Outside structures control learners' bodies and voices. The genres of interaction are alienated, whether they are the genres that students consume, such as textbooks that nobody would want to consult if they were given a choice, or the lectures that are completely packaged summaries of some learning. The genres of production are also alienated, forms that do not occur outside schools, whether tests, or papers, or projects. We have encountered alienating question-asking, where the questions are not real questions but devices to determine whether students have actually obeyed and complied and learned what they have been told to learn. We find alienation in the kinds of technology that are employed in schools, where the technology is artificially constrained and unique to school. Sometimes the students' own work can't even be retained outside school—not that they would care enough about it to want it.

And we find alienated bodies, bodies that are confined and constrained and made to conform to predetermined actions, even though those actions may not meet so many actual learners' needs.

In all these ways the prototypical school is alienating of the humanity, the fully embodied, fully relating being, of learners. No wonder students dread going, and find excuses to avoid it. No wonder students drop out of college. No wonder students have trouble paying attention, and no wonder there is so much stress, anxiety, and depression associated with schools.

Alienated Learning

Alienation is other, separate, removed. It can be helpful in seeing as if from afar, anew—*Entfremdung*—as in the first weeks of fieldwork.

Alienation is experienced when an activity or quality is perceived as "liquid" or shifting, arbitrary, replaceable as a means, indifferent in its own terms, not connected to the subject, and not valuable for itself. Effects are unpredictable. It is outside, other than, the experiencer. A sense of the "random" may be included, as may be boredom. Quintessential examples include learning to memorize the order of a professor's point system for a required class. Alienated experiences can be painful themselves, such as getting a bad grade, but they are magnified by the fact that they are alienated. Descriptions of alienation may include *meaningless, useless, waste of time, incomprehensible, random, arbitrary.* Alienation may accompany bureaucracy, and also attempts to overcome, to dominate the natural world either through manufacture or staving off the true price of our methods, as in industrial agriculture. When students have to learn how each individual teacher conducts class, which form of citation a teacher prefers, whether or not students can write in the first person, whether they have to show their work in math classes or merely provide an answer, all this is arbitrary and not connected to the content of learning.

When the subjects roll by, first biochemistry, then gender and film, then Spanish, then accounting, unmotivated by the learners' needs or interests, it's hard to keep any of it straight. It's both bad for learning and bad for being.

Arbitrariness

A colleague lamented a student's protest over a grade. Both protests, and laments about protests, are common. I suggested to this colleague that his decision to count participation at 40 percent and tests at 60 percent was entirely arbitrary. Another colleague muttered, correcting me (mansplaining, but I digress), "*subjective.*" But it *is* arbitrary. Why 40 percent and not 35 percent? Why not 10 percent? He said he had very specific and precise ways of assessing participation.

And so this leads students to wonder: *Will the teacher like this? Will this count? How should I spend my time? How do I figure out what this particular teacher wants?*

The relationship between a teacher's authority and arbitrariness, between authenticity and alienation, are evident in the game of school, as we saw.

We learned in COVID times how arbitrary everything was.

Arbitrariness is the condition of not being rule-governed or predictable, of lacking an intrinsic connection between items. In linguistics, Ferdinand de Saussure wrote of the arbitrariness of the linguistic sign, emphasizing that for many signs, there was no necessary relationship between the signifier and the signified. There is no inherent reason for the idea or object of "fish" to be called by the word *fish* in English or *poisson* in French or *yú* in Chinese. This idea was radical in Saussure's day, because arguments at the time focused on which language had the true terms—Latin, Greek, etc.? Which was the real name of the object? This idea of *convention* was shocking but important for understanding the nature of linguistic and, in turn, semiotic and cultural variation.[1] In language it is arbitrary, from an objective position, a position from nowhere, whether we call a young female a *girl, una ragazza, una niña, une fille, ein Mädchen, yíge nǚháizi,* etc.—though for speakers it does come quickly to feel necessary. (What else could a *girl* possibly be called!), and when it combines with other units it is only *relatively* arbitrary: *girlfriend* or *schoolgirl,* etc. And schools are filled with arbitrariness, explainable only by historical contingency.

A life filled with arbitrariness comes to seem absurd, unpredictable, senseless, meaningless, and is a sure way to create anxiety or even mental illness, not knowing what is coming or why. . . . Even saber-toothed tigers had behavioral patterns; monsoons usually come in their season. In Deuteronomy 11.14, God promises "I will give you the rain of your land in its due season." That's the hope.

Experientially, as captured by Kafka, Weber, and others, modernity and postmodernity make life feel like a series of arbitrary, disconnected edicts, rules, frameworks. One day you have to do X, the next day Y. You plop a Doric column on a log cabin.

And this is one thing that students often feel. Rules of citation, rules about collaboration, whether notes may be consulted on tests, page lengths of papers, length of class period or semester . . . all seems arbitrary. Psychologically this takes its toll.

Some students who strive for academic and expressive perfection "lose their sense of 'authenticity' because in their view the pedagogic relationship is inauthentic, not meaningful and deeply affected as it coldly fails to engage with who they feel they 'really' are."[2] This can lead to eating disorders, according to a study showing high school girls who limited their consumption as a way to resist the inauthentic self through controlling it.[3] "The body becomes just another way of achieving 'performances' to meet the criteria of excellence, control and so on, by which they feel they are judged by teachers or their peers. Conversely, it is also a resource for challenging inauthenticity."[4] Some students claim their own selfhood through bodily control. "In cultures of performativity and corporeal perfection, where 'the body' is constantly subject to authoritative gaze, health educators, teachers, doctors and others simply assume right of judgement over the 'others' body and its health."[5]

For whom does one perform?

Estrangement, Schoolish Affect, Genuine and Artificial: Emotional Labor and Emotional Coercion

The brilliant sociologist Arlie Hochschild first published *The Managed Heart* in 1983; it was republished in 2012, long after airlines had dramatically changed.[6] This book haunts me. My students adore it. Hochschild studied flight attendants, who were *required* to *appear genuinely*—sincerely, authentically—*happy* to see passengers, and to muster "real" smiles—and in the process to erase any evidence of "effort."[7] Extrapolating from this domain, she wrote of the damage such "emotional labor" causes to those—often but not only women—whose work requires not just technical skills but the emotional bestowal of the self. Such workers experience stress partly as a result of the "estrangement between self and feelings and between self and display," leading to "a challenge to a person's sense of self."[8] This "deep acting" may even lead to a sense of "false self," a "socio-centric, other-directed self,"[9] or uncertainty about whether there are two (or more) selves—one at work/school and one when on one's own—or one *real* and one *phony*.[10] Middle-class children are "more likely to be asked to shape their feelings according to the rules they are made aware of."[11] In relinquishing "a healthy sense of wholeness," the flight attendants (or students) accept "the tension we feel between our own 'real' and our 'on-stage' selves."[12] This estrangement, this doubleness, "the lie to oneself," may come to be experienced as "a sign of human weakness, of bad faith."[13]

Schoolishness, too, increasingly, teaches people to perform a specific version of affect, and I believe that this takes its toll, just as it did with flight attendants. The longer students stay in school, the more emotional requirements are attached to schooling, the higher the stakes of school success, the more intrusion school makes into the home and social life— the more likely it is that estrangement, or bad faith, alienation, will be the affective fabric of everyday life, with no respite, no place, no time, when it is possible to kick back and just relax. As students are constantly wondering how they will be seen, how they will be evaluated, the norms of others are internalized and replace any sense of their own nature.

You saw in chapter 5, "Questions," how school teaches dependence on others, in the discussions surrounding the so-called language gap, and the default imperative to engage in initiation-response-evaluation. While it is true, as sociologist George Herbert Mead says, that self must be created in dialogue with others, we must attend both to *being for oneself* and to some degree to *being for others*. In his ambitious book *Escaping Alienation: A Philosophy of Alienation and Dealienation*, Warren Frederick Morris reminds us that though "oversocialized selves" are alienated, nonetheless "a willful egoistic self . . . defined by unbridled self-seeking desire must be tamed in order to exist within a society conferring collective benefits and requiring commonality of purpose. There must be reciprocity between the egoistic self driven by desires and social self driven by roles and behavioral expectations."[14] We can't be all about ourselves, nor all about others. There's a dialectic. As Frantz Fanon has shown, students whose own cultural backgrounds are distant from the one dominant in schooling also feel especially alienated, required to don a mask just to avoid offending their white, or majority, peers.

The absolute distinction between "authentic" and "fake" may be too simplistic and romantic; yet however we might want to regard "authenticity" as a social construction, it's hard to argue against the phenomenological, lived experience of contemporary life as alienated. Zygmunt Bauman calls it "liquid" in contrast to solid, as in a contrast between "solid modernity" and "liquid modernity." Marshall Berman quotes Marx and Engels's claim that under capitalism, "all that is solid melts into air."[15] Evidence from psychology and politics shows genuine painful alienation in a wide variety of domains, and that this helpful concept can aid in unifying disparate cultural analyses.

Faculty Alienation

Faculty suffer when they feel compromised—what is sometimes called "moral injury." I referred to this in the opening of the book, when

I invoked the Buddhist idea of "right livelihood." The more that people feel their work is a "calling," the more painful it is if it can't be practiced as desired. As Stephen J. Ball writes in his compassionate article "The Teacher's Soul and the Terrors of Performativity," many teachers feel torn between their own views and those of the system: "A kind of values schizophrenia is experienced by individual teachers where commitment, judgement and authenticity within practice are sacrificed for impression and performance. Here there is a potential 'splitting' between the teachers' own judgements about 'good practice' and students' 'needs' and the rigours of performance."[16]

One of the teachers he interviewed had lost self-respect when she felt compelled by "inspection," or outside evaluation: "What is produced," Ball said, "is a spectacle, or game-playing, or cynical compliance, or what one might see as an 'enacted fantasy' . . . which is there simply to be seen and judged a fabrication. . . . And, as the teacher ["Diane"] also hints, the heavy sense of inauthenticity in all this may well be appreciated as much by the Inspectors as the inspected; Diane is 'playing the game' and 'they know I am.'"[17]

Even the important dimension of "care" can be mandated, as in Hochschild's invocation of emotional labor. If it is mandatory, then can it become a mere performance of care, contributing to a sense of falseness?

Ball writes, "While we may not be expected to care about each other, we are expected to 'care' about performances and the performances of the team and the organization and to make our contribution to the construction of convincing institutional spectacles and 'outputs.' We are expected to be passionate about excellence. Our performances and those of the organization cannot be constructed without 'care.' Presentation, 'front' impressions 'given' and 'given off' must be carefully crafted and managed. They are part of the currency and substance of performance. As individuals and organizational actors the performances must be constructed or fabricated with artifice and with an eye to the competition."[18]

The invocation of Goffman's notion of "impression management" and "front stage," impressions "given" and "given off," connect this to the earlier discussion of authenticity and alienation.

During COVID return-to-campus, a particularly tone-deaf email from our generally reasonable learning experts urged us to "express our happiness" at "welcoming" (a verb that became the default, in contrast, say, to "allowing") students back to campus. Many faculty balked at being told how to feel.

Less-Schoolish Learning: Authentic Learning and Being

If there's any justification for the expansion of schooling into decades of young life, it has to have genuine, authentic outcomes and goals. It can't just be a decades-long rite of passage that students have to endure. Learning for a test is part of the game. Learning something fun, fascinating, useful, or necessary has immediate payoffs and is more likely to stick. That doesn't mean everything has to be prosaic and obvious, like how to pay taxes. It could be about why we don't have to worry about meteors, usually (though see the 2022 film *Don't Look Up*).

But so much of schooling is artificial, disconnected, not unlike the idea of nutritionism, the tendency to reduce food to the identifiable, measurable component parts, to specify precisely what they are and put them back together, almost always with a diminution of the experience. Alice Miller laments the artificial and dead nature of schoolish learning: "It is among the commonplaces of education that we often first cut off the living root and then try to replace its natural functions by artificial means. Thus we suppress the child's curiosity, for example (there are questions one should not ask), and then when he [*sic*] lacks a natural interest in learning he is offered special coaching for his scholastic difficulties."[19]

When schooling goes well, as it likely has for many faculty, everything is aligned. Students play the game, happily, and get rewarded. They find meaning in their accomplishments and enjoy what they are learning. At its best, students find authenticity and meaning in school. They revel in its structure, identifying enthusiastically with its goals, as this student—let's call him Chet—an applied math and liberal studies major and a chess aficionado, explained in an interview:

> I really like math. I have always liked math. I especially fell in love with math, doing . . . integrals, integration. I love, they're just like little puzzles. . . . I played a lot of chess as a kid. I fell in love with chess, I think . . . it was kinda a special thing between my dad and me, around fourth grade, somehow I kinda got the bug. . . . I think he started picking it up and started playing online and kinda refreshed me on rules, and I just picked it up.

He has deep affect, *love*, for both math and chess and for his father (now deceased), and this has led him to love his math classes (even though he also says frankly that in one of them he "knocks out" problem sets while attending class lectures). He finds that elusive *flow* in chess, as the hours go by: "From fourth to sixth grade especially I would play chess online at least two hours every day, at least, sometimes like on the weekends it would be four hours." And seminar-type classes suit him perfectly.

> The thing I really like about that well, *A*, it's really engaging, *B*, I just learn really pretty well that way, but, *C*, It's also really neat for me, it's kind of a creative enterprise. You're creating your own kind of education, but you're also creating your own discussion. But to me it's like . . . your own little project you are working on, and yeah, I just really like that style of learning and I think it's . . . one of the best ways to learn.

For many college faculty, this student is exactly the kind we like: he finds freedom and joy in learning and identifies with it all the way through. Not only that, but as a religious young man, he clarifies his own notion of *authenticity*, being consistent, as a goal that he can realize through school.

> Something that has become a priority for me is to be authentic, so being authentic in my relationship with other people, being authentic in regards to the motivation I have for doing things. So now . . . I got to make sure that . . . when I'm learning and when I'm studying that it's always with the proper intention in mind, the proper end in mind.

Few students explicitly speak so openly of authenticity. But he shows the way education in school can work, at least for some.

In stark contrast is a student—pseudonym Bruno—who had gotten a perfect score of 36 on his ACT test yet had been expelled from college, at least for a semester. Spending nearly every morning smoking "a decent amount of weed" before he could muster an appetite, he was not really enthusiastic about school at any level. Asked if he liked school (before coming to college) he answered, "Not particularly." Why? "Uh, it was school. Most kids don't like school." He acknowledged that there were good times in school: "It was alright. We had fun. . . . Some kids cracked me up all the time. Some ridiculous stuff happened." But "school was more of a chore, though. Actually trying to learn. Came pretty easy, and I cheated a lot, so I got really good grades . . . without much work. . . . It was just easy. Everyone took turns doing papers, and we'd copy each other's." He was adept: "I could cram three essays out in forty minutes like nobody's business." Like Chet, Bruno liked his seminars, but he "didn't really feel like as close to all the rest of the kids that were in the [honors] program as they really were to each other." He looked forward to Fridays so he could "not think about any work at all" and get right to "drinking and pre-gaming" and "trying to find something to do." He did say "I really like the whole college experience"—drinking, smoking, partying included. This insightful former student wanted to learn, as he explained elsewhere in the interview; knew how to play the game; knew why he suffered; and knew where he could find enjoyment.

Authenticity

The concept of authenticity has been celebrated and deplored and distorted and stretched. It means many things: It means the authentic self as experienced by an individual, or it means an authentic experience. It can be *demanded*, in which case it's a kind of false authenticity, as can happen when people of minoritized backgrounds are expected to represent their particular group. They may not wish to do it. It can happen when people are forced to share in ways and in settings and among people whom they don't trust and for whom they have no desire to perform an authentic self.

Authenticity is problematic, and it's useful, in the existentialist sense of Simone de Beauvoir and Jean-Paul Sartre, to contrast to bad faith. Authenticity is not having to perform for others—even though Goffman argued that we are always performing. I ask my students sometimes about performance selves and authentic selves. Authenticity is *experienced*—because it is phenomenological, not ontological—when an activity or quality is perceived as solid, intrinsically motivated, irreplaceable as a means, real in its own terms, and an end in itself. The line of cause and effect is predictable. Authentic experience is beautiful, meaningful, useful, desired. It is connected or attached in some important way to the subject. It could even be painful, as is childbirth. Examples include learning to get water to a sapling; growing food using rain and compost. Authenticity is the natural state of animals and of nature. Authenticity is connected to wholeness, integrity, connection, unification. When people experience authenticity, they feel motivation and meaning. Things feel real, understandable, genuine. They know where they stand. They are at home in the world.

On the more authentic side of the scale, in terms of learning, I would place things like learning to walk and learning to cook. More alienated would be memorizing a syllabus for a required class in a degree that is needed to get a raise at work, which is needed to pay for a new car. In terms of food, more authentic would be food that does not even require agriculture, such as wild edibles like berries and mushrooms. More alienated would be foods created in laboratories, such as Twinkies. In terms of art, more authentic would be a poem that arrives, fully formed, after sleep. More alienated would be a copy of a commercial painting that is intended to be hung over all the rooms in an apartment complex. Midway might be a copy, with variation, for joy.

Similarly, even the notion of simulation and simulacrum might exist on a scale. Pilots learning to fly begin with simulations. But a simulacrum, such as of a safari ride at Disney World, might come to replace the authentic because it's more convenient, predictable, and instantly satisfying than hoping animals actually appear for tourists in the savannah. In this sense nature becomes alienated. Learning in a classroom may include simulations, prototypes, models, and theories, while application outside the classroom may be a measure of authenticity.

Aristotle's and Marx's notions of *use value* and *exchange value* map onto these. *Use value* emphasizes the transparency and inevitability of means to an end: you have to strengthen your arm to play tennis well, even if the repeated exercise might be boring or painful. *Exchange value* emphasizes opacity and interchangeability of means to an end: you can get an A by learning the material or by attending class or by getting extra-credit points. Onomatopoeia, what anthropologists call an *icon*, where the sign resembles the thing depicted, is authentic: cats everywhere say something like *meow*; you can't substitute *moo* for a cat's utterance. In this sense it is iconic: the word resembles in a necessary, if incomplete, way, that which it represents. Ordinary words are arbitrary: we can refer, more or less, to the same object by saying *library* or *túshūguǎn* or *biblioteca*. You can study Spanish because you want to communicate with your sister's husband, or you can study Spanish to do well enough to pass the competency test and get the requirement out of the way, in which case German or Chinese would also work. Authentic learning can happen in school: you can learn calculus because you recognize how valuable this will be when you are an engineer calculating the rush of water into a sewer or because math fascinates you. Alienated "learning" (which is often phony learning, sham learning) can also occur in school: you can learn calculus because it is on the list of required subjects for entrance into a highly selective college, or because you will be tested on it in the MCAT, or it is needed to enter medical school, needed to practice medicine, which could be done in the service of healing others or to make money, which in turn is used for . . .

The more steps between the activity and the goal, the more likely it is that someone may be alienated. Directness is often diagnostic of authenticity: I drop the exercise weight on my toe and it hurts. Authentic agony! If I substituted a stretchy band to increase my strength, I might also get the strength, but I wouldn't get the purple toe. I do my homework—or copy my homework from a friend—for my chemistry class because I get points for homework, and I need the points to get a good grade in each class so that my GPA is high, which will help me when I apply to vet school, which is competitive. In one case, there is no possibility of substitution; the heavy metal equipment gets different results at the moment than the stretchy plastic. In the other, all kinds of similar things could be substituted: I could take biology instead of chemistry; I could find the answers to the problem sets online; I could change the grade by hacking; I could butter up the professor and get her to raise my grade; I could focus my efforts on excelling on labs and tests rather than homework; I could make sure my participation either in person or online is noticeably high; I could try to scrounge all the extra credit I can. All these would contribute to the GPA-to-vet-school goal.

Individuals in Society

Romantic and existentialist ideas of authenticity emphasized a timeless individual essence that required no practice or action or interaction and verged quite close to solipsism. In that sense, isolation, retreat, and defiance were typical components of this notion of authenticity, where conformity and pressure from outside or society were seen as some of the greatest problems facing individual self-actualization.

Some versions of the authentic self celebrate separation of the person and society. This self is distrustful of convention and even of success, since worldly success means somehow meeting the expectations and desires of the larger populace. Vincent van Gogh represents this version of an "authentic" self: he had his own, singular style, suffered during his lifetime, and was not commercially successful. The hero of Ayn Rand's *The Fountainhead*, Howard Roark, was an individual unbeholden to others' views—a view of an authentic individual as inevitably at odds with any collective norms. Former UK prime minister Margaret Thatcher claimed that there is no such thing as *society*—an ideological stance favoring only individuals. Yet all of social science has shown that even individual behavior needs to be explained, at least in part, by larger-than-individual patterns. "My sense of self as a stable entity comes about largely through interactions with others,"[20] says David Detmer, commenting on Sartre's concepts of bad faith and authenticity.

For short, we call the people involved in these emergent patterns *society*. I share Hochschild's *social theory of self*: neither an individual, organismic model, such as Darwin's, nor merely a performance such as Goffman portrays.

Hermits, for instance, retreat in socially and culturally understandable ways. Authenticity does not require rejection of others or of social convention. One could imagine individuals formed by their social interaction and biography quite comfortable following social norms and acting authentically (Lionel Trilling would have called it, rather, *sincerely*), which might even be unconsciously, in ways that resemble the actions of others.[21] In this sense, conformity is not an automatic sign of alienation. All humans emerge only in constant interaction with others, and in large part the unit of analysis for human beings is interaction, as analysts from George Herbert Mead to Erving Goffman to Jack Sidnell and all the conversation analysts have shown. This is not to say that individuals, as some kind of density in the gaseous universe, in Latour's words, cannot be a useful focus; and experientially, phenomenologically, we emphasize—especially in the twentieth- and twenty-first-century Euro-American context—our uniqueness. But observations do not necessarily bear out claims of uniqueness. Our language, our musical forms, our ways of interacting bodily in our environments, our food preferences—all come from experience with others and the world. It is part of our nature, our species-being.

Wholeness and Meaning: Authenticity Moderated by the Real

It's easy to exaggerate the possibility of authenticity. The Romantic long-ing for another place where and time when things were real and solid, when actions were pure and done for simple, unself-conscious reasons of need, comes from an ideology that aims to get at something impossible.

Performance—as doing actions focused on the audience and on re-sults, rather than on intrinsic, inward criteria—is also an enduring part of the human condition. The balance may alter from one time to another. Members participate in ritual; audiences observe performances. Cheung distinguishes "live and interactive" experiences from "dead and hard" memorials.[22] My students talk constantly about "performative" courtesy, political positions, hygiene, etc.

And yet . . . there is superreal, and superfake, and the continuum be-tween them. We will never attain genuine, full-fledged authenticity. We always compromise, for a variety of very good reasons. But our hunger for authenticity is enormous now, because people feel a lack in their own con-nections to the world. If everything is available, then there is no reason to select one thing as opposed to another. We are too free, and our being has become unbearably light, paraphrasing Milan Kundera's perfect phrase.

Authenticity ties us to a time and place, a style and a self. It is not free. It is anchored, local, necessary, unchanging.

Theodor Adorno argued against "the jargon of authenticity." Eric Hobsbawm and Terence Ranger pointed out how much of "tradition" has actually been invented.[23] If the quest for authenticity paralyzes us, then we should discard it. If it inspires us, we should embrace it.

The prototype of schoolishness is bleak.

But along the way I have also introduced mitigating practices of vari-ous sizes, from very small tweaks to proposals for overhauls of entire systems. All the ten key elements of schoolishness that I enumerated in chapters 3 through 12, however, are intertwined, Nothing fundamental can change until multiple dimensions are simultaneously changed—and yet we know that there are multiple entrenched interests and con-sequences, given the embedded pathways of so many dimensions of schools. To the extent that we can replace alienation with some kind of authentic experience, in authentic settings, with authentic payoff, to that extent we may improve things.

One concerted effort to improve things is called high-impact practices. These practices have been broadly highlighted in higher education because of the recognition that some things were amiss. George Kuh has with other colleagues created lists of high-impact practices, some of which are very small, and some of which are much larger.[24] They range from having a freshman seminar to doing senior theses to studying abroad and more. One of the practices is experiential, community-based learning, where students work with community partners in real-world settings, to analyze and possibly solve problems. In the next chapter you will see an example of a successful community-based summer internship program that essentially goes against every one of the ten elements of schoolishness that you saw, and has spectacular results.

"The Trees Need Water"

Authentic Learning in an Educational Ecosystem

> It is not enough to insist upon the necessity of experience, nor even
> of activity in experience. Everything depends upon the quality of the
> experience.
>
> John Dewey, *Experience and Education*

In this chapter I tell the story of tiny trees, of student interns, of learning, and of an internship experience—one that produced effective, enjoyable, authentic, and enduring learning emergent through constantly evolving expectations.[1] This ongoing paid community-based internship was almost a job, almost an apprenticeship, a project built on an engineering foundation but which had early spilled into adjacent fields, and which a team of faculty and undergraduates studied ethnographically. My point is to demonstrate the effectiveness of a complex, embodied cooperative social experience with authentic responsibility, which contrasts in important ways with conventional education, with schoolishness. I begin with an ethnographic moment: a weekly report from the team responsible for a tree nursery on a vacant lot.

The student intern who chose as his pseudonym "Mufasa" [all names are pseudonyms chosen by the participants themselves based on their "spiritual animal avatars"] ended his weekly update with a comment about the urgency of his team's task: "We need to do this really fast 'cuz the trees need water!" There was no room for excuses. The team had to figure out how to water the small trees in the tree nursery on the neighborhood vacant lots—or the trees would die.

Mufasa's team of three had schematic drawings, which were sometimes wrong. They had plans to route drip-hoses from neighbors' spouts, but some spouts didn't work and others were in the wrong places. Plans changed and time passed as it took days to schedule meetings with adjacent neighbors. They persisted. They enlisted the help of plumbers who provided estimates and suggested locations for underground pipes. They met with city planners and had long conversations with the neighbors. They learned, within a week or so, that their plans required frequent revisions, and that they, as student interns with plans, had no particular power. Yet by summer's end, the trees got their water. How this happened isn't obvious. It wasn't efficient; there were false starts and frustrations. But it was effective in many ways. Both learning and doing happened. The experience was emotional, sometimes scary, and ultimately felt triumphant.

For me, it showed how authentic learning can occur when there's a problem to be solved in a particular place, with other people, for a real purpose. And it's a lot different from what happens in prototypical conventional classrooms, from schoolishness. Instead of the stereotype of alienated, disengaged, unhappy, nonlearning students, it was a different kind of learning, one that can be extremely successful when it has social, emotional, place-based dimensions, when it solves problems, and when it offers tangible, authentic outcomes that matter beyond the individual. Responsibility and involvement contribute, as do adequate time and scaffolded permission for failure.[2] I'll identify elements that contribute to its success—and ultimately suggest contrasts with conventional schoolish practices in all ten dimensions.

The Bowman Creek Educational Ecosystem is an example of authentic learning—an extremely unschoolish project supported by a school.

The Bowman Creek Educational Ecosystem: Authentic Education

The Bowman Creek Educational Ecosystem project, BCe2, is a partnership with two universities, a community college, a high school, the city, a neighborhood association, and several other entities. The project took place in my hometown, South Bend, Indiana, a small Rust Belt city recovering from decades of economic decline, and emerged out of pollution, in the aftermath of deindustrialization. The Environmental Protection Agency issued a Consent Decree in 2011 for violations of the Clean Water Act, with Bowman Creek a major component.[3] Cleaning up the creek required technical expertise in water chemistry, in civil engineering, in biological understanding of the biota present in the water. This city, like many other recovering Rust Belt cities, also has a problematic number of vacant lots.

A Notre Dame club, the Society for Women Engineers, decided to take on the vacant lot problem. They developed a technical tool for determining the optimal use of some of the vacant lots: whether to turn them into pocket parks, to see if the adjoining neighbors wanted to incorporate them into their own land, or to see if new houses could be built on them. At the same time, a colleague, a professor of engineering and later dean of community engagement, Jay Brockman, became interested in this project. He got involved the first summer, with eight college interns, all from Notre Dame, who were working on the water quality of Bowman Creek and on the vacant lots. He worked with a former city engineer, Gary Gilot, and the two of them made magic happen.

Jay and Gary diverted some other funding to address problems with the water quality of polluted Bowman Creek. Their effort quickly expanded into the Bowman Creek neighborhood, one of the poorest in the city of South Bend. The neighborhood constitutes one square mile out of South Bend's forty-four square miles.

Jay is a creative scientist, an engineer, educator, and musician who keeps generating new ideas and procuring new grants, starting new projects and racking up new job titles for himself. He got the Third Coast Percussion group, an ensemble with whom he had collaborated during their residency at Notre Dame, in 2013–2018, and which had just won a Grammy award, to come give a master class and concert to his little side project on music education as a way to learn math (STEM + Arts = STEAM).[4] Gary is similar: when given a problem, he generates fifty ways to solve it. One of the orientation programs asked people to identify where they fell on a continuum between those who liked to imagine and those who liked to implement (innovators—bridgers—adaptors). Gary and Jay were off-the-charts innovators.

Gary was critical of conventional engineering education because when companies hire new college graduates there's usually "some assembly required": they have a "school degree," as one of the local residents put it, but not a "street degree." This internship intentionally mimicked authentic professional practice, having complex problems and a true risk of failure. Gary reiterated, "I could spoon feed you really simple problems where there's only a narrow range of correct solutions [like in school], but I actually prefer the idea of giving really high-level conceptual assignments and see you go through an iterative process with false starts and dead ends forcing you to turn around and get back on track. That's what we are aiming for: authentic, real, complex learning." Such learning is accomplished in ways contrasting substantially with conventional lecture-and-test college courses. The "syllabus" couldn't be more different from the standard week-by-week specified-in-advance list of tasks to be accomplished uniformly by each individual, alone, inside a building.

Methods

In the summer of 2015, Jay and Gary, in conjunction with our Center for Social Concerns, assembled a National Science Foundation grant proposal to fund more of the Bowman Creek project as it contributed to the "STEM pipeline" and workforce development. The idea was that we would recruit students from a variety of institutions, including high schools, and work with the city and other partners who have a stake in the outcomes, to provide hands-on engineering experience and explore whether, and how, "multidimensional diversity" contributed. (Since then the project has been renamed and expanded; by 2021 almost three hundred interns had participated.)

The grant writers, Jay and Danielle Wood of the Center for Social Concerns, had the insight that it could be useful to include social scientists—in this case anthropologists. They invited me in fall 2015. I agreed in part because I was going to work with my colleague, Gabriel Torres, who was our department's director of undergraduate studies and therefore had access to undergraduates. Besides, I really like Gabriel. Gabriel and I took months to understand what this project was, although we didn't truly grasp it until the summer of 2016 when we actually saw it in action. But even before it began, Gabriel had found a job at another university, and though he graciously helped to recruit our ethnographic interns, he left before any of the activities began.

We were fortunate enough to have another wonderful colleague take over the position as director of undergraduate studies, Eric Haanstad. Eric and I took on the work (with Eric doing the lion's share) of overseeing our two ethnographic interns, Asha Barnes and Kenzell Huggins. These two interns observed how social categories contributed to the qualities of interaction, how questions of power intersected with actual versus formal leadership. That summer, 2016, there were twenty-two interns altogether, and they completed nine projects, including analyzing vacant lots and installing eight or ten rain gardens using equipment called Arduino technology. (Arduinos are small, easily programmed computer components that can automate simple tasks, like sensing moisture in soil.)

After observing the project all summer, by the fall it occurred to me that the Bowman Creek project exemplified *authentic learning*, and that I could study that dimension. The interns came with preconceived ideas about what they were going to be doing and seeing, but they soon discovered things on the way that were not predictable and required them to learn about and master many different skills and kinds of knowledge, including navigating social relations within the team, figuring out about bureaucratic regulations, learning who were the key figures, and creating workarounds, as well as dealing with other social, technical, and even ethical concerns. There would have been no way to predict the full, robust assortment of learning that the students were to undergo. I applied for a small grant, which allowed me to hire an intern whose task would be to study the learning that occurred in and around the Bowman Creek project, possibly in direct contrast with learning in a classroom.[5]

I observed and participated part-time in the summer of 2017, including the entire first two weeks of orientation, doing icebreaking exercises with the interns and participating in the full-day leadership training workshop. The students got used to me, and they certainly got used to the ethnographers, who were ubiquitous. I subsequently attended the weekly meetings and some other events, including picnics.

We recruited a diverse research team, with five students (supported
by the project) and three faculty: Terri Hebert, a professor of education at a different institution, Jay Brockman, and me, as an anthropologist of education. Our five "embedded ethnographic interns" (Gabrielle
Robinson, Kirill Gillespie, Maeve Mallozzi-Kelly, Missy Norberg, and
Saliyha Webb), all social science majors, spent the entire summer studying the project—forty hours a week for ten weeks—as paid members of
the project. They began with varying degrees of anthropological study
but very little experience doing actual ethnography. None had worked on
a project that went beyond the classroom, at least in their anthropology
classes. They were uneasy to varying degrees at the beginning. One in particular seemed somewhat angry at the lack of direction she received from
the two anthropology advisers, Eric and me. *What*, she asked, *were they
supposed to be doing? What were they supposed to do every day?*

The ethnographers nevertheless learned well, fast, and deeply. They
organized themselves, deciding that they were not going to neatly divide
up the four projects involved but would keep all of them in mind all
summer. They wrote field notes, recorded interviews, conducted focus
groups, and more, all for the first time. Their data include hundreds of
pages of field notes, interview transcripts, and reflections, shared on
Google Drive. I also have a notebook full of field notes. Two of the interns remained after the summer ended to help analyze the abundant data
that they had amassed. Several written products emerged, many with students as coauthors.[6]

At first the five ethnographers planned to work with one of the eight
project teams. This ended up being an effective strategy, though later
they limited their work with the teams. They had each gotten to know
the dynamics of particular groups very well. At first the twenty-five non-
ethnographers didn't really know what ethnography was and were uncomfortable, indeed suspicious, of the ethnographers' motives. Were they
spies? Were they judges? Were they going to report them if they didn't
act properly? All but one eventually signed the consent form, agreeing
to be studied. Only at the midway point were they comfortable with the
ethnographers, even sometimes seeking them out because they recognized
that the ethnographers had the big picture.

Including the student ethnographers, there were thirty interns altogether, ranging in age from fifteen to fifty-something, selected through a

process of written application followed by interviews, from thirteen different educational institutions (local high schools, community colleges, regional and flagship public universities, private universities); a few were recent graduates. They differed along many dimensions: race and ethnicity, social class, nationality, college major, and gender; they spoke many languages. Only a few interns were familiar with the neighborhood; even fewer had grown up there. Others had scarcely stepped out of the bubble of the selective, national university that provided the core administrative support. Interns earned $4,000 for ten weeks, and worked 8 a.m. to 5 p.m., with a lunch break, unless there were evening events. Every one of the thirty interns also had a personal project. A set of twenty-one mentors, with varying commitments, was also involved.

The "stakeholders" included city partners, churches, NGOs, academic institutions, and more, for a total of 168 people who had expressed interest in the project. News coverage was not lacking—even the mayor came to some of the events—and piqued interest from many people, although perhaps not adequately from the neighbors themselves. This is a common challenge to university-neighborhood partnerships and community-service projects, which typically last only a summer. The neighbors have seen countless projects come and go over the years and are weary and wary of the good intentions of the apparently privileged students who pass in and out of their orbit.

It was breathtaking. It was complex. It was an ecosystem of humans operating within an ecosystem of a neighborhood operating within an ecosystem of a planet.

Back to the Tree Nurseries

The project's three-person "Urban Natural Resources and Smart Green Infrastructure" team illustrates well the arc of learning. One of their tasks was to plant and care for three tree nurseries. The tiny, inexpensive trees, called *whips* (costing about $20 apiece), would grow at low cost into more valuable larger trees (worth around $500 apiece), to be transplanted into newly developed areas. In the meantime, the trees would improve the feel of the neighborhood; instead of vacant lots inviting trash accumulation or illicit behavior, they would provide beauty, shade, and oxygen while increasing the diminished tree canopy of South Bend. This was year 3 of the internship, so some tree nurseries were already in place. But there was a challenge: How do you get water to the fragile, tiny trees? (Once established they wouldn't need this pampering.) Nobody knew a surefire method. Unlike a lab experiment, there was no single right answer to this real-life problem. And—this was urgent. Heat was predicted. This all had to be solved quickly. There was no negotiating the due date. The deadline was authentic.

The problems were numerous: Even when an adjacent house had a functioning spigot, and even though the project was willing to pay the increased water bill, there had to be a signed contract. Neighbors were often at work during business hours. If spigots failed, the interns had to identify the reason and then devise a solution, whether technical, interpersonal, or bureaucratic: Did the problem stem from the water line from the street (the city would be responsible), the pipe under the ground (to be repaired by a plumber), or the spigot itself (plumber)? And though the project had money to repair the spigots, some neighbors didn't want strangers on their property. Residents who rented could lack the authority to authorize the repairs. The interns had to figure out how to contact the actual owners, who might live elsewhere, or to go through property management companies.

Over the weeks, the team operated on a number of fronts. They learned how to negotiate with neighbors. They found property records. They requested estimates from plumbers. They worked with the technically advanced Arduino team. They developed skills and vocabulary, and both technical and bureaucratic knowledge. They also learned to wait.

There was so much waiting. In the first weeks, the interns moved from confidence that their problems would be quickly solved to frustration that their plans had not yielded immediate results; even after settling on technical solutions (rerouting irrigation lines), they faced unexpected social and practical obstacles, such as when a resident changed her mind about permitting city officials and plumbers to enter her house in her absence.

In week 3 (the first week of the team presentations), "Peanut" reported on the native tree nurseries and their challenges, including the original plan to run an irrigation system through a homeowner's backyard. Pointing to the images, he lamented, "We soon learned that that was just not gonna happen. There's a concrete pathway that goes through here." And the problems multiplied. "He also doesn't have a spigot on this side. It's on this side. And that spigot also doesn't work [*laughter from the group*]. So we just adapted to the situation." He hesitated slightly before relatively new terms such as *schematic*, *drip hose*, *irrigation system*, or *spigot*, as some of the interns were still becoming familiar with them.

They were still struggling in week 5; one intern lamented that "everything takes longer than we think." In week 6, this team was still waiting for plumbers. (They were also waiting to hear about another dimension of their project: rain garden locations—native plantings with deep roots to absorb heavy rains and prevent excessive strain on the city's stormwater system. One admitted, "It's possible that no rain gardens will be installed.") One of the neighbors, a renter, didn't want to sign the contract to allow their water to be used for the trees. During this presentation, Mufasa expressed his pressing alarm: "We need to get water to the trees 'cuz the trees are gonna die."

The Trees Got Their Water

Interns' familiarity with bureaucratic processes grew rapidly over the course of the summer as they realized that nobody could magically make everything happen the way they had envisioned. While they spoke haltingly at first of *crimp lines* (a type of water line for irrigation), having to explain the meaning each time, after a few weeks they rattled off the names of key people, local organizations, city offices, equipment, the commonly used terminology of *deliverables* and *prototyping*, *milestones* and *Gantt charts*, *whips*, *Arduinos*, *timer belts*, and more. One morning, in the first few weeks, the Affordable Housing team advised the Lead Information team about how regulations are set up, how to avoid risks, how the city's inspection process works, and how one may encounter "fogginess" when contacting residents and landlords about current house conditions. By the final week, they embraced their few triumphs, and the atmosphere was much more relaxed. Everyone understood all the projects well, and they were all eager to laugh and respond. The last update on the tree nurseries was much more positive than the earlier ones. (See table 4.1 for a list of the teams.)

> So . . . the tree nursery project is almost done. We promise [*group laughter*].
> . . . Last week we dug trenches. . . . That's a strong understatement. I think
> most of us feel like we've been digging nonstop last week just to get this all
> done before the end of the summer. . . . The entire system on all three lots,
> it's about like ninety-nine percent done. We just have a few PVC . . . issues
> that we need to correct. . . . The timer belts . . . those should be coming in
> today, and ideally we can get those implemented either today or tomorrow
> depending on when they come in.

This group had technical knowledge that they were still teaching their colleagues, though all interns already shared much understanding, such as
the use of Gantt charts, project management tools, which all teams were
required to update weekly.

> This is the specific Gantt chart for the tree nursery. We are . . . almost done
> with most of the components. The only things we have left are installing the
> timer belts and then also using the tree teepees. So, we need to work out a
> way to . . . do sort of a long-term experimentation to see if these tree tee-
> pees are useful.

As the expert, he explained what the tree teepees were:

> If you haven't seen 'em, they're basically the black plastic . . . cone-shaped
> things that are . . . just randomly in the room over there. So you can take
> a look at those. They just wrap around the trees. They're marketed to hold
> ninety percent more moisture than without 'em. I feel like that's . . . really
> a huge number. So we'll see how that goes, and . . . we can work something
> out with just anyone else who's gonna be here and keeping the project going
> to make sure we get good data over time.

The interns had become experts in their own areas and taught the others—
without sheepishness for taking on an expert rather than novice role, as
students often do in classroom settings. By the final weeks the work had
been completed, and all the interns knew substantial amounts about all
the teams' work. All the tree nurseries had water. Rain gardens had been
installed. Sensors were monitoring moisture levels. The problems had
been solved.

Comparing Schoolishness and Bowman Creek / Authentic Learning

One of our initial research questions involved a comparison between classroom learning and what anthropologist David Thornton Moore in the 1980s called "field" learning.[7] In many interviews and reflections, interns explicitly, and often voluntarily, contrasted the BCe2 work with experiences in classrooms. Using the dimensions addressed throughout this book, we show how the two differ.

Experiencing School: How It Felt

With few exceptions, students loved this internship. One said explicitly, "This internship has been perhaps the greatest experience of my life." Interns reflected that they felt closer to the people on the project than to anyone they had ever been involved with before, that they were sad to see it end, that they looked forward to coming to work in the morning, even though it was 8 a.m., and that they felt very proud of themselves for what they had accomplished. This contrasts with students' feelings about their ordinary classroom experiences. During the first weeks, interns expressed nervousness about knowing what needed to be done each day and week and about their potential ability to deliver, worried they might not meet goals or produce something tangible in time for the final presentations. Some perceived their role as quite limited, given their educational background, which had taught them to compare themselves to others. "Snake," a local student in his late twenties, was concerned that he lacked exposure to DNA barcoding (a technique to identify species by using portions of genetic material), unlike others in his team, feeling as if he were a "little fish in a big pond," or an "outsider looking in." Early concerns were amplified by pressure from the city, and professional and academic mentors' high expectations.

The Qualities of the Experiences   The English word *quality* has at least two meanings: one is *evaluative* ("high quality," "low quality," according to measures), and the other is simply *descriptive* of the nature of the thing itself, its characteristics. As Dewey noted in his book *Experience and*

Education, "everything depends on the quality of the experience," yet despite the fact that all students engage in experiences, some experiences are more genuinely "educative" than others.[8]

Over the course of the summer, every intern experienced changes—the definition of learning. They spoke with much greater ease about local entities, the neighborhood organizations, various people in city government, the practicalities of doing things like installing crimp lines or working with "smart sensors." They had learned to consider a variety of "stakeholders"—people and organizations to be affected by their actions. Overall, there was a kind of arc of excitement that began early on, with perhaps unrealistic expectations, a dip in the middle when limitations and realities set in, and a strong rebound toward the end when they saw what had in fact been accomplished. Because they had different backgrounds, their growth differed. Some interns had arrived confident of their academic abilities but without any exposure to the realities of life in a low-income urban environment. Others were perhaps "weaker" academically but stronger in terms of life experience. Final interviews and surveys showed gains in many areas, such as making public presentations. Increased confidence about public speaking is evident in the self-assessment in the surveys (see figure 14.1).

The Aims and the Ends, Values and Value: Real Responsibility and Outcomes

In contrast with schoolish aims and ends, the projects' aims and ends were varied and numerous, but also emergent throughout the summer. The goals of the project as a whole were to work with the community to improve both water quality and quality of life in this neighborhood. The teams' aims were often quite ambitious, and sometimes even impossible. Individuals had their own specific goals, which ranged from professional ambitions to become civil engineers to finding a way to engage in community partnerships. There had been two previous seasons, so the interns did not have carte blanche to begin afresh; a number of projects were already in place. Interns were excited to do something useful and make a difference, excited about turning the creek area into something vibrant and healthy, excited for field days, excited to see how projects would turn out,

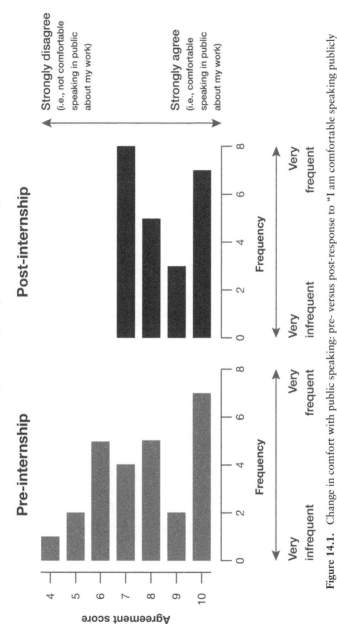

Figure 14.1. Change in comfort with public speaking: pre- versus post-response to "I am comfortable speaking publicly about my work."

Source: Redrawn from image by Rahul Oka.

and excited to show the mayor the results. In addition to looking forward to the project-related activities and progress, the interns also expressed excitement about personal fulfillment: to grow as individuals and to apply what they learned to future careers and activities. Some were also drawn to this for their résumés and for the summer salary.

As I mentioned in chapter 10, one group initially planned to work on lead present in the soil in this impoverished neighborhood, but they discovered that a city neighborhood association, with many prominent personnel, was also engaged in this work, serving as the coordinator for a Notre Dame–run project. The Notre Dame partners would not permit our interns to work independently because they were worried that this would be too much redundancy for the city. So our students, who had planned to accomplish something important over the course of the summer, had to regroup. I spoke with them around week 6 or 7, and they were completely despondent. But they ended up salvaging their work by reducing the length (151 to 35 pages) and grade level (to 8.6 years) of the brochure that the city handed out when people had their soil or their paint tested. One Monday morning they showed it to someone who recommended dozens of further changes; they revised it again.

College faculty, pay attention: Professors know that it is often impossible to get students to do revision, that they don't feel the need to get something to a point where they're proud of it; they only need to complete tasks, check them off the list. But in this case, because there were *actual consequences*, an actual audience, purpose, whether it was for a neighborhood meeting or the end of the internship, they revised, even though they were tired and they had already done it several times.

In so many projects of this complex ecosystem—rain gardens, a summer camp for high school students, helping to get streetlights installed— *the questions and problems that the interns confronted directed their learning*. They did not begin with the precise plan that ended up guiding them, but the gains in learning were nonetheless impressive.

Grade Focus and Failure   Another contrast has to do with the nature of assessment.[9] In school, almost every activity is completed for a grade. Even when school projects require community outreach or collaboration, students often do the work just for the grade, rather than out of genuine interest in a cause or relationships with the community. In much community-based learning, the students never even bother to show it to the community. Here the assessment was authentic: Did the project get done? How well? How did people honor the stakeholders in the process? The activities had real-world consequences, not grades or points, though there was ample feedback in the form of both self-assessments and narratives written by the project managers. The consequences included accountability to the community, tangible results, and the final public presentations. The assessments and feedback came from outcomes, constant interactions, and the many dimensions of the ultimate results, which did not require perfection.

Pedagogy and Pedagogizing: Independent Learning

This experiential learning-by-doing contrasts with what most of the interns had encountered in school. One of the project managers had given a day's lesson on design thinking, which involves five steps: empathize, design, ideate, prototype, and test—reassuring them that failures were useful. From initial suspicion of "learning by doing" rather than being first instructed abstractly, and in the experiential fashion that Deweyists would support, the interns had been persuaded largely of the effectiveness of that experiential learning (see figure 14.2).

BCe2 provided both the freedom and responsibility of working independently. The interns had to discover how they would fulfill their initial promises. Often they had to define the problems themselves and figure out where to turn to find information or skills. As one intern explained it, "Right now I am learning how to work ArcGIS. There really isn't anyone to teach me. There is a training today, which should be fun. I'm excited for that. But as of right now there really has not been anyone around to teach me. I did some research on it, but one of the things that I have learned from here is how to build up a relationship really quick. . . . It's kinda weird, but I like it."

Another explained that they had "already learned the basics of building a website, tinkering with Arduino. . . . I've already been using stuff I already know, and I've just been floating around between groups and been learning stuff from them." Interns sought multiple places to learn and consult.

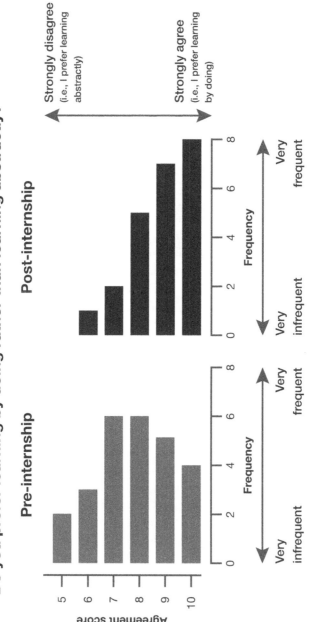

Figure 14.2. Change in attitude preference toward learning by doing: pre- versus post-response to "I prefer learning by doing rather than learning abstractly."

Source: Redrawn from image by Rahul Oka.

Teachers, Students, Classes: Communities of Varied Independent Learners

The relationships were one of the most important dimensions of this project.

Mentors   Instead of all-knowing "sages on the stage," the academic and professional mentors were truly "guides on the side." City and neighborhood officials, including the mayor, also offered their time and expertise.

Project managers, mentors, and consultants aimed generally to allow the students to learn on their own, intervening only if there was going to be a great obstacle.[10]

Respect for Learners' Capacities: Autonomy, Responsibility, Trust   Interns were free to generate their own questions and solutions and to take whatever steps they deemed appropriate. They could come and go as they wished, though they were generally expected to be engaged during work hours, which they reported on the electronic payroll system. Small teams went out into the neighborhood, downtown, to offices, to campuses. Nobody was monitored. There were no bells, no surveillance. Much time was spent outdoors, in environments without specific boundaries. The building where the project was based was open to the public.

Teams: Cooperative and Diverse   In communities, knowledge and skills are often distributed unevenly, and it's common for experts and novices to work together for a shared purpose.[11] BCe2 was deliberately shaped to welcome a high level of diversity, requiring participants to contribute their particular skills and knowledge to various aspects of each project. Despite differences in personal backgrounds, life experiences, and areas of educational focus, interns were eager to bring what they could to their teams.

In 2017 the facilitator-led exercises held during the first two weeks focused on the importance of incorporating multiple cognitive styles. Only after these first two weeks were the interns assigned to their particular three-person teams on the basis of their choices and the supervisors' sense of people's skills. There were eight major teams.

TABLE 14.1. Project teams, BCe2 2017

1	Urban Sustainability and Smart Green Infrastructure	• Tree nurseries • Rain gardens
2	Integrated Stormwater Management	Green technology to reduce stormwater entering the sewer system
3	Vacant Lots	Develop positive use for the approximately 25 percent vacant Southeast neighborhood lots
4	Daylighting Bowman Creek	Restore the creek aboveground
5	Southeast Neighborhood Redevelopment	• Seek new home construction on vacant lots • Add street and property lighting to improve neighborhood safety
6	Arduino Technology	Uses low-cost microprocessor systems (Arduino) for environmental sensing and control and other applications
7	DNA Barcoding	Catalog plant life in the neighborhood
8	Healthy Neighborhoods	• Develop plan for detecting lead in homes built before 1970 • Recommend low-cost solutions for minimizing risks of lead exposure

Participants were uniformly enthusiastic about their fellow interns. Interns appreciated their mutual support and the relatively informal social relations, positive even in the course of stress:

> I loved the unique energy between the interns. Even when we were working hard or under a lot of stress, they still had a smile on their face and were joking. . . . I've never worked anywhere that was more fun or productive than at BCe2. The energy was infectious. Even when I was exhausted the other interns were able to keep me going and happy. I loved how we were directly involved in the community, getting to know people and truly meeting them where they are.

Everyone seemed to look forward to seeing each other at work every day. In fact, most interns usually chatted for ten to fifteen minutes in the main office room each morning before spreading throughout the building with their project teams.

They often commented on their relationships. "The friendship between interns and an opportunity to make a difference was the most exciting part of the internship." "Red Panda" wrote about solidifying her intention to work for improving the world in an unconventional workplace and on a team.

> One thing about this internship that I did not anticipate is how close I would become to these people that I have known for a relatively short time. I truly believe that our bond as a team is centered around us working towards a large common goal of making the neighborhood better and making Bowman Creek a fun, innovative, and creative place to work. I also liked learning about technical and practical things that I wouldn't learn in my normal curriculum as an economics major. I feel that overall being immersed with all these different project teams has made me a more well-rounded academic and person. I also learned that I can do more than I think I am capable of and that my abilities are a direct reflection of how much work and effort I put towards learning something new.

The friendly, casual, respectful relationships had been carefully nurtured by the project managers from the beginning; the interns reported that they felt connected to everyone. One said that she felt closer to the other twenty-nine people in this internship than she had to anyone since she began college. The lack of competition between teams and individuals and the lack of a zero-sum assumption provided positive motivation for all involved. During a focus group held near the end of the summer, participants pointed out the lack of competition between teams; nobody was vying to be the best intern or accomplish the most. Teams' willingness to help one another was striking, and consistent. They gave examples of the Arduino team's generosity in teaching the Stormwater team about sensors and helping analyze the data, or the several times that the DNA Barcoding team members accompanied the Green Infrastructure team to inspect rain gardens.

Interns were conscious of the diversity of others' backgrounds. Snake observed, "Here, it is more organic, in that people aren't scared of being open to ideas." One intern wrote in anonymous post-survey comments,

> I honestly feel like Bowman Creek is the ideal working environment. We had such an influx of diversity bringing forth torrents of new ideas and perspectives. Since we all had such different projects, we didn't have the negative competition that is seen in schools or work environments when everyone is

doing the same projects and comparing their success to others. We felt free to try and fail and make faster, more innovative and deeper progress than in other ways of learning or working. I wish this was a real job so I could keep furthering our research and making our projects even better. I feel like we only just scratched the surface.

"Beaver" felt as if the ten weeks had flown by. He enjoyed gaining skills, especially in terms of presentations, and noted,

> Bowman Creek's format as experiential learning immersed in talent of different backgrounds and styles was different than anything I've experienced in my academic or professional career. The other interns have been great resources in themselves, offering fresh perspectives to develop ideas with. Working with them was fun, and it made our project better off as well as myself. . . . One part of the BCe2 experience that stood out to me the most was . . . getting to pitch the big-picture vision of the Daylighting project to members of the city, community, the school district, and the University of Notre Dame. These experiences in meetings and at our final presentation really made me feel like an advocate for the ecosystem and for the neighborhood, which was a great feeling.

Interns contrasted schoolish group work with their BCe2 experience. In group work for class, they said, students typically procrastinate, waiting until the last minute possible to complete their projects. Group work is often unevenly completed. In BCe2, they understood the necessity of each person working steadily. Cramming wasn't an acceptable tactic.

"Nemo," a member of the Arduino team, emphasized that "it's . . . a lot more fun to come here and work despite waking up at eight and learning about circuits and learning about new technology, whereas in class I'm just stressed about meeting deadlines." Moore writes that "in classrooms, students rarely have the opportunity to be truly responsible—not just punctual or obedient, but to have others actually count on them for something meaningful."[12] Students were aware of this: on written reflections, another pointed out the interns' responsibility to others: "When I'm in the classroom the only one who my work affects is me, whereas in the internship, I have a whole community—both in terms of the neighborhood and my fellow interns that are reliant upon me to do my work, which is a much better motivator than grades." Another pointed out, "Here, everyone wants to do the same work, and even if someone does more work, it does not really matter; it is about the common goal and finished product. The environment is more conducive to creativity, not as much about getting it done as quickly as possible. It is about taking the time to find the best possible solution. Everyone wants to do it."

While schools include great diversity, a sense of uniformity—of age, learning outcomes, practices, assessment, languages—is often idealized. Here, diversity was *needed* and celebrated, in a way far beyond tokenism.

Questions: Problems and Problem-Solving

The interns continually encountered unforeseen complications and obstacles, forcing them to plan on the fly and revise their plans. The early stages brought some frustrations, which, interns noted, would have typically been foreseen in a classroom or lab. Activities and inquiry were *led by questions and problems* rather than a preordained syllabus; even students interested in technical or economic dimensions of neighborhood revitalization or sustainability had to grapple with all these unexpected dimensions. It would have been impossible to set out "learning outcomes" for such a project, or a list of skills that would be developed.

Improvising, Emergence, and Open-Ended Learning The tasks were not "closed" as in conventional classes, but rather "open" and emergent. Sometimes interns seemed to wish there were right answers because they wanted to get the job done by summer's end; but over the summer they began to acknowledge the limits of their power, accepting that they might not be able to accomplish their goals, or at least not in their entirety, unlike schoolish goals where it would be a risk to one's grade not to accomplish the goals. Already in week 3, for instance, one group admitted they'd had to jettison their original plans because of the actual conditions. There was a lot of improvisation, with unpredictable timelines.

Time: Humane, Variation, and Harvest

Time operated differently at BCe2 from how it did in schoolish settings. Scheduling was not all-efficient. One member of the Healthy

Neighborhoods team spent five hours redoing the website after she re-named the domains. In week 6 the Arduino team's battery chargers blew up. The Stormwater team created simulated rain gardens to test the ef-fectiveness of different types of soils in absorbing water and to learn how the Arduino sensors functioned, but they needed to observe actual "rain events," obviously dependent on the weather, and revise their end goals to be more realistic. The Green Infrastructure team experimented with dif-ferent piping and connections so that they would know how to connect to the piping system in the neighborhood. The DNA Barcoding team had to collect data from the creek but had not discussed their methods and ended up "wasting" a day—because they had not properly documented the sam-ples, only afterward brainstorming about how to do so. The Stormwater team had installed sensors into one of their soil containers to assess mois-ture levels, realizing only the next day that their SD (secure digital) card had not been plugged in and they had no data.

Ample but Authentic Time Constraints   There was ample time and un-even external pressure. Unlike conventional classroom learning, much of the use of time would not have been possible to specify in advance. There were also simply a lot of hours: ten weeks of forty hours a week (four hundred hours), in contrast to a typical fifteen-week semester with perhaps six to nine hours devoted to each course (total 135 hours, if we use nine hours). But also there were *authentic deadlines* presented by the summer's constraints—not arbitrarily imposed, and palpably consequential.

Most members of the project teams seem panicked by week 8, feel-ing real responsibility to the community partners who had helped them develop their plans and visions. Some seemed surprised that things were taking longer than they had expected, almost as if they brought with them their expectations from classes where professors ensure that projects can be completed within the space of a semester, or a lab period. According to "Sitka," "Since this is independent work you really have the opportunity to just slack and go onto the internet and do whatever, but it is all up to the individual; you have to want to learn something—no one is going to micromanage you. You have to figure it out by yourself." Sometimes in-terns were astonished that they didn't get answers to questions overnight, from overworked city agencies, or that there were limitations to what they were allowed to share or gain access to. Mufasa commented about the surprising number of unforeseen problems that arose and the lengthy waiting that often had to be endured. "For some of them, it seems like we can't really do anything about it until we hear back from someone, and I'm just trying to think of things to do while we are waiting. And I'm really surprised that we don't, not exactly learn, but get to experience that when we're in college." In authentic experience, there's no constant efficiency.

Work, Labor, Play: Worth, Meaning, Play, and Use

Was it a job? Was it labor? Clearly it was work, paid labor to some extent, and sometimes even play.

For most of the interns this was their sole activity during the summer. It was a paid forty-hour-a-week "job." Thus most interns felt their financial needs were taken care of. One intern reveled in the technical work, calling it *play*: "I was really excited to make new friends and play with new technology. Being able to say that I piloted a beta software from Esri—the leader in intelligent mapping—is truly incredible. And I had a really enjoyable time doing it. I hope that my work ends up impacting the neighborhood, but even if it doesn't I enjoyed doing it."

Spaces and Places: Sanctuaries and Connection

Because we've seen how significant place and bodily experience were, it's important to describe the physical location of the internship:

Headquarters   Headquartered in the Bowman Creek neighborhood at a former warehouse repurposed as a multipurpose incubator space known as LangLab, the group rented the main room at one end of the L-shaped building, with couches, plywood tables, whiteboards, storage, walls for sticky notes. Several small rooms were available for quiet, focused, sometimes-solitary technical work and experiments with sensors, filtering, and soil. Scrounged coffeemakers, cups, and refrigerators served to care for the interns' bodily needs. The space housed other small businesses, including a café and coffee roaster, ecological printer, art exhibits, performances, community gatherings—even Mayor Pete Buttigieg's wedding took place there the next summer. Cast-off books, many academic or creative, lined the walls in a hodgepodge of shelves. The headquarters was three short blocks from a small park on Bowman Creek, the renovation of which had drawn much of the program's attention the first several years, and four blocks from a recently built large city park. The flexibility of the space facilitated flexible interactions within it.

Connection to Community and Place   Connections to the city and the neighborhood, to *place*, were nurtured in multiple ways every day. The wide variety of activities that interns engaged in included community outreach. They had to interact with the city government. Every few weeks BCe2 hosted late-afternoon cookout picnics in parks in the neighborhood, advertised and open to all. Several interns cooked hamburgers and veggie burgers over as many grills as possible. Neighbors brought children, city officials popped in, and people sat together at picnic tables eating burgers and chips, potato salad, watermelon, cookies. These unscripted interactions demonstrated commitment both to the project and to the neighbors, revealed each other's humanity, and fed often-underresourced people. Other outdoor activities, such as installation of rain gardens, required the entire group's physical participation. Local professionals and community leaders dropped by, and periodically the BCe2 interns met with members of a separate city-promoted engineering-technology internship. Some evenings and weekends the interns attended minor-league baseball games or went to bars or restaurants, sometimes organized and sometimes informally. Even interns from the area discovered new dimensions of their hometown.

As you can see in figure 14.3, from an initial lack of interest or involvement in the community, by the internship's end the interns were very much committed to this specific place.

Genres of Consumption: Abundance, as Needed

There was no textbook. Interns consulted whatever resources they needed—books, websites, training, articles, videos, podcasts—to solve their problems. They didn't complain about the reading. They were motivated purely by need and curiosity.

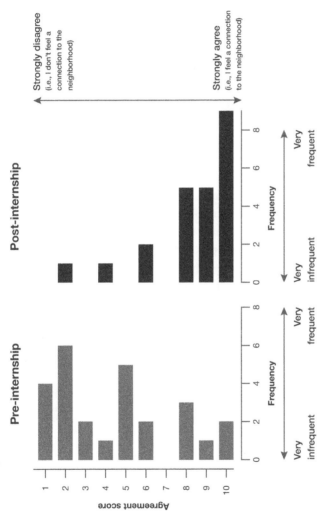

Figure 14.3. Change in connection to Bowman Creek neighborhood: pre- versus post-response to "I feel a connection to the Bowman Creek neighborhood."

Source: Redrawn from image by Rahul Oka.

Genres of Production: Authenticity and Freedom

The interns produced multiple types of works, demanded by both the project's structure and the real-world expectations of engineers. It was all bracketed between the weekly Monday morning presentations and the end-of-summer summary presentations and reports. Between those times interns discovered that they needed to research technical problems, plan how to proceed, build websites, write brochures, learn technical skills, assist other teams, and conduct local surveys, often on foot. One team ran a one-week camp for children. None of these were schoolish genres at all. They were often challenging.

Weekly Presentations   Because the project designers emphasized the real-world practices of engineers, which often required convincing stakeholders of the value of the work, each Monday morning at eight, every team presented an update, with slides, to the entire BCe2 community. Typically this included the thirty interns, the project manager, the faculty gurus, and several mentors. Other interested community members often attended. Many interns, like most people, were especially anxious about presenting before large groups.[13] These weekly team presentations (we recorded five weeks of presentations) took place in the large, dim gallery, with surplus chairs arranged in two rows before the screen. The teams spent the final hours on each Friday afternoon preparing the update for the following Monday morning. Though there was no formal clocking in, nearly everyone was present at that very early hour each Monday—a rare and punishing requirement for most college students. Many had coffee, or water bottles. Some slouched or even appeared to be closing their eyes, but nobody looked at any devices. (I've double-checked my field notes. Really. Nobody.)

Final Products   Every group was expected to prepare a final presentation at an open house, to which the community, mentors, and even the mayor were invited. Each group produced a final report with an accompanying website—all real-world products for engineers. They were aware of the upcoming presentation all summer; it motivated them to have something to show.

Tech and Media: Real and Eclectic

In their weekly updates many interns nonchalantly stated that they had had to learn a new software system, or work on their HTML, or learn to use new equipment, or read hundred-page manuals, or work their way through a body of research, because it was necessary for them to function properly on their project team. None of this could have been predicted but emerged out of necessity.

To aid in planning processes, multiple groups used visual aids, such as diagrams or flowcharts, to organize ideas. The Vacant Lots team drew thought diagrams on multiple occasions. One day at the University of Notre Dame, a group of interns, discussing how ArcGIS, a cloud-based online mapping tool, might be used to combine already existing data from the city and previous interns, created a diagram of possibilities on the whiteboard. Another day, the group left to investigate a lot in an old park that they wanted to clean. After surveying the area and talking with a neighbor about the Miami Village Association (which was supposed to be maintaining the park), they used a giant sketch pad to draw how they could organize a cleanup.

One of the leaders, Red Panda, once brought a big paper pad to the back room and, on the floor, began making a logic flow chart of the vacant lots, explaining that it was an organizing method that would allow her to later add information to her website in a more visually appealing way. Other groups used diagrams and maps to represent the geographic areas and urban zoning layouts they needed for their projects.

The tech was high-tech and low-tech. Media were old and new. These tools did not follow a preordained sequence of use but were selected on the fly as needed.

Bodies: Multimodal Involvement

The learning was not all cognitive or verbal. Throughout the summer, interns engaged in substantial amounts of physical labor and what linguistic anthropologists call multimodal activities, such as hauling compost, digging holes, and lounging in LangLab's irregular furniture. They pasted sticky notes and moved among each other, getting physically close. At picnics and in rain gardens, being outside, struggling with materials and conveyances, walking and grilling, they became involved with all their being. The learning was "extended," as Andy Clark puts it, by the body, the world, objects, and other beings.[14]

From Alienation to Authenticity: Wholeness and Meaning

Interns took their responsibility seriously. "Wolf"'s awareness of her responsibility was "motivating and intimidating." "Tantor" was "more afraid of failing in this situation than with GPA in school." Snake said that because he "always wanted to have an impact on the world" the internship and the work were fulfilling, even if what he did lacked immediate large-scale results. "Tiger" emphasized autonomy and responsibility, saying, "It makes me feel great . . . because that means I get to decide on something, that means I have to really work on being as safe as I can. It means that I will really have an impact on people's lives."

Sitka admitted that the feelings could vary, precisely because of the real-world responsibility. "It depends, it feels good, but if you mess up one thing then everyone will remember that, so you will have to do like four good things to make it go away. So it's kinda scary, but when you do something good, then it makes you feel great. So it depends on the problem."

Snake—the one who was so worried initially about his relative lack of preparation—claimed that this job was the best he had ever had, given his personal creativity, because BCe2 provided the freedom to solve problems, and he was not constrained to do it in a certain way. In his words, "it's not A, B, and C, do this, but rather allows teams to create their own way of doing." Tiger reflected, "I am excited about [giving] this my best, leaving this place and feeling like I can't blame myself for anything, like I gave it all I had." One intern noted that "since we were all given tasks that we really had to define ourselves as much as actually work on them, having such an energized and talented group of coworkers was essential."

Lessons for Schoolishness

Every dimension of schoolishness that I've presented throughout this book was challenged by this complicated, unique (and well-funded) project. The results—learning, experiencing—have been positive.

It's important to understand how successful learning works, not only because it's valuable in its own right, but also to provide a model for ideal learning environments. "Field learning" in a project like Bowman Creek is the opposite of everything schoolish: it takes place in many places; time is abundant; social dimensions are central; failure is information; assessment is multifaceted; cooperation is necessary; people grow to trust each other; emotional and physical elements are essential. Internships like this one can demonstrate how learning almost-in-the-wild leads to effective and enjoyable experiences that engage the full learner.

Many know that this is so. The final question, though, is how to change schoolish schools.

15

MAKING SCHOOLS LESS SCHOOLISH

Of Evolutions and Revolutions

> The American university has become the final stage of the most all-
> encompassing initiation rite the world has ever known. . . . We
> cannot begin a reform of education unless we first understand that
> neither individual learning nor social equality can be enhanced by the
> ritual of schooling. . . . The project of demythologizing which
> I propose cannot be limited to the university alone.
>
> IVAN ILLICH, *Deschooling Society*

You've seen all the problems associated with schoolishness: gaming the system, over-pedagogizing society, endless deferral, suffering, unsatisfied bodies, alienation. You've also seen one example of what authentic learning might look like.

But can we get more of this authentic learning into existing schools? Must we discard schools entirely, start from scratch, to eliminate schoolishness? Can existing schools become less schoolish?

Do we need revolution, or can evolution help?

In *I Love Learning*, I wrote that we need revolution. We need to change the systems of institutional learning in profound ways, I said, maybe even get rid of school entirely—or at least question its existence, structures, ubiquity. All assumptions were up for grabs.

A review of that book in the *Chronicle of Higher Education* by strangely parallel education writer James Lang contrasted my "revolutionary" approach to his own more evolutionary approach, as presented in his popular, incrementalist, *Small Teaching*. Joshua Eyler in *How Humans Learn* also called me an unrealistic, idealistic revolutionary. (Both Jim and Josh are now dear colleagues.) Josh has just begun a new enterprise, to try to change institutions.[1]

Yet a graduate student of mine, one with whom I worked very closely on education topics, came in one day for our weekly meeting to discuss his independent reading course on critical education and said that while *he* wants to "blow up the system," I'm more content to work within it.

This surprised me.

I too want to "blow up the system." I wish we could start from scratch. I feel that way about the internal combustion engine, about the Haber-Bosch process of nitrogen fixation that gave rise to industrial agriculture, about slavery and the continuing aftermath of this tragic and immoral system.

I worked for two years, with five cherished colleagues, on a project to reimagine public higher education, entirely.[2] Our proposal didn't look anything like the current system. Everything—time, space, roles, products—was determined by questions learners wanted to ask.

Which is it? Is it a revolution, where everything changes? Or evolution, small, slow alterations that may in time add up to greater changes?

Revolution?

My primary graduate and scholarly training was in China studies. China had revolutions, including a "cultural revolution," which did not turn out so well; the overnight imposition of one person's vision of utopia, using the power of the regime to enforce compliance, in the name of equality and justice (and largely to consolidate power), did not yield a social paradise. Millions died in the name of eradicating old views.

That's not my approach. In case you can't tell, I'm not a murderer, strongman, autocrat. I'm actually torn between polite timidity and outraged impassioned courage, which has been increasing.

But things do change, sometimes completely. Sometimes it happens only through violent struggle ("revolution comes out of the barrel of a

gun," Mao said): think of the abolition of slavery, the civil rights movement, women's voting rights. Sometimes they change through both gradual and sudden transformation, like the struggle for LGBTQ acceptance:
Stonewall and Act Up and *Will and Grace* and Obama's "evolution" and
a lot of other factors contributed. In the summer of 2020, as I was working on this book, after George Floyd was killed and Black Lives Matter
entered mainstream US awareness, Confederate flags were coming down
and Princeton's Woodrow Wilson School was getting renamed, and suddenly 75 percent of the US population agreed that racism is real.

In scientific revolutions, slow understanding that the old system
isn't working accumulates, and then it appears as if there is a sudden
change—Ptolemaic (Earth-centered) to Copernican (Sun-centered) as-
tronomy, germ theory—and then the old system is repudiated by almost
everyone.

But the point is that revolutions need preparatory work, and they
need to spread not by fiat but by persuasion, by changing "hearts and
minds."

These things happen slowly, and with a lot of resistance. Some people
benefit from the status quo.

But COVID propelled us to change with lightning speed, whether we
wanted to or not. All through the summer of 2020 I read articles about the
"speed of innovation" and about "two decades of change in two weeks,"
about not returning to the status quo, and so on.[3] And the battle, tension, disagreement between evolution and revolution—and stasis—were
everywhere.

My edited volume, *Ungrading*, was published in late fall 2020 and
caught the attention of a lot of educators. By the first months of 2022
people were calling it "the ungrading movement." In April 2022, someone at a Zoom talk I gave at the Claremont Colleges called it a "revolution." In fall 2023 alternative assessment is increasing.

The good news is that ours is a new golden age of progressive education,
at all levels from preschool to higher education and beyond, into graduate and professional education. Challenges to conventional schooling
take many forms: getting rid of conventional disciplines; having student-
driven inquiry, with problem-, project-, and place-based learning;
"flipping the classroom"; focusing on application rather than theory;

implementing hands-on learning, active learning, participatory research. Career education is bubbling up as a new enthusiasm. There are forest kindergartens and farm schools, polytechnics and apprenticeships, Khan Academy and MOOCs, coding academies, badges, microcredentials, and other demonstrations of proficiency. We're in a moment of intense educational ferment, which is exciting. It's also evidence that our current model is problematic.

The bad news is that we've been here before. There have been many waves of educational change and transformation, some enduring but most fleeting. Many changes have simply evaporated or been reversed partly because of the pull of schoolishness and partly because all dimensions of institutional education are so intertwined. Educational change is really hard.

Educational experimentation out there has been going on for decades— a century, actually, as Tyack and Cuban show in their book *Tinkering toward Utopia*.[4] At times I feel as if my book is just an expanded version of John Dewey's eighty-page 1938 book, *Experience and Education*, or an extended meditation of Neil Postman's 1996 *The End of Education*. Many of the changes people are pushing so fervently now have been tried before:

In the 1920s Helen Parkhurst developed the Dalton Plan. One element was essentially contract grading.

In the 1930s three high school teachers in Canton, Mississippi, had students spending five hours a day on an integrated, wicked problem or question that the students generated.

In the 1960s the Eight-Year Study proposed that "the young should be seen as active, intellectually curious, and capable of taking charge of their own learning."[5]

Sound familiar?

Are we merely reinventing the wheels that never rode the roads?

Progressive and Traditional Schooling

Tension between what we might call "traditional" and "progressive" education has been in play for at least the last hundred or so years since Dewey, Piaget, and Vygotsky, or two and a half times that if we count

Rousseau (and that's just the European tradition). Theorists such as Foucault, Elias, Bourdieu, Rose, Freire, Illich, Kohn, hooks, Emdin, and Cottom have looked hard at the discipline and race-class-gender-sexuality-subjectivity instilled via schools at all levels. The twentieth century saw both the spread of traditionalist schools and a strand of utopian experimentation, from small to enormous changes.

In *The Learning Rainforest: Great Teaching in Real Classrooms*, Tom Sherrington presents multidimensional contrasts between "traditional" and "progressive" classrooms: "expert knowledge delivered by teacher" versus "experiential learning"; "power and control" versus "trust and openness"; "desks in rows" versus "desks in groups"; "19th-century skills" versus "21st-century skills" (ultimately he'll find a balance between them).[6] Metaphors and models of industrial efficiency and uniformity of factories, with ranking, sorting, assessing, testing, have been central to the dominant model, challenged by an alternative model of natural development, human cultivation and unfolding.

Kieren Egan in *Starting from Scratch* proposes something that he sees as unlike both progressive education, with its focus on natural development, and conventional education. In some of his work he calls this "imaginative education."[7] Whether we call it "progressive" or something else, all these reforms question some or all dimensions of schoolishness: grades, deadlines, attendance, points, disciplines, curriculum, requirements, false objectivity, scientism, metrics fixation, obedience, compliance. Yet many who claim to be "reinventing" various forms of education retain a lot of the current practices (age grading, a predetermined curriculum, accreditation . . .) because it's "not possible" or "not realistic" to question everything.

But it all depends on the reformer's/revolutionary's scale, ambition, and sense of *what's untouchable*. Remember foot binding. It was "just the way it was"—until it was gone.

Change

Experts in institutional, educational change note different levels of transformation, and diverse models of the process. One very linear image of institutional change, "transformation of a practice," comes from Kate

White and colleagues in a book devoted to, as its title has it, *Transforming Institutions*.[8] First is awareness of a transformative practice, followed by interest in the practice. Then evaluation, trial, and finally adoption of the practice. It's no wonder that such transformation often gets stopped before the whole sequence can unfold. "Practice" tends to appear relatively modest, such as shifting from lecturing to active-learning practices, which will eventually be transformative.

A messier version, by Thompson and Marbach-Ad, shows many more dimensions, including faculty intentions and beliefs about teaching (see figure 15.2).

Many note the challenge of active-learning practices to take hold, despite robust evidence about their benefits. As I mentioned in chapter 9, students *feel* that they learn more in lectures, but they *actually* learn less than in active-learning classes.[9]

Again, the structures of schoolishness are intertwined, and it's impossible to change one without changing many others. Brittnee Earl and colleagues note, "Despite decades of work documenting the effectiveness of [evidence-based instructional practices] in STEM courses, high levels of adoption have been elusive."[10] I'm uncomfortable with the constant invocation of "evidence-based" whatever, because there are lots of kinds of evidence, but the point here is that no matter how convincing is the support for practices like active learning, people revert to the familiar. Ungrading is an example of a transformation entering widespread awareness; I'll talk about it below.

Changes can go from small tweaks to course changes; from programs to institutions. Theoretically entire networks of institutions could work together for change, which would result in the entire sector changing.

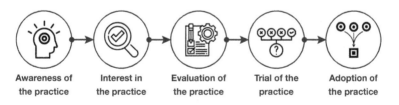

| Awareness of the practice | Interest in the practice | Evaluation of the practice | Trial of the practice | Adoption of the practice |

Figure 15.1. Transformation, idealized

Source: Redrawn from White et al., *Transforming Institutions*, 14 (adapted from Rogers's Innovation Decision Process).

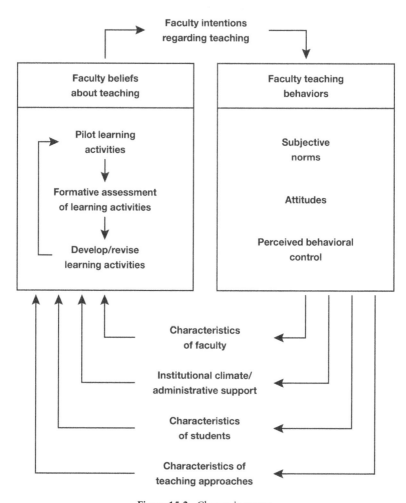

Figure 15.2. Change is messy

Source: Redrawn from Katerina Thompson and Gili Marbach-Ad, "The Characteristics of Dissemination Success (CODS) Model as a Framework for Changing the Culture of Teaching and Learning," in White et al., *Transforming Institutions*, 38.

But change is affected by, and in turn affects, multiple participants and factors: students, faculty, leadership, local culture, funding, all the schoolish structures, and the training, socialization, experience, and expectations of each of these entities. I've started to call ungrading a "workaround in a problematic structure," a hack, to amplify Starr Sackstein.

Small Tweaks

Least pervasive and easiest to implement are what James Lang calls "small teaching," changes that can be done in the *very next class session*. These include think-pair-share exercises, where students are given time to reflect, then to talk with a neighbor or classmate, and finally to present to the class. The advantages are that students are engaged; shy or anxious students don't have to present to the whole class.

Some of the best proponents of such tweaks are James Lang; Cathy Davidson and Christina Katopodis in their book *The New College Classroom*; and Kelly Hogan and Viji Sathy in their instant classic, *Inclusive Teaching: Strategies for Promoting Equity in the College Classroom*.[11] Ideas such as entrance and exit tickets, polls, or anything that is not just a lecture-and-test format is an improvement.

I have included many of these ideas in the preceding chapters. Some fall under the "active learning" heading. These tweaks are realistic and unthreatening. Though if you do enough of them, they add up.

Course Changes: Critical Pedagogical Praxis

Next are *course-by-course* changes, such as ungrading, which has affected at least tens of thousands of students, especially if we include all variations, as I do, under my capacious "ungrading umbrella" (I'm a lumper, not a splitter; some prefer to be more precise about each variant).[12] And other methods of class improvement, explained under the labels of "instructional design" or the "Science of Teaching and Learning," or teaching-and-learning centers, foreground social-emotional learning, antiracist, trauma-informed, or trauma-sensitive pedagogies.

My approach is to make the learning my students do in my classes as much as possible like learning that they do outside classes, as I showed in the previous chapter, "The Trees Need Water." The shifts I've undertaken personally since about 2003 in my own teaching—shifts that are more aspirational than completed, though some are well under way—include at least the following. Although they amount to a grand restructuring in my classes—enough so that students are unbalanced for a time—the scale is small.

Each semester I begin anew the daunting task of untraining my successful students' helplessness—or rather inviting them to acknowledge and

TABLE 15.1. Progress(ive) Shifts

Before	Toward	Now (and eventually?)
teacher driven	→	student driven
uniformity	→	diversity
saying/ telling (referential/semantic)	→	doing / showing (pragmatic)
judgment	→	support
known in advance	→	discovered, emergent
product	→	process
sage on the stage	→	guide on the side
for the teacher	→	for others or the self
individual	→	social (but not all the time)* *introverts
intellectual/cognitive	→	emotional/affective
"hard" and "rigorous"	→	comfortable or manageable (optimal challenge) (like Suzuki)
mind	→	body
judgment	→	conversation
control	→	trust
"cover the content"	→	discover the questions
order	→	liveliness
children	→	adults
compliance	→	responsibility and accountability
rigor	→	flexibility, responsiveness
fixity and isolation	→	emergence from interaction, unfolding, and iteration
arbitrariness	→	connection
alienation	→	authenticity

accept their own substantial roles in the community of learners, and trying to let them feel *the power of the floor*, the power to ask a genuine question, and a release from the game of trivia that they have mastered with such earnestness, and with such problematic effects.

Programs

More sweeping are *programmatic* changes, such as the Science Education Initiative overseen by physics Nobel laureate Carl Wieman or the

Red House program at Georgetown, which "seeks to shape a new learning paradigm that expands high-impact practices at Georgetown University, confronts systemic injustice, improves wellbeing and healing, while controlling the rising costs of a transformative education."[13] You've already read a little (chapter 2) about the Mastery Transcript Consortium's aims to alter the way information about students' learning moves from secondary schools to college admissions departments by including a portfolio and other detailed information about specific skills, knowledge, and dispositions.[14] Such changes almost always require a powerful, charismatic champion, such as someone with a Nobel prize or people who have been presidents and provosts, who then take on a huge project of changing the status quo. The changes rarely, from what I've seen, begin as grassroots projects, though they also require ordinary faculty to join in the effort.

Other examples of programmatic change include concerted efforts in first-year writing programs to use versions of ungrading techniques (often contract grading or labor-based grading, where what matters is just the completion or the time spent, not a single external measure of "quality"); and preclinical science courses in medical schools that have changed to ungraded programs. (This is welcome, of course, but as a paper by Creighton University medical school professors James F. Smith Jr. and Nicole M. Piemonte shows, when the sorting still must be done, "tiered grading," no matter what it is labeled, still persists—even when it has deleterious psychological and moral effects.)[15]

A $7.2 million initiative at the University of Michigan aims to transform "large, foundational courses" through focus on pedagogically informed redesign.[16] In Australia, about a third (eight out of twenty-three) units in the graduate design degree at Swinburne University were changing to a pass/fail system, to move away from grades in an effort to focus on creativity and safety for risk taking.[17] Clare McNally, academic lead for assessment and evaluation, has been active in moving the highly ranked (eleventh in the world for clinical and health studies in 2021, according to the Times Higher Education World University Rankings) University of Melbourne Dental Higher Education program from conventional grades to e-portfolios and other measures of learning. Arts educators in higher education in the UK are discussing the value of pass/fail assessment for student belonging and learning.[18]

An innovative project within conventional public schools is the Edible Schoolyard founded by Alice Waters, chef of Chez Panisse in Berkeley, California, who is often credited with helping to transform the US food system. This project aims to be simultaneously a way of educating children about the realities of the food production system and to entice them to eat healthier foods.[19]

Institutions

Among the grandest changes are entirely new *institutions*. Some are founded as unconventional and over time "revert to the mean" of schoolishness.

Some innovative K–12 schools are cooperative institutions in which school is supposed to be more like life outside school and less schoolish in at least several dimensions. Examples include the John Dewey–founded Chicago Laboratory Schools (1896);[20] child-centered Montessori schools (1906); the Reggio Emilia schools (1913);[21] freedom-emphasizing Summerhill in England (1921); forest kindergartens that function entirely outdoors and aim to be child-driven, connected with nature, and have an emergent curriculum (1952); freedom-and-responsibility-focused Sudbury schools (1968); and the Haja Production School (1999) in South Korea (which I have visited) for students with "school refusal through social entrepreneurship," helping students who have "refused" to attend school find a community with a focus on real-world revenue-generating projects that address social problems.[22] Some of these emphasize that teachers merely guide rather than act as central authorities. They often challenge the space and time expectations of schoolishness. Their curricula and interactive structures look nothing like prototypical schoolish structures; their measurements of success may not match the standardized-testing regime, either. From 1919 to 1955 the Progressive Education Association convened meetings, supported publications, and commissioned studies of progressive education in primary and secondary schools in the United States advocating child-centered and unschoolish schools.[23]

Some colleges were designed with radical, fundamental, reconceptualization: Bennington College in Vermont (1932) was founded as a "laboratory" emphasizing self-directed learning.[24] Some of these schools have entirely unconventional structures, such as Goddard College in Vermont, founded in 1938 by Royce "Tim" Pitkin (a student of John Dewey), with "low-residency" requirements and its tagline "progressive education for creative minds," learning by doing, and explicit invocation of the principles of John Dewey.[25]

The 1960s (extending to the early 1970s) were a period of great experimentation. For example, the New College of Florida emphasized personalized educational goals and freedom from the "lock-step curriculum and a focus on credit hours and a GPA" (1960).[26] In 2023 this public, overtly progressive college became the target of Florida governor Ron DeSantis, who fired the president and appointed new members of the board of trustees, in order to replace its progressive orientation with a far more conservative structure and curriculum.[27]

The University of California, Santa Cruz, began with its founding in 1965 to challenge many conventional structures in pursuit of social and environmental justice. Its early years were filled with experimentation, and no grades.[28] But its structures are more conventional now. While the school began with only narrative evaluations, in 2000, because of *both student and faculty* demands, it changed to a system that included grades.[29] (Narrative evaluations take a lot of faculty time and require knowing students well.) This shows the intertwined nature of the system. Surely the students were not saying that grades made them happier or better at learning; they just were interested in mundane hurdles like medical school applications.

The Open University in the UK (1969) aimed to make education available to every adult.[30] Hampshire College in Massachusetts was founded through collaboration among Amherst, Mount Holyoke, and Smith Colleges and the University of Massachusetts at Amherst, to "examine the assumptions and practices of liberal arts education" (1970).[31] Best known for its use exclusively of narrative evaluations, not grades, Hampshire was one of the first liberal arts colleges to integrate a campus farm with pedagogy in the twentieth century. It has no majors and emphasizes a student-designed curriculum.[32] Evergreen State College in Washington State has no majors or minors and similarly uses narrative evaluations (1971).[33]

A more recently (2002) founded innovative school is the Olin School of Engineering in Massachusetts, a small, top-notch program that centers project-based learning in accordance with contemporary notions of learning.[34]

Deschooling, Unschooling, School Abolition

In contrast to efforts to work within the framework of institutional education are minority calls to abolish schools, to *deschool* entirely, sometimes termed "unschooling" or the college rejection narrative. Motivations can be libertarian and antisocietal, or utopian and anticapitalist.

Ivan Illich called for *Deschooling Society* in a broad philosophical and psychological analysis of the harms of schooling. John Holt called for unschooling. Gina Riley has published the first academic study of contemporary unschooling.[35]

The Human Restoration Project goes beyond the mere curricular to address the many dimensions of being human—educational, psychological, political, philosophical—and the roles of schools in fostering harm or good.[36]

Those in favor of retaining schools point out that schools are, or potentially could be, democratic institutions, especially at lower levels, and should be supported by public funding. Neil Postman makes this case in *The End of Education.*

Schools may be engines of equality or inequality, depending how they're set up and funded, and how participation is determined. In some settings, they may be students' only reliable safety net.

The Limits of Relativism

Throughout the book I've argued for "what's better." Any shifts really need to be grounded in a set of axioms, principles, and values. "What works" must be clearly articulated as "what works for whom and in what sense?" In this book I've tried to spell out my framework. You may disagree, but at least we can locate the sources of our disagreement.

In this sense, the book addresses the anthropological challenge of the limits of relativism, in which we look at what causes the elasticity, plasticity, of human flexibility to go beyond the breaking point, resulting in suffering, misery, and ill-being, and argues in favor of not merely observing but actively advocating for change.[37]

Anthropology in its earliest years combated racism and ideas of the "ladder of civilization" with ideas of relativism. Yet a fully relativist approach has in turn been challenged: What about evil, about darkness?

From accounts such as Edgerton's discussion of the "myth of primitive harmony" in *Sick Societies* to most of the work in applied anthropology and recent calls for "anthropology of the good," notions of the good are often implicit.[38] So debates about *better* education must first ask "Better in what sense?" And how would we measure? Would we measure a liberated education by means of standardized tests? In writing about "the schools our children deserve," Alfie Kohn warns that "it is assumed that the standardized test scores used to draw all these conclusions [about the relative failure of US schools] are valid indicators of the quality of education. You or I could design a test in half an hour that would be failed by most of the children, and even the adults, who took it. . . . Many of the specific tests being used to generate speeches and articles about the desperate plight of American education . . . are seriously deficient."[39] But also we must ask, What are the views of ideal human flourishing driving each claim of "better"? Putting salves on injuries from harmful political and economic systems in order to succeed in their metrics may be necessary but is not sufficient.

Humility and Not Knowing Everything

But it's not easy.

Teaching, in any event, is humbling. Redoing one's teaching top to bottom is beyond difficult.

If we temporarily set aside institutional imperatives and social expectations of perfection—easier said than done—then we can acknowledge that profound change may lead to failures, sometimes spectacular. But if we apply what we know about learning in general not only to student learning but to learning new forms of pedagogy, then failures and mistakes are information.

We just need humility (and not humiliation, or at least not too often).

In "real life" people learn from mistakes and failure. Mistakes provide information; they show the climber that the foot must be further from the edge, the flutist that the inhale needs to be quicker, the baker that the dough needs more water, the computer user that the mouse has to be clicked twice. Errors, failure, are critical for learning to play an instrument, learning sports, learning to be a parent, or struggling to become a decent teacher. These are *information*. Design thinking employs prototyping, relatively low-cost attempts to try things that might not work. New clichés, "fail forward" and "fail often and fast," have emerged as schools try to foster entrepreneurship and innovation, destruction of the old.[40]

As most school is structured, though, this is penalized. If possible we need to figure out ways to encourage students and teachers to be courageous and to fail spectacularly, if necessary. Ungrading helps with that. Certainly the mistakes through which people learn, the false starts, the tentative beginnings, should never be averaged in.

But however much teachers may *claim* that mistakes are information, we often don't feel we're allowed to make them ourselves.

When you completely transform your teaching, when you go against the grain, it's very likely that you'll experience all kinds of mistakes, at least. Uncertainty. Lack of confidence. Sometimes humiliation. Resistance. Failure. Doubt.

Transforming education does not happen with a single epiphany. It's a slow, gradual, humbling process.

It requires safety—professional safety that many lack. So, for many colleagues in precarious positions, I understand that you may not feel you can take this risk.

Boy did the COVID pivot allow me to demonstrate failure! Trying new tools, making mistake after mistake, showing humility. . . . If ever there was a moment in schools for teachers to show students what learning— real, consequential, learning—looks like, it was during spring, summer, fall 2020.

A Failure

One semester I tried something. It didn't work very well.

I was teaching a new class called The Culture of College. In my long-standing effort to have the classroom mirror life outside the classroom as much as possible, given the structures of the university where I teach and my own disciplinary responsibilities, I reserved slots for students at every level. I had four first-year students, in their very first months of college, one sophomore, two juniors, and five seniors. I decided I would teach it as a radically liberated class. We'd co-construct the syllabus, generate ideas for projects, discuss standards. Students would bring their own questions, share their own experience, and we would challenge all the dogmas, both about college in general and about the ways courses operate.

It was a big bust. I knew it at the time; I couldn't turn it around, couldn't salvage it. Discussions were icy, painful. It should have been the perfect course, with a perfect dozen students. But as I walked into the room, my stomach clenched. Instead of gratitude for liberation, I faced steely resistance.

I tried a lot of activities to shake things up: lots of movement the first day, chatting anonymously on a Google Doc about college before the first substantive discussions, having them talk in small groups or pairs. We watched *Animal House* one evening—my first shocked full viewing—and I had them over to my house to see *Good Will Hunting*, which nobody wanted to talk about—even with what I thought was a very user-friendly discussion guide. (Students often need guidance about how to analyze, not just watch, TV and movies, and they talk mostly about plot and character rather than point of view or editorial decisions.) All semester our discussions were tepid, with students only really coming alive when talking about alcohol and sexual assault.

I blamed the room, the time of day (5 p.m.), whatever.

At a certain point I tried to invite them to "co-create the curriculum," and they had no idea what I was talking about. *What do YOU want to learn?*

Huh?

And I decided that we needed variety, student ownership, etc., after the truly silent moments. Students would each, in pairs, take over responsibility for leading the class.

They wanted to know what to do. What I wanted. How long things should be.

I tried to leave things open-ended, to keep asking them to think about what they wanted to do for the final project, building on the sometimes fabulous smaller writing that they were doing nearly every week: interviews, ethnographies, mapping of campus, reflecting on experience, going to another campus. They thought my ungrading approach was really weird, though some came to like it.

They weren't slackers. Just about all of them did just about all the reading.

But I offered them a space for developing their own questions. It wasn't a joyous celebration of discovery, though they were fascinated with discussions about alcohol, and their discovery that "college" doesn't only mean highly selective private residential schools like our own.

There was no embrace of this freedom.

What should they do?

Someone, please, tell them!

Finally, one of the seniors I'd had in several previous courses, heading for medical school and engaged in a "leadership" course for honors students, took charge. She helped them organize themselves, and finally, during the final two weeks of class, there was some excitement.

The final product was fine. For a group of college students, they had very few technical skills. iMovie was pretty much as far as they could go.

They resisted seeking technical assistance from our library, which offers fabulous sessions staffed by capable undergraduates.

They weren't interested in reflecting on the class project. I consider it a not entirely abysmal failure. But it was definitely not what I had hoped for.

(The very next semester, in the same room, my two courses went *great*! It wasn't, it seems, the room.)

I thought about it obsessively. I lost sleep over it.

Several strong, silent personalities seemed to dominate through their quiet disapproval. (One, whom I'd assumed to be very disapproving, took another class with me as a senior. My reading of body language may be somewhat unreliable, colored by insecurity.)

I'm not sure what else was going on.

I planned to teach it again the following year but chickened out.

But I have also discovered an article by Robert FitzSimmons on higher education in Finland, using Freire's notion of "pedagogy of the heart." Finnish students, in thrall to neoliberalism, don't want freedom.[41] Freire describes the "fear of freedom" as one of the attributes of the oppressed because they have internalized the laws and rules of the oppressor. Accordingly, they have accepted the oppressors' guidelines in how to act and do life. Freire has called this "prescribed behavior" because it focuses on the prescription of the oppressor.[42]

They want rules. They want tasks.

Give us our lists. Tell us what to do to get our A's, our credits, our degrees, our jobs in this competitive sphere.

Here are some jottings I wrote at the time.

A Month In: Triumphs and Struggles   (Mid-September 2018)

In the class where I'm aiming for democratic and feminist pedagogy, The Culture of College, it is mostly not quite working. I have twelve students, mostly fairly quiet. At least three are first-year students; five have taken classes with me before. One has me for both classes.

I have not scaffolded this very well yet. They want to know what to do. I want them to want things, to be curious, to bring questions. They are busy; they do what I ask. If I ask them to find three articles, they find three. If I ask them to visit another campus and do fieldwork, they do, but they may stay only half an hour.

They are busy. Have I mentioned that before?

I have told them that I'm not in charge; if there is something that needs solving—a folder to post work in—they should do it, just like if their neighborhood needs a recycling bin, they should figure out how to arrange it.

It's not quite jelling yet. A work in progress, and a lot of sleep lost.

I tried everything. Addressing it openly. Small groups. Reflections. One-on-one meetings. Talking with students I knew from the past. Nothing really turned it around.

Two Months In   (October 10, 2018)

Talking about students leading discussion, to get more "ownership" and involvement (a reset, with food and sitting on the floor and a "game" and a frank discussion . . . about how we're lacking zest, oomph . . .).

"Why don't *you* just do it?" asks one of my first-year students.

Not because I'm lazy; not because I don't know this stuff.

Precisely because I have done it, read it, chosen it . . . thought about it. It works much better if it comes from you.

I don't think she buys it. She pouts, a little. Polite in person, aloof in the group.

I do a lot of soul-searching. How can I meet these particular students partway? If they rebel, am I not succeeding in accepting them, and their particularity?

How can I explain? I research. Explaining doesn't work for pedagogy, just like it doesn't work for anything else. Show, don't tell. So I have to show them that they learn more, better, this way.

I think it is working, a little, even when the students don't ask great questions, or the questions are a little boring.

And in private meetings, one-on-one with every student (ten minutes each), one student confessed: "We try harder to answer questions, to be honest, when other students are leading. When the professor asks a question, we're willing to let it just go."

So. A little validation from a thoughtful and honest student.

Another demands more structure: Students want direction. When is this due? How long should it be?

I argue that I'm giving them radical freedom.

They want structure. "You have to acknowledge that we're in the system."

Students admit that they prioritize in their very clear-eyed neoliberal task-oriented fashion that their organic chemistry, the curved classes, the ones that will get them into med school, will get them internships with finance and consulting firms. They look at me blankly when I point out a passage that defines neoliberalism as applying economic concepts, such as competition, to noneconomic realms, such as education. Duh. Isn't it obvious that that's the reality? What fantasy and romantic universe am I living in that doesn't see that?

I ask about religion, values, the ND family, the community, and how that plays against the competitive nature of academics.

They tell me that they compartmentalize academics and everything else.

I ask if that is healthy, to do this?

One says, maybe holism is ideal. Another says, don't be silly and seek authenticity and integrity. Everyone knows that this isn't possible. We're one person with our friends and another with parents.

Resistance

Each of the changes I describe in this chapter encounters resistance, because faculty, administrators, students, and the public think they know what "real school" is—that is, schoolishness. People studying educational and institutional change have observed, for instance, that despite abundant scholarship and "evidence-based findings," such as in the Scholarship of Teaching and Learning, in many domains there's virtually no uptake. Walk down the hall; tally the lectures. Why, researchers want to know, has physics education been virtually unchanged when there are so many better ideas? Student resistance is only one reason. Incentive structures for higher education are another: faculty in higher education are rewarded for research. Teaching is often devalued. Class sizes may be too big for meaningful interaction. Teachers' employment conditions are often risky; only the secure may be willing to take on the ideologies of direct instruction. And the structures are so powerful. The costs of education are enormous, at all levels. The buildings are built. The software processes the grades. High school counselors know how to coach students. How much of the system can change?

Students often resist new approaches: Students want (often) what they know, what is secure, what has worked in the past, a recipe for success. Research continually shows that students learn more from "active learning" classes than from conventional lecture-based classes, but they think they learn more the other way. Any "tinkering with utopia" is suspect. Students, their parents, the public are confident that they already know what a "real school" is, and anything different from it may appear inadequate, incompetent, lazy, guilty of malpractice. A professor who tries new things may be dinged in the student evaluations of teaching.

Just as students want a surefire recipe for success, faculty who will be evaluated by students may have a hard time risking anything on something new, which may be rejected by students. True experimentation means not knowing how things are going to turn out. This means the institution must make allowances.

I've suggested things to colleagues who can't imagine turning their classes upside down. Their reactions are the same: But what about X? But what about Y? Won't they take advantage of you? How will you get the work out of them? What about my employment conditions? What about my identity as a Z?

I've also found myself struggling. I have so many years with conventional learning. . . . I've had to unlearn, relearn. My learning is imperfect.

It's hard, and it is time-consuming to do it right. But if we don't want to do it right, we probably shouldn't bother doing it at all.

Taking It Apart to Put It Back Together: Maybe Don't Take It Apart in the First Place

Schoolish thinking is like nutritionism in food—the industrial belief that foods are merely combinations of identifiable and sometimes manufacturable micro- and macronutrients, and that if you take them apart, simplify, and add some artificial ingredients that resemble food, people will be nourished. Michael Pollan writes of this pernicious approach in his book *In Defense of Food*, and Gyorgy Scrinis devotes a whole book to *Nutritionism*.[43] Like nutritionism, schoolishness takes something vibrant and exuberant—human learning in a complex world, often with others—and removes it from its contexts, breaks it down into measurable and uniform parts, and then tries to put it back together several decades later.

School is nearly universal in the experience of contemporary humans, and it both creates and reflects cultural values. As schools aim to fashion the kind of person who is acceptable—outgoing, team- and group-oriented, able to sit still, learn from lectures, respond when called—anyone who deviates must be disciplined, medicated, counseled. People too energetic, people who are introverted, people who take longer. People who mono-task, people who are distracted. There is such a strong current of normalization, of "governmentality," of "neoliberal branding" with just the right amount of apparent authenticity and quirkiness, but not to the point of being antisocial, asocial, etc., that one might wonder how anyone at all gets to succeed in such a system without feeling as if they have sold their soul or twisted their own heart.

To the extent that the outcomes of school make sense on their own terms, that students feel that as human beings they are doing something that resonates with their own articulated goals, to that extent we might find schooling a positive contributor to the well-being of students. They can be learning and be fulfilled at the same time.

But not with random, arbitrary hoop-jumping. All *that* teaches is behaviorist tricks, easily taught to any mammal—and surely we want more for ourselves than that, especially at this high price.

Meanwhile, we have stunted growth and created pathologies: students don't like it, or the ones who do are damaged. The ill effects are known, multiple and multifaceted: depression, anxiety, suicidality, nightmares, malevolent interactions, superficiality, not-learning, dependence. After decades, how can the survivors easily recover? How can they emerge into the world as confident, joyous, independent actors, who know how to learn and how to accomplish their own positive ends?

As I've been implementing as many changes as I can, and as I give students space and time to learn on their own, I cherish what each student brings. I'm much *less cynical*. I know that in most of human life, people learn because they want to or have to use what they learn. The more we can mimic this, the more likely it is that we can succeed in our goals of fostering student engagement, learning, well-being. The less we emphasize the game of school, the less energy we will encourage students to expend on the alienated practices. It's all an imperfect, unfinished work in progress.

But when teaching works, it is a glorious accomplishment with many actors working in harmony.

Dreams, Idealism, Being "Unrealistic"

If we don't try, nothing will change. It's hard. Hell, it's probably impossible. Schoolishness is probably here to stay, but maybe not all of its elements are inevitable. Entrenched, yes. But inevitable? I don't think so. In my own lifetime I have seen amazing changes in the world. When I was very young people threw litter out their car windows. Decent people, people who otherwise were responsible and respectable. It's hard to understand that, but it's just the way things were: nature was ours, and we used it. In 1969 the Cuyahoga River caught fire because it was so polluted. The waterways were just ours for use. Until 1974 women still had to request permission from their husbands to open a credit card. In my youth Black people in the South were denied the right to vote, by law. My husband grew up with segregated water fountains and bathrooms in the South. Gay and lesbian people were not allowed to demonstrate affection publicly, let alone marry. Interracial marriage was prohibited by law in many states. Birth control was not available or reliable, and many women found themselves pregnant and in desperate situations. I grew up eating Wonder Bread and Twinkies and canned vegetables and sugar candy and sugared cereal. People died in car accidents because there were no seat belts. Polio vaccinations began just before I was born. Measles was rampant.

In terms of equality, health, safety, the environment, so many things have changed in my six-plus decades. But these changes didn't come overnight, and they required concerted effort, simultaneously technical, scientific, and moral, on the part of many. And many people may not agree with the changes—in fact we know that there is opposition, some sincere and some contrived.

To change as pervasive an institution as school will require the same kind of technical, scientific, and moral commitment. We have so much evidence and information. And the need for change is also everywhere.

From mental health, to expense, to nonlearning, to anxiety, we know the ills of our current schoolish systems and know that these systems are not effective and are often harmful. Some of this knowledge is a hundred years old. Some of it is thousands of years old. But what is new, I think, is the large-scale experimentation and the large-scale research that are combining to suggest new ways. New *ways* because there cannot be a uniform solution to a problem that is by its nature about uniformity. The more a one-size-fits-all solution is proposed, the less it is a solution.

I am hopeful, barely. There are tendencies toward increasing schoolishness everywhere, but at the same time there are tendencies fighting schoolishness. Possibly we will see a disappointing future where the poor get more schoolishness and the wealthy get less. It's possible that more and more people opt out entirely of the schoolish rat race. It's possible that some incremental changes, like ungrading, take hold. It's possible that we revert to the mean, as has been the case in so much educational transformation. It's possible that I won't live to see wholesale change. But it's also possible, given what I know about millennials and gen Z, that they will change things. They've stopped buying new clothes and paper napkins, and in the United States they've stopped getting driver's licenses. I will not be surprised if they also rethink the whole anxious inevitability of higher ed.

And what has helped more than anything else is sharing the questioning with others—having company.

In fall 2020, faculty and students were burned out. Exhausted, depleted. We worked so hard. Everything felt imperfect. We all got advice about how to improve our wellness. How to improve our classes. More webinars, workshops, talks. I did many of them myself.

We can't ask for perfection—from students or ourselves. The lessons are many; I haven't digested them all yet. And that's okay, because if there's one thing we know it is that schoolishness demands perfection, completion, closure.

And real life yields imperfection, continuity, openness.

Humbled, I keep working. It is all a work in progress.

Consider this book my progress report.

CONCLUSION

Creating the World We Want to Live In

Schoolishness is a problem. So what's the alternative?

Alternatives range from no school and unschooling, to better school, to self-directed learning. There can be idleness, as the Victorians deplored, or labor for wages, as child rights advocates campaigned against. There can be a whole host of alternatives. Some of them are an improvement, but some may not be.

When families are in desperate situations, or unable to rely on a community to pick up their child's needs, it may be preferable, as it is in the United States, to have an institution devoted to caring for the young. It may be that until we fix poverty, we can't fix schools, or at least we can't fix them for everyone. If schools are uniform, then they will suit only some. If schools aren't uniform, then some schools may be preferable to others, and guess who tends to get the preferable ones.

This is a wicked problem, the kind of thing that we all need to be thinking about. If someone sells you a simple one-size-fits-all solution, then you know it's not the right answer. There is no single right answer.

I believe my days of giving pedagogy workshops are numbered, because how could I give a forty-five-minute talk on all this? What use would it be? I can point out the complex, intertwined nature of the dilemma. I can make a few suggestions. I can point to some improvements. But how can Professor Overwhelmed implement this in her class on Tuesday? Obviously I can't fix any of the problems in one paragraph. I can't sell a package that promises to deliver on all this.

But I can say that the education gospel is a problem if we don't examine it, scrutinize it.

So in this book I've provided some tools for scrutiny, some suggestions of how strange our schoolish educational institutions are, and I've nodded here and there to some better versions, some tweaks, some fixes, some improvements.

For me, this quest has been personal and professional. It's been a burning question for me for at least a decade. I don't know how other people stay calm. I get so upset when I hear about unnecessary rigidity and unnecessary suffering through the insistence on inhumane and arbitrary, if unquestioned, structures.

I'm not saying all mental health, all inequality, all superficial learning, is a consequence of our schoolish structures. But our school structures, to the extent that they are alienating, make authentic learning, authentic being, near impossible.

And as the years go by, and the years of schoolish experience pile up, they are bound to have an effect. Either students internalize the arbitrary perfectionistic metrics, or they perform them falsely, leading to a different kind of alienation.

Either way, they put the power in others' hands, creating helplessness, dependence, insecurity. As Yong Zhao pointed out, these are not mere side effects. If they are pervasive, if so many people wish they could not go to school, if it's harmful, then we can't just keep administering this medicine. We have to look at the dose. Perhaps it should not be as all-encompassing for so many hours and so many years. We have to look at the mechanism, the processes, the structures of interaction. We have to look at the outcomes. We have to look at the cross indications. And if the side effects are worse than the disease, then in some cases we need to discontinue it and use the body's own healing practices.

We need to learn with others. We need dignity. We need to feel truly immersed in our actual lives, not just wait them out for the future. There is so much space between forest kindergartens, where children slide in the mud, and schools for students with disabilities where the police are called every other day and children are confined in bare rooms.[1] There's room between "breaking" children and letting them roam freely in packs. We need to shed the inhumane foot-binding version of school, to discard schoolishness and let the toes spread out, letting those small appendages provide support for a body that may run, jump, and even soar, letting them spread with pleasure in mud, or in the sky, not break for someone's contemplation.

If, as I've said repeatedly, the only positive reason to have schools is to make my classes as much as possible like the world I wish to live in—democratic, joyful, calm, cooperative—and if the way to do this is to foster confident, independent, joyous, effective learners who can ask questions, and to do so without harm, then we need to make our schools places where learners can live as authentic beings, to gather with others for learning, undamaged. So they can find a place to be at home in the world.

ALLIES AND ACKNOWLEDGMENTS

Having Company

> You do what you can within the confines of the current structure, trying to minimize harm. You also work with others to try to change that structure, conscious that nothing dramatic may happen for a very long time.
>
> ALFIE KOHN, *Punished by Rewards: The Trouble with Gold Stars, Incentive Plans, A's, Praise, and Other Bribes*

I haven't invented the ideas for this book from thin air. My outlook derives from reading and teaching about the anthropology of learning, the anthropology of childhood, cognitive studies of learning, linguistic anthropology of education, the philosophy of education, the scholarship of teaching and learning, my own teaching since 1988, fieldwork among undergraduates since 2003, experimentation since at least 2009, research on critical pedagogy, and a lot of self-examination. Since 2016 when I published *"I Love Learning; I Hate School": An Anthropology of College*, I've engaged in a large number of what I thought were side projects, all with collaborators: (1) ethnographic fieldwork in the local Bowman Creek Educational Ecosystem internship, which you read about in chapter 14 of this book; (2) a digital crowdsourced citizen science project, "School Stories," which I run with students; (3) a six-person attempt over two years to imagine what public higher education might be if invented from scratch, "A Theory of Public Higher Education"; (4) a long inquiry into the nature of the so-called word gap or language gap; and (5) a deep plunge into the world of ungrading, which has taken me virtually and in embodied form into nearly a hundred settings and engagement with thousands of educators at all levels and in several countries.

All this is to say: I stand on pyramids of colleagues, not just shoulders.

It has made all the difference to have company.

I'm an independent thinker and self-sufficient, a borderline introvert. I didn't mind the 2020 coronavirus isolation at all for the first week. But still, the company of others feels like a set of pillows on a rocky landscape, like a line of hands cushioning my fall, like an auditorium of nodding faces, smiling as I bare my soul on the stage.

I published *I Love Learning* in 2016. That same year I discovered Starr Sackstein and the whole Hacking Learning crew. I started ungrading. I gave some talks that didn't quite work; in fact, they were fairly alienating, demoralizing. Was I a fraud? Who was I to give pedagogy workshops?

I worked on my own classes, and wrote, trying to figure out what I was trying to figure out. I called it The Quest.

After I published a short article online in 2017 that I called "Ungrading: The Significant Learning Benefits of Getting Rid of Grades," or "Just One Change; Just Kidding," I was invited to a secret Facebook group called Teachers Going Gradeless, TG2.[1] There was already a group that Starr Sackstein had been part of called "Teachers Throwing Out Grades." Then I discovered more and more evidence of faculty going gradeless— most at the secondary (middle and high school) level, but increasingly in higher ed.

All anyone I talked to wanted to talk about was the fact that I'd stopped giving grades, so I decided to edit a book about it, a side project to assemble some of the practices faculty have devised to question the apparently central, unchanging, unyielding fact of schooling (especially according to students). I went out and solicited a dozen writers, both established, like Cathy Davidson, and new, like Christina Katopodis, Marcus Schultz-Bergin, Rissa Sorensen-Unruh, and Gary Chu. I pitched the book to the series just launched in 2016, Teaching and Learning in Higher Education, at the West Virginia University Press. At the time they had published only two books (Sarah Rose Cavanagh's *The Spark of Learning* and Joshua Eyler's *How Humans Learn*). I knew of the series editor, James Lang, whose work had overlapped in strange ways with mine (his *Cheating Lessons* and my *My Word! Plagiarism and College Culture* were both published in 2009, his *Small Teaching* and my *I Love Learning* in 2016), and he'd written a somewhat challenging but mostly positive review of *I Love Learning* in the *Chronicle of Higher Education*. We both saw me as a revolutionary, and him as an incrementalist.

I believed that the WVU Press series, though brand new, would be perfect for the ungrading project, though I was also committed to including both K–12 and higher ed writers, and the series focused on higher ed. I also learned, after I'd pitched the proposal, that they had established a rule that they wouldn't publish edited volumes. But they accepted it, enthusiastically. Alfie Kohn, whose work literally changed my life, honored us with a brilliant foreword that was a call to action. Even before the book was published, it got a kind of legendary presence, mostly through our collective social media, especially Twitter. Shameless self-promotion, yes, but I was also determined, along with people like Jesse Stommel and Alfie Kohn, to change things. #MeToo and #BlackLivesMatter were "hashtag movements." Why not #ungrading?

The other WVU Press authors have become comrades, sibling-authors—very significant people in my world. I finally met Jim Lang in person, and I hope to meet many more. The press proposed an actual physical meeting—but then COVID hit. The "WVU Crew" created a set of free resources, "Pedagogies of Care," for teaching in a pandemic. I met with them several times, on Zoom, and contributed a podcast.

As a result of the buzz around the book, many other things occurred.

I did a podcast with Will Richardson on his Modern Learners series in 2018 about learning and schooling.

Colleen Flaherty—herself a former high school teacher, and now a reporter from *Inside Higher Ed*—heard about this in 2019. She wrote a quick article—which attracted the concerned attention from a Notre Dame alum, who contacted the provost, who contacted the dean, who contacted my department chair. "What?" they were shocked, "She said she'll never grade an assignment again?"

A terrific reporter, Beckie Supiano, from the *Chronicle of Higher Education*, did a four-month project, also in 2019. She came to Notre Dame to observe all my final portfolio conferences (with signed consent; I'd previously polled my students, anonymously, to see if they wanted to do this at all, because I had concerns about privacy—though as one student said to me, "It's just classes"), to interview me and my students, and spoke with others in the ungrading world. She wrote a magnificent piece of long-form journalism, "Grades Can Hinder Learning. What Should Professors Use Instead?"[2]

Another podcast happened, thus time from the Human Restoration Project (August 2019), whose every word evokes agreement in me. They express their goals as "aimed at transforming school systems, restoring students as human beings rather than a vessel for standards."

All that's just on the ungrading side.

I was also invited to give a talk in 2019 to a group called the Society for Values in Higher Education (now renamed the Society for the Future of Higher Education), and then to participate in a funded project to entirely reimagine public higher ed. I've been delighted to have the company of these five progressive pedagogy folks (Oscar Fernandez, Mays Imad, Ryan Korstange, Tom Nelson Laird, Kate Pantelides), who are very knowledgeable, open, humble. Many of them run centers, are in charge of training other faculty. We have met in person several times (two meetings curtailed by COVID-19) and often on Zoom. These people, my "Theory of Public Higher Education" siblings, are truly meaningful people in my life.

I'm not sure where all this is going, but I am sure, now, that I'm not alone.

I'd been afraid, yet determined despite the fear, of some kind of negative reaction from the administration at my university. All this attention and all the others doing it too have given me courage.

And it is so much more fun to have company, whether it's virtual or face to face.

There's an incomparable thrill of being in a room with others who are known and present. That's not only fun. It's a joy. It is the peak of meaning.

It keeps me going.

Probably in a few years I'll write the next iteration of my progress.

Before all this, I had not necessarily realized how difficult it was—mostly in terms of morale—to be the only person I knew in higher ed undertaking this fundamental change in pedagogy, until I had company. This is not my challenge alone. An article about "critical pedagogy" puts it clearly: "There are several challenges to maintaining a dedication to critical pedagogy, whether one teaches in K–12 or postsecondary educational settings. A major challenge is isolation."[3]

But the risks are not uniform: "Having full time faculty take the lead [in a certain project] was strategic because they were the least vulnerable among the group members and instrumental for advancing the vision of the new curricular and pedagogical approaches."[4] I take seriously my obligation to use my own security to protect others, to take on the first challenges.

At my university, and especially in my department, I have graduate students, postdocs, and young colleagues who have wholeheartedly embraced ungrading and alternative practices. A former postdoc in our department, Marc Kissel, has taken the "unessay" and ungrading to heart. Marc and I coauthored an "Ungrading + UnEssay" piece for biological anthropologists called "Let's Talk Teaching." Cara Ocobock, a current younger colleague, does the same, enticing brilliant, creative, responsible work out of her students—and posting evidence all around the department walls. I feel a great responsibility, given the relative security and seniority of my position, to be protective of others.

But the key point remains: Everywhere I look, now, I have company.

Two Tracks

All over the United States and in some parts of the world that I know, people are earnestly grappling with the questions I raise in this book. It is only the sense that I have company that makes this tolerable.

At Notre Dame, "Catholic social teaching" is encouraged. It can be a wonderful way to deal with injustice, far better than simply giving alms. The key notion, popularized by the late anthropologist/physician and cofounder of Partners in Health Paul Farmer and originally borrowed from liberation theology, is "accompaniment." Sitting with. Walking with. Eating with. Being with.[5] Apparently its Latin origins resonate, like those for *company*, with the idea of eating bread with someone. (Etymology is not *meaning*—but I love the resonances anyway.)

"Slow food," that quasi-elite movement originating in France in opposition to American fast food, encourages not only knowing where your food is from, but also purchasing local foodstuffs directly from growers, cooking from scratch.

It also means you sit, and eat, without haste, in company, for however long it takes to complete the conversation and to reach satisfaction.

Patience. Tasting the sauce. Adding salt. Adding spice. Laughing at a joke.

That's the model—conviviality—of a community of learners thriving together, along with their guides, coaches, advisers. We're all in this together. Let us work. Grow the ingredients, or shop carefully for the right ones from the right growers. Assemble the company. Clear the calendar. Sit, laugh, talk, wonder, taste the subtle flavors of place and toil and earth. Take your time. This is how we feast. This is how we might learn. And thus nourished, how we might live.

Gratitude

I am filled with gratitude. For this project, and others, I've received institutional and financial support from the University of Notre Dame, the College of Arts and Letters, the Department of Anthropology, the Kellogg Institute for International Studies, the Notre Dame Institute for Advanced Study, the Office of Research, and the Institute for Scholarship in the Liberal Arts, which has provided support for all my books, including support for the images, permissions, and indexing for this one. I'm grateful for the Department of Anthropology's Ethnography Salon and our camaraderie. The research for chapter 14 was supported by NSF and the entire Bowman Creek community, the City of South Bend, the University of Notre Dame, Indiana University South Bend, Riley High School, St. Mary's College, and Ivy Tech Community College. I've also received support from the Society for the Future of Higher Education, Indiana University, the University of Oklahoma, and the Haja school in Seoul, South Korea. Librarians and support staff from the Hesburgh Libraries at Notre Dame, especially Jessica Kayongo and Leslie Morgan, and the St. Joseph County Public Library have generously offered assistance and sanctuary. Eileen Barany and Michelle Thornton in the Department of Anthropology provide friendship, humanity, competence, and support.

I've had the pleasure of working on various projects with undergraduate and graduate students, including Pamela Alvarado-Alfaro, Analina Barnes, Asha Barnes, Ivoline Budji Kefen, Nick Clarizio, Gabi De Leon

Fuentes, Sarah Galbenski, Kirill Gillespie, John (Jack) Harkin, Yuanmeng He, Kenzell Huggins, Laila Ibrahim, Lauren Jhin, Lily Jingting Kang, Maeve Malozzi-Kelly, Julia McKenna, Brandon Moskun, Veronica Navarro, Middi Norberg, Gabrielle Robinson, Claire Squire, Taylor Still, Monica vanBerkum, Anne Viesser, Saliyha Webb, Matthew Williams, Attina Xueheng Zhang.

I've tried out my ideas in all my classes, especially in many incarnations of Anthropology of Childhood and Education and Fundamentals of Linguistic Anthropology. I've also gained enormously from my experiments in Food and Culture and its transformation into What Should We Eat? I'm grateful to the graduate students in the fall 2019 Writing Anthropology class for their essential feedback on the draft of "The Trees Need Water."

I've had the honor of presenting my work, and getting probing questions and much ethnographic material, at AP / College Board, Boise State University, Boston University, California Community Colleges, California Virtual Campus, California State University Fresno, California State University Poly Pomona, California State University Stanislaus, Carthage College, the Claremont Colleges, College of the Holy Cross (Massachusetts), Colorado College, Cornell University (Office of Teaching Excellence), Council on Basic Writing (Conference on College Composition & Communication), CUNY (Hunter College, Transformative Learning in the Humanities), Deans' Equity and Inclusion Initiative, Duke Kunshan University, Oxford College at Emory University, Georgia Tech, Hamilton College, Indiana University South Bend, Indiana University Career EDGE, Indiana University SoTL series, Johns Hopkins Center for Educational Resources, Kern Community College District, King's College London, Lawrence University, London School of Economics and Political Science, Middle Tennessee State University, Middlebury College, Midwest Conference on Scholarship of Teaching and Learning, North Carolina State University, Northeastern State University, Northwestern University, Oklahoma State University, Pennsylvania State University, Pepperdine University and Seaver College, Plymouth State University, Purdue University, San José State University, Smith College, Southern Oregon University, St. Mary's College of Maryland, SUNY Westchester Community College, Trinity College, Trinity University (Texas), Tufts University (New England Consortium), University of Delaware, University of Greenwich,

University of Manchester, University of Michigan Flint, University of Mississippi, University of Northern Colorado, University of Notre Dame (Department of American Studies, Department of Romance Languages, Kaneb Center), University of South Dakota, Washington and Lee University, Western Carolina University, Western Michigan University (Community of Practice), Wofford College.

I've done podcasts on ungrading and other topics with *Anarchy and Higher Ed* (Roger Kerry), *Higher Ed Spotlight* (Ben Wildavsky), the *Human Restoration Project* (Chris McNutt), *Learning and Forgetting* (Kevin Currie-Night), *Lecture Breakers* (Barbi Honeycutt), *The Sausage of Science: Hackademics* (Cara Ocobock and Chris Lynn), *Tea for Teaching* (John Kane and Rebecca Mushtare), *Teachers Going Gradeless* (Aaron Blackwelder), *Teaching and Learning Collaborative* (Josh Luckens), *Teaching for Student Success* (Steve Robinow), *Teaching in Higher Ed* (Bonni Stackoviak), *Teaching in the CTEI* (Rush University, Angela Solic), *Think UDL* (Lillian Nave), *Tomayto Tomahto* (Talia Sherman), *What's the Big Idea* (Dan Kearney), and more—lots of podcasts.

I've benefited from conversations with colleagues and friends near and far, recent and long ago, fleeting and enduring (and many I'm sure I'm forgetting to list; please forgive me): Maurizio Albahari, Alex Ambrose, Hal Aqua, Risa Aqua, Sevda Arslan, Eric Bain-Selbo, Maha Bali, Chris Ball, Kevin Barry, Jim Bellis, Jada Benn-Torres, Aaron Blackwelder, Martin Bloomer, Diane Blum, Cat Bolten, Jay Brockman, David Buck, Ivoline Budji Kefen, Ayşe Bursalı, Tracie Canada, Alex Chávez, Meredith Chesson, Arthur Chiaravalli, Gary Chu, Judith Cohn, Ann Marie Conrado, Giovanni da Col, Cathy Davidson, Greg Downey, Carolyn Edwards, Josh Eyler, Lizzie Fagen, Oscar Fernandez, Christina Finnan, Lauren Finnigan, Chelly Freel, Rabbi Michael Friedland, Agustín Fuentes, Father Patrick Gaffney, Suzanne Gaskins, Carey Gaudern, Ilana Gershon, Lee Gettler, Laura Gibbs, Meredith Gill, Gary Gilot, Donna Glowacki, Mark Golitko, Stuart Greene, Alisa Zornig Gura, Eric Haanstad, Buster Hall, Terri Hebert, Chris Hebron, Michel Hockx, Helen Hockx-Yu, Zachary Howlett, Mays Imad, Barb Inwald, Christina Katopodis, Marc Kissel, Alfie Kohn, Ryan Korstange, Matthew Koss, Julia Kowalski, Jill Kuharic, Derek Krissoff, Ian Kuijt, David Lancy, Jim Lang, Jean Lave, Helen Lees, Blake Leyerle, April Lidinsky, Cecilia Lucero, Neil MacDonald (Mac), Joanne Mack, Todd Marek, Jim McKenna, Maria McKenna, Sarah McKibben, Father Aaron Michka, Tami Moore, Brandon Moskun, Luis Felipe

Murillo, Tom Nelson Laird, Sarah Nerenberg, Myriam Nicodemus, Cara Ocobock, Rahul Oka, Rev. Hugh Page, Jacquetta Page, Kate Pantelides, Jeff Peterson, Diane Johnson Prosser, Rebecca Pope-Ruark, Ann Marie Power, Will Richardson, Chris Riesbeck, Gina Riley, Rebecca Ritter, Patrícia Rodrigues-Niu, Barbara Rogoff, Starr Sackstein, Leslie Schaeffer, Marcus Schultz-Bergin, Mark Schurr, Aidan Seale-Feldman, Sue Sheridan, Vania Smith-Oka, EJ Sobo, Rissa Sorensen-Unruh, Jesse Stommel, Beckie Supiano, Tom Tobin, Gabriel Torres, Elliott Visconsi, John Warner, Karen Wasserman, Danielle Wood, Yun Xie. Thanks to Karen Gottschang for asking the question: "How did you go from being a China scholar to giving pedagogy workshops?" Local poet and friend Ken Smith spontaneously wrote the book a poem, which serves as one of the epigraphs of the book. Rahul Oka provided analysis of some of the Bowman Creek data. Nick Clarizio helped with research.

On my various projects, I've been enriched by colleagues from the Language and Social Justice Task Group of the Society for Linguistic Anthropology, especially those working with me on the so-called language gap. I've benefited from various groups working on ungrading: Teachers Going Gradeless; Let's Talk Ungrading; Teachers Throwing Out Grades. And just as this book was in production, I became a member of the Self-Directed Education discussion group, comrades all.

At Cornell University Press, initially with the astute steering of Fran Benson and more recently with Jim Lance and Clare Jones, I have found an enthusiastic home for three books over the course of a decade and a half. I'm grateful to anonymous readers and to Amy Weldon, with whom I have a lot to discuss! Copy editor Glenn Novak and production editor Jennifer Savran Kelly improved a shaggy manuscript as much as they could; indexer Lisa DeBoer put order to it for questing readers. Nuria Melisa Morales Garcia honored me with the illustrations for the book, thanks to the generosity of the Institute for Scholarship in the Liberal Arts, College of Arts and Letters, at Notre Dame, which also provided support for the index.

I am profoundly grateful to my family—especially our Friday night Shabbat zooms beginning in March 2020, which connected the thirty-odd members of our four generations beyond anything we'd ever enjoyed previously. My parents, Dr. George and Joyce Blum, keep us connected to a wish for the normal. My siblings and their partners (Kathi Moss, Dr. Bobby Blum and Tracye Valasco, Linda and Ken Long, Barbara and Mitch

Blum-Alexander, David Moss and Sharon Mayone), their children and partners (Leah and Adam Sachs, Dr. Henry Moss and Jackie Pilcowitz, Drs. Natalie Bum and Kevin Garfield, Madeline Blum and Riley McCullagh, Cameron and Kassidy Blum, Weston Blum, Veronica Long, Sara Long, Mario Blum-Alexander, Leídy Blum-Alexander), and now my parents' grandchildren (Estrella, Sally, Andy, and Rose), keep things complicated! My own little family, Lionel Jensen, Rabbi Hannah Jensen, Elena and Gerson Coronado-Jensen, and of course Estrella, keeps us in a state of protection. Without you five, I'd be adrift in so many ways. You are my readers, listeners, counselors, companions, laughers, audience. These last years have brought authentic joy and meaning to a life filled with so much complexity. Lionel, I can't imagine anyone else I could spend 24/7 with for eighteen months of a pandemic! Gratitude is too feeble a word to describe what I feel for all of you.

I dedicate this book to Estrella. Her parents don't want me to use her full name. May the world you learn in be gentler and more loving than the one I describe here. Con miles abrazos y mucha esperanza.

Appendix

SCHOOLISHNESS CHECKLIST

While prototypes can never be fully enumerated by a list of features, and membership in categories is a matter of degree, for those to whom this provides some use, I present here a checklist of schoolish features. It may be helpful for thinking about whether a particular setting, class, or experience is schoolish—or to understand how schoolish it is.

For each item, give it a 3 (just about always), 2 (usually), 1 (never or rarely).

___ Students have no choice about attending
___ The power to determine activity lies in the hands of the teacher
___ Teachers are authorities
___ Students are competitors
___ Questions concern compliance
___ Stillness and isolation are the norm
___ Time is predetermined
___ Work feels laborious

___ Space is disconnected from the world

___ Genres are school-only

___ Students are told exactly how to accomplish their work

___ Happens indoors

___ Happens with students sitting in rows

___ Syllabus prepared before semester begins, and no modifications occur

___ Begins with "the field" and content

___ Primary form of interaction is lecture

___ Uses the LMS

___ Students are assumed to be uniform "minds on a stick" (per Hrach)

___ Students cannot consult outside sources for tests

___ All class material is textbook or scientific papers

___ Rubrics are always given

___ The kinds of questions students ask are always about "What do you want?" and "How many . . . do I have to do?" and "What do I need to do to get an A?"

___ Class time is spent frequently on grades

___ Grades are calculated to the fraction

Results:

60–72	Pretty schoolish
37–59	Schoolish-ish
24–36	Not too schoolish

NOTES

Preface

1. Harber 2004, 8, 9, 24, 65.
2. Blum 2016.

Introduction

1. Brink 2013.
2. Sterelny 2021, 6, 8, 13; Tomasello 2009; Kline 2015 vs. Lancy 2010.
3. Blum 2020a.
4. My only encounter with the term *schoolish* was from Lindblom (2015), who contrasted "schoolish writing" and "authentic writing," but I have subsequently learned—as the book went to press—that Peter Gray had also used this term in 2014 in speaking of a "schoolish view" of child rearing, in that children are supposed to be directed by adults and to learn mostly from school. Our senses of the term are similar, though not identical.
5. Grubb and Lazerson 2004.
6. Bernstein 1971; Elias (1939) 2000; Foucault (1977) 1979.
7. Kipnis 2011.
8. Seth 2002.
9. Cho 2022.
10. "Youth, Rebellion, and the Pressure of Korea's Education Fever," Seoulbeats, December 17, 2021, https://seoulbeats.com/2021/12/youth-rebellion-and-the-pressure-of-koreas-education-fever/.

11. Thorsten 1996.

12. "Over 97% of Japan's New Univ. Graduates Employed amid Labor Shortage," Kyodo News, May 26, 2023, https://english.kyodonews.net/news/2023/05/b2e7a3830941-over-97-of-japans-new-univ-graduates-employed-amid-labor-shortage.html.

13. Bolten, n.d.

14. See Rosch 1973 on the concept of prototypes.

15. N. Anderson 2020.

16. Biesta 2010.

17. I build here on the work I've done with the TPHE Collective—Theory of Public Higher Education. Our proposal for how we would reimagine public higher education if we were creating it from scratch is published in Korstange et al. 2021. See also hooks 1994; Morris and Stommel 2018.

18. Berman and Smith (2021) challenge the naturalization of the "novice" in their article "De-naturalizing the Novice."

19. Muir (1911) 1988, 110.

20. See, e.g., Ko 2001, 2005.

21. Arnett 2018.

1. Experiencing School

1. Yerkes and Dodson 1908.

2. Zhao 2018, 115–16.

3. Zhao 2018, chap. 3.

4. Stambach 1998; Lancy 2022.

5. Warner 2016.

6. Cavanagh 2016; Damasio 1999; Immordino-Yang 2015; Immordino-Yang and Damasio 2007.

7. Premack 2007.

8. Panksepp and Biven 2012.

9. Damasio 1994, xi–xii; Damasio 1999; but see Leys 2011.

10. Damasio 1994, xii.

11. Paul 2021, 24.

12. Shelton, n.d. a, 3.

13. Cavanagh 2016; Pekrun and Linnenbrink-Garcia 2014.

14. Zull 2002.

15. Leys 2010.

16. Evans, Rich, and Holroyd 2004, 139.

17. Carolyn Jackson, an education researcher at Lancaster University in the UK, has written about "fear in education"—something that many hesitate to notice yet is a large part of people's experience at all levels (Jackson 2010).

18. Ndiaye 2019, 11.

19. Ndiaye 2019, 12.

20. Harber 2004.

21. "US Indian Boarding School History," National Native American Boarding School Healing Coalition, n.d., https://boardingschoolhealing.org/education/us-indian-boarding-school-history/; Ridgely 2019.

22. "Campus Sexual Violence: Statistics," RAINN, n.d., https://www.rainn.org/statistics/campus-sexual-violence. But it's not only on-campus students who face this; the risk for the 18–24 age is even higher off campus.

23. Venet 2018; "Trauma-Informed Teaching," Center for Teaching and Learning, n.d., University of Georgia, https://ctl.uga.edu/faculty/teaching-resources/trauma-informed-teaching/.

24. Imad 2021. Alex Shevrin Venet argues that we should only aim for "trauma-aware teaching" because true "trauma-informed teaching" takes years to develop.

25. Stearns 2017, 2.

26. Elias (1939) 2000; Foucault (1977) 1979, 1978, 1988; N. Rose 1999.

27. Shelton, n.d. b, 17.

28. Sjöberg, Nilsson, and Leppert 2005, e392.

29. O. Davis 2013.

30. Jessica Villegas and WikiHow, "How to Not Be Bored during Class," n.d., https://www.wikihow.com/Not-Be-Bored-During-Class; Amanda Morin, "Why Kids Get Bored at School—and How to Help," n.d., verywellfamily, https://www.verywellfamily.com/reasons-kids-are-bored-at-school-620804.

31. Jason 2017.

32. Jason 2017.

33. Toppo 2015.

34. Bryner 2007.

35. Bauerlein 2013. In college, where students have fewer hours of class than students at earlier levels of schooling, they may be bored in class, or if they are on a residential campus (only about 40 percent of full-time public college students live on campus, but that number is 64 percent for private colleges and universities), they may be bored just in general—and turn to drugs and alcohol, sex, video games, porn, or other streaming and social media outlets.

36. Wiggins 2014.

37. Smith and Piemonte 2022.

38. Wieman 2014.

39. Evans, Rich, and Holroyd 2004, 132.

40. Evans, Rich, and Holroyd 2004, 131.

41. Evans and Davies 2004.

42. Evans, Rich, and Holroyd 2004, 136.

43. Evans, Rich, and Holroyd 2004, 137.

44. Evans, Rich, and Holroyd 2004, 138.

45. Evans, Rich, and Holroyd 2004, 138.

46. Berlant 2011.

47. Bateson et al. 1963.

48. Luthar, Kumar, and Zillmer 2020; Wallace 2019; National Academies 2019, 264.

49. Bregnbæk 2016.

50. M. Townsend 2017.

51. Purser 2019.

52. Eliza Abdu-Glass, Steven Scholzman, and Gene Beresin, "The College Mental Health Crisis: A Call for Cultural Change—Part 2," Clay Center for Young Healthy Minds, https://www.mghclaycenter.org/parenting-concerns/college-mental-health-crisis-call-cultural-change-part-2/.

53. Jessica Colarossi, "Mental Health of College Students Is Getting Worse," April 21, 2022, https://www.bu.edu/articles/2022/mental-health-of-college-students-is-getting-worse.

54. GBD 2019 Mental Disorders Collaborators 2022.

55. Christakis 2016.

56. During the 2020 presidential primary, Kamala Harris's support from progressives was hindered in part because during her time as attorney general of California she'd had parents arrested for their children's truancy, believing that she was helping to motivate children's attendance (Mason and Finnegan 2019). In the summer of 2020 a terrible story circulated of a fifteen-year-old Black student in suburban Detroit—coincidentally at the high school where most of my nieces and nephews have gone—who was on probation for other misdeeds and was given jail time for failing to do her online schoolwork during the pandemic. In August 2020, the judge was ordered by an appeals court to release her from probation. Associated Press 2020; J. Cohen 2020.

57. Lancy 2022; L. C. Moore 2006; Tyack and Berkowitz 1977.

58. Bregnbæk 2016; Chu 2017; Fong 2011; Howlett 2021; Kipnis 2011.

59. Beresin 2017.

60. Albrecht et al. 2022; Davies 2005.

61. Fisher 2021.

62. Fisher, "As a clinical psychologist . . .," Tweet, August 18, 2022, https://twitter.com/naomicfisher/status/1560218145125814273?s=20&t=_DliFcJwTVXYXV9wmg76Wg.

63. Mayo Clinic 2018.

64. "College Enrollment in the United States from 1965 to 2022 and Projections Up to 2030 for Public and Private Colleges," Statista, June 2, 2023, https://www.statista.com/statistics/183995/us-college-enrollment-and-projections-in-public-and-private-institutions/; "Percentage of 18- to 24-Year-Olds Enrolled in College, by Level of Institution and Sex and Race/Ethnicity of Student: 1970 through 2021," Digest of Education Statistics, National Center for Education Statistics, table 302.60, https://nces.ed.gov/programs/digest/d22/tables/dt22_302.60.asp.

65. Purser 2019, 7, 8.

66. Purser 2019, 9.

2. The Aims and the Ends, Values and Value

1. "What Is School For?," *New York Times*, September 1, 2022, https://www.nytimes.com/interactive/2022/09/01/opinion/schools-education-america.html.

2. Marples 1999.

3. Secretary Miguel Cardona, "Every Student Should Have Access . . . ," Tweet, December 16, 2022, https://twitter.com/SecCardona/status/1603831119962570771?s=20&t=AUK1qtBwvKawQxdLKO51CQ.

4. Pascarella and Terenzini (2005) note the same thing in *How College Affects Students*, conducting surveys beginning in the 1960s.

5. The notion of "moral panic" arose from the understanding of idle adolescents. See S. Cohen 1972; G. S. Hall 1904; Savage 2007.

6. Freire (1970) 2000.

7. Lepore 2022.

8. B. Anderson (1983) 1991.

9. Komline 2020.

10. Jung 2007.

11. Labaree 2010.

12. Davidson 2017.

13. Abramson 2007; Kennedy 2005.

14. Hirsch 1988.

15. Hirsch 1988, 2.

16. David Lancy (2022) points out that some societies regard children as inherently good and in need of gentle nurturing ("cherubs"); others as inherently bad and in need of discipline, punishment, and correction ("changelings"); and others as useful and to be made instruments ("chattel"). Tension in fundamental views of child development sometimes pits those favoring the "natural unfolding" of children, such as Piaget and Vygotsky, against those who focus on reinforcement, control, and discipline.

17. Jessica Furr (Waggener), "A Brief History of Mathematics Education in America," University of Georgia, Spring 1996, http://jwilson.coe.uga.edu/EMAT7050/HistoryWeggener.html.

18. "Mathematics Framework," California Department of Education, n.d., https://www.cde.ca.gov/ci/ma/cf/; Boaler 2022.

19. Boaler and Levitt 2019; Fortin 2021.

20. OECD 2011.

21. Bourdieu and Passeron (1970) 1990; Knoll 2009.

22. Collins 1979.

23. McNamee 2018, 104.

24. Caplan 2018.

25. Lieber 2022.

26. Caplan 2018.

27. Jeremy Bauer-Wolf, "Over 1,700 Colleges Won't Require SAT, ACT for Fall 2023, Up from Same Point Last Year," Higher Ed Dive, July 27, 2022, https://www.highereddive.com/news/over-1700-colleges-wont-require-sat-act-for-fall-2023-up-from-same-poin/628267/.

28. Warner 2022.

29. Zachary Howlett's book *Meritocracy and Its Discontents* (2021) is based on two years of participant observation in a Chinese high school.

30. Graeber and Wengrow 2021.

31. Saini 2020.

32. Guinier 2015; Lemann 2000; McNamee 2018; Stevens 2007.

33. Appiah 2018; Bradbury 2021; Littler 2017; Markovits 2019; McNamee 2018; Sandel 2021; "Is Meritocracy a Myth?," Fabiola Cineas, Vox, April 2, 2021, https://www.vox.com/videos/2021/4/2/22349990/education-inequality-meritocracy-myth.

34. Stone 2020, 12.

35. Blum 2016, chap. 5.

36. See Kohn (1993) 2018, esp. chaps. 1–4 and appendix A; Kohn 2019.

37. Lepper 1983; Lepper and Greene 1975.

38. Deci 1971.

39. Deci 1971; see Ryan and Deci 2000 for a summary of this research.

40. Strickland and Strickland 1998, 3.

41. "Research Excellence Framework 2021," 2023, https://www.ref.ac.uk/.

42. Mirya Holman, Ellen Key, and Rebecca Kreitzer, "Evidence of Bias in Standard Evaluations of Teaching," 2019, https://docs.google.com/document/d/14JiF-fT--F3Qaefjv2jMRFRWUS8TaaT9JjbYke1fgxE/edit.

43. "The History of College Rankings," CollegeRank.net, 2023, https://www.collegerank.net/history-of-college-rankings/.

44. US Department of Education, "College Scorecard," n.d., https://collegescorecard.ed.gov/.

45. "World University Rankings," Times Higher Education, 2023, https://www.timeshighereducation.com/world-university-rankings; "Academic Ranking of World Universities,"

Shanghai Ranking, 2023, https://www.shanghairanking.com/; "QS World University Rankings: Top Global Universities," QS Quacquarelli Symonds Limited, 2023, https://www.topuniversities.com/qs-world-university-rankings.

46. Walt Gardner, "The College Rankings Game: How Students and Parents Are Being Played," James G. Martin Center for Academic Renewal, May 27, 2022, https://www.jamesgmartin.center/2022/05/the-college-rankings-game-how-students-and-parents-are-being-played/; Scott Jaschik, "'Breaking Ranks' with 'U.S. News,'" Inside Higher Ed, April 10, 2022, https://www.insidehighered.com/admissions/article/2022/04/11/breaking-ranks-new-book-attacks-us-news.

47. This section reworks Blum 2015.

48. Kirschenbaum, Simon, and Napier 1971.

49. Demerath 2009 shows how mostly white "point-hungry" students at an affluent suburban high school cajole their teachers into giving them extra credit because they "need" the good grades to get into the good colleges that the school advertises. This topic permeates the book: pp. 105, 110–11, 115–18, 125, 134, 182.

50. The anthropology of play and games shows a fascinating contrast between societies whose games require competition and those that simply institute moments of enjoyment, like singing and dancing together. See, e.g., Schwartzman 1976.

51. Pope 2001.

52. Calarco 2020; Jack 2019.

53. Lees 2022.

54. Henry (1967) 1973, 125.

55. Eaton et al. 2022; Tomar 2012; Young 2020.

56. Academia, journalism, and science struggle with faked peer review, multiply submitted papers, fraudulent results, invented data, plagiarism (and the misnamed self-plagiarism), fueled by a system that rewards both authors and publishers for sheer quantity of publication. Professors game the system with publications. Institutions game the metrics of prestige by focusing on the numbers tracked by *US News & World Report*, Times Higher Education World University Rankings, or the Shanghai Ranking. In fake and corrupt publishing, benefits go to several parties: to scientists credited with publications, to brokers who find publication outlets and sometimes even manuscripts to publish, and to journal editors, especially of high-impact journals. Everyone keeps an eye on the rankings, and publications in Thomson Reuters' Science Citation Index (SCI)-tracked journals are required for promotion. Hvistendahl 2013, 1036; Normile 2017.

57. Blum 2007, 2009; Elman 2000; Howlett 2021; Miyazaki (1963) 1981; Suen and Yu 2006; Zhao 2009.

58. Flaherty 2020; Harwell 2020. But see Chin 2020b for what this feels like to students. See Chin 2020a on the lawsuit against Ian Linkletter by Proctorio because he revealed the truth about their practices. See Manolev, Sullivan, and Slee 2019 on ClassDojo and discipline.

59. R. White 1959.

60. Sackstein 2015; Kohn (1993) 2018.

61. Blum 2020a, 2021.

62. Smith and Piemonte 2022.

63. See R. White 1959 for the original formulation of the distinction between "intrinsic and extrinsic motivation."

64. Willingham 2021.

65. Dashiell 1925.

66. Darwin 1882, 71–72.

67. E.g., Loewenstein 1994; Markey and Loewenstein 2014.

68. Livio 2017, 1.

69. Schwartz and Bransford 1998; Lom 2012; Waldrop 2015. Read about the Carl Wieman Science Education Initiative in Chasteen and Code 2018, and at Carl Wieman Science Education Initiative, https://cwsei.ubc.ca/home.

70. Dewey (1916) 1966, 27.

71. Noddings 2013.

72. Davidson 2011b.

73. Blum 2022.

74. "Mastery Transcript Consortium," 2021, https://mastery.org/.

75. Orbey 2022.

76. Jaschik 2019, 2022.

77. Sharma 2022.

78. Lat 2022.

79. Liebowitz and Margolis 1995.

80. Fischman and Gardner 2022; Moner, Motley, and Pope-Ruark 2020; Korstange et al. 2021; Staley 2019.

81. Bringhurst 2008, 54.

82. "What Is Career EDGE?," Indiana University Career Edge, 2023, https://edge.iu.edu/about/index.html.

83. Monaghan 1998.

3. Pedagogy and Pedagogizing

1. Enfield 2017, 58.

2. See Birner 2022.

3. E. Clark 2017.

4. The nature of language is quite unsettled. A good discussion of the theoretical approaches can be found in P. Austin 2021.

5. ZeroToThree.org 2004.

6. Henrich 2020; Henrich, Heine, and Norenzayan 2010. Critiques by K. Clancy and Davis 2019 and Fuentes 2022 emphasize that the default assumption is that WEIRD populations are white.

7. Arnett 2018.

8. Calls to increase schooling in developing countries, or to improve girls' access, have everything to do with equity. Whether more school is inherently good, bad, or neutral depends on the context, content, and structures of that schooling.

9. Grubb and Lazerson 2004.

10. A. Lareau 2003. See also Gopnik 2016 on parents as "gardeners."

11. See Levine 2006.

12. Suskind 2022; see Leung 2020 on the harms of concerted cultivation.

13. P. Clancy 1986; Heath 1983; McCarty 2015; Ochs and Schieffelin 1984, 1986; Stack 1974; Zentella 2015.

14. "Learn," WordSense, https://www.wordsense.eu/learn/.

15. Kaiser 2011.

16. Foucault (1977) 1979; Freud (1930) 1961; N. Rose 1999.

17. Foucault (1977) 1979, 304.

18. Gray 2013, 2014; Hari 2022; Louv 2005; Skenazy 2021.

19. Solomon 2021.

20. Labaree 2010; Spindler and Spindler 1989; Varenne and McDermott 1998.
21. Ochs and Shohet 2006, 35.
22. Blum-Kulka 1997; Counihan 2004; Elias (1939) 2000; Ochs and Shohet 2006; Ochs and Taylor 1992; Paugh and Izquierdo 2009.
23. Snow and Beals 2006; Fishel 2015.
24. Fishel 2016.
25. KIPP: Public Schools, kipp.org, n.d. Education is expected to create social and economic equality. For a rare negative view see John Marsh's brutal *Class Dismissed: Why We Cannot Teach or Learn Our Way Out of Inequality* (2011).
26. Kohn 2020.
27. Mervosh 2022.
28. Kramer 2021.
29. Tehrani and Riede 2008 on craft apprenticeship and nonlinguistic instruction; Lancy 2022; Csibra and Gergely 2011; Gärdenfors and Högberg 2017. There's a robust debate about the necessity and evolution of teaching, and of pedagogy.
30. Lancy 2022.
31. Pollan 2022.
32. Gaskins 2008, 2013; Greenfield 2004; Lave 1988.
33. *"The Beatles: Get Back,"* Wikipedia, June 29, 2023, https://en.wikipedia.org/wiki/The_Beatles:_Get_Back.

4. Teachers, Students, Classes

1. Cazden 2001, 40.
2. Berman and Smith (2021) "de-naturalize" the novice in the context of the enormously influential language socialization research in linguistic anthropology, questioning assumptions of the novice's lack of agency and calling attention to the sociopolitical forces that create the category of novice.
3. Huston 2009.
4. Black, n.d.
5. Doi 1971.
6. Philips 1983.
7. Rebecca Traister, "Elizabeth Warren's Classroom Strategy," the Cut, August 6, 2019, https://www.thecut.com/2019/08/elizabeth-warren-teacher-presidential-candidate.html.
8. Melton 1988.
9. "FAQ's," Sudbury Valley School, 2020, https://sudburyvalley.org/faqs.
10. Malcolm Knowles wrote about self-direction for adult education, both formal and other; https://infed.org/mobi/malcolm-knowles-informal-adult-education-self-direction-and-andragogy/.
11. Cooper and Klymkowsky 2020.
12. Bowen and Cooper 2022.
13. Coral Murphy Marcos, "New York University Professor Fired after Students Say His Class Was Too Hard," *Guardian*, October 6, 2022, https://www.theguardian.com/us-news/2022/oct/06/nyu-professor-fired-maitland-jones-jr-student-petition.
14. Eric Levitz, "The Whiny Grade-Grubbing NYU Students Have a Point," Intelligencer, October 5, 2022, https://nymag.com/intelligencer/2022/10/nyu-professor-fired-cancel-culture-doctor-shortage.html.
15. Katopodis and Davidson 2020, 115–16.
16. Hull 2002, 30.

17. Tobin, Hsueh, and Karasawa 2009.

18. "Japan: A Story of Sustained Excellence," in *Strong Performers and Successful Reformers in Education: Lessons from PISA for the United States* (OECD.org, 2010), https://www.oecd.org/japan/46581091.pdf.

19. See Blum 2016, chap. 6, on "campus delights."

20. Lave and Wenger 1991.

21. Susan D. Blum, "Human Scavenger Hunt," Equity Unbound/OneHE, https://onehe.org/eu-activity/human-scavenger-hunt/.

22. Elbow 1998.

23. Bellah et al. 1985.

24. Cain 2012; Neuhaus 2019.

25. von Eschenbach 2020.

5. Questions

1. Denworth 2019, 2021.

2. Conversation is mostly studied using neurotypical, not neurodivergent, speakers. One symptom of neurodivergence is out-of-rhythm interaction, as some analysts are starting to note. See, e.g., Christensen 2021; Ochs et al. 2004; Ochs and Solomon 2010.

3. J. L. Austin 1962.

4. Enfield 2017, 18.

5. Blum 1997; P. Brown 2002; Daniels 1984; Duranti 1997.

6. This is a lively topic, summarized well in Ladd 2001.

7. Huddleston 1994.

8. E. Carr (2010, 50–55), writes of the "travel" of written intake documents in the institutional treatment of addiction.

9. Cazden 2001.

10. Compton 2022.

11. Hart and Risley 1995.

12. But see Blum 2017; Johnson and Johnson 2022; Sperry, Sperry, and Miller 2019.

13. Gatto (1992) 2005.

14. Emdin 2016.

15. Michael Wesch, "The End of Wonder in the Age of Whatever," Cornell Center for Teaching Excellence, October 3, 2013, https://www.youtube.com/watch?v=B0Ghq7UWqpQ.

16. Rothstein and Santana 2011.

17. Pedaste et al. 2014.

18. Hanstedt 2018, 9.

19. Mullaney and Rea (2022) have written *Where Research Begins: Choosing a Research Project That Matters to You (and the World)*, which leads to the generation of a researchable and meaningful question.

6. Time

1. Thompson 1967, 60, 82.

2. Thompson 1967, 84.

3. Thompson 1967, 89.

4. Thompson 1967, 95.

5. Chudacoff 1989, 15.

6. David Lancy writes of the Anglo-American desirability of "precocity," or children demonstrating the early mastery of skills, in contrast to many other societies where this is undesirable and children are—or were, until the Anglo-American model spread—ideally kept from doing things too early. See Lancy 2022, 138, 205.

7. Chudacoff 1989, 15.

8. Chudacoff 1989, 17.

9. Chudacoff 1989.

10. "Sustainable Development Goal 4" (SDG4), UNESCO, Education 2030, n.d., https://www.sdg4education2030.org/the-goal.

11. Elise Berman's book *Talking Like Children: Language and the Production of Age in the Marshall Islands* (2019) shows how children are *taught* to differentiate themselves from adults and older people, through their behavior and speech. The burgeoning of "childhood studies" and its development into "lifecourse studies" reflects the discovery that ages are not tracked identically across all societies. Also see Kurt 2020 on Malcolm Knowles, who is credited with popularizing the study of adult learning and the term *andragogy*.

12. "German Education System," Study in Germany, 2022, https://www.studying-in-germany.org/german-education-system/; Bleiker 2015.

13. Moskun 2022.

14. Silva, White, and Toch 2015.

15. Silva, White, and Toch 2015.

16. David 1997.

17. Melanie Hanson, "College Graduation Statistics," Education Data Initiative, June 12, 2022, https://educationdata.org/number-of-college-graduates#. See Caplan 2018 for an economist's case "against education."

18. Silva, White, and Toch 2015.

19. Silva, White, and Toch 2015.

20. Crosier and Parveva 2013; European Commission, Directorate-General for Education, Youth, Sport and Culture 2017.

21. Silva, White, and Toch 2015.

22. See, e.g., Lester 2014 for a critique.

23. "National Center on Time & Learning," 2017, https://www.timeandlearning.org/.

24. Farbman 2015.

25. Coonan 2014.

26. Diem, Levy, and VanSickle, n.d.

27. Che 2021; Ye 2021.

28. NCEE 2018.

29. Schleicher 2019.

30. Xiong et al. 2017.

31. Zhao 2018.

32. Jan et al. 2020.

33. Price 2011, 63.

34. Mischel 2014.

35. The literature is enormous. See, e.g., Duckworth 2016; Dweck 2006; Dweck, Walton, and Cohen 2014; and Kohn 2014 for a critique.

36. Visser 1991, 138–46.

37. Freud (1930) 1961.

38. Kritz 2018.

39. Zhao 2018.

40. Collins 1979.

41. I'm not going to obsess about the specific terms. They form a family. There is further discussion and analysis about the ontological status of the terms, which I will also not engage: What, exactly, are hope, aspiration, optimism? Are they emotions? Stances? Positions? Practices? Dispositions? Ploys? You can read Eagleton 2015 for some discussion.

42. Barbara Ehrenreich (2009) writes that this future orientation is messianic and a feature of Christianity.

43. Mischel 2014.

44. Mischel 2014, 107.

45. This is really based on the Protestant ethic and future orientation connected with ideas of progress and individual self-creation, as Keane (2007) shows, but it is so pervasive that it's hard to untangle causality.

46. Foucault (1977) 1979.

47. Mischel 2014, 102–6.

48. And then what happens when these kids, including George, get to college, even at Yale? While some people, such as Harris (2018), are concerned about something called "undermatching," whereby very smart kids ("high ability") in poverty fail to adequately aim for ambitious, elite schools, others, such as Anthony Abraham Jack (2019), worry about what actually happens to disadvantaged students when they *do* arrive at elite institutions (Rosenberg 2019). Warner (2020) also challenges the "undermatching" narrative in his chapter on Betsy DeVos, former secretary of education under President Donald Trump.

49. "Cup of Joe—Serving Students on the Path to College and Heaven," Alliance for Catholic Education, University of Notre Dame, 2023, https://ace.nd.edu/blog/cup-joe-serving-students-path-college-and-heaven.

50. Ravitch 2014; Thomas 2014.

51. Kohn 2014.

52. Dweck, Walton, and Cohen 2014, 32.

53. Mehta 2015.

54. Kohn (1993) 2018. New research is demonstrating neurobiological reasons that make shared rhythms and predictable patterns pleasing, soothing, and even healthy for our species, with its likely evolutionary selection for sociality. Bergland 2017.

55. Xiang 2018, 88.

56. Xiang 2018, 89.

57. My brother recently found a record of the passage from Hungary in 1929 of my paternal grandmother and grandfather, just in time to survive the Holocaust that would kill their relatives.

58. Carpena-Méndez 2017; Finnan 2021; Hoffman 2017.

59. M. Anderson (2017) writes of the "myth of meritocracy" hurting students of color.

60. Clegg 2010, 350.

61. Clegg 2010, 348, and citing Marginson and Considine 2000; Clegg 2010, 350.

62. Khattab 2015, 747.

63. Davidson 2017, 69.

64. Mischel 2014, 272.

65. Mischel 2014, 272.

66. Dunlap 2016.

67. "We Call It Competency-Based Education. Grads Call It the Best Way to Learn," Western Governors University, 2023, https://www.wgu.edu/about/story/cbe.html.

68. "What's a Block?," the Block Plan, Colorado College, December 17, 2020, https://www.coloradocollege.edu/basics/blockplan/whats-a-block.html.

69. Cavanagh 2016; Livio 2017; Panksepp and Biven 2012.

70. Noddings 2003.

71. Kabat-Zinn 2005.

72. A book called *The Slow Professor: Challenging the Culture of Speed in the Academy* clearly recognized the issue but addressed it from the perspective of faculty, not students: Berg and Seeber 2016.

7. Work, Labor, Play

1. "Doing the Work Externally and Internally: Race, Equity, Diversity and Inclusion," Web Junction, OCLC, 2023, https://www.webjunction.org/events/webjunction/doing-the-work-race-equity-diversity-inclusion.html; "Doing the Work of the Social Justice Movement through Storytelling," BrandStoryTelling.TV, 2023, https://www.brandstorytelling.tv/single-post/doing-the-work-of-the-social-justice-movement-through-storytelling; Angela Barbuti, "A Calling to Do the Work of Social Justice in New York," Our Town, October 4, 2021, https://www.ourtownny.com/news/a-calling-to-do-the-work-of-social-justice-in-new-york-KX1808738.

2. Aniesa, "What 'Doing the Work' in Therapy Looks Like," Hanson Complete Counseling, 2023, https://aniesahanson.com/what-doing-the-work-in-therapy-looks-like/; "What Does 'the Work' Mean in Therapy," Reddit, 2021, https://www.reddit.com/r/TalkTherapy/comments/m2tgc0/what_does_the_work_mean_in_therapy/; Byron Katie, "The Work," the Work Foundation, 2023, https://thework.com/.

3. Seabrook 2013.

4. "Freedom Not Licence," A. S. Neill Summerhill School, https://www.summerhillschool.co.uk/freedom-not-licence. See also Neill 1960.

5. "Child Work, Child Labour," ECLT Foundation, 2023, https://www.eclt.org/en/news/what-is-child-labour.

6. "Born of Controversy: The GI Bill of Rights," US Department of Veterans Affairs, n.d., https://www.va.gov/opa/publications/celebrate/gi-bill.pdf.

7. Erik Schmidt, "Census Shows Great Recession's Impact on College Enrollment," High Unemployment, High College Enrollment, US Census Bureau, June 13, 2018, https://www.census.gov/library/stories/2018/06/going-back-to-college.html.

8. Kang 2022.

9. "Faculty Workload Model," Faculty of Arts, Macquarie University, December 2, 2020, https://staff.mq.edu.au/intranet/arts-intranet/documents/Faculty-of-Arts-Workload-Model.pdf. I'm grateful to Greg Downey for helping me think about this.

10. Marcus 2022.

11. Inoue 2019, 130, 132, 214, 215.

12. Carillo 2021, 12.

13. Carillo 2021, 18.

14. Inoue 2019, 16.

15. Carillo 2021, 22.

16. Blum 2022.

17. Carillo 2021, 58.

18. Gray 2013, x.

19. "Pedagogy of Play," Project Zero, Harvard Graduate School of Education, 2022, https://pz.harvard.edu/projects/pedagogy-of-play.

20. Lancy 2022.

8. Spaces and Places

1. Tuan 2001.

2. Zaidel 2019 and others argue that our sense of aesthetics, an appreciation of beauty, *evolved* in humans as a species.

3. Moskun 2022.

4. Zimmerman 2015.

5. "School Buildings and Student Performance in Developing Countries," OECD, n.d., https://www.oecd.org/education/innovation-education/schoolbuildingsandstudentperformanceindevelopingcountries.htm.

6. P. Barrett et al. 2019.

7. Blum 2007, 28.

8. Trow 2007.

9. Staggs and Ambrose 2021.

10. E. Hall 1969.

11. "Learning Space Rating System," Educause, 2023, https://www.educause.edu/eli/initiatives/learning-space-rating-system.

12. Barnum 2018; Strauss 2018.

13. Goffman 1961; Jacka, Kipnis, and Sargeson 2013.

14. Lewis 1970; Vanover and DeBowes 2013.

15. Dzieza 2014; Olson 2005.

16. "Spotlight on: School Safety," YouthTruth, n.d., http://youthtruthsurvey.org/wp-content/uploads/2018/04/YouthTruth-Spotlight-On-School-Safety.pdf.

17. "The Tools You Need for Campus Safety and Security Analysis," Campus Safety and Security, US Department of Education, n.d., https://ope.ed.gov/campussafety/#/.

18. Watters 2022.

19. Connery 2020.

20. Ajemu et al. 2020; Cole, Chorba, and Horan 1990; Jarvi, Jackson, Swenson, and Crawford 2013.

21. Hrach 2021.

22. Bloomer 2011.

23. Edwards et al. 2013.

24. R. Lareau 2019; "Celebrating 25 Years of Edible Education," Edible Schoolyard Project, 2023, https://edibleschoolyard.org/; Louv 2005; "Sudbury Valley School," 2020, https://sudburyvalley.org/.

25. "Promoting Social, Emotional, and Physical Wellness," EL Education, 2023, https://eleducation.org/core-practices/curriculum/promoting-social-emotional-and-physical-wellness/.

26. "For a Better Society and a Better World," Prescott College, 2023, https://prescott.edu/about/; "Our Mission, Our Vision, Our Values," Prescott College, 2023, https://prescott.edu/about/mission-vision-values/.

27. Diner 2017.

28. Burns 2022; Diner 2017.

9. Genres of Consumption

1. Briggs and Bauman 1992.

2. Wolf 2018.

3. Goffman 1981.

4. Friesen 2011, 97–99.

5. Friesen 2011, 101.

6. Friesen 2011, 100.

7. Goffman 1981, 167.

8. Schwartz and Bransford 2009.

9. There are numerous sources for good ideas. See especially Davidson and Katopodis 2022; Lang 2021.

10. Freeman et al. 2014.

11. Deslauriers et al. 2019, 19251.

12. Haynie and Spong 2022; G. Smith 2015.

13. Hammond 2019; May 2014.

14. Weldon 2018.

15. Ingold (2009) 2017.

16. Casper 2010.

17. The "Reading Wars" in the United States contest the best way to teach reading, especially given the complexity of the orthography (writing system) of English, but also the diverse linguistic, cultural, and economic backgrounds of our students. Like so much else, it is a hugely political as well as a financial issue. People disagree about what constitutes "evidence" for the success of particular reading programs, about whether motivation or pleasure should be included, and over questions of students' engagement. These fights, according to education professor Jon Reyhner (2020), mirror behaviorist and constructivist fights throughout education: "traditional" (schoolish) and "progressive" (antischoolish).

18. Amy Watson, "Estimated Textbook Publishing Revenue in the United States from 2010 to 2020," Statista, January 2, 2023, https://www.statista.com/statistics/185042/us-publishing-revenue-from-textbooks-since-2005/.

19. B. Barrett 2019.

20. On Pakistan, Ali Abbas, "Uniform National Curriculum and Our Educational System," MM News, March 20, 2020, https://mmnews.tv/uniform-national-curriculum-and-our-educational-system/; on China, Cantoni et al. 2015; for an international summary, "International Curricula," Mempowered, n.d., http://www.mempowered.com/children/international-curricula; on Papua New Guinea, "Papua New Guinea's First National Textbook: Japan's Knowledge Is Fully Localized," Japan International Cooperation Agency, March 26, 2020, https://www.jica.go.jp/english/news/field/2019/20200326_01.html.

21. Chang 2018.

22. Wieman 2014.

23. Cohn 2021.

24. Kalir, personal communication, July 30, 2023; Kalir forthcoming; see Kalir and Garcia 2021 for a discussion of annotation.

25. NPR 2013.

26. "Information Literacy," ALA Literacy Clearinghouse, 2023, https://literacy.ala.org/information-literacy/.

27. Claudio Aspesi, "Research Companies: Springer Nature," Scholarly Publishing and Academic Resources Coalition, n.d., https://infrastructure.sparcopen.org/landscape-analysis/springer-nature-group#; Resnick and Belluz 2019.

28. Barrett 2019.

29. "Plan S," Plan S: Making Full & Immediate Open Access a Reality, European Science Foundation, 2023, https://www.coalition-s.org/.

10. Genres of Production

1. Goldstein 2017.

2. Mintz (2020) lost me when he said teachers should supply a rubric.

3. Kellaghan and Greaney 2019.

4. Gascoigne 1984.

5. Liang et al. 2021.

6. Watanabe 2013.

7. Kellaghan and Greaney 2019; Zeng 1999.

8. Atkinson and Geiser 2015; Tai 2020.

9. Michael Winerip, "S.A.T. Increases the Average Score, by Fiat," *New York Times*, June 11, 1994, https://www.nytimes.com/1994/06/11/us/sat-increases-the-average-score-by-fiat.html.

10. Newton 2011.

11. B. G. Davis 1999.

12. M. Miller 2022.

13. van Gog and Sweller 2015, 248.

14. E.g., Goldstein 2017.

15. Stewart 1982.

16. Zaretsky 2019.

17. Cleary 2014; Graham et al. 2012.

18. McCulloch 2019.

19. Lenhart et al. 2008.

20. Lunsford, n.d.; Stanford University, n.d.

21. Sztabnik 2015.

22. Eodice, Geller, and Lerner 2016, 137, 140.

23. Warner 2013.

24. Bartholomae 1986, 10.

25. See Klebanov and Madnani 2020 for a fairly even-handed summary of the developments and refinements, as well as challenges, of Automated Writing Evaluation. Their institutional affiliation with the Educational Testing Service does suggest that they are believers in the project, whatever misgivings they might have.

26. Lindblom 2015.

27. Warner 2018, 144.

28. Strauss 2019.

29. Kissel and Blum 2021; O'Donnell (2012) 2018.

30. "The UnEssay," Marc Kissel's Website, May 7, 2018, https://marckissel.netlify.app/post/on-the-unessay/.

31. Cara Ocobock, "Un-essay," University of Notre Dame, http://sites.nd.edu/cara-ocobock/un-essay/.

32. Slagle 1997.

33. Roberts 2018.

34. Watson and Hagood 2017.

35. See, e.g., Lovett et al. 2023; Day and Goldstone 2012.

11. Tech and Media

1. Cabrera-Álvarez and Clayton 2020.

2. Gershon 2017.

3. Here are a few sources on media, but the list is enormous. Heyer and Urquhart 2019; Jones and Hafner 2021; Poe 2011.

4. Umble 2003.

5. Bernstein 1971.

6. Cazden 2001.

7. Gibson 1979.

8. Kelley and Oliver 2020; J. Rose 2022.

9. Lee 2020.

10. Feathers 2020.

11. Watters 2014, 2015a, 2015b, 2016, 2017, 2021; Williamson 2021, 51; Zuboff 2019.

12. Gilliard 2017.

13. Laura Gibbs, Tweet, January 27, 2020, https://twitter.com/OnlineCrsLady/status/1221879650424709121?s=20&t=Es2pvcepVh8TF2dV5hZavw.

14. See Stommel, Friend, and Morris's (2020) analysis of how to assess tools and their costs and benefits.

15. Lieberman 2019.

16. Others (in 2022) use Discord, a communication tool that arose from gaming, so that players could simultaneously talk and play.

17. Bruff 2019; Cohn 2021; M. Miller 2022.

18. Cohn 2021, 278–86.

19. M. Miller 2022, 209–10.

20. Berry 1994.

21. Slightly edited from Blum 2020b.

22. "Our Brains Synchronize during a Conversation," Science Daily, July 20, 2017, https://www.sciencedaily.com/releases/2017/07/170720095035.htm.

23. Tannen 1981, 145.

24. Enfield 2017; Goodwin 2018.

25. Levinson and Torreira 2015.

26. Tomasello et al. 2007.

27. Griswold 2020.

28. Gaver 1991.

29. Norman 1998; Rayner 2018.

30. Leader 2020.

12. Attending (to) Bodies

1. Winnicott 1960, 147.

2. Hrach 2021, 17.

3. Foucault 1978, 1988.

4. Cisney and Morar 2015.

5. Dunbar 1996.

6. McKenna and Gettler 2015.

7. Panksepp and Biven 2012.

8. Dworkin-McDaniel 2011; *Neurocritic* 2012; Peled-Avron, Perry, and Shamay-Tsoory 2016; Trudeau 2010.

9. Mauss 1934; Vergunst and Ingold 2016.

10. Lacan (1964) 1978; P. Lee 2003. Also see Thibierge and Morin 2010.

11. Mulvey 1975.

12. Ungar 2020.

13. boyd 2014.

14. Fawns, Aitken, and Jones 2019; Gourlay 2021.

15. Baron 2008; Twenge 2018.

16. See in Davidson (2011a) the chapter "Against Technophobia." This is connected both to "generation theory" and moral panic, in which new communicative technologies are held monocausally responsible for many social ills: Gen-Experts, in Jessica Kriegel's term, are selling reductive stereotypes (Kriegel 2016). W. Strauss and Howe started it with their book *Generations* (1992); N. Carr continued with "Is Google Making Us Stupid?" (2008); Jean Twenge's books *Generation ME* (2006) and *iGen* (2018) are statistics- and graph-filled explanations of why the current generation is entirely different from the one that preceded it. Yes,

things done by people at fifteen in 2016 are different from what people did at fifteen in 1986—but so are the things done by people at forty-five in 2016. By contrasting only the years, she is making "young people today" into aliens. Yes, they sleep with their phones—but so does my husband when he wants to be sure to hear his alarm, and he's sixty-eight. He didn't do that forty years ago, true, but that makes him more like today's fifteen-year-olds and less like his own fifteen-year-old self.

17. Zull 2002.

18. Craft and Perna 2004; Hari 2022, 127–28; Van Der Kolk 2014.

19. I am really going beyond my expertise here. Check out Linda Cole, "Tunicates—Not So Spineless Invertebrates," Ocean: Find Your Blue, Smithsonian, June 2018, https://ocean.si.edu/ocean-life/invertebrates/tunicates-not-so-spineless-invertebrates; "Phylum Chordata," Exploring Our Fluid Earth: Teaching Science as Inquiry, Curriculum Research & Development Group, College of Education, University of Hawai'i, n.d., https://manoa.hawaii.edu/exploringourfluidearth/biological/invertebrates/phylum-chordata; Fodor et al., 2021; "How the Brain Works: The Brain Is Mostly for Movement," Centre for Educational Neuroscience, University College London, March 11, 2019, http://www.educationalneuroscience.org.uk/2019/03/11/how-the-brain-works-the-brain-is-mostly-for-movement/.

20. Rubin 1992.

21. Franz and Intagliata 2017; Furey 2020; Reynolds 2021; Willingham 2009.

22. "World Report on Disability," World Health Organization, December 14, 2011, https://www.who.int/publications/i/item/9789241564182.

23. Paúl and Branigin 2022.

24. I put this term in scare quotes because sometimes this has to do with genuine integrity but more often to do with arbitrary and random prohibitions imposed by faculty, such as against checking outside sources during an exam. The schoolishness of such prohibitions is breathtaking in its lack of preparation for life beyond school, when the whole world is available with a quick verbal question posed to Alexa, Siri, or Google Assistant. See, e.g., the earnest struggle of faculty such as Hallowell 2022; Chin 2020b.

25. J. Lee 2020.

26. Zuboff 2019.

27. "#AgainstSurveillance: A Fundraiser in Defence of Ian Linkletter," n.d., https://againstsurveillance.net/.

28. Zoë Corbyn, "'I'm Afraid': Critics of Anti-cheating Technology for Students Hit by Lawsuits," *Guardian*, August 26, 2022, https://www.theguardian.com/us-news/2022/aug/26/anti-cheating-technology-students-tests-proctorio.

29. Davidson 2011a; Hari 2022.

30. Hartnett 2017.

31. Yeshurun, Nguyen, and Hasson 2021.

32. Gaskins 2013; Gaskins and Paradise 2010.

33. Hari 2022, 219–20.

34. Zeller 2017.

35. Hanna 2015, 172.

36. Hu 1944.

37. Philips 1983.

38. Kidmas, Ashman, and Short 2017, 80.

39. Chapman 2011.

40. Arbouin 2012, 206.

41. Cavanagh 2019.

42. Cavanagh 2023.

43. Leanna Garfield, "What School Lunch Looks Like in 19 Countries around the World," Insider, September 27, 2019, https://www.businessinsider.com/school-lunches-around-the-world-photos-2017-4.

44. Baltag, Pachyna, and Hall 2015; Zwiebel and Thompson 2022.

45. Abelson et al. 2020.

13. Selves

1. Subsequently three modifications arose: (1) Emphasizing that some signs were "relatively motivated," which is to say once a language had an item like *fish*, then things like *fish sticks* and *fishing for compliments* were understood quickly and were not arbitrary. Michael Silverstein and others began to speak of these apparently arbitrary signs becoming *iconized* for their speakers (Silverstein 2023). That is, speakers began to feel as if there was something fishlike about the words. But for a long time this focus in the conventional nature of signs drove discussions about meaning. (2) There was a reminder that only some signs ("symbols") were arbitrary. There were other types of signs, notably icons, which resemble their referent, and indexes, which are associated by habit or logic with their referent. (3) There was some simple and later complex research on the possibility of universal connections between signifiers and signifieds. This is evident in things like high vowels indicating smallness (*eek*) and low vowels indicating largeness (*low*).

2. Evans et al. 2005, 140.

3. Evans et al. 2005, 140.

4. Evans et al. 2005, 140–41.

5. Evans et al. 2005, 142.

6. Hochschild 2012.

7. Hochschild 2012, 167.

8. Hochschild 2012, 131.

9. Hochschild 2012, 194.

10. Hochschild 2012, 133.

11. Hochschild 2012, 158, 136.

12. Hochschild 2012. In what are called the "caring professions"—e.g., social work, nursing, teaching, clergy—this is usually regarded as unforced, voluntary, and there is a professional mask or shield, compartmentalizing, that puts up a line between the client and the worker. These professions tend not to be well paid and are feminized.

13. Hochschild 2012, 47.

14. Morris 2002, 51–52.

15. M. Berman 1982; Marx and Engels (1848) 1964.

16. Ball 2003, 221.

17. Ball 2003, 222.

18. Ball 2003, 222, 224.

19. A. Miller (1979) 1981, 75.

20. Detmer 2008, 25.

21. Trilling 1972.

22. Cheung 2002.

23. Adorno (1964) 1973; Hobsbawm and Ranger 2012.

24. Kuh 2008.

14. "The Trees Need Water"

1. This chapter is a revised version of "'The Trees Need Water' and the Students Need Authentic Responsibility: Learning Almost-in-the-Wild in a Community-Based

Internship," by Susan D. Blum, Terri Hebert, Gabrielle Robinson, Kirill Gillespie, Maeve Mallozzi-Kelly, Melissa Norbert, Saliyha Webb, and Jay B. Brockman and published in *Other Education*, 2022.

2. Hanstedt 2018.

3. "City of South Bend—Indiana Settlement," US Environmental Protection Agency, 2022, https://www.epa.gov/enforcement/city-south-bend-indiana-settlement; "United States District Court Northern District of Indiana South Bend Division, Consent Decree," Environmental Protection Agency, n.d., https://www.epa.gov/sites/default/files/documents/cityof southbend-cd.pdf.

4. Walton 2017. STEM stands for "science, technology, engineering, and mathematics."

5. Comparison of such magnitude is tricky; it's about more than manipulating a single variable. Thus the comparison is more suggestive than conclusive. William Sewell Jr. elaborated on Marc Bloch's consideration of the comparative method, concluding that narrow comparison is more useful than broad comparison (Bloch 1928, discussed in Sewell 1967). I got this reference from Bernie McGinn, when we were both fellows at the Notre Dame Institute for Advanced Study in fall 2017.

6. See Blum et al. 2018; Coward 2020; Haanstad, Robinson, and Webb 2020.

7. Moore 1983, 1986.

8. Dewey 1938.

9. See Blum 2020a.

10. But sometimes they told the interns what and how to do what they were doing, reverting to conventional roles of "sage on the stage." Mentor interaction with the interns was uneven. In one case it seemed that a faculty mentor directed the interns to carry out a project conceived by the mentor rather than responding to needs perceived by the community.

11. Hoadley 2012.

12. Moore 1983, 43.

13. Grieve 2020.

14. Clark 2008. See also Hrach 2021; Paul 2021.

15. Making Schools Less Schoolish

1. "Eyler Warner & Associates, LLC," n.d., https://eylerwarner.com/.

2. Korstange et al. 2021.

3. Crenshaw 2020; Dignan 2020; Tam and El-Azar 2020.

4. Tyack and Cuban 1995.

5. Tyack and Cuban 1995, 95, 97, 102.

6. Sherrington 2017. See especially pp. 49, 51, 54.

7. Egan 2010.

8. White et al. 2020.

9. Deslauriers et al. 2019.

10. Earl et al. 2020, 19.

11. Lang 2021; Davidson and Katopodis 2022; Hogan and Sathy 2022.

12. Blum 2022.

13. "Welcome to the Red House," Georgetown University, n.d., https://redhouse.georgetown.edu/.

14. "Carl Wieman Science Education Initiative," University of British Columbia, n.d., https://cwsei.ubc.ca/home; "Welcome to the Red House," Georgetown University; "Mastery Transcript Consortium," 2021, https://mastery.org/.

15. Smith and Piemonte 2022.

16. "Transforming Large Foundational Courses," Foundational Course Initiative, CRLT, University of Michigan, 2021, https://crlt.umich.edu/fci.

17. Precel 2022.

18. "Interrogating Spaces: Pass/Fail Assessment in Arts Higher Education," UAL Teaching, Learning and Employability Exchange," University of the Arts London, December 1, 2021, https://interrogatingspaces.buzzsprout.com/683798/9644305.

19. "The Edible Schoolyard Project," 2023, https://edibleschoolyard.org/.

20. "125 Years of Scholarship, Curiosity & Creativity," University of Chicago Laboratory Schools, n.d., https://www.ucls.uchicago.edu/about-lab/lab-history.

21. "Reggio Emilia Approach," Scuole e Nidi d'Infanzia, 2022, https://www.reggiochildren.it/en/reggio-emilia-approach/.

22. "Denmark's Forest Kindergartens," Special Broadcasting Service Dateline (Australia), February 23, 2016, https://www.youtube.com/watch?v=Jkiij9dJfcw; "History," American Forest Kindergarten Association, n.d., https://www.forestkindergartenassociation.org/history; "Sudbury Valley School," 2020, sudburyvalley.org; "Haja Center for Youth and Social Enterprises, South Korea, Bon Voyage E. 36," MakeChangeTV, November 22, 2012, https://www.youtube.com/watch?v=55RjuwgZk60.

23. Biebrich, n.d.

24. Cappel 1999; "Vision and History," Bennington College, n.d., https://www.bennington.edu/about/vision-and-history.

25. "The Goddard Difference," Goddard College, 2023, https://www.goddard.edu/; "Ten Reasons Why Goddard Is Distinctly Different," Goddard College, 2023, https://www.goddard.edu/blog/featured-posts/10-reasons-why-goddard-is-different/; "Mission," Goddard College, 2023, https://www.goddard.edu/about-goddard/mission/.

26. "New College History," New College of Florida, 2023, https://www.ncf.edu/about/history/.

27. Gecker 2023.

28. P. Townsend 2015.

29. Schevitz 2000b, 2000a.

30. "Learn about the Open University," Open University, 2023, https://www.open.ac.uk/about/main/.

31. "Mission and Vision," History, Hampshire College, n.d., https://www.hampshire.edu/hampshire-experience/mission-and-vision/history#.

32. "Why Hampshire? To Know Is Not Enough," Hampshire College, 2022, https://www.hampshire.edu/hampshire-experience/why-hampshire; "Hampshire College," Colleges That Change Lives, https://ctcl.org/hampshire-college/.

33. "About," Evergreen State College, 2023, https://www.evergreen.edu/about/about.

34. "History," Olin College of Engineering, n.d., https://olin.smartcatalogiq.com/en/2018-19/Catalog/Information-about-Olin/History#.

35. Holt (1976) 2004; Illich 1970; Riley 2020.

36. "Human Restoration Project," 2023, humanrestorationproject.org/.

37. Brown 2008.

38. Edgerton 1992; Ortner 2016; Robbins 2013.

39. Kohn 1999, 19.

40. "The five stages of Design Thinking, according to d.school, are as follows: Empathise, Define (the problem), Ideate, Prototype, and Test," "Design Thinking, Define Stage SWOT and TOWS Analysis," Litt Agile Transformation, July 24, 2020, https://www.youtube.com/watch?v=qTQ-7LNhj-I. See also IDEOU 2022. Some versions of "design thinking" remind

their users to "fail" and to "fail fast" ("fail often and fast"), e.g., Babineaux and Krumboltz 2013. Whether or not our students are "customers," as in business, they are certainly the beneficiaries of our work (putting aside the research part of our profession).

41. FitzSimmons 2015.

42. FitzSimmons 2015, 222; Freire 1998, 48.

43. Pollan 2008; Scrinis 2015.

Conclusion

1. Richards and Cohen 2022.

Allies and Acknowledgments

1. Blum 2017.

2. Supiano 2019.

3. Foley et al. 2015, 124.

4. Foley et al. 2015, 126.

5. Paul Farmer, "Accompaniment as Policy," Office of the Secretary-General's Special Adviser on Community-Based Medicine & Lessons from Haiti, May 25, 2011, https://www.lessonsfromhaiti.org/press-and-media/transcripts/accompaniment-as-policy/.

SOURCES

Abelson, Jenn, Nicole Dungca, Meryl Kornfield, and Andrew Ba Tran. 2020. "At College Health Centers, Students Battle Misdiagnoses and Inaccessible Care." *Washington Post*, July 13. https://www.washingtonpost.com/investigations/2020/07/13/college-health-centers-problems/.

Abramson, Larry. 2007. "Sputnik Left Legacy for U.S. Science Education." NPR, September 30. https://www.npr.org/2007/09/30/14829195/sputnik-left-legacy-for-u-s-science-education.

Adorno, Theodor. (1964) 1973. *The Jargon of Authenticity*. Translated by Knut Tarnowski and Frederic Will. London: Routledge.

Ajemu, Kiros Fenta, Tewolde Wubayehu Weldearegay, Nega Mamo Bezabih, Yrgalem Meles, Goytom Mehari, Abraham Aregay Desta, Asfawosen Aregay Berhe, et al. 2020. "Mass Psychogenic Illness in Haraza Elementary School, Erop District, Tigray, Northern Ethiopia: Investigation to the Nature of an Episode." *Psychiatry Journal* 2693830, July 23. https//doi.org/10.1155/2020/2693830.

Albrecht, Joëlle N., Helene Werner, Noa Rieger, et al. 2022. "Association between Homeschooling and Adolescent Sleep Duration and Health during COVID-19 Pandemic High School Closures." *JAMA Network Open*, January 5. https:// doi.org/10.1001/jamanetworkopen.2021.42100.

Anderson, Benedict. (1983) 1991. *Imagined Communities: Reflections on the Origin and Spread of Nationalism*. 2nd ed. London: Verso.

Anderson, Melinda D. 2017. "Why the Myth of Meritocracy Hurts Kids of Color." *Atlantic*, July 27. https://www.theatlantic.com/education/archive/2017/07/internaliz ing-the-myth-of-meritocracy/535035/.

Anderson, Nick. 2020. "Colleges Are Ditching Required Admission Tests over Covid-19. Will They Ever Go Back?" *Washington Post*, June 15. https://www.washingtonpost. com/local/education/coronavirus-sat-act-admission/2020/06/15/18c406dc-acca-11ea-a9d9-a81c1a491c52_story.html.

Appiah, Kwame Anthony. 2018. "The Myth of Meritocracy: Who Really Gets What They Deserve?" *Guardian*, October 19. https://www.theguardian.com/news/2018/oct/19/the-myth-of-meritocracy-who-really-gets-what-they-deserve.

Arbouin, Lee. 2012. *The Nottingham Connection*. Bloomington, IN: AuthorHouse.

Arnett, Jeffrey Jensen. 2018. *Adolescence and Emerging Adulthood: A Cultural Approach*. 6th ed. New York: Pearson.

Associated Press. 2020. "Judge: Michigan Teen Jailed over Homework Released from Probation." August 11. https://www.clickondetroit.com/news/michigan/2020/08/11/judge-michigan-teen-jailed-over-homework-released-from-probation/.

Atkinson, Richard C., and Saul Geiser. 2015. "The Big Problem with the New SAT." *New York Times*, May 4. https://www.nytimes.com/2015/05/05/opinion/the-big-problem-with-the-new-sat.html.

Austin, J. L. 1962. *How to Do Things with Words*. Oxford: Oxford University Press.

Austin, Patrik. 2021. "Theory of Language: A Taxonomy." *SN Social Sciences* 1 (78). https://doi.org/10.1007/s43545-021-00085-x.

"Authentic Writing: What It Means and How to Do It." 2017. http://21stcentury englisheducation.blogspot.com/2017/11/authentic-writing-is-not-five-paragraph.html.

Babineaux, Ryan, and John Krumboltz. 2013. *Fail Fast, Fail Often: How Losing Can Help You Win*. New York: Penguin.

Ball, Stephen J. 2003. "The Teacher's Soul and the Terrors of Performativity." *Journal of Education Policy* 18 (2): 215–28.

Baltag, Valentina, Anastasiya Pachyna, and Julia Hall. 2015. "Global Overview of School Health Services: Data from 102 Countries." *Health Behavior and Policy Review* 2 (4): 268–83. https://doi.org/10.14485/HBPR.2.4.4.

Barnum, Matt. 2018. "Do Community Schools and Wraparound Services Boost Academics? Here's What We Know." Chalkbeat, February 20. https://www.chalkbeat. org/2018/2/20/21108833/do-community-schools-and-wraparound-services-boost-academics-here-s-what-we-know.

Baron, Naomi S. 2008. *Always On: Language in an Online and Mobile World*. New York: Oxford.

Barrett, Brian. 2019. "The Radical Transformation of the Textbook." *Wired*, August 4. https://www.wired.com/story/digital-textbooks-radical-transformation/.

Barrett, Peter, Alberto Treves, Tigran Shmis, Diego Ambasz, and Maria Ustinova. 2019. "The Impact of School Infrastructure on Learning: A Synthesis of the Evidence." International Development in Focus. Washington, DC: World Bank. https://doi. org/10.1596/978-1-4648-1378-8.

Bartholomae, David. 1986. "Inventing the University." *Journal of Basic Writing* 5 (1): 1–20. https://wac.colostate.edu/jbw/v5n1/bartholomae.pdf.

Bateson, Gregory, Don D. Jackson, Jay Haley, and John H. Weakland. 1963. "A Note on the Double Bind—1962." *Family Process* 2 (1): 154–61. https://doi.org/10.1111/j.1545-5300.1963.00154.x.

Bauerlein, Mark. 2013. "Boredom in Class." EducationNext, September 20. https://www.educationnext.org/boredom-in-class/.

Bellah, Robert N., Richard Madsen, William M. Sullivan, Ann Swidler, and Steven M. Tipton. 1985. *Habits of the Heart: Individualism and Commitment in American Life*. New York: Harper & Row.

Beresin, Eugene. 2017. "The Problem of School Refusal; Back to School: A Joy to Most, a Nightmare for Others." *Psychology Today*, September 18. https://www.psychologytoday.com/us/blog/inside-out-outside-in/201709/the-problem-school-refusal-0.

Berg, Maggie, and Barbara K. Seeber. 2016. *The Slow Professor: Challenging the Culture of Speed in the Academy*. Toronto: University of Toronto Press.

Bergland, Christopher. 2017. "The Neurobiology of Music-Induced Pleasure." *Psychology Today*, January 8. https://www.psychologytoday.com/us/blog/the-athletes-way/201701/the-neurobiology-music-induced-pleasure.

Berlant, Lauren. 2011. *Cruel Optimism*. Durham, NC: Duke University Press.

Berman, Elise. 2019. *Talking Like Children: Language and the Production of Age in the Marshall Islands*. New York: Oxford University Press.

Berman, Elise, and Benjamin Smith, 2021. "De-naturalizing the Novice: A Critique of the Theory of Language Socialization." *American Anthropologist* 123 (3): 590–602.

Berman, Marshall. 1982. *All That Is Solid Melts into Air: The Experience of Modernity*. New York: Simon & Schuster.

Bernstein, Basil. 1971. *Class, Codes and Control: Theoretical Studies towards a Sociology of Language*. New York: Schocken Books.

Berry, Wendell. 1994. "Why I Am Not Going to Buy a Computer." In "Field Observations: An Interview with Wendell Berry," by Jordan Fisher-Smith. *Sun*, February. http://tipiglen.co.uk/berrynot.html.

Biebrich, Caitlin. n.d. "Progressive Education Association Founded." http://njdigitalhistory.org/1919/progressive-education-association-founded/.

Biesta, Gert J. J. 2010. *Good Education in an Age of Measurement: Ethics, Politics, Democracy*. New York: Routledge.

Birner, Betty. 2022. "How Do Children Acquire Language? Do Parents Teach Their Children to Talk?" Language Acquisition. Linguistic Society of America. https://www.linguisticsociety.org/resource/faq-how-do-we-learn-language.

Black, Carol. n.d. "Children, Learning, and the 'Evaluative Gaze' of School." Teachers Going Gradeless. https://www.teachersgoinggradeless.com/blog/evaluative-gaze.

Bleiker, Carla. 2015. "Stressed Out Fourth Graders." DW, May 5. https://www.dw.com/en/the-pressures-of-being-a-fourth-grader/a-18423632.

Bloch, Marc. 1928. "Pour une histoire comparée de sociétés européennes." *Revue de synthèse historique* 46:15–50.

Bloomer, W. Martin. 2011. *The School of Rome: Latin Studies and the Origins of Liberal Education*. Berkeley: University of California Press.

Blum, Susan D. 1997. "Naming Practices and the Power of Words in China." *Language in Society* 26 (3): 357–79.

Blum, Susan D. 2007. *Lies That Bind: Chinese Truth, Other Truths*. Lanham, MD: Rowman & Littlefield.

Blum, Susan D. 2009. *My Word! Plagiarism and College Culture*. Ithaca, NY: Cornell University Press.

Blum, Susan D. 2015. "The Game of School." Academia. https://www.academia. edu/19672842/The_Game_of_School.

Blum, Susan D. 2016. *"I Love Learning; I Hate School": An Anthropology of College*. Ithaca, NY: Cornell University Press.

Blum, Susan D. 2017. "Unseen WEIRD Assumptions: The So-Called Language Gap Discourse and Ideologies of Language, Childhood, and Learning." *International Multilingual Research Journal* 11 (1): 23–38.

Blum, Susan D., ed. 2020a. *Ungrading: Why Rating Students Undermines Learning (and What to Do Instead)*. Morgantown: West Virginia University Press.

Blum, Susan D. 2020b. "Why We're Exhausted by Zoom." Inside Higher Ed, April 22. https://www.insidehighered.com/advice/2020/04/22/professor-explores-why-zoom-classes-deplete-her-energy-opinion.

Blum, Susan D. 2021. "So You Want to Take the Grades Out of Teaching? A Beginner's Guide to Ungrading." Times Higher Education: Campus, November 30. https://www.timeshighereducation.com/campus/so-you-want-take-grades-out-teaching-beginners-guide-ungrading.

Blum, Susan D. 2022. "The Ungrading Umbrella." Teachers Going Gradeless. https://www.teachersgoinggradeless.com/blog/the-ungrading-umbrella.

Blum, Susan D., Asha Barnes, Kenzell Huggins, and Eric Haanstad. 2018. "Practicing Anthropology and 'Ethnographic Engineering' in a Community-Based Ecological Project." *Practicing Anthropology* 40 (1): 26–28. https://doi.org/10.17730/0888-4552.40.1.26.

Blum, Susan D., Terri Hebert, Gabrielle Robinson, Kirill Gillespie, Maeve Mallozzi-Kelly, Melissa Norberg, Saliyha Webb, and Jay B. Brockman. 2022. "'The Trees Need Water' and the Students Need Authentic Responsibility: Learning Almost-in-the-Wild in a Community-Based Internship." *Other Education: The Journal of Educational Alternatives* 11 (1): 9–41.

Blum-Kulka, Shoshana. 1997. *Dinner Talk: Cultural Patterns of Sociability and Socialization in Family Discourse*. Mahwah, NJ: Erlbaum.

Boaler, Jo. 2022. "How Can We Make More Students Fall in Love with Math?" *Los Angeles Times*, March 14. https://www.latimes.com/opinion/story/2022-03-14/math-framework-california-low-achieving.

Boaler, Jo, and Steven D. Levitt. 2019. "Modern High School Math Should Be about Data Science—Not Algebra 2." *Los Angeles Times*, October 23. https://www.latimes.com/opinion/story/2019-10-23/math-high-school-algebra-data-statistics.

Bolten, Catherine E. n.d. "Jumping into Elderhood: Schooling, Apprenticeships, and the Right to Sit Comfortably in Sierra Leone." Manuscript.

Bourdieu, Pierre, and Jean-Claude Passeron. (1970) 1990. *Reproduction in Education, Society, and Culture*. Translated by Richard Nice. Newbury Park, CA: Sage.

Bowen, Ryan S., and Melanie M. Cooper. 2022. "Grading on a Curve as a Systemic Issue of Equity in Chemistry Education." *Journal of Chemistry Education* 99 (1): 185–94.

boyd, danah. 2014. *It's Complicated: The Social Lives of Networked Teens*. New Haven, CT: Yale University Press.

Bradbury, Alice. 2021. *Ability, Inequality and Post-pandemic Schools: Rethinking Contemporary Myths of Meritocracy*. Bristol: Policy.

Bregnbæk, Susanne. 2016. *Fragile Elite: The Dilemmas of China's Top University Students*. Stanford, CA: Stanford University Press.

Briggs, Charles L., and Richard Bauman. 1992. "Genre, Intertextuality, and Social Power." *Journal of Linguistic Anthropology* 2 (2): 131–72. http://www.jstor.org/stable/43102167.

Bringhurst, Robert. 2008. *The Tree of Meaning: Language, Mind and Ecology*. Berkeley, CA: Counterpoint.

Brink, Susan. 2013. *The Fourth Trimester: Understanding, Protecting, and Nurturing an Infant through the First Three Months*. Berkeley: University of California Press.

Brown, Michael F. 2008. "Cultural Relativism 2.0." *Current Anthropology* 49 (3): 363–83.

Brown, Penelope. 2002. "Everyone Has to Lie in Tzeltal." In *Talking to Adults: The Contribution of Multiparty Discourse to Language Acquisition*, edited by Shoshana Blum-Kulka and Catherine E. Snow, 241–75. Hoboken, NJ: Lawrence Erlbaum Associates.

Bruff, Derek. 2019. *Intentional Tech: Principles to Guide the Use of Educational Technology in College Teaching*. Morgantown: West Virginia University Press.

Bryner, Jeanna. 2007. "Most Students Bored at School." LiveScience, February 28. https://www.livescience.com/1308-students-bored-school.html.

Buranyi, Stephen. 2017. "Is the Staggeringly Profitable Business of Scientific Publishing Bad for Science?" *Guardian*, June 27. https://www.theguardian.com/science/2017/jun/27/profitable-business-scientific-publishing-bad-for-science.

Burns, Nick. 2022. "Elite Universities Are Out of Touch. Blame the Campus." *New York Times*, August 2.

Cabrera-Álvarez, María J., and Nicola S. Clayton. 2020. "Neural Processes Underlying Tool Use in Human, Macaques, and Corvids." *Frontiers in Psychology* 11 (September 23). https://doi.org/10.3389/fpsyg.2020.560669.

Cain, Susan. 2012. *Quiet: The Power of Introverts in a World That Can't Stop Talking*. New York: Broadway.

Calarco, Jessica McCrory. 2020. *A Field Guide to Grad School: Uncovering the Hidden Curriculum*. Princeton, NJ: Princeton University Press.

Cantoni, Davide, Yuyu Chen, David Y. Yang, Noam Yuchtman, and Y. Jane Zhang. 2015. "Curriculum and Ideology." October 7. http://davidyyang.com/pdfs/curriculum_draft.pdf.

Caplan, Bryan S. 2018. *The Case against Education: Why the Education System Is a Waste of Time and Money*. Princeton, NJ: Princeton University Press.

Cappel, Constance. 1999. *Utopian Colleges*. New York: Peter Lang.

Carillo, Ellen C. 2021. *The Hidden Inequities in Labor-Based Contract Grading*. Logan: Utah State University Press.

Carpena-Méndez, Fina. 2017. "Indigenous Youth and the Production of Hope: Migration, Radical Uncertainty, and Knowing/Livelihood Anxieties." Paper presented at the annual meeting of the American Anthropological Association, Washington, DC. November.

Carr, E. Summerson. 2010. *Scripting Addiction: The Politics of Therapeutic Talk and American Sobriety.* Princeton, NJ: Princeton University Press.

Carr, Nicholas. 2008. "Is Google Making Us Stupid?" *Atlantic*, July/August.

Casper, Scott E. 2010. "McGuffey Readers." In *The Oxford Companion to the Book*, edited by Michael Suarez and H. R. Woudhuysen. Oxford: Oxford University Press.

Cavanagh, Sarah Rose. 2016. *The Spark of Learning: Energizing the College Classroom with the Science of Emotion.* Morgantown: West Virginia University Press.

Cavanagh, Sarah Rose. 2019. "The Best (and Worst) Ways to Respond to Student Anxiety." *Chronicle of Higher Education*, May 5. https://www.chronicle.com/article/ The-Best-and-Worst-Ways-to/246226.

Cavanagh, Sarah Rose. 2023. *Mind over Monsters: Supporting Youth Mental Health with Compassionate Challenge.* Boston: Beacon.

Cazden, Courtney B. 2001. *Classroom Discourse: The Language of Teaching and Learning.* 2nd ed. Portsmouth, NH: Heinemann.

Chang, Julie. 2018. "Texas Education Board Approves Curriculum That Challenges Evolution." *Austin American-Statesman*, September 25. https://www.statesman.com/ story/news/2017/02/02/texas-education-board-approves-curriculum-that-challenges-evolution/10153292007/.

Chapman, Ben. 2011. "10-Year-Old Autistic Boy, Brandon Strong, Punished for Behavior Caused by His Condition." *New York Daily News*, February 15. https://www. nydailynews.com/new-york/brooklyn/10-year-old-autistic-boy-brandon-strong-punished-behavior-caused-condition-article-1.136258.

Chasteen, Stephanie V., and Warren J. Code. 2018. *The Science Education Initiative Handbook: A Practical Guide to Fostering Change in University Courses and Faculty by Embedding Discipline-Based Education Specialists within Departments.* https:// pressbooks.bccampus.ca/seihandbook.

Che, Chang. 2021. "After Online Tutoring, Why Is China Cracking Down on Private Schools?" China Project, September 9. https://supchina.com/2021/09/09/after-online-tutoring-why-is-china-cracking-down-on-private-schools/.

Cheung, Sidney. 2002. "Traditional Dwellings, Conservation, and Land Use: A Study of Three Villages in Sai Kung, Hong Kong." In *Tensions of Preservation.* Traditional Dwellings and Settlements Working Paper Series, 33–51. Vol. 153. Berkeley, CA: International Association for the Study of Traditional Environments.

Chin, Monica. 2020a. "An Ed-Tech Specialist Spoke Out about Remote Testing Software— and Now He's Being Sued." Verge, October 20. https://www.theverge.com/2020/10/22/ 21526792/proctorio-online-test-proctoring-lawsuit-universities-students-coronavirus.

Chin, Monica. 2020b. "Exam Anxiety: How Remote Test-Proctoring Is Creeping Students Out." Verge, April 29. https://www.theverge.com/2020/4/29/21232777/ examity-remote-test-proctoring-online-class-education.

Cho, Mun Young. 2022. "The Precariat That Can Speak: The Politics of Encounters between the Educated Youth and the Urban Poor in Seoul." *Current Anthropology* 63 (5): 491–518.

Christakis, Erika. 2016. "The New Preschool Is Crushing Kids." *Atlantic*, January/February. https://www.theatlantic.com/magazine/archive/2016/01/the-new-preschool-is-crushing-kids/419139/.

Christensen, Fie Lund Lindegaard. 2021. "Synchronization and Syncopation: Conceptualizing Autism through Rhythm." *Culture, Medicine, and Psychiatry* 45: 683–705. https://doi.org/10.1007/s11013-020-09698-y.

Chu, Lenora. 2017. *Little Soldiers: An American Boy, a Chinese School, and the Global Race to Achieve*. New York: HarperCollins.

Chudacoff, Howard P. 1989. *How Old Are You? Age Consciousness in American Culture*. Princeton, NJ: Princeton University Press.

Cisney, Vernon W., and Nicolae Morar. 2015. *Biopower: Foucault and Beyond*. Chicago: University of Chicago Press.

Clancy, Kathryn B. H., and Jenny L. Davis. 2019. "Soylent Is People and WEIRD Is White: Biological Anthropology, Whiteness, and the Limits of the WEIRD." *Annual Review of Anthropology* 48: 169–86.

Clancy, Patricia M. 1986. "The Acquisition of Japanese Communicative Style." In *Language Acquisition and Socialization across Cultures*, edited by Elinor Ochs and Bambi B. Schieffelin, 213–50. New York: Cambridge University Press.

Clark, Andy. 2008. *Supersizing the Mind: Embodiment, Action, and Cognitive Extension*. Oxford: Oxford University Press.

Clark, Eve V. 2017. *Language in Children*. London: Routledge.

Cleary, Michelle Navarre. 2014. "The Wrong Way to Teach Grammar." *Atlantic*, February 25. https://www.theatlantic.com/education/archive/2014/02/the-wrong-way-to-teach-grammar/284014/.

Clegg, Sue. 2010. "Time Future: The Dominant Discourse of Higher Education." *Time and Society* 19 (3): 345–64.

Cohen, Jodi S. 2020. "A Teenager Didn't Do Her Online Schoolwork. So a Judge Sent Her to Juvenile Detention." ProPublica Illinois, July 14. https://www.propublica.org/article/a-teenager-didnt-do-her-online-schoolwork-so-a-judge-sent-her-to-juvenile-detention.

Cohen, Stanley. 1972. *Folk Devils and Moral Panic: The Creation of the Mods and Rockers*. London: Routledge.

Cohn, Jenae. 2021. *Skim, Dive, Surface: Teaching Digital Reading*. Morgantown: West Virginia University Press.

Cole T. B., T. L. Chorba, and J. M. Horan. 1990. "Patterns of Transmission of Epidemic Hysteria in a School." *Epidemiology* 1 (3): 212–18. https//doi.org/10.1097/00001648-199005000-00006. PMID: 2081255.

Collins, Randall. 1979. *Credential Society: An Historical Sociology of Education and Stratification*. New York: Columbia University Press.

Compton, Martin. 2022. "How Effective Are Your Questions?" January 10. https://reflect.ucl.ac.uk/mcarena/2022/01/10/how-effective-are-your-questions/.

Connery, Chelsea. 2020. "The Prevalence and the Price of Police in Schools." UConn NEAG School of Education, October 27. https://education.uconn.edu/2020/10/27/the-prevalence-and-the-price-of-police-in-schools/.

Coonan, Clifford. 2014. "Home from School at 1 am in South Korea Where Education Rules." *Irish Times,* July 21. https://www.irishtimes.com/business/home-from-school-at-1am-in-south-korea-where-education-rules-1.1869562.

Cooper, Melanie M., and Mike Klymkowsky. 2020. "Curbing the Malpractice of Curved Grades and High-Stakes Exams." *ASBMB Today: The Member Magazine of the American Society for Biochemistry and Molecular Biology,* November 18. https://www.asbmb.org/asbmb-today/opinions/111820/curbing-the-malpractice-of-curved-grades-and-high.

Counihan, Carole M. 2004. *Around the Tuscan Table: Food, Family, and Gender in Twentieth-Century Florence.* New York: Routledge.

Coward, Kyle. 2020. "The Creek Will Rise." *Stanford Social Innovation Review* 18 (1): 15–17. https://doi.org/10.48558/RPX7-6K33.

Craft, Lynette L., and Frank M. Perna. 2004. "The Benefits of Exercise for the Clinically Depressed." *Primary Care Companion to the Journal of Clinical Psychiatry* 6 (3): 104–11. https//doi.org/10.4088/pcc.v06n0301.

Crenshaw, Alan. 2020. "How Innovation Is Accelerating to Meet Coronavirus Challenges." US Chamber of Commerce. https://www.uschamber.com/series/above-the-fold/how-innovation-accelerating-meet-coronavirus-challenges.

Crosier, David, and Teodora Parveva. 2013. *The Bologna Process: Its Impact on Higher Education Development in Europe and Beyond.* Paris: UNESCO, International Institute for Educational Planning.

Csibra, Gergely, and György Gergely. 2011. "Natural Pedagogy as Evolutionary Adaptation." *Philosophical Transactions of the Royal Society of London.* Series B, Biological Sciences, 366: 1149–57.

Damasio, Antonio R. 1994. *Descartes' Error: Emotion, Reason, and the Human Brain.* New York: Penguin.

Damasio, Antonio R. 1999. *The Feeling of What Happens: Body and Emotion in the Making of Consciousness.* New York: Harcourt Brace.

Daniels, E. Valentine. 1984. *Fluid Signs: Being a Person the Tamil Way.* Berkeley: University of California Press.

Darwin, Charles. 1882. *The Descent of Man, and Selection in Relation to Sex.* 2nd ed. New York: D. Appleton.

Dashiell, J. F. 1925. "A Quantitative Demonstration of Animal Drive." *Comparative Psychology* 5: 205–8.

David, Paul A. 1997. "Path Dependence and the Quest for Historical Economics: One More Chorus of the Ballad of QWERTY." University of Oxford: *Discussion Papers in Economic and Social History* no. 20.

Davidson, Cathy N. 2011a. *Now You See It: How the Brain Science of Attention Will Transform the Way We Live, Work, and Learn.* New York: Viking.

Davidson, Cathy N. 2011b. "Strangers on a Train." AAUP, September–October. https://www.aaup.org/article/strangers-train#.Y435QuxufBE.

Davidson, Cathy N. 2017. *The New Education: How to Revolutionize the University to Prepare Students for a World in Flux.* New York: Hachette.

Davidson, Cathy N., and Christina Katopodis. 2022. *The New College Classroom.* Cambridge, MA: Harvard University Press.

Davies, Leah. 2005. "Overcoming School Phobia." http://www.kellybear.com/Teacher Articles/TeacherTip51.html.

Davis, Barbara Gross. 1999. *Tools for Teaching*. San Francisco: Jossey-Bass.

Davis, Obasi. 2013. "Bored in 1st Period." Power Poetry, November 17. https://power poetry.org/poems/bored-1st-period.

Day, Samuel B., and Robert L. Goldstone. 2012. "The Import of Knowledge Export: Connecting Findings and Theories of Transfer of Learning." *Educational Psychologist* 47 (3): 153–76. https://doi.org/10.1080/00461520.2012. 696438.

Deci, Edward L. 1971. "Effects of Externally Mediated Rewards on Intrinsic Motivation." *Journal of Personality and Social Psychology* 18: 105–15.

Demerath, Peter. 2009. *Producing Success: The Culture of Personal Advancement in an American High School*. Chicago: University of Chicago Press.

Denworth, Lydia. 2019. "'Hyperscans' Show How Brains Sync as People Interact." *Scientific American*, April 10. https://www.scientificamerican.com/article/hyperscans-show-how-brains-sync-as-people-interact/.

Denworth, Lydia. 2021. "Making Eye Contact Signals a New Turn in a Conversation." *Scientific American*, September 21. https://www.scientificamerican.com/article/making-eye-contact-signals-a-new-turn-in-a-conversation/.

Deslauriers, Louis, Logan S. McCarty, Kelly Miller, Kristina Callaghan, and Greg Kestin. 2019. "Measuring Actual Learning versus Feeling of Learning in Response to Being Actively Engaged in the Classroom." *PNAS* 116 (30): 19251–57. https://www.pnas.org/doi/pdf/10.1073/pnas.1821936116.

Detmer, David. 2008. *Sartre Explained: From Bad Faith to Authenticity*. Chicago: Open Court.

Dewey, John. (1916) 1966. *Democracy and Education: An Introduction to the Philosophy of Education*. New York: Free Press.

Dewey, John. 1938. *Experience and Education*. New York: Macmillan.

Diem, Richard, Tedd Levy, and Ronald VanSickle. n.d. "South Korean Education." Asia Society: Center for Global Education. https://asiasociety.org/education/south-korean-education.

Dignan, Larry. 2020. "Online Learning Gets Its Moment Due to COVID-19 Pandemic: Here's How Education Will Change." ZDNet, March 22. https://www.zdnet.com/article/online-learning-gets-its-moment-due-to-covid-19-pandemic-heres-how-education-will-change/.

Diner, Steven J. 2017. *Universities and Their Cities: Urban Higher Education in America*. Baltimore: Johns Hopkins University Press.

Doi, Takeo. 1971. *The Anatomy of Dependence*. Translated by John Bester. New York: Kodansha.

Duckworth, Angela. 2016. *Grit: The Power of Passion and Perseverance*. New York: Scribner.

Dunbar, Robin. 1996. *Grooming, Gossip, and the Evolution of Language*. Cambridge, MA: Harvard University Press.

Dunlap, Rika. 2016. "Hope without the Future: Zen Buddhist Hope in Dōgen's *Shōbōgenzō*." *Journal of Japanese Philosophy* 4: 107–35.

Duranti, Alessandro. 1997. "Universal and Culture-Specific Properties of Greetings." *Journal of Linguistic Anthropology* 7 (1): 63–97.

Dweck, Carol S. 2006. *Mindset: The New Psychology of Success.* New York: Random House.

Dweck, Carol S., Gregory M. Walton, and Geoffrey L. Cohen. 2014. *Academic Tenacity: Mindsets and Skills That Promote Long-Term Learning.* Bill and Melinda Gates Foundation.

Dworkin-McDaniel, Norine. 2011. "Touching Makes You Healthier." CNN, January 5. http://www.cnn.com/2011/HEALTH/01/05/touching.makes.you.health ier.health/index.html.

Dzieza, Josh. 2014. "A History of Metaphors for the Internet." Verge, August 20, 2014. https://www.theverge.com/2014/8/20/6046003/a-history-of-metaphors-for-the-internet.

Eagleton, Terry. 2015. *Hope without Optimism.* Charlottesville: University of Virginia Press.

Earl, Brittnee, Karen Viskupic, Anthony Marker, Amy Moll, Tony Roark, R. Eric Landrum, and Susan Shadle. 2020. "Driving Change: Using the CACAO Framework in an Institutional Change Project." In *Transforming Institutions: Accelerating Systemic Change in Higher Education*, edited by Kate White, Andrea Beach, Noah Finkelstein, Charles Henderson, Scott Simkins, Linda Slakey, Marilyne Stains, Gabriela Weaver, and Lorne Whitehead. Pressbooks. http://openbooks.library. umass.edu/ascnti2020/.

Eaton, Sarah Elaine, Guy J. Curtis, Brenda M. Stoesz, Joseph Clare, Kiata Rundle, and Josh Seeland, eds. 2022. *Contract Cheating in Higher Education: Global Perspectives on Theory, Practice, and Policy.* Cham, Switzerland: Palgrave Macmillan.

Edgerton, Robert B. 1992. *Sick Societies: Challenging the Myth of Primitive Harmony.* New York: Free Press.

Edwards, Carolyn Pope, Keely Cline, Lella Gandini, Alga Giacomelli, Donatella Giovannini, and Annalia Galardini. 2013. "Books, Stories, and the Imagination at 'The Nursery Rhyme': A Qualitative Case Study of the Learning Environment at an Italian Preschool." In *Learning In and Out of School: Education across the Globe*, edited by Susan D. Blum. Conference proceedings. https://kellogg.nd.edu/calendar/5151.

Egan, Kieran. 2010. *Learning in Depth: A Simple Innovation That Can Transform Schooling.* Chicago: University of Chicago Press.

Ehrenreich, Barbara. 2009. *Bright-Sided: How the Relentless Promotion of Positive Thinking Has Undermined America.* New York: Metropolitan Books.

Ehrenreich, Ben. 2021. *Desert Notebooks: A Road Map for the End of Time.* Berkeley, CA: Counterpoint.

Elbow, Peter. 1998. *Writing without Teachers.* New York: Oxford University Press.

Elias, Norbert. (1939) 2000. *The Civilizing Process.* Oxford: Blackwell.

Elman, Benjamin A. 2000. *A Cultural History of Civil Examinations in Late Imperial China.* Berkeley: University of California Press.

Emdin, Christopher. 2016. *For White Folks Who Teach in the Hood—and the Rest of Y'all Too: Reality Pedagogy and Urban Education.* Boston: Beacon.

Enfield, N. J. 2017. *How We Talk: The Inner Workings of Conversation.* New York: Basic Books.

Eodice, Michele, Anne Ellen Geller, and Neal Lerner. 2016. *The Meaningful Writing Project: Learning, Teaching, and Writing in Higher Education.* Logan: Utah State University Press.

European Commission, Directorate-General for Education, Youth, Sport and Culture. 2017. *ECTS Users' Guide 2015.* Publications Office. https://data.europa.eu/doi/10.2766/87192.

Evans, John, and Brian Davies. 2004. "Endnote: The Embodiment of Consciousness." In *Body Knowledge and Control: Studies in the Sociology of Physical Education and Health*, edited by John Evans, Brian Davies, and Jan Wright. London: Routledge.

Evans, John, Emma Rich, Brian Davies, and Rachel Allwood. 2005. "The Embodiment of Learning: What the Sociology of Education Doesn't Say about 'Risk' in Going to School." *International Studies in Sociology of Education* 15 (2): 129–48. http://dx.doi.org/10.1080/09620210500200136.

Evans, John, Emma Rich, and Rachel Holroyd. 2004. "Disordered Eating and Disordered Schooling: What Schools Do to Middle Class Girls." *British Journal of Sociology of Education* 25 (2): 123–42.

Farbman, David A. 2015. "The Case for Improving and Expanding Time in School: A Review of Key Research and Practice." National Center on Time & Learning. https://www.timeandlearning.org/sites/default/files/resources/caseformorelearningtime.pdf.

Fawns, Tim, Gill Aitken, and Derek Jones. 2019. "Online Learning as Embodied, Socially Meaningful Experience." *Postdigital Science and Education* 1: 293–97. https://doi.org/10.1007/s42438-019-00048-9.

Feathers, Todd. 2020. "An Exam Surveillance Company Is Trying to Silence Critics with Lawsuits." Vice, October 21. https://www.vice.com/en/article/7k9zjy/an-exam-surveillance-company-is-trying-to-silence-critics-with-lawsuits.

Finnan, Christine. 2021. "Enacting Identity in the Constrained Academic Space of a Boarding School for Indigenous Students." In *Agency in Constrained Academic Spaces: Explorations of Space in Educational Anthropology*, edited by Aprille J. Phillips and Tricia Gray, 69–86. Lanham, MD: Rowman & Littlefield.

Fischman, Wendy, and Howard Gardner. 2022. *The Real World of College: What Higher Education Is and What It Can Be.* Cambridge, MA: MIT Press.

Fishel, Anne. 2015. "The Most Important Thing You Can Do with Your Kids? Eat Dinner with Them." *Washington Post*, January 12. https://www.washingtonpost.com/posteverything/wp/2015/01/12/the-most-important-thing-you-can-do-with-your-kids-eat-dinner-with-them/.

Fishel, Anne. 2016. "The Family Dinner Project." http://thefamilydinnerproject.org/resources/faq/.

Fisher, Naomi. 2021. *Changing Our Minds: How Children Can Take Control of Their Own Learning.* London: Robinson.

FitzSimmons, Robert. 2015. "Countering the Neoliberal Paradigm: A Pedagogy of the Heart from a Finnish Higher Learning Perspective." *Journal for Critical Education Policy Studies* 13 (1): 210–37.

Flaherty, Colleen. 2020. "Big Proctor: Is the Fight against Cheating during Remote Instruction Worth Enlisting Third-Party Student Surveillance Platforms?"

Inside Higher Ed, May 11. https://www.insidehighered.com/news/2020/05/11/online-proctoring-surging-during-covid-19.

Fodor, Alexander, Jiatai Liu, Lindsay Turner, and Billie J. Swalla. 2021. "Transitional Chordates and Vertebrate Origins: Tunicates." In *Evolutionary Developmental Biology* 141, edited by Scott F. Gilbert, 149–71. Cambridge, MA: Academic.

Foley, Jean Ann, Doug Morris, Panayota Gounari, and Faith Agostinone-Wilson. 2015. "Critical Education, Critical Pedagogies, Marxist Education in the United States." *Journal for Critical Education Policy Studies* 13 (3): 110–44.

Fong, Vanessa L. 2011. *Paradise Redefined: Transnational Chinese Students and the Quest for Flexible Citizenship in the Developed World*. Stanford, CA: Stanford University Press.

Fortin, Jacey. 2021. "California Tries to Close the Gap in Math, but Sets Off a Backlash." *New York Times*, November 17. https://www.nytimes.com/2021/11/04/us/california-math-curriculum-guidelines.html.

Foucault, Michel. (1977) 1979. *Discipline and Punish: The Birth of the Prison*. Translated by Alan Sheridan. New York: Vintage Books.

Foucault, Michel. 1978. *The History of Sexuality*. Translated by Robert Hurley. New York: Pantheon Books.

Foucault, Michel, 1988. *Technologies of the Self*. Edited by Luther H. Martin, Huck Gutman, and Patrick H. Hutton. Amherst: University of Massachusetts Press.

Franz, Julia, and Christopher Intagliata. 2017. "Consider Yourself a 'Visual' or 'Auditory' Learner? Turns Out, There's Not Much Science behind Learning Styles." *World*, September 17. https://theworld.org/stories/2017-09-17/consider-yourself-visual-or-auditory-learner-turns-out-there-s-not-much-science.

Freeman, Scott, Sarah L. Eddy, Miles McDonough, Michelle K. Smith, Nnadozie Okoroafor, Hannah Jordt, and Mary Pat Wenderoth. 2014. "Active Learning Increases Student Performance in Science, Engineering, and Mathematics." *PNAS* 111 (23): 8410–15. https://doi.org/10.1073/pnas.1319030111.

Freire, Paulo. (1970) 2000. *Pedagogy of the Oppressed*. Translated by M. B. Ramos. New York: Continuum.

Freire, Paulo. 1998. *Pedagogy of the Heart*. Translated by Donaldo Macedo and Alexandre Oliveira. New York: Continuum.

Freud, Sigmund. (1930) 1961. *Civilization and Its Discontents*. Translated and edited by James Strachey. New York: W. W. Norton.

Friesen, Norm. 2011. "The Lecture as Trans-medial Pedagogical Form: A Historical Analysis." *Educational Researcher* 40 (3): 95–102. https://doi.org/10.3102/0013189X11404603.

Fromm, Erich. 1955. *The Sane Society*. New York: Henry Holt.

Fuentes, Agustín. 2022. "WEIRD Indeed, but There Is More to the Story: Anthropological Reflections on Henrich's *The Weirdest People in the World*." *Religion, Brain & Behavior* 12 (3): 284–90.

Furey, William. 2020. "The Stubborn Myth of 'Learning Styles': State Teacher-License Prep Materials Peddle a Debunked Theory." *Education Next* 20 (3): 8–12. https://www.educationnext.org/stubborn-myth-learning-styles-state-teacher-license-prep-materials-debunked-theory/.

Gärdenfors, Peter, and Anders Högberg. 2017. "The Archaeology of Teaching and the Evolution of *Homo docens.*" *Current Anthropology* 58 (2): 188–208. https://doi.org/10.1086/691178.

Gascoigne, John. 1984. "Mathematics and Meritocracy: The Emergence of the Cambridge Mathematical Tripos." *Social Studies of Science* 14: 547–84.

Gaskins, Suzanne. 2008. "Children's Daily Lives among the Yucatec Maya." In *Anthropology and Child Development: A Cross-Cultural Reader,* edited by Robert A. LeVine and Rebecca S. New, 280–88. Malden, MA: Blackwell.

Gaskins, Suzanne. 2013. "Open Attention as a Cultural Tool for Observational Learning." In *Learning In and Out of School: Education across the Globe,* edited by Susan D. Blum. Conference proceedings. https://kellogg.nd.edu/calendar/5151.

Gaskins, Suzanne, and Ruth Paradise. 2010. "Learning through Observation in Daily Life." In *The Anthropology of Learning in Childhood,* edited by David F. Lancy, John Bock, and Suzanne Gaskins, 85–118. Lanham, MD: AltaMira.

Gatto, John Taylor. (1992) 2005. *Dumbing Us Down: The Hidden Curriculum of Compulsory Schooling.* Gabriola Island, BC: New Society.

Gaver, William W. 1991. "Technology Affordances." *Proceedings of the SIGCHI Conference on Human Factors in Computing Systems,* 79–84. https://doi-org.proxy.library.nd.edu/10.1145/108844.108856.

GBD 2019 Mental Disorders Collaborators. 2022. "Global, Regional, and National Burden of 12 Mental Disorders in 204 Countries and Territories, 1990–2019: A Systematic Analysis for the Global Burden of Disease Study 2019." *Lancet Psychiatry* 9: 137–50. https://doi.org/10.1016/ S2215-0366(21)00395-3.

Gecker, Jocelyn. 2023. "A College in Upheaval: War on 'Woke' Sparks Fear in Florida." Associated Press, March 30. https://apnews.com/article/ron-desantis-new-college-florida-woke-15d61ab52724dc447ba6d03238f7719e.

Gershon, Ilana. 2017. "Language and the Newness of Media." *Annual Review of Anthropology* 46:15–31.

Gibson, James J. 1979. "The Theory of Affordances." In *The Ecological Approach to Visual Perception,* 127–37. Boston: Houghton Mifflin.

Gilliard, Chris. 2017. "Pedagogy and the Logic of Platforms." *EDUCAUSE Review* 52 (4) (July 3). https://er.educause.edu/articles/2017/7/pedagogy-and-the-logic-of-platforms.

Goffman, Erving. 1961. *Asylums: Essays on the Social Situation of Mental Patients and Other Inmates.* New York: Anchor Books.

Goffman, Erving. 1981. "The Lecture." In *Forms of Talk,* 160–96. Philadelphia: University of Pennsylvania Press.

Goldstein, Dana. 2017. "Why Kids Can't Write." *New York Times,* August 2. https://www.nytimes.com/2017/08/02/education/edlife/writing-education-grammar-students-children.html?_r=0.

Goodwin, Charles. 2018. "Why Multimodality? Why Co-operative Action?" Transcribed by J. Philipsen. *Social Interaction: Video-Based Studies of Human Sociality* 1 (2). https://doi.org/10.7146/si.v1i2.110039.

Gopnik, Alison. 2016. *The Gardener and the Carpenter: What the New Science of Child Development Tells Us about the Relationship between Parents and Children.* New York: Farrar, Straus and Giroux.

Gourlay, Lesley. 2021. "There Is No 'Virtual Learning': The Materiality of Digital Education." "No hay 'aprendizaje virtual': La materialidad de la educación digital." *Journal of New Approaches in Educational Research* 10 (1). https://naerjournal. ua.es/article/view/v10n1-4.

Graeber, David, and David Wengrow. 2021. *The Dawn of Everything: A New History of Humanity*. New York: Farrar, Straus and Giroux.

Graham, Steve, Debra McKeown, Sharlene Kiuhara, and Karen R. Harris. 2012. "A Meta-analysis of Writing Instruction for Students in the Elementary Grades." *Journal of Educational Psychology* 104 (4): 879–96. https://doi.org/10.1037/a0029185.

Gray, Peter. 2013. *Free to Learn: Why Unleashing the Instinct to Play Will Make Our Children Happier, More Self-Reliant, and Better Students for Life*. New York: Basic Books.

Gray, Peter. 2014. "School Overload: How the Schoolish Approach to Child Rearing Is Hurting Children." EdCan Network, April 1. https://www.edcan.ca/articles/ school-overload/.

Greenfield, Patricia Marks. 2004. *Weaving Generations Together: Evolving Creativity among the Mayas of Chiapas*. Santa Fe, NM: School of American Research.

Grieve, Rob. 2020. *Stand Up and Be Heard: Taking the Fear Out of Public Speaking at University*. London: Sage.

Griswold, Charles L. 2020. "Plato on Rhetoric and Poetry." *The Stanford Encyclopedia of Philosophy*, Spring 2020 ed., edited by Edward N. Zalta. https://plato.stanford. edu/archives/spr2020/entries/plato-rhetoric/.

Grubb, W. Norton, and Marvin Lazerson. 2004. *The Education Gospel: The Economic Power of Schooling*. Cambridge, MA: Harvard University Press.

Guinier, Lani. 2015. *The Tyranny of the Meritocracy: Democratizing Higher Education in America*. Boston: Beacon.

Haanstad, Eric, Gabrielle Robinson, and Saliyha Webb. 2020. "The Crucial Role of Community Liaisons in Place-Based Experiential Education Organizations." *Collaborations: A Journal of Community-Based Research and Practice* 3 (1): 12. https://doi. org/10.33596/coll.64.

Hall, Edward T. 1969. *The Hidden Dimension*. Garden City, NY: Doubleday.

Hall, G. Stanley. 1904. *Adolescence: Its Psychology and Its Relations to Physiology, Anthropology, Sociology, Sex, Crime, Religion, and Education*. New York: D. Appleton.

Hallowell, Sunny G. 2022. "An Educator's Challenge: Maintaining Academic Integrity during Remote Proctoring." Harvard Macy Institute, May 10. https://harvardmacy. org/blog/an-educators-challenge-maintaining-academic-integrity-during-remote-proctoring.

Hammond, Claudia. 2019. "When the Best Way to Take Notes Is by Hand." BBC, November 27. https://www.bbc.com/future/article/20191122-when-the-best-way-to-take-notes-is-by-hand.

Hanna, Judith Lynne. 2015. *Dancing to Learn: The Brain's Cognition, Emotion, and Movement*. Lanham, MD: Rowman & Littlefield.

Hanstedt, Paul. 2018. *Creating Wicked Students: Designing Courses for a Complex World*. Sterling, VA: Stylus.

Harber, Clive. 2004. *Schooling as Violence: How Schools Harm Pupils and Societies.* London: RoutledgeFalmer.

Hari, Johann. 2022. *Stolen Focus: Why You Can't Pay Attention—and How to Think Deeply Again.* New York: Crown.

Harris, Adam. 2018. "When Disadvantaged Students Overlook Elite Colleges." *Atlantic,* April 18. https://www.theatlantic.com/education/archive/2018/04/when-dis advantaged-students-overlook-elite-colleges/558371/.

Hart, Betty, and Todd Risley. 1995. *Meaningful Differences in the Everyday Experiences of Young American Children.* Baltimore: Brookes.

Hartnett, Kevin. 2017. "A Path Less Taken to the Peak of the Math World." Quanta Magazine, June 27. https://www.quantamagazine.org/a-path-less-taken-to-the-peak-of-the-math-world-20170627/.

Harwell, Drew. 2020. "Mass School Closures in the Wake of the Coronavirus Are Driving a New Wave of Student Surveillance." *Washington Post,* April 1. https://www.washingtonpost.com/technology/2020/04/01/online-proctoring-college-exams-coronavirus/.

Haynie, Aeron, and Stephanie Spong. 2022. *Teaching Matters: A Guide for Graduate Students.* Morgantown: West Virginia University Press.

Heath, Shirley Brice. 1983. *Ways with Words: Language, Life and Work in Communities and Classrooms.* Cambridge: Cambridge University Press.

Henrich, Joseph. 2020. *The WEIRDest People in the World: How the West Became Psychologically Peculiar and Particularly Prosperous.* New York: Farrar, Straus and Giroux.

Henrich, Joseph, Steven J. Heine, and Ara Norenzayan. 2010. "The Weirdest People in the World?" *Behavioral and Brain Sciences* 33: 61–135. https://doi.org/10.1017/S0140525X0999152X.

Henry, Jules. 1963. *Culture against Man.* New York: Random House.

Henry, Jules. (1967) 1973. "Sham." In *On Sham, Vulnerability and Other Forms of Self-Destruction,* 120–27. New York: Vintage Books.

Heyer, Paul, and Peter Urquhart. 2019. *Communication in History: Stone Age Symbols to Social Media.* 7th ed. London: Routledge.

Hirsch, E. D., Jr. 1988. *Cultural Literacy: What Every American Needs to Know.* New York: Houghton Mifflin.

Hoadley, Christopher. 2012. "What Is a Community of Practice and How Can We Support It?" In *Theoretical Foundations of Learning Environments,* 2nd ed., edited by David Jonassen and Susan Land, 287–300. New York: Routledge.

Hobsbawm, Eric, and Terence Ranger, eds. 2012. *The Invention of Tradition.* Cambridge: Cambridge University Press.

Hochschild, Arlie Russell. 2012. *The Managed Heart: Commercialization of Human Feeling.* Berkeley: University of California Press.

Hoffman, Diane M. 2017. "Making Hope: Youth and Cultural Practice in Haiti." Paper presented at the annual meeting of the American Anthropological Association, Washington, DC. November.

Hogan, Kelly A., and Viji Sathy. 2022. *Inclusive Teaching: Strategies for Promoting Equity in the College Classroom.* Morgantown: West Virginia University Press.

Holt, John. (1976) 2004. *Instead of Education*. Boulder, CO: Sentient.

hooks, bell. 1994. *Teaching to Transgress: Education as the Practice of Freedom*. New York: Routledge.

Howlett, Zachary M. 2021. *Meritocracy and Its Discontents: Anxiety and the National College Entrance Exam in China*. Ithaca, NY: Cornell University Press.

Hrach, Susan. 2021. *Minding Bodies: How Physical Space, Sensation, and Movement Affect Learning*. Morgantown: West Virginia University Press.

Hu, Hsien Chin. 1944. "The Chinese Concepts of 'Face.'" *American Anthropologist* 46 (1): 45–64.

Huddleston, Rodney. 1994. "The Contrast between Interrogatives and Questions." *Journal of Linguistics* 30 (2): 411–39. http://www.jstor.org/stable/4176277.

Hull, Kathleen. 2002. "*Eros* and Education: The Role of Desire in Teaching and Learning." *NEA Higher Education Journal*, Fall, 19–31. http://www.margie-pignataro. com/uploads/4/2/8/2/4282040/taa_02_03.pdf.

Huston, Therese. 2009. *Teaching What You Don't Know*. Cambridge. MA: Harvard University Press.

Hvistendahl, Mara. 2013. "China's Publication Bazaar." *Science* 342 (November 29): 1035–39.

IDEOU. 2022. "Design Thinking." https://www.ideou.com/pages/design-thinking.

Illich, Ivan. 1970. *Deschooling Society*. London: Marion Boyars.

Imad, Mays. 2021. "Transcending Adversity: Trauma-Informed Educational Development." *Educational Development in the Time of Crises* 39 (3). https://doi.org/10.39 98/tia.17063888.0039.301.

Immordino-Yang, Mary Helen. 2015. *Emotions, Learning, and the Brain: Exploring the Educational Implications of Affective Neuroscience*. New York: W. W. Norton.

Immordino-Yang, Mary Helen, and Antonio Damasio. 2007. "We Feel, Therefore We Learn: The Relevance of Affective and Social Neuroscience to Education." *Mind, Brain, and Education* 1 (1): 3–10.

Ingold, Tim. (2009) 2017. "In Defence of Handwriting." In *Knowing from the Inside: Correspondences*, 90–93. University of Aberdeen. https://knowingfromtheinside.org/ files/correspondences.pdf.

Inoue, Asao. 2019. *Labor-Based Grading Contracts: Building Equity and Inclusion in the Compassionate Writing Classroom*. Fort Collins, CO: WAC Clearinghouse.

Jack, Anthony Abraham. 2019. *The Privileged Poor: How Elite Colleges Are Failing Disadvantaged Students*. Cambridge, MA: Harvard University Press.

Jacka, Tamara, Andrew B. Kipnis, and Sally Sargeson. 2013. *Contemporary China: Society and Social Change*. Cambridge: Cambridge University Press.

Jackson, Carolyn. 2010. "Fear in Education." *Educational Review* 62 (1): 39–52.

Jan, Catherine, Ling Li, Lisa Keay, Randall S. Stafford, Nathan Congdon, and Ian Morgan. 2020. "Prevention of Myopia, China." *Bulletin of the World Health Organization* 98 (6) (June 1): 435–37. https://doi.org/10.2471/BLT.19.240903.

Jarvi, Stephanie, Benita Jackson, Lance Swenson, and Heather Crawford. 2013. "The Impact of Social Contagion on Non-suicidal Self-Injury: A Review of the Literature." *Archives of Suicide Research* 17 (1): 1–19. https://doi.org/10.1080/13811118.2013. 748404.

Jaschik, Scott. 2019. "Reed Students Challenge 'U.S. News,' and Magazine Challenges Some Colleges." Inside Higher Ed, July 28. https://www.insidehighered.com/admissions/article/2019/07/29/reed-students-challenge-us-news-formula.

Jaschik, Scott. 2022. "'Breaking Ranks' with 'U.S. News.'" Inside Higher Ed, April 10. https://www.insidehighered.com/admissions/article/2022/04/11/breaking-ranks-new-book-attacks-us-news.

Jason, Zachary. 2017. "Bored Out of Their Minds." Harvard Graduate School of Education. Ed. Magazine, Winter, January 8. https://www.gse.harvard.edu/news/ed/17/01/bored-out-their-minds.

Johnson, David Cassels, and Eric J. Johnson. 2022. *The Language Gap: Normalizing Deficit Ideologies.* New York: Routledge.

Jones, Rodney H., and Christoph A. Hafner. 2021. *Understanding Digital Literacies: A Practical Introduction.* 2nd ed. Abingdon, UK: Routledge.

Jung, Hyang Jin. 2007. *Learning to Be an Individual: Emotion and Person in an American Junior High School.* New York: Peter Lang.

Kabat-Zinn, Jon. 2005. *Coming to Our Senses: Healing Ourselves and the World through Mindfulness.* New York: Hyperion.

Kaiser, Matthew. 2011. *The World in Play: Portraits of a Victorian Concept.* Stanford, CA: Stanford University Press.

Kalir, Remi H. Forthcoming. *Remarkable Legacies.* Cambridge, MA: MIT Press.

Kalir, Remi H., and Antero Garcia. 2021. *Annotation.* Cambridge, MA: MIT Press.

Kang, Jay Caspian. 2022. "The Movement to End Homework Is Wrong." *New York Times,* July 25. https://www.nytimes.com/2022/07/25/opinion/end-of-homework.html.

Katopodis, Christina, and Cathy N. Davidson. 2020. "Contract Grading and Peer Review." In *Ungrading: Why Rating Students Undermines Learning (and What to Do Instead),* edited by Susan D. Blum, 105–22. Morgantown: West Virginia University Press.

Keane, Webb. 2007. *Christian Moderns: Freedom and Fetish in the Mission Encounter.* Berkeley: University of California Press.

Kellaghan, Thomas, and Vincent Greaney. 2019. *Public Examinations Examined: A Brief History of Written Examinations.* New York: World Bank Group. https://elibrary.worldbank.org/doi/10.1596/978-1-4648-1418-1_ch3.

Kelley, Jason, and Lindsay Oliver. 2020. "Proctoring Apps Subject Students to Unnecessary Surveillance." Electronic Frontier Foundation, August 20. https://www.eff.org/deeplinks/2020/08/proctoring-apps-subject-students-unnecessary-surveillance.

Kennedy, Ian. 2005. "The Sputnik Crisis and America's Response." Electronic Theses and Dissertations, 2004–2019. 579. https://stars.library.ucf.edu/etd/579.

Khattab, Nabil. 2015. "Students' Aspirations, Expectations, and School Achievement: What Really Matters?" *British Educational Research Journal* 41 (5): 731–48.

Kidmas, Lois, Greg Ashman, and Megan Short. 2017. "My Friends Were There for Me: Exploring the Pedagogical Adaptations of Secondary Nigerian-Australian Students in Tasmania." *Australasian Review of African Studies* 38 (1): 65–85.

Kipnis, Andrew. 2011. *Governing Educational Desire: Culture, Politics, and Schooling in China.* Chicago: University of Chicago Press.

Kirschenbaum, Howard, Sidney B. Simon, and Rodney W. Napier. 1971. *Wad-ja-get? The Grading Game in American Education*. New York: Hart.

Kissel, Marc, and Susan D. Blum. 2021. "Let's Talk Teaching: Progressive Pedagogy in Anthropology Courses." *American Journal of Human Biology* 34 (S1): e23706. https://doi.org/10.1002/ajhb.23706.

Klebanov, Beata Beigman, and Nitin Madnani. 2020. "Automated Evaluation of Writing—50 Years and Counting." In *Proceedings of the 58th Annual Meeting of the Association for Computational Linguistics*, 7796–810. https://aclanthology. org/2020.acl-main.697.pdf.

Kline, Michelle Ann. 2015. "How to Learn about Teaching: An Evolutionary Framework for the Study of Teaching Behavior in Humans and Other Animals." *Behavioral and Brain Sciences* 38 (January): e31.

Knoll, Michael. 2009. "From Kidd to Dewey: The Origin and Meaning of 'Social Efficiency.'" *Journal of Curriculum Studies* 41 (3): 361–91. https://doi.org/10.1080/ 00220270801927362.

Ko, Dorothy. 2001. *Every Step a Lotus: Shoes for Bound Feet*. Berkeley: University of California Press.

Ko, Dorothy. 2005. *Cinderella's Sisters: A Revisionist History of Footbinding*. Berkeley: University of California Press.

Kohn, Alfie. (1993) 2018. *Punished by Rewards: The Trouble with Gold Stars, Incentive Plans, A's, Praise, and Other Bribes*. Boston: Houghton Mifflin.

Kohn, Alfie. 1999. *The Schools Our Children Deserve: Moving beyond Traditional Classrooms and "Tougher Standards."* Boston: Houghton Mifflin.

Kohn, Alfie. 2014. "Grit: A Skeptical Look at the Latest Educational Fad." *Independent School*. Fall. https://www.alfiekohn.org/article/grit/.

Kohn, Alfie. 2019. "The Crucial Steps Are Those We May Have Skipped." *Education Week*, September 3. https://www.alfiekohn.org/article/skipped/.

Kohn, Alfie. 2020. "Is Learning Lost When Kids Are Out of School?" *Boston Globe*, September 6. https://www.alfiekohn.org/article/loss/.

Komline, David. 2020. *The Common School Awakening: Religion and the Transatlantic Roots of American Public Education*. New York: Oxford University Press.

Korstange, Ryan, Susan D. Blum, Oscar Fernandez, Mays Imad, Thomas F. Nelson Laird, and Kate L. Pantelides. 2021. "A Theory of Public Higher Education." *Soundings: An Interdisciplinary Journal* 104 (2–3): 141–251. https://doi.org/10.5325/ soundings.104.2-3.0141.

Kramer, Karen L. 2021. "What Industrial Societies Get Wrong about Childhood." Sapiens, November 18. https://www.sapiens.org/culture/children-social-learning/.

Kriegel, Jessica. 2016. *Unfairly Labeled: How Your Workplace Can Benefit from Ditching Generational Stereotypes*. Hoboken, NJ: Wiley.

Kritz, Ben. 2018. "A Little Less 'Resiliency' May Be in Order." *Manila Times*, August 14. https://www.manilatimes.net/2018/08/14/business/a-little-less-resiliency- may-be-in-order/430172/.

Kuh, George D. 2008. *High-Impact Educational Practices: What They Are, Who Has Access to Them, and Why They Matter*. Washington, DC: Association of American Colleges and Universities.

Kurt, Serhat. 2020. "Andragogy Theory—Malcolm Knowles." *Educational Technology*, July 11. https://educationaltechnology.net/andragogy-theory-malcolm-knowles/.

Labaree, David F. 2010. *Someone Has to Fail: The Zero-Sum Game of Public Schooling*. Cambridge, MA: Harvard University Press.

Lacan, Jacques. (1964) 1978. "The Split between the Eye and the Gaze." In *The Four Fundamental Concepts of Psychoanalysis*, translated by Alan Sheridan, 67–78. New York: W. W. Norton.

Ladd, D. R. 2001. "Intonational Universals and Intonational Typology." In *Language Typology and Language Universals: An International Handbook*, edited by Martin Haspelmath, Ekkehard König, Wulf Oesterreicher, and Wolfgang Raible, 1380–90. Berlin: Mouton de Gruyter.

Lancy, David F. 2010. "Learning 'from Nobody': The Limited Role of Teaching in Folk Models of Children's Development." *Childhood in the Past* 3: 79–106.

Lancy, David F. 2016. "Teaching: Natural or Cultural?" In *Evolutionary Perspectives on Child Development and Education*, edited by David C. Geary and Daniel B. Berch, 33–65. Cham, Switzerland: Springer. https://link.springer.com/book/10.1007/978-3-319-29986-0.

Lancy, David F. 2022. *The Anthropology of Childhood*. 3rd ed. Cambridge: Cambridge University Press.

Lang, James. 2021. *Small Teaching: Everyday Lessons from the Science of Learning*. 2nd ed. San Francisco: Jossey-Bass.

Lareau, Annette. 2003. *Unequal Childhoods: Class, Race, and Family Life*. Berkeley: University of California Press.

Lareau, Renée. 2019. "South Bend School Farm Program Connects Students to the Land." *Edible Michiana*, April 16. https://ediblemichiana.ediblecommunities.com/food-thought/south-bend-school-farm-program.

Lat, David. 2022. "Why Six Top-Ranked Law Schools Left U.S. News in the Dust This Week." Slate, November 19. https://slate.com/human-interest/2022/11/yale-law-school-harvard-law-berkeley-georgetown-us-news-rankings.html.

Lave, Jean. 1988. *Cognition in Practice: Mind, Mathematics and Culture in Everyday Life*. Cambridge: Cambridge University Press.

Lave, Jean, and Étienne Wenger. 1991. *Situated Learning: Legitimate Peripheral Participation*. Cambridge: Cambridge University Press.

Leader, George M. 2020. "Why Social Distancing Feels So Strange." Sapiens, March 30. https://www.sapiens.org/biology/covid-19-social-distancing/.

Lee, Jennifer 8. 2020. "When Bias Is Coded into Our Technology." NPR. Codeswitch. February 8. https://www.npr.org/sections/codeswitch/2020/02/08/770174171/when-bias-is-coded-into-our-technology.

Lee, Phil. 2003. "Eye and Gaze." Theories of Media, Keywords Glossary, the University of Chicago. Winter. https://csmt.uchicago.edu/glossary2004/eyegaze.htm.

Lees, Helen E. 2022. *Playing the University Game: The Art of University-Based Self-Education*. London: Bloomsbury.

Lefebvre, Henri. 1991. *Critique of Everyday Life*. London: Verso.

Lemann, Nicholas. 2000. *The Big Test: The Secret History of the American Meritocracy*. New York: Farrar, Straus and Giroux.

Lenhart, Amanda, Sousan Arafeh, Aaron Smith, and Alexandra Macgill. 2008. "Writing, Technology and Teens." Pew Research Center, Internet & Technology. April 24. http://www.pewinternet.org/2008/04/24/writing-technology-and-teens/.

Lepore, Jill. 2022. "Why the School Wars Still Rage." *New Yorker*, March 21. https://www.newyorker.com/magazine/2022/03/21/why-the-school-wars-still-rage.

Lepper, Mark R. 1983. "Extrinsic Reward and Intrinsic Motivation." In *Teacher and Student Perceptions: Implications for Learning*, edited by John M. Levine and Margaret C. Wang, 281–317. Hillsdale, NJ: Erlbaum.

Lepper, Mark R., and David Greene. 1975. "Turning Play into Work: Effects of Adult Surveillance and Extrinsic Rewards on Children's Intrinsic Motivation." *Journal of Personality and Social Psychology* 3 (3): 479–86.

Lester, Jaime. 2014. "The Completion Agenda: The Unintended Consequences for Equity in Community Colleges." In *Higher Education: Handbook of Theory and Research*, edited by Michael B. Paulsen, vol. 29, 423–66. Dordrecht: Springer. https://doi.org/10.1007/978-94-017-8005-6_10.

Leung, Janet T. Y. 2020. "Concerted Cultivation and Adolescent Psychopathology over Time-Mediation of Parent-Child Conflict." *International Journal of Environment Research and Public Health* 17 (24): 9173. https://doi.org/10.3390/ijerph17249173.

Levine, Madeline. 2006. *The Price of Privilege: How Parental Pressure and Material Advantage Are Creating a Generation of Disconnected and Unhappy Kids*. New York: HarperCollins.

Levinson, Stephen C., and Francisco Torreira. 2015. "Timing in Turn-Taking and Its Implications for Processing Models of Language." *Frontiers in Psychology*, June 12. https://doi.org/10.3389/fpsyg.2015.00731.

Lewis, Guy. 1970. "The Beginning of Organized Collegiate Sport." *American Quarterly* 22 (2): 222–29.

Leys, Ruth. 2010. "How Did Fear Become a Scientific Object and What Kind of Object Is It?" *Representations* 110 (1): 66–104. https://www.jstor.org/stable/10.1525/rep.2010.110.1.66.

Leys, Ruth. 2011. "The Turn to Affect: A Critique." *Critical Inquiry* 37 (3): 434–72.

Liang, Zhengyan, Minqiang Zhang, Feifei Huang, Derong Kang, and Lingling Xu. 2021. "Application Innovation of Educational Measurement Theory, Method, and Technology in China's New College Entrance Examination Reform." *Chinese/English Journal of Educational Measurement and Evaluation*. 教育测量与评估双语季刊 2 (1), Article 3. https://www.ce-jeme.org/journal/vol2/iss1/3.

Lieber, Ron. 2022. "Some Colleges Don't Produce Big Earners. Are They Worth It?" *New York Times*, August 24. https://www.nytimes.com/2022/08/20/your-money/college-graduate-earnings.html.

Lieberman, Mark. 2019. "Discussion Boards: Valuable? Overused? Discuss." Inside Higher Ed, March 27. https://www.insidehighered.com/digital-learning/article/2019/03/27/new-approaches-discussion-boards-aim-dynamic-online-learning.

Liebowitz, S. J., and Stephen E. Margolis. 1995. "Path Dependence, Lock-In, and History." *Journal of Law, Economics, and Organization* 11 (1): 205–26.

Lindblom, Ken. 2015. "School Writing vs. Authentic Writing." Writers Who Care, July 27. https://writerswhocare.wordpress.com/2015/07/27/school-writing-vs-authentic-writing/.

Littler, Jo. 2017. *Against Meritocracy: Culture, Power and Myths of Mobility.* Abingdon, UK: Routledge.

Livio, Mario. 2017. *Why? What Makes Us Curious.* New York: Simon & Schuster.

Loewenstein, George. 1994. "The Psychology of Curiosity: A Review and Reinterpretation." *Psychological Bulletin* 116 (1): 75–98.

Lom, Barbara. 2012. "Classroom Activities: Simple Strategies to Incorporate Student-Centered Activities within Undergraduate Science Lectures." *Journal of Undergraduate Neuroscience Education* 11 (1): A64–71.

Louv, Richard. 2005. *Last Child in the Woods: Saving Our Children from Nature-Deficit Disorder.* Chapel Hill, NC: Algonquin.

Lovett, Marsha C., Michael W. Bridges, Michele DiPietro, Susan A. Ambrose, and Marie K. Norman. 2023. *How Learning Works: Eight Research-Based Principles for Smart Teaching.* 2nd ed. San Francisco: Jossey-Bass.

Lunsford, Andrea. n.d. "Our Semi-Literate Youth: Not So Fast." https://ssw.stanford.edu/sites/default/files/OPED_Our_Semi-Literate_Youth.pdf.

Luthar, Suniya S., Nina L. Kumar, and Nicole Zillmer. 2020. "High-Achieving Schools Connote Risks for Adolescents: Problems Documented, Processes Implicated, and Directions for Interventions." *American Psychologist* 75 (7): 983–95. https://doi.org/10.1037/amp0000556.

Manolev, Jamie, Anna Sullivan, and Roger Slee. 2019. "The Datafication of Discipline: ClassDojo, Surveillance and a Performative Classroom Culture." *Learning, Media and Technology* 44 (1): 36–51. https://doi.org/10.1080/17439884.2018.1558237.

Marcus, Jon. 2022. "America's Next Union Battlefield May Be on Campus." *Washington Post*, March 25. https://www.washingtonpost.com/education/2022/03/25/colleges-faculty-unions-labor/.

Markey, Amanda, and George Loewenstein. 2014. "Curiosity." *International Handbook of Emotions in Education*, edited by Reinhard Pekrun and Lisa Linnenbrink-Garcia, 228–45. New York: Routledge. https://doi.org/10.4324/9780203148211.

Markovits, Daniel. 2019. *The Meritocracy Trap: How America's Foundation Myth Feeds Inequality, Dismantles the Middle Class, and Devours the Elite.* New York: Penguin.

Marples, Roger, ed. 1999. *The Aims of Education.* London: Routledge.

Marsh, John. 2011. *Class Dismissed: Why We Cannot Teach or Learn Our Way Out of Inequality.* New York: Monthly Review.

Marx, Karl, and Friedrich Engels. (1848) 1964. *The Communist Manifesto.* New York: Monthly Review.

Mason, Melanie, and Michael Finnegan. 2019. "Kamala Harris Regrets California Truancy Law That Led to Arrest of Some Parents." *Los Angeles Times*, April 17. https://www.latimes.com/politics/la-na-pol-kamala-harris-truancy-20190417-story.html.

Mauss, Marcel. 1934. "Techniques of the Body." Translated by Ben Brewster. *Journal de psychologie normal et pathologique* 32 (1935): 271–93. https://monoskop.org/images/c/c4/Mauss_Marcel_1935_1973_Techniques_of_the_Body.pdf.

May, Cindi. 2014. "A Learning Secret: Don't Take Notes with a Laptop." *Scientific American*, June 3. https://www.scientificamerican.com/article/a-learning-secret-don-t-take-notes-with-a-laptop/.

Mayo Clinic. 2018. "Oppositional Defiant Disorder." https://www.mayoclinic.org/diseases-conditions/oppositional-defiant-disorder/symptoms-causes/syc-20375831.

McCarty, Teresa L. 2015. "How the Logic of Gap Discourse Perpetuates Education Inequality: A View from the Ethnography of Language Policy." *Journal of Linguistic Anthropology* 25 (1): 70–72.

McCulloch, Gretchen. 2019. *Because Internet: Understanding the New Rules of Language*. New York: Riverhead.

McKenna, James J., and Lee T. Gettler. 2015. "There Is No Such Thing as Infant Sleep, There Is No Such Thing as Breastfeeding, There Is Only *Breastsleeping*." *Acta Paediatrica* 105 (1): 17–21. https://doi.org/10.1111/apa.13161.

McNamee, Stephen J. 2018. *The Meritocracy Myth*. 4th ed. Lanham, MD: Rowman & Littlefield.

Mehta, Jal. 2015. "The Problem with Grit." *Learning Deeply* (blog). *Education Week*, April 27. http://blogs.edweek.org/edweek/learning_deeply/2015/04/the_problem_with_grit.html.

Melton, James Van Horn. 1988. *Absolutism and the Eighteenth-Century Origins of Compulsory Schooling in Prussia and Austria*. Cambridge: Cambridge University Press.

Mervosh, Sarah. 2022. "The Pandemic Erased Two Decades of Progress in Math and Reading." *New York Times*, September 1. https://www.nytimes.com/2022/09/01/us/national-test-scores-math-reading-pandemic.html.

Miller, Alice. (1979) 1981. *The Drama of the Gifted Child: The Search for the True Self*. Translated by Ruth Ward. New York: Basic Books.

Miller, Michelle D. 2022. *Remembering and Forgetting in the Age of Technology: Teaching, Learning, and the Science of Memory in a Wired World*. Morgantown: West Virginia University Press.

Mintz, Steven. 2020. "Next-Generation Writing Instruction." Inside Higher Ed, November 24. https://www.insidehighered.com/blogs/higher-ed-gamma/next-generation-writing-instruction.

Mirel, Jeffrey. 2006. "The Traditional High School: Historical Debates over Its Nature and Function." *Education Next* 6 (1). https://www.educationnext.org/the-traditional-high-school/.

Mischel, Walter. 2014. *The Marshmallow Test: Mastering Self-Control*. New York: Little, Brown.

Miyazaki, Ichisada. (1963) 1981. *China's Examination Hell: The Civil Service Examinations of Imperial China*. Translated by Conrad Schirokauer. New Haven, CT: Yale University Press.

Monaghan, E. Jennifer. 1998. "Reading for the Enslaved, Writing for the Free: Reflections on Liberty and Literacy." *Proceedings of the American Antiquarian Society* 108: 308–41.

Moner, William, Phillip Motley, and Rebecca Pope-Ruark. 2020. *Redesigning Liberal Education: Innovative Design for a Twenty-First-Century Undergraduate Education*. Baltimore: Johns Hopkins University Press.

Moore, David Thornton. 1983. "Perspectives on Learning in Internships." *Journal of Experiential Education* 6 (2): 40–44. https://doi.org/10.1177/10538259830 0600207.

Moore, David Thornton. 1986. "Learning at Work: Case Studies in Non-school Education." *Anthropology & Education Quarterly* 17 (3): 166–84.

Moore, L. C. 2006. "Learning by Heart in Qur'anic and Public Schools in Northern Cameroon." *Social Analysis: The International Journal of Cultural and Social Practice* 50 (3): 109–26.

Morris, Sean Michael, and Jesse Stommel. 2018. *An Urgency of Teachers: The Work of Critical Digital Pedagogy*. Madison, WI: Hybrid Pedagogy.

Morris, Warren Frederick. 2002. *Escaping Alienation: A Philosophy of Alienation and Dealienation*. Lanham, MD: University Press of America.

Moskun, Brandon. 2022. "The Student Body and Covid-19: An Anthropological Perspective on Higher Education Organization during a Pandemic." PhD diss., University of Notre Dame.

Muir, John. (1911) 1988. *My First Summer in the Sierra*. Boston: Houghton Mifflin; repr., Sierra Club.

Mullaney, Thomas S., and Christopher Rea. 2022. *Where Research Begins: Choosing a Research Project That Matters to You (and the World)*. Chicago: University of Chicago Press.

Muller, Jerry Z. 2018. *The Tyranny of Metrics*. Princeton, NJ: Princeton University Press.

Mulvey, Laura. 1975. "Visual Pleasure and Narrative Cinema." *Screen* 16 (3): 6–18.

National Academies of Sciences, Engineering, and Medicine. 2019. *Vibrant and Healthy Kids: Aligning Science, Practice, and Policy to Advance Health Equity*. Washington, DC: National Academies Press. https://doi.org/10.17226/25466.

NCEE. 2018. "How Much Time Do Students Spend in School in Top-Performing School Systems and the U.S.?" http://ncee.org/wp-content/uploads/2018/02/School YearStatv5.pdf.

Ndiaye, Marie. 2019. *The Cheffe: A Cook's Novel*. Translated by Jordan Stump. New York: Alfred A. Knopf.

Neill, A. S. 1960. *Summerhill: A Radical Approach to Child Rearing*. New York: Hart.

Neuhaus, Jessamyn. 2019. *Geeky Pedagogy: A Guide for Intellectuals, Introverts, and Nerds Who Want to Be Effective Teachers*. Morgantown: West Virginia University Press.

Neurocritic. 2012. "Paul Zak, Oxytocin Skeptic?" Blog post. July 18. https://neuro critic.blogspot.com/2012/07/paul-zak-oxytocin-skeptic.html.

Newton, Paul. 2011. "A-Level Pass Rates and the Enduring Myth of Norm-Referencing." *Research Matters: A Cambridge Assessment Publication*. Special Issue 2: Comparability. https://www.cambridgeassessment.org.uk/Images/567580-a-level-pass-rates-and-the-enduring-myth-of-norm-referencing.pdf.

Noddings, Nel. 2003. *Happiness and Education*. Cambridge: Cambridge University Press.

Noddings, Nel. 2013. *Caring: A Relational Approach to Ethics and Moral Education*. 2nd ed. Berkeley: University of California Press.

Noguera, Pedro A., and Morgan Polikoff. 2022. "How We Can Finally End the 'Math Wars.'" *Education Week*, August 24. https://www.edweek.org/teaching-learning/opinion-how-we-can-finally-end-the-math-wars/2022/08.

Norman, Donald A. 1998. *The Design of Everyday Things*. Cambridge, MA: MIT Press.

Normile, Dennis. 2017. "China Cracks Down after Investigation Finds Massive Peer-Review Fraud." *Science*, July 31. https://www.sciencemag.org/news/2017/07/china-cracks-down-after-investigation-finds-massive-peer-review-fraud.

NPR. 2013. "The Myth of Multitasking." Talk of the Nation, May 10. https://www.npr.org/2013/05/10/182861382/the-myth-of-multitasking.

Ochs, Elinor, and Carolina Izquierdo. 2009. "Responsibility in Childhood: Three Developmental Trajectories." *Ethos* 37 (4): 391–413.

Ochs, Elinor, Tamar Kremer-Sadlik, Karen Gainer Sirota, and Olga Solomon. 2004. "Autism and the Social World: An Anthropological Perspective." *Discourse Studies* 6 (2): 147–83.

Ochs, Elinor, and Bambi B. Schieffelin. 1984. "Language Acquisition and Socialization: Three Developmental Stories." In *Culture Theory: Essay on Mind, Self, and Emotion*, edited by Richard A. Shweder and Robert A. LeVine, 276–320. Cambridge: Cambridge University Press.

Ochs, Elinor, and Bambi B. Schieffelin, eds. 1986. *Language Acquisition and Socialization across Cultures*. New York: Cambridge University Press.

Ochs, Elinor, and Merav Shohet. 2006. "The Cultural Structuring of Mealtime Socialization." *New Directions for Child and Adolescent Development* 111: 35–49.

Ochs, Elinor, and Olga Solomon. 2010. "Autistic Sociality." *Ethos* 38 (1): 69–92.

Ochs, Elinor, and Carolyn Taylor. 1992. "Family Narrative as Political Activity." *Discourse and Society* 3 (3): 301–40.

O'Donnell, Daniel Paul. (2012) 2018. "The Unessay." https://people.uleth.ca/~daniel.odonnell/Teaching/the-unessay.

OECD (Organisation for Economic Co-operation and Development). 2011. "Japan: A Story of Sustained Excellence." In *Lessons from PISA for the United States*. Paris: OECD. https://doi.org/10.1787/9789264096660-7-en.

Olson, Kathleen K. 2005. "Cyberspace as Place and the Limits of Metaphor." *Convergence* 11 (1): 10–18.

Orbey, Eren. 2022. "How the Pandemic Remade the SAT." *New Yorker*, May 24. https://www.newyorker.com/news/annals-of-education/how-the-pandemic-remade-the-sat.

Ortner, Sherry B. 2016. "Dark Anthropology and Its Others: Theory since the Eighties." *Hau: Journal of Ethnographic Theory* 6 (1). https://doi.org/10.14318/hau6.1.004.

Panksepp, Jaak, and Lucy Biven. 2012. *The Archaeology of Mind: Neuroevolutionary Origins of Human Emotions*. New York: W. W. Norton.

Pascarella, Ernest T., and Patrick T. Terenzini. 2005. *How College Affects Students: A Third Decade of Research*. San Francisco: Jossey-Bass.

Paugh, Amy, and Carolina Izquierdo. 2009. "Why Is This a Battle Every Night? Negotiating Food and Eating in American Dinnertime Interaction." *Journal of Linguistic Anthropology* 19 (2): 185–204.

Paul, Annie Murphy. 2021. *The Extended Mind: The Power of Thinking outside the Brain*. Boston: Houghton Mifflin Harcourt.

Paúl, María Luisa, and Anne Branigin. 2022. "A School Made Girls Wear Skirts. A Court Ruled It Unconstitutional." *Washington Post*, June 15. https://www.washingtonpost.com/nation/2022/06/15/north-carolina-dress-code-skirts/.

Pedaste, Margus, Mario Mäeots, Leo A. Siiman, Ton de Jong, Siswa A. N. van Riesen, Ellen T. Kamp, Constantinos C. Manoli, Zacharias C. Zacharia, and Eleftheria Tsourlidaki. 2014. "Phases of Inquiry-Based Learning: Definitions and the Inquiry Cycle." *Educational Research Review* 14: 47–61. http://dx.doi.org/10.1016/j.edurev.2015.02.003.

Pekrun, Reinhard, and Lisa Linnenbrink-Garcia, eds. 2014. *International Handbook of Emotions in Education*. New York: Routledge.

Peled-Avron, Leehe, Anat Perry, and Simone G. Shamay-Tsoory. 2016. "The Effect of Oxytocin on the Anthropomorphism of Touch." *Psychoneuroendocrinology* 66: 159–65. https://doi.org/10.1016/j.psyneuen.2016.01.015.

Philips, Susan U. 1983. *The Invisible Culture: Communication in Classroom and Community on the Warm Springs Indian Reservation*. Long Grove, IL: Waveland.

Poe, Marshall T. 2011. *A History of Communications: Media and Society from the Evolution of Speech to the Internet*. Cambridge: Cambridge University Press.

Pollan, Michael. 2008. *In Defense of Food: An Eater's Manifesto*. New York: Penguin.

Pollan, Michael. 2022. *How to Change Your Mind*. Film. Netflix. https://www.netflix.com/title/80229847.

Pope, Denise Clark. 2001. *"Doing School": How We Are Creating a Generation of Stressed Out, Materialistic, and Miseducated Students*. New Haven, CT: Yale University Press.

Postman, Neil. 1996. *The End of Education: Redefining the Value of School*. New York: Vintage Books.

Precel, Nicole. 2022. "Swinburne Dumps Grades, Says Marking Hinders Creative Process." *Age* (Melbourne, Australia), March 4. https://www.theage.com.au/national/victoria/swinburne-dumps-grades-says-marking-hinders-creative-process-20220304-p5a1vs.html.

Premack, David. 2007. "Human and Animal Cognition: Continuity and Discontinuity." *PNAS* 104 (35): 13861–67. https://www.ncbi.nlm.nih.gov/pmc/articles/PMC1955772/.

Price, Margaret. 2011. *Mad at School: Rhetorics of Mental Disability and Academic Life*. Ann Arbor: University of Michigan Press.

Purser, Ronald E. 2019. *McMindfulness: How Mindfulness Became the New Capitalist Spirituality*. London: Repeater.

Ravitch, Diane. 2014. "Ex-KIPP Teacher: Why I Could Not Teach Like a Champion." *Diane Ravitch's Blog*, February 13. https://dianeravitch.net/2014/02/13/ex-kipp-teacher-why-i-could-not-teach-like-a-champion/.

Rayner, Tim. 2018. "Hacking Is Not a Crime. It's a Problem Solving Activity—and the Key to Innovating Like a Startup." Medium, January 29. https://timrayner01.medium.com/hacking-is-not-a-crime-its-the-key-to-innovating-like-a-startup-1ccd6208563a.

Resnick, Brian, and Julia Belluz. 2019. "The War to Free Science: How Librarians, Pirates, and Funders Are Liberating the World's Academic Research from Paywalls." Vox, July 10. https://www.vox.com/the-highlight/2019/6/3/18271538/open-access-elsevier-california-sci-hub-academic-paywalls.

Reyhner, Jon. 2020. "The Reading Wars: Phonics vs. Whole Language." https://jan.ucc.nau.edu/~jar/Reading_Wars.html.

Reynolds, Emily. 2021. "The 'Learning Styles' Myth Is Still Prevalent among Educators—and It Shows No Sign of Going Away." *Research Digest: The British Psychological Society*, February 4.

Richards, Jennifer Smith, and Jodi S. Cohen. 2022. "The School That Calls the Police on Students Every Other Day." ProPublica, December 17. https://www.propublica.org/article/students-police-arrests-illinois-garrison-school.

Ridgely, Susan B. 2019. "Centering the Children in the Catholic Sex Abuse Crisis." *American Catholic Studies* 130 (2) (Summer): 8–11. https://doi.org/ 10.1353/acs.2019.0036.

Riley, Gina. 2020. *Unschooling: Exploring Learning beyond the Classroom.* Cham, Switzerland: Palgrave Macmillan.

Robbins, Joel. 2013. "Beyond the Suffering Subject: Toward an Anthropology of the Good." *JRAI* 19 (3): 447–62.

Roberts, Meghan. 2018. "Role-Playing the French Revolution, Reacting to the Past in the Classroom." Age of Revolutions, September 24. https://ageofrevolutions.com/2018/09/24/role-playing-the-french-revolution-reacting-to-the-past-in-the-classroom/.

Rosch, Eleanor. 1973. "Natural Categories." *Cognitive Psychology* 4 (3): 328–50.

Rose, Janus. 2022. "Proctorio Is Going After Digital Rights Groups That Bash Their Proctoring Software." Vice, February 23. https://www.vice.com/en/article/epxqgw/proctorio-is-going-after-digital-rights-groups-that-bash-their-proctoring-software.

Rose, Nikolas. 1999. *Governing the Soul: The Shaping of the Private Self.* London: Free Association.

Rosenberg, John S. 2019. "Adjacent but Unequal." *Harvard Magazine*, March/April. https://harvardmagazine.com/2019/03/first-gen-elite-students.

Rosin, Hanna. 2015. "The Silicon Valley Suicides: Why Are So Many Kids with Bright Prospects Killing Themselves in Palo Alto?" *Atlantic*, December. http://www.theatlantic.com/magazine/archive/2015/12/the-silicon-valley-suicides/413140/.

Rothstein, Dan, and Luz Santana, 2011. *Make Just One Change: Teach Students to Ask Their Own Questions.* Cambridge, MA: Harvard Education Press.

Rubin, Donald L. 1992. "Nonlanguage Factors Affecting Undergraduates' Judgments of Nonnative English-Speaking Teaching Assistants." *Research in Higher Education* 33 (4): 511–31.

Ryan, Richard M., and Edward L. Deci. 2000. "Intrinsic and Extrinsic Motivations: Classic Definitions and New Directions." *Contemporary Educational Psychology* 25 (1): 54–67.

Sackstein, Starr. 2015. *Hacking Assessment: 10 Ways to Go Gradeless in a Traditional Grades School.* Cleveland: Times 10.

Saini, Angela. 2020. *Superior: The Return of Race Science.* Boston: Beacon.

Sandel, Michael J. 2021. *The Tyranny of Merit: Can We Find the Common Good?* New York: Picador.

Savage, Jon. 2007. *Teenage: The Creation of Youth Culture.* New York: Viking.

Schevitz, Tanya. 2000a. "Evaluations Stay at UC Santa Cruz / Students Will Get Them along with Grades." SF Gate, November 28. https://www.sfgate.com/education/arti cle/Evaluations-Stay-at-UC-Santa-Cruz-Students-will-2725580.php.

Schevitz, Tanya. 2000b. "UC Santa Cruz to Start Using Letter Grades." SF Gate, February 24. https://www.sfgate.com/education/article/UC-Santa-Cruz-To-Start-Using-Let ter-Grades-2773570.php.

Schleicher, Andreas. 2019. "PISA 2018, Insights and Interpretations." OECD. https:// www.oecd.org/pisa/PISA%202018%20Insights%20and%20Interpretations%20 FINAL%20PDF.pdf.

Schroeder, Joanna. 2020. "What If Some Kids Are Better Off at Home?" *New York Times,* August 10. https://www.nytimes.com/2020/08/10/opinion/coronavirus-school-closures.html.

Schwartz, Daniel L., and John D. Bransford. 2009. "A Time for Telling." *Cognition and Instruction* 16 (4): 475–522. https://doi.org/10.1207/s1532690xci1604_4.

Schwartzman, Helen B. 1976. "The Anthropological Study of Children's Play." *Annual Review of Anthropology* 5: 289–328.

Scrinis, Gyorgy. 2015. *Nutritionism: The Science and Politics of Dietary Advice.* New York: Columbia University Press.

Seabrook, Jeremy. 2013. "The Language of Labouring Reveals Tortured Roots." *Guardian,* January 14. https://www.theguardian.com/commentisfree/2013/jan/14/ language-labouring-reveals-tortured-roots1.

Seth, Michael J. 2002. *Education Fever: Society, Politics, and the Pursuit of Schooling in South Korea.* Honolulu: University of Hawai'i Press.

Sewell, William H., Jr. 1967. "Marc Bloch and the Logic of Comparative History." *History and Theory* 6 (2): 208–18.

Sharma, Yojana. 2022. "Three Major Universities Quit International Rankings." University World News, May 11. https://www.universityworldnews.com/post. php?story=20220511170923665.

Shelton, Leslie. n.d. a. "School-Induced Shame: Research Overview." http://www.rp forschools.net/articles/ASP/Shelton%20(nd)%20School-Induced%20Shame%20 -%20Research%20Overview.pdf.

Shelton, Leslie. n.d. b. "Transforming the Shame of Early School Difficulties." https:// learningandviolence.net/original/violence/shame/shelton.pdf.

Sherrington, Tom. 2017. *The Learning Rainforest: Great Teaching in Real Classrooms.* Melton, Woodbridge, UK: John Catt Education.

Silva, Elena, Taylor White, and Thomas Toch. 2015. *The Carnegie Unit: A Century-Old Standard in a Changing Education Landscape.* Stanford, CA: Carnegie Foundation for the Advancement of Teaching.

Silverstein, Michael. 2023. *Language in Culture: Lectures on the Social Semiotics of Language.* Cambridge: Cambridge University Press.

Sjöberg, Rickard L., Kent Nilsson, and Jerzy Leppert. 2005. "Obesity, Shame, and Depression in School-Aged Children: A Population-Based Study." *Pediatrics* 116 (3): 3389–92.

Skenazy, Lenore. 2021. *Free-Range Kids: How Parents and Teachers Can Let Go and Let Grow*. Hoboken, NJ: Jossey-Bass.

Slagle, Patricia. 1997. "Getting Real: Authenticity in Writing Prompts." *Quarterly* 19 (3) (Summer). nwp.org/cs/public/print/resource/882.

Smith, Gary A. 2015. "Why College Faculty Need to Know the Research about Learning." *InSight: A Journal of Scholarly Teaching* 10:9–18.

Smith, James F., Jr., and Nicole M. Piemonte. 2022. "The Problematic Persistence of Tiered Grading in Medical School." *Teaching and Learning in Medicine*, May 26. https://doi.org/10.1080/10401334.2022.2074423.

Snow, Catherine E., and Diane E. Beals. 2006. "Mealtime Talk That Supports Literacy Development." *New Directions for Child and Adolescent Development* 111 (Spring): 51–66.

Socol, Ira, Pam Moran, and Chad Ratliff. 2018. *Timeless Learning: How Imagination, Observation, and Zero-Based Thinking Change Schools*. San Francisco: Jossey-Bass.

Solomon, Mark R. 2021. "10 Ways to Help Your Child Succeed in School." Metro Parent, September 1. http://www.metroparent.com/daily/education/school-issues/ways-help-child-succeed-school-right-way/.

Sperry, Douglas E., Linda L. Sperry, and Peggy J. Miller. 2019. "Reexamining the Verbal Environments of Children from Different Socioeconomic Backgrounds." *Child Development* 90 (4): 1303–18. https://doi.org/10.1111/cdev.13072.

Spindler, George, and Louise Spindler. 1989. "There Are No Dropouts among the Arunta and the Hutterites." In *What Do Anthropologists Have to Say about Dropouts?*, edited by Henry T. Trueba, George Spindler, and Louise S. Spindler, 7–15. New York: Falmer.

Stack, Carol B. 1974. *All Our Kin: Strategies for Survival in a Black Community*. New York: Harper & Row.

Staggs, Jess, and Alex Ambrose. 2021. "The Effects of COVID-19 on Learning Space Rating System Scores." *Educause Review*, November 11. https://er.educause.edu/articles/2021/11/the-effects-of-covid-19-on-learning-space-rating-system-scores.

Staley, David J. 2019. *Alternative Universities: Speculative Design for Innovation in Higher Education*. Baltimore: Johns Hopkins University Press.

Stambach, Amy. 1998. "'Too Much Studying Makes Me Crazy': School-Related Illnesses on Mount Kilimanjaro." *Comparative Education Review* 42 (4): 497–512.

Stanford University. n.d. "Stanford Study of Writing." https://ssw.stanford.edu/.

Stearns, Peter N. 2017. *Shame: A Brief History*. Champaign: University of Illinois Press.

Sterelny, Kim. 2012. *The Evolved Apprentice: How Evolution Made Humans Unique*. Cambridge, MA: MIT Press.

Sterelny, Kim. 2021. *The Pleistocene Social Contract: Culture and Cooperation in Human Evolution*. Oxford: Oxford University Press.

Stevens, Mitchell L. 2007. *Creating a Class: College Admissions and the Education of Elites*. Cambridge, MA: Harvard University Press.

Stewart, Donald C. 1982. "Some Facts Worth Knowing about the Origins of Freshman Composition." *CEA Critic* 44 (4): 2–11. https://www.jstor.org/stable/44376093.

Stommel, Jesse, Chris Friend, and Sean Michael Morris, eds. 2020. *Critical Digital Pedagogy: A Collection.* Washington, DC: Hybrid Pedagogy. https://hybridpedagogy. org/critical-digital-pedagogy/.

Stone, Deborah. 2020. *Counting: How We Use Numbers to Decide What Matters.* New York: Liveright.

Strauss, Valerie. 2018. "What Research Really Says about Closing Schools—and Why It's a Bad Idea." *Washington Post,* February 28. https://www.washingtonpost.com/news/ answer-sheet/wp/2018/02/28/what-research-really-says-about-closing-schools-and-why-its-a-bad-idea-for-kids/.

Strauss, Valerie. 2019. "Today's Kids Might Be Digital Natives—but a New Study Shows They Aren't Close to Being Computer Literate." *Washington Post,* November 16. https://www.washingtonpost.com/education/2019/11/16/todays-kids-may-be-digital-natives-new-study-shows-they-arent-close-being-computer-literate/.

Strauss, William, and Neil Howe. 1992. *Generations: The History of America's Future, 1584 to 2069.* New York: Quill.

Strickland, Kathleen, and James Strickland. 1998. *Reflections on Assessment: Its Purposes, Methods and Effects on Learning.* Portsmouth, NH: Heinemann.

Suen, H. K., and L. Yu. 2006. "Chronic Consequences of High-Stakes Testing? Lessons from the Chinese Civil Service Exam." *Comparative Education Review* 50 (1): 46–65.

Supiano, Beckie. 2019. "The Problem with Grades: Grades Can Hinder Learning; What Should Professors Use Instead?" *Chronicle of Higher Education,* August 2. https:// www.chronicle.com/interactives/20190719_ungrading.

Suskind, Dana, with Lydia Denworth. 2022. *Parent Nation: Unlocking Every Child's Potential, Fulfilling Society's Promise.* New York: Dutton.

Sztabnik, Brian. 2015. "Let's Bury the 5-Paragraph Essay: Long Live Authentic Writing." Talks With Teachers. [No longer available.]

Tam, Gloria, and Diana El-Azar. 2020. "Three Ways the Coronavirus Pandemic Could Reshape Education." World Economic Forum, March 13. https://www.weforum. org/agenda/2020/03/3-ways-coronavirus-is-reshaping-education-and-what-changes-might-be-here-to-stay/.

Tannen, Deborah. 1981. "New York Jewish Conversational Style." *International Journal of the Sociology of Language* 30: 133–49.

Tehrani, Jamshid J., and Felix Riede. 2008. "Towards an Archaeology of Pedagogy: Learning, Teaching and the Generation of Material Culture Traditions." *World Archaeology* 49 (3): 316–31.

Thibierge, Stéphane, and Catherine Morin. 2010. "The Self and the Subject: A Psychoanalytic Lacanian Perspective." *Neuropsychoanalysis* 12 (1): 81–93. https://hal.ar chives-ouvertes.fr/hal-01519835/document.

Thomas, P. L. 2014. "The 'Grit' Narrative, 'Grit' Research, and Codes That Blind." Radical Eyes for Equity. https://radicalscholarship.wordpress.com/2014/01/30/ the-grit-narrative-grit-research-and-codes-that-blind/.

Thompson, E. P. 1967. "Time, Work-Discipline, and Industrial Capitalism." *Past and Present* 38: 56–97.

Thorsten, Marie. 1996. "A Few Bad Women: Manufacturing 'Education Mamas' in Postwar Japan." *International Journal of Politics, Culture, and Society* 10 (1): 51–71.

Tobin, Joseph Jay, Yeh Hsueh, and Mayumi Karasawa. 2009. *Preschool in Three Cultures Revisited: China, Japan, and the United States.* Chicago: University of Chicago Press.

Tomar, Dave. 2012. *The Shadow Scholar: How I Made a Living Helping College Kids Cheat.* London: Bloomsbury.

Tomasello, Michael. 2009. *Why We Cooperate.* Cambridge, MA: MIT Press.

Tomasello, Michael, Brian Hare, Hagen Lehmann, and Josep Call. 2007. "Reliance on Head versus Eyes in the Gaze Following of Great Apes and Human Infants: The Cooperative Eye Hypothesis." *Journal of Human Evolution* 52 (3): 314–20. https://doi.org/10.1016/j.jhevol.2006.10.001.

Toppo, Greg. 2015. "Our High School Kids: Tired, Stressed and Bored." *USA Today*, October 23. https://www.usatoday.com/story/news/nation/2015/10/23/survey-students-tired-stressed-bored/74412782/.

Townsend, Mary. 2017. "The Walking Wounded." *Hedgehog Review.* Spring. https://hedgehogreview.com/issues/the-post-modern-self/articles/the-walking-wounded.

Townsend, Peggy. 2015. "The Birth of UC Santa Cruz: Audacious and Academic." UC Santa Cruz Newscenter, January 1. https://news.ucsc.edu/2014/12/birth-of-ucsc.html.

Trilling, Lionel. 1972. *Sincerity and Authenticity.* Cambridge, MA: Harvard University Press.

Trow, Martin. 2007. "Reflections on the Transition from Elite to Mass to Universal Access: Forms and Phases of Higher Education in Modern Societies since WWII." In *International Handbook of Higher Education*, edited by James J. F. Forest and Philip G. Altbach, 243–80. Dordrecht: Springer.

Trudeau, Michelle. 2010. "Human Connections Start with a Friendly Touch." NPR Morning Education, September 20. https://www.npr.org/2010/09/20/128795325/human-connections-start-with-a-friendly-touch.

Tuan, Yi-Fu. 2001. *Space and Place: The Perspective of Experience.* Minneapolis: University of Minnesota Press.

Twenge, Jean M. 2006. *Generation Me: Why Today's Young Americans Are More Confident, Assertive, Entitled—and More Miserable Than Ever Before.* New York: Free Press.

Twenge, Jean M. 2018. *iGen: Why Today's Super-Connected Kids Are Growing Up Less Rebellious, More Tolerant, Less Happy—and Completely Unprepared for Adulthood—and What That Means for the Rest of Us.* New York: Atria.

Tyack, David, and Michael Berkowitz. 1977. "The Man Nobody Liked: Toward a Social History of the Truant Officer, 1840–1940." *American Quarterly* 29 (1): 31–54. https://doi.org/10.2307/2712260.

Tyack, David, and Larry Cuban. 1995. *Tinkering toward Utopia: A Century of Public School Reform.* Cambridge, MA: Harvard University Press.

Umble, Diane Zimmerman. 2003. "Sinful Network or Divine Service: Competing Meanings of the Telephone in Amish Country." In *New Media 1740–1915*, edited by Lisa Gitelman and Geoffrey B. Pingree, 139–56. Cambridge, MA: MIT Press.

Ungar, Peter S. 2020. "Why We Have So Many Problems with Our Teeth." *Scientific American*, April 1. www.scientificamerican.com/article/why-we-have-so-many-prob lems-with-our-teeth/.

Van Der Kolk, Bessel A. 2014. *The Body Keeps the Score: Brain, Mind, and Body in the Healing of Trauma*. New York: Viking.

van Gog, Tamara, and John Sweller. 2015. "Not New, but Nearly Forgotten: The Test ing Effect Decreases or Even Disappears as the Complexity of Learning Materials Increases." *Educational Psychology Review* 27: 247–64. https://doi.org/10.1007/ s10648-015-9310-x.

Van Horn Melton, James. 2003. *Absolutism and the Eighteenth-Century Origins of Compulsory Schooling in Prussia and Austria*. Cambridge: Cambridge University Press.

Vanover, Eric T., and Michael M. DeBowes. 2013. "The Impact of Intercollegiate Ath letics in Higher Education." *Higher Education Politics & Economics* 1 (1). https:// digitalcommons.odu.edu/cgi/viewcontent.cgi?article=1003&context=aphe.

Varenne, Hervé, and Ray McDermott. 1998. *Successful Failure: The School America Builds*. Boulder, CO: Westview.

Venet, Alex Shevrin. 2018. "The How and Why of Trauma-Informed Teaching." Edutopia, August 3. https://www.edutopia.org/article/how-and-why-trauma-informed-teaching.

Vergunst, Jo Lee, and Tim Ingold, eds. 2016. *Ways of Walking: Ethnography and Practice on Foot*. Abingdon, UK: Routledge.

Visser, Margaret. 1991. *The Rituals of Dinner: The Origins, Evolution, Eccentricities, and Meaning of Table Manners*. New York: HarperCollins.

von Eschenbach, Warren. 2020. "Being-for-Others and Integral Human Development." Blog post. Keough School of Global Affairs, University of Notre Dame. November 16. https://nanovic.nd.edu/news/being-for-others-and-integral-human-development/.

Waldrop, M. Mitchell. 2015. "Why We Are Teaching Science Wrong, and How to Make It Right." *Nature* 523: 272–74. https://doi.org/10.1038/523272a.

Wallace, Jennifer Breheny. 2019. "Students in High-Achieving Schools Are Now Named an 'At-Risk' Group, Study Says." *Washington Post*, September 26. https://www. washingtonpost.com/lifestyle/2019/09/26/students-high-achieving-schools-are-now- named-an-at-risk-group/.

Walton, Jack. 2017. "Third Coast Percussion and Community Musicians Play Terry Riley's 'In C' at Riley High School." *South Bend Tribune*, July 27. https://www. southbendtribune.com/entertainment/inthebend/music/third-coast-percussion-and- community-musicians-play-terry-riley-s/article_b7463cd5-f736-596f-a622-8aa64bd dd0e3.html.

Warner, John. 2013. "The Search for the Origins of Pseudo-academic B.S." Inside Higher Ed, October 20. https://www.insidehighered.com/blogs/just-visiting/search- origins-pseudo-academic-bs.

Warner, John. 2016. "School Is Bad for Students." Inside Higher Ed, July 6. https:// www.insidehighered.com/blogs/just-visiting/school-bad-students.

Warner, John. 2018. *Why They Can't Write: Killing the Five-Paragraph Essay and Other Necessities*. Baltimore: Johns Hopkins University Press.

Warner, John. 2020. *Sustainable. Resilient. Free. The Future of Public Higher Education*. Cleveland: Belt.

Warner, John. 2022. "A Course in Organic Chemistry Doesn't Need to Be a Living Hell." Slate, October 7. https://slate.com/human-interest/2022/10/does-organic-chemistry-need-to-be-hard.html.

Watanabe, Yoshinori. 2013. "The National Center Test for University Admissions." *Language Testing* 30 (4): 565–573. https://doi.org/10.1177/0265532213483095.

Watson, C. Edward, and Thomas Chase Hagood, eds. 2017. *Playing to Learn with Reacting to the Past: Research on High Impact, Active Learning Practices*. Cham, Switzerland: Springer International.

Watters, Audrey. 2022. "The History of the School Bell." Hackeducation.com, January 30. http://hackeducation.com/2022/01/30/bell.

Watters, Audrey. 2014, 2015a, 2015b, 2016, 2017, 2021. https://books.audreywatters.com/.

Weldon, Amy E. 2018. *The Hands-on Life: How to Wake Yourself Up and Save the World*. Eugene, OR: Cascade.

White, Kate, Andrea Beach, Noah Finkelstein, Charles Henderson, Scott Simkins, Linda Slakey, Marilyne Stains, Gabriela Weaver, and Lorne Whitehead, eds. 2020. *Transforming Institutions: Accelerating Systemic Change in Higher Education*. Pressbooks. http://openbooks.library.umass.edu/ascnti2020/.

White, Robert W. 1959. "Motivation Reconsidered: The Concept of Competence." *Psychological Review* 66 (5): 297–333. https://doi.org/10.1037/h0040934.

Wieman, Carl. 2014. "Stop Lecturing Me." *Scientific American*, July 15. https://www.scientificamerican.com/article/stop-lecturing-me/.

Wiggins, Grant. 2014. "Attention, Teachers! Why Students Are Bored." HuffPost, January 23. https://www.huffpost.com/entry/why-students-are-bored_b_4274474.

Williamson, Ben. 2021. "Making Markets through Digital Platforms: Pearson, Edu-business, and the (E)valuation of Higher Education." *Critical Studies in Education* 62 (1): 50–66. https://doi.org/10.1080/17508487.2020.1737556.

Willingham, Daniel T. 2009. "The Learning Styles Myth." Psych Files, episode 90. March 29. http://thepsychfiles.com/2009/03/episode-90-the-learning-styles-myth-an-interview-with-daniel-willingham/.

Willingham, Daniel T. 2021. *Why Don't Students Like School? A Cognitive Scientist Answers Questions about How the Mind Works and What It Means for the Classroom*. 2nd ed. Hoboken, NJ: Jossey-Bass.

Winnicott, D. W. 1960. "Ego Distortion in Terms of True and False Self." In *The Maturational Processes and the Facilitating Environment*, 140–52. New York: International Universities Press.

Wolf, Maryanne. 2018. *Reader, Come Home: The Reading Brain in a Digital World*. New York: HarperCollins.

Wood, Tara. 2017. "Cripping Time in the College Composition Classroom." *College Composition and Communication* 69 (2): 260–86.

Xiang, Xin. 2018. "My Future, My Family, My Freedom: Meanings of Schooling for Poor, Rural Chinese Youth." *Harvard Educational Review* 88 (1): 81–102.

Xiong, Shuyu, Padmaja Sankaridurg, Thomas Naduvilath, Jiajie Zang, Haidong Zou, Jianfeng Zhu, Minzhi Lv, Xiangui He, and Xun Xu. 2017. "Time Spent in Outdoor Activities in Relation to Myopia Prevention and Control: A Meta-analysis and Systematic Review." *Acta Ophthalmologica* 95 (6): 551–66. https://doi.org/10.1111/aos.13403.

Ye, Wendy. 2021. "China's Harsh Education Crackdown Sends Parents and Businesses Scrambling." CNBC, August 5. https://www.cnbc.com/2021/08/05/chinas-harsh-education-crackdown-sends-parents-businesses-scrambling.html.

Yerkes, R. M., and J. D. Dodson. 1908. "The Relation of Strength of Stimulus to Rapidity of Habit Formation." *Journal of Comparative Neurology & Psychology* 18 (5): 459–82. https://doi.org/10.1002/cne.920180503.

Yeshurun, Yara, Mai Nguyen, and Uri Hasson. 2021. "The Default Mode Network: Where the Idiosyncratic Self Meets the Shared Social World." *Nature Reviews: Neuroscience* 22: 181–92. https://doi.org/10.1038/s41583-020-00420-w.

Young, Jeffrey R. 2020. "What Colleges Are Doing to Fight the 'Contract Cheating' Industry." EdSurge, January 30. https://www.edsurge.com/news/2020-01-30-what-colleges-are-doing-to-fight-the-contract-cheating-industry.

Zaidel, Dahlia W. 2019. "The Evolution of Aesthetics and Beauty." In *The Oxford Handbook of Empirical Aesthetics*, edited by Marcos Nadal and Oshin Vartanian. Oxford Handbooks Online. https://doi.org/10.1093/oxfordhb/9780198824350.013.8.

Zaretsky, Robert. 2019. "Our Students Can't Write. We Have Ourselves to Blame." *Chronicle of Higher Education*, May 29. https://www.chronicle.com/article/Our-Students-Can-t-Write-We/246385.

Zeller, Jessica, 2017. "On Dance Pedagogy and Embodiment." *Society of Dance History Scholars* 38:17–20.

Zeng, Kangmin. 1999. *Dragon Gate: Competitive Examinations and Their Consequences*. London: Cassell.

Zentella, Ana Celia. 2015. "Books as the Magic Bullet." *Journal of Linguistic Anthropology* 25 (1): 75–77.

ZeroToThree.org. 2004. "Getting Ready for School Begins at Birth: How to Help Your Child Learn in the Early Years." http://www.zerotothree.org/child-development/social-emotional-development/gettingreadyforschoolbeginsatbirth.pdf.

Zhao, Yong. 2009. *Catching Up or Leading the Way: American Education in the Age of Globalization*. Alexandria, VA: ASCD.

Zhao, Yong. 2018. *What Works May Hurt: Side Effects in Education*. New York: Teachers College Press.

Zimmerman, Jonathan. 2015. *Small Wonder: The Little Red Schoolhouse in History and Memory*. New Haven, CT: Yale University Press.

Zuboff, Shoshana. 2019. *The Age of Surveillance Capitalism: The Fight for a Human Future at the New Frontier of Power*. New York: Hachette.

Zull, James E. 2002. *The Art of Changing the Brain: Enriching the Practice of Teaching by Exploring the Biology of Learning*. Sterling, VA: Stylus.

Zwiebel, Hannah, and Lindsay A. Thompson. 2022. "What Are School-Based Health Clinics?" *JAMA Pediatrics* 176 (4): 428. https://doi.org/10.1001/jamapediatrics.2021.6579.

INDEX

Page numbers in italics refer to figures and tables.

Printed in the USA
CPSIA information can be obtained
at www.ICGtesting.com
CBHW031250060524
8103CB00002B/68